**BROWN
FLEMING
AND THE
HAARLEM
COLLECTION**

BROWN FLEMING AND THE HAARLEM COLLECTION

The European production of Dutch wax prints for West Africa

HELEN ELANDS

SilvanaEditoriale

Introduction

I still vividly remember my first visit to the Vlisco archives in Helmond in 1986, where I was kindly received by Cees Krantz, then recently retired after three decades as Head of the Design Department. Hanging on metal racks up to the ceiling were 350,000 textile samples. Another 25,000 original drawings of textile designs, all produced for the African market, were stored in a long wall of white cardboard tubes. Even after so many years I still remember how dizzy I felt. It was almost impossible to decide where to focus my attention. I also recall that, while contemplating the immensity of the collection, I realised each one of these designs must have a story; none could have been created haphazardly. I determined that if I were to do research about Vlisco's most important product, its wax prints, my goal would be to discover the nucleus of these designs, the backbone to these stories. But at the time, I was involved in other research projects and soon my inspirational visit dwindled among more pressing matters.

Almost three decades later, then living in the UK and looking for a new research subject, my fascination with wax prints had remained intact and I decided to pay a visit to ABC Wax in Hyde near Manchester. The company had printed for the African market until 2007 when production was transferred to Ghana. Only the design studio and the archives were left operating, the latter then in an almost derelict building.

Looking around the archives I felt even more lost than on my visit to Vlisco: another huge mass of cloth closely packed on hangers and countless sample books with company names I had never heard of. On the last afternoon of my visit, I was talking in a corridor to David Bradley, Managing Director of the company. Next to him was a clothing rail with some of the oldest samples he had put there to protect them from possible water damage from the leaky ceiling. I suddenly realized that I was looking at the samples that I would have to start with, but not knowing exactly what they were. They came the closest to the very first wax prints, the nucleus I wanted to understand. Many of them would turn out to be early registration samples from Ebenezer Brown Fleming, a Scottish merchant who introduced a substantial number of designs from 1895 to 1912, designs that are still in print today. These samples, kept in Glasgow after his death by his son-in-law Ronald Herbertson, travelled to Manchester in 1939 in three hampers on the back of a motorbike. The Calico Printers' Association had bought the company from Herbertson including the rights to this famous collection of designs, with the intention of printing them at Newton Bank Print Works, the precursor of ABC Wax. Known more widely within the wax print industry as the *Haarlem Collection* after the place of their initial production, these patterns and motifs were to become the classics that formed core references for European companies that started wax printing after 1910. While several attempts had been made by other textile printers to acquire knowledge of the Haarlem company's production process, it was only around 1910 that several companies in the Netherlands, the United Kingdom and Switzerland managed to produce a quality of wax print that compared to that of Haarlem's Prévinaire and Son. These companies started printing the designs of the Haarlem Collection, sometimes with impunity despite their registration, and these precedents would later lead to a dispute about their ownership that ran for several decades. This acrimony ended only when all parties realized that by then the designs had become part of the cultural heritage and no longer belonged to a specific company.

With this direction established for my preliminary research I wanted to understand how these Dutch wax prints had become so firmly embedded in African cultures that many of Brown Fleming's patterns remain popular in Africa to this day. And even after the death of Brown Fleming many more designs, introduced by other companies, have become classics. Most of these were created by Vlisco, which is the last remaining wax printer in Europe today. Printing wax for African export continues to be challenging, with varying qualities of cloth and copying of patterns remaining as much an issue as in the early days. Vlisco has been able to retain the same prestige once held by the Brown Fleming brand. Crucial for success, as from the start, is the combination of high quality of cloth with designs that are deeply integrated within African cultures.

Just as anywhere in the world, clothing in Africa is closely linked to identity and social status. Throughout the African continent, social and cultural identities of ethnicity, gender, age, rank and status are signalled via a range of personal adornments, especially cloth. Such cultural meanings and values take precedence over personal preference. It was the acquisition of cultural meaning that allowed designs of the Haarlem Collection to become classics. In societies where culture was passed on through oral tradition, the spoken word had to be treated with care. If you communicated something directly, it could be misinterpreted. In this context, the unspoken messages of patterns on garments gain a powerful expressive function. Classic patterns, re-issued on a regular basis, accumulate layers of cultural value and prestige through longstanding use.

The classic wax prints were generally of a better quality and durability than ordinary prints. There has been a long-standing interest, especially in West Africa, in high quality imported cloth with an exclusive *signature*. Clothing was not simply obtained locally, but through regional, national and even international markets (Allman 2004). Indeed, fine quality cloth from India and China was transported to West Africa via trans-Saharan and Indian Ocean routes from the eleventh century onwards (Lydon 2009). From the fifteenth century, European trading companies entered these pre-existing trading markets that involved the exchange of Indian cloth.

The history of Dutch wax print begins at the start of the nineteenth century when British and Dutch and later also Swiss companies saw the potential of developing and selling machine-made versions of batik for the Indonesian market. Batik is a handmade, resist-dyed method of creating patterned cloth, perfected to an art in Indonesia, and much sought after there at the beginning of the nineteenth century. In the Netherlands, J.-B. T. Prévinaire founded a company that was to specialise in the most outstanding quality of batik imitations. He developed the *Javanaise*, a block printing machine capable of applying a warm resinous wax resist to each side of the cloth. To further increase productivity, this was later replaced by a duplex roller printing machine. Prévinaire died in 1854, but his son continued to run the business and in the early 1860s Indonesian demand for these imitation batiks, especially the high-quality products of Prévinaire, began to increase. From 1863 to 1867, the company made huge profits. But when Indonesians developed their own technology, a wax stamping tool to speed the traditional process, export of batik imitations went into sharp decline. Some European producers made attempts to improve their quality by experimenting with wax printing like Prévinaire, but only for a short time. Most European manufacturers reduced production or ceased altogether. Prévinaire's son maintained his belief in the future of the batik imitations and continued to make further improvements. From 1875 onwards, under the name of the *Haarlemsche Katoen Maatschappij* (HKM, or Haarlem Cotton Company), the company struggled along with poor sales. But Prévinaire's contacts with a British merchant, Ebenezer Brown Fleming (1858-1912), was to result in a sharp upturn of his business.

When Brown Fleming introduced his imitation batiks, printed with wax, onto the West African market around 1890, they became a huge success. Rising standards of living had stimulated demand for luxury products. By the end of the nineteenth century there was clearly a market for up-scale and exclusive cloth that appealed specifically to the tastes of the wealthy African customer – in sharp contrast to the earlier batik imitations, produced in Europe for Indonesia, and destined for the lower classes. The English colonial power, later taken over by the Dutch, was to make as much profit as possible for the Empire without consideration for local values. The West Africans were not passive recipients of European goods, but actively expressed their discerning taste, knowing precisely what to ask for, which initially proved an unsettling challenge for European merchants.

In 1895 Brown Fleming founded his own company and developed collections, not only with Indonesian-inspired motifs, but with new designs based on African cultures, and adapting the batik styling. His collection of wax prints printed by HKM was the best on the market. But it was not only the outstanding quality of the printed cloth that appealed to West African customers: HKM stood out from its competitors because of the high standard of design, suggesting that its designers had formal training. These aspects, combined with Brown Fleming's willingness to adapt designs to his customers' tastes, were the key to his success. As the sole merchant for HKM's wax prints, he used his extensive sales network in West Africa to provide their designers with market information (Ingenbleek 1998). Such market expertise was essential to the manufacturer whose business depended on overseas buyers, and information was assembled about consumer preferences via a network of trade relationships and communications (Launert 2002).

Until around 1910 Brown Fleming dominated the market for imitation batiks on the West African coast. Increasing demand in combination with limited production led to frustration on the part of traders in Africa. However, while several attempts had been made to gain an insight into Prévinaire's production process, it was only in the years directly leading up to 1910 that a few other companies in the Netherlands, the United Kingdom and Switzerland managed to produce a quality of wax print that compared to that of Prévinaire and could capture sales in the West African markets. Other companies that already made imitation batik started to produce imitations of his famous wax prints, but sometimes in cheapened versions that did not use wax.

After Brown Fleming's death in 1912, his company continued trading until 1939 when it was acquired by the Calico Printers' Association for printing at its Newton Bank branch, later known as ABC Wax. Until recently, this firm was still printing designs that were introduced by Brown Fleming, Vlisco and others continue to do so today.

Dutch wax prints, the first on the market, and maintaining their reputation for quality, came to hold an important role in affirming West African cultural identity into the post-colonial period. British, Dutch and Swiss merchants obviously traded in this type of cloth for economic reasons, but underlying this trade were local conditions and individuals with a crucial determining role, as sales could only succeed with African patronage (Picton 1995). Textiles are simultaneously a product of artistic expression and an economic commodity, requiring an inordinate number of design, production and marketing variables. Minor aspects of motif, colour, texture and finish can be the determinant of eventual saleability, especially in the African market accustomed to high standards (Steiner 1985). Merchants and manufacturers of Euro-African styles had to invest enormous time and effort in conceptualising, producing and distributing their wax prints. Although introduced and made profitable in times of European imperialism, the local practices of circulation, exchange and cultural assimilation acted to defeat the colonial order (Hendrickson 1996, Hansen 2013).

The designs of Dutch wax have become a sign of authenticity and have been integrated within African identity. They are not only the result of locally identifiable cultural expressions but an amalgamation resulting from the complex processes of cultural exchange and integration (Allman 2004, Kriger 2006, Maynard 2004). Wax prints are an example of complex appropriation and re-appropriation of an elite craft. Batik, produced in one part of the world – Java, became the object of substitute merchandise for nations with distant trade routes – the Netherlands and the United Kingdom, and subsequently acquired a new identity in another part of the world – West Africa (Rabine 2002). The power of this appropriation led to a shift of identity attributes: in adopting wax prints the Africans linked their own cherished traditions to global culture, embracing modernity while retaining authenticity. Africans transformed a colonial commodity into a truly African material, incorporating African aesthetics and meaning (Picton 1995).

Searching for the nucleus of these designs, I systematically researched the surviving Brown Fleming material from the 1890s until 1912. Between the Brunnschweiler Archive (ABC Wax and its predecessors) in Hyde near Manchester, the Patent Office registered designs at The National Archives in Kew, London and sixty sample books of the HKM in the Vlisco Archives in Helmond, I located a near-complete series of the designs. These searches enabled the chronological arrangement of patterns otherwise randomly presented in a collection of 220 black-and-white photographs of swatches made in 1939 when Brown Flemings Ltd was sold. The first 162 samples seem to constitute the original Brown Fleming collection, the remaining designs having been introduced later. Only fragmentary sales figures for designs are available, but the photos indicate designs still in the Brown Fleming portfolio upon sale of the company. The Brunnschweiler Archives and Vlisco Archives each document developments after the death of Brown Fleming, especially since these archives incorporate the archives of other wax printers and merchants, acquired on their closure. Many other sources turned out to be useful. To name a few: the British Museum which holds Indonesian batik and its imitations collected by the merchants Blakely and Beving; De Lakenhal in Leiden which holds cloth and sample books of the Leidsche Katoen Maatschappij; Museum Rotterdam, which holds cloth and sample books of the Kralingsche Katoen Maatschappij; and the Dutch National Archives in The Hague (the Netherlands). Correspondence in the Basel Mission Archive revealed much about trading relationships. I am especially indebted for family information about Brown Fleming to his great-grandson, a keen genealogist.

Up to now, research on printed textiles for Africa has been undertaken largely from the standpoint of anthropology and ethnography. My research, based on archival records, is viewed from the perspective of the history of design. It is a new story of design, textiles, global trade and the circulation of visual ideas. It reveals the actual patterns that launched the fashion for wax print in Africa, patterns that had a complex genesis in the competition between the Netherlands and Britain for export markets, a confrontation that eventually entangled a family of Dutch printers, the Scottish entrepreneur Brown Fleming and market women on the Gold Coast of Africa in an unlikely design collaboration. It is a collaboration that has transformed the history of dress in West Africa.

Helen Elands

Acknowledgements

This study was only made possible with the help, support and patience of many individuals and institutions, both in the United Kingdom and in Europe. To all of them, too numerous to mention by name, I am immensely grateful.

The impetus to start this project came from Jana Sheena, for which I cannot thank her enough. The idea for the topic of this study came from Ellinoor Bergvelt.

My research started at the archives of ABC in Hyde (UK), where I was welcomed by Marilyn Hoyle and David Bradley. I would like to thank Joanne Worthington, Rob Evans, Philip Poole and Steven Dutton of ABC Wax for their advice and support.

Many other people and institutions in the United Kingdom were of great help: Malcolm Fleming, George English (Research Through People), The National Archives in Kew (Dinah Eastop, Julie Halls and the Conservation Care Department), the British Museum in London (Helen Wolfe), Duncan Clarke of Adire African Textiles, the Pitt Rivers Museum in Oxford (Philip Grover and Katherine Clough) and the Royal Anthropological Institute of Great Britain and Ireland (Amanda Vinson and Andrei Nacu).

Ruud Sanders, responsible for the archives of Vlisco Netherlands BV in Helmond, has provided me with invaluable assistance for many years. The recently appointed head of archives, Fabian Kolobaric, has been equally very supportive. Other employees and former staff of Vlisco I would like to thank are Roger Gerards, Karl-Heinz Hegmann, Frans van Rood and Joop Martens, the latter especially for his technical knowledge. I am also grateful for the help of Willem Ankersmit who wrote a study about the company of his family, Paul Faber (former curator Africa Tropenmuseum Amsterdam), Marit Feld (inventory Ankersmit Archives Collectie Overijssel), Itie van Hout (batik expert and former curator Textiles at the Tropenmuseum in Amsterdam), Derk Jordaan (Archief Twentse Textielfamilies), Dan van Lunsen who researched the family history of Prévinaire, and René van Walsem (Professor Emeritus Egyptology in Leiden).

Frieda Sorber of the MoMu in Antwerp gave me insight into the early batik imitations in Belgium. In Switzerland, Anne Wanner and Barbara Karl of the Textilmuseum in Sankt Gallen and Claudia Wirthlin of the Basel Mission Archives provided precious help and information. In France, I would like to thank Corinne Tuncq (head of the Archives Départementales de la Seine Maritime in Darnetal), David Gadanho (head of collections of the Musées de Honfleur) and especially Ghislain Inaï of the Société des Missions Africaines in Lyon. Conversations with Maria Wronska-Friend, an anthropologist and batik specialist at the James Cook University in Cairns, Australia, were inspiring.

Throughout this journey – from the very beginning of my research all the way through the long and often lonely process of writing and revising – I have been blessed with the expert advice, excellent editing skills, patience, and above all the most remarkable supportive friendship of Philip Sykas. I cannot thank him enough…

Contents

12
Imitating Indonesian batik in Europe: the beginnings

32
The introduction of machine-made batik into West Africa

48
Ebenezer Brown Fleming and the Haarlemsche Katoen Maatschappij

66
The creation of the Haarlem Collection by Brown Fleming 1895–1912

146
The rise of Brown Fleming's competitors in wax printing

166
Production and trade of wax prints during the First World War and the interwar period

184
Production and trade in wax prints after the Second World War

204
Epilogue
The *Contentious* Designs: the legacy of Brown Fleming

215
Addenda

Imitating Indonesian batik in Europe: the beginnings

The early nineteenth century saw machine-made versions of Indonesian batik made in Europe for export to Indonesia and South East Asia. From the 1840s, after an arduous start, a successful trade ensued for about three decades. Prévinaire and Son became the market leader for true wax resist printing. Declining sales forced other companies to divert from imitation batik production around 1870, but Prévinaire maintained faith in his product and continued to improve quality and technique.

With more than 17,000 islands, Indonesia is a large and populous country situated in South East Asia on the Indian Ocean trade route between India and China. Indonesian port cities became international trading centres, contributing to a cosmopolitan society that absorbed neighbouring cultures into its own rich blend. In the field of textiles, Indonesia developed some of the finest dyeing and weaving traditions in the world, notably batik, a time-consuming method of producing designs by hand-applied wax resist and dyeing. Batik was accorded high status in Indonesian society, playing an important role in court etiquette by the eighteenth century. This was especially the case on Java in the central principalities of Surakarta, Yogyakarta, Pakualaman and Mangkunegara as well as the northern coast around Pekalongan. Patterns indicated social rank with some reserved for royalty. Nevertheless, batik for clothing was produced for all social classes in great variety and degrees of refinement.[1]

Towards the beginning of the nineteenth century Indonesia attracted European textile manufacturers looking for new markets for their industrial, mass-produced cloth, bleached, unbleached and printed. Despite the cost of transport, these could be sold at a lower price than local handmade fabrics, especially those using labour-intensive techniques such as batik. There was an opportunity for machine-made versions of batik aimed at the middling sectors of Indonesian society if these could successfully substitute for traditional batik.

The development of Indonesian batik and European encounters

The earliest precursors that have been found date from the tenth century Fustat (Old Cairo) where resist-printed cloth exported from India shows evidence of a wax resist batik technique.[2] Indian cloth was already exported to Java by the ninth century.[3] Rouffaer suggested that the technique was introduced there by merchants from India and Sri Lanka. Jan Wisseman Christie posited that an early form of batik *tulis warnna* (cloth drawn in colour) was used in Indonesia by the end of the twelfth century.[4] The fifteenth century witnessed the growth of ports on the Javanese north coast due to the expanding Indian Ocean trade for Indonesian spices, bringing a greater volume and variety of Indian cloths to Indonesia. Early Indonesian batik designs imitated woven patterning, notably the expensive *patola*, double ikat weaves of Gujarat. Also appreciated were printed floral patterns realised with a combination of mordant and resist dyeing. Inger McCabe Elliott suggested that Indian textiles could have inspired arrangement of the batik as a bordered, framed rectangle to be filled with something other than stripes or checks.[5]

Batik started to flourish from around 1500, when specifically Indonesian designs and styles, now seen as traditional, were formulated.[6] The *batik tulis* technique was developed, using a hand tool called *canting* or *tjanting* to apply hot beeswax in fine lines to both surfaces of a cloth, a skilled and lengthy process.[7] The wax hardens on cooling, giving a protective layer that prevents dye from penetrating the cloth. After dyeing in a tepid bath, removal of the wax in hot water reveals the pattern against the dyed background. Incidental cracks in the wax allowed dye to seep through creating an unplanned pattern of little veins. Some veining was inevitable, but in the best qualities, cracks were avoided. For each colour added, wax application and removal had to be repeated. The beeswax residue gives batik a typical scent much appreciated and characteristic of an authentically produced piece.

A distinctive batik iconography developed over centuries. Regional or ethnic forms and colours were used to express identity and social position and could hold symbolic meanings. Specific designs could be reserved for the ruling family, codified, and regulated to enable continuity but also differentiating one court from another. On Java, especially on the North Coast, a mixture of Hindu, Buddhist and Islamic motifs evolved, later with European influence.[8]

From 1595 to 1597 the Dutch made their first expedition to Indonesia. In 1602 they founded the Dutch East India Trading Company, known by its initials VOC (Vereenigde Oost-Indische Compagnie) to engage in trade with Asia. It also had a commercial settlement on Java, known as Batavia (present day Jakarta). In 1641, the word *batick* is first mentioned on shipping documents from boats sailing from Batavia to Sumatra, describing multi-colour textiles.[9] The British East India Company was founded in 1600, and a trading post (known as a factory) was opened in 1602 at Bantam, west of Batavia, on its first trip to the archipelago. The Company records contain a ledger of 1669 to 1671 mentioning *batteck* cloth.[10]

By the end of the eighteenth century, the Indian textile industry that had dominated the Indian Ocean markets was in decline due to European interference; costs of local materials and production could no longer compete with European mill-spun cotton. With the decline of the Indian imports, batik manufacture increased.[11] This helped to relieve shortages of Indian cloth and to circumvent its high prices. Batik produced within the Javanese courts gained in importance, and the development of the batik stamp technique (*batik cap*) in the 1840s served to speed production of cheaper styles.

Europeans also imitated Indian cottons to create more widely affordable versions. Initially these imitations were made by hand, but machine spinning of cotton was introduced in the late 1700s, and mechanical weaving in the first half of the 1800s. Export to countries that previously purchased Indian cloth was economically attractive. The growing popularity of batik in Indonesia did not go unnoticed in Europe. In the early 1800s, printed imitation of batik was seen as holding potential for export market growth. By the 1850s, Indonesia was to be inundated by fabrics from Dutch and English mills.[12]

Imitating Indonesian batik in the United Kingdom
Sir Thomas Stamford Raffles was a British East India Company official who served as Lieutenant Governor of Java between 1811 and 1816.[13] His book *The History of Java* (1817) was the first detailed European description of the history, culture, architecture and contemporary civilisation of the island. This includes a description of the making of batik:

> Of the several kinds of coloured cottons and silks there is a great diversity of patterns, particularly of the bátik, of which not less than an hundred are distinguished by their appropriate names. Among these are the patterns exclusively worn by the sovereign […] and others which designate the wearer, and are more or less esteemed, as well on this account as their comparative beauty of design and execution.[14]

Raffles collection of Indonesian objects
His book includes sixty-six engravings of which ten coloured aquatints by William Daniell illustrate Javanese life and costume with careful precision.[15] Daniell almost certainly used a collection of painted wooden models of clothed figures that Raffles commissioned in Indonesia as models for these illustrations. The purpose of the models was to accurately show people in their local costumes.[16] Raffles also collected objects representative of Indonesian culture. The British Museum holds more than 2000 objects donated by his heirs in 1859, with accruals in 1908 and 1939.[17] The collection helped him to validate his belief that the British could improve the future of Java. A second collection, acquired between 1818 and 1824 when he was Lieutenant Governor of Bencoolen in southwestern Sumatra, unfortunately sank on its way back to Britain.[18]

Indonesia's location between India and China was crucial for global trade. Dutch control had long hampered free commerce for the British in the region. No time was wasted in taking advantage of the weak situation of the Dutch under Napoleonic rule, at first imposing a naval blockade of Java in 1795, and then taking control of the former Dutch colony in 1811. As governor, Raffles acted in the interests of the East India Company, looking toward financial profit.[19] A firm believer in the superiority of European civilisation, he was convinced Java could be more prosperous under British colonial rule and criticized the limitation of Dutch policy to trade interests only.[20]

One of the first changes was to replace the relationship with Javanese rulers, which the Dutch had built on mutual understanding, with a colonial system of government. He introduced the *landrentestelsel* (land interest system), which meant that land belonged to the coloniser and locals had to pay rent to use it, which led to impoverishment and privation of the peasantry despite the natural fertility of the soil. The Dutch would replace this system in 1830 by the *cultuurstelsel* (Cultivation System), which tied peasants to their land, forcing them to work in government-owned plantations. The system brought the Dutch an enormous wealth and was only abolished after 1870.

Raffles's investigations into Javanese culture were directed towards effective colonial prosperity. An important area for development was the textile trade. The East India Company started in this period with selling copies of Indian cloth to India, transforming it from a production capital in the seventeenth century into an export market for British made textiles from the 1820s.

In Indonesia there was already a profitable trade of imported plain cloth as a base for locally produced batik, as well as striped and checked cottons for clothing, imitations of Indian types such as *ginghams*. Raffles was the first European to promote the possibility of making imitation batiks.[21] John Crawfurd, working closely with Raffles, thought batik an awkward artisanal substitute for English factory-printed cottons with their reduced labour requirements and consistent quality.[22]

Raffles was convinced that imitation batik could find a ready market in Java:

> I am most sanguine in my expectations of success, provided strict attention is paid to the patterns and sizes as well as

to the other suggestions which accompany the musters; the consignments, however, should, in the first instance, be considered rather as an experiment; and, afterwards, if the cloths are once generally and advantageously introduced, there will be no difficult in increasing the quantity to an unlimited extent.[23]

Raffles was aware that patterns were important to commercial success. Soon after his arrival in Indonesia he negotiated a treaty with Sultan Hamengkubuwono II in Yogyakarta that 'His Highness engages not to prohibit to any class of his subjects the use of any particular article or wearing-apparel, ornament or luxury'.[24] He insisted on repealing controls over exclusivity of specific patterns because such restrictions hindered trade.[25] To him, batik was primarily a commodity, irrespective of its role in Javanese culture.

The aim was not to compete with original batiks on high-quality of print cloth, but to use a coarser quality acceptable to a broad range of classes. Economies of large-scale production put the focus on quantity rather than quality. Competition with local production was not relevant because, according to Raffles, it was not the primary source of income for the locals. Given the abundance of unused land, he rather wanted them to focus on agriculture. But he also saw possibilities of a wider market:

> The Java cloths are also generally in use among the neighbouring Islands and are in request in the Malay Peninsula to which considerable quantities were formerly exported. [...It would be profitable if] it should be found that the Cloths can be exported from Europe and offered for sale at a cheaper rate than the present Manufacturer in Java.[26]

In January 1813 he wrote to the Directors of the East India Company in London about the possibility of sale of batik imitations on Java, stressing that the fabrics needed to suit the taste and the requirements of the Javanese people. This was initially difficult for the European traders, accustomed to producing imitations of simple Indian types rather than complex patterns. Manufacturers required precise specifications from traders, resident in Indonesia to obtain a readily saleable product.

In the middle of 1814, eighty-eight cases containing printed batik imitations arrived in Batavia, advertised as *Europe Cloth imitated from Javanese Patterns*.[27] Raffles wrote:

> A very extensive and valuable assortment of these cottons, imitated after the Javan and Malayan patterns, was recently imported into Java by the East-India Company, and on the first sale produced very good prices; but before a second trial could be made, the natives had discovered that the colours would not stand, and the remainder were no longer in any demand.[28]

Indonesian scholar Maria Wronska-Friend believes further issues were at play, such as faulty imitations of colours and patterns and cloth sizes that were not acceptable for the intended garments. The Company did not want to continue the trial, but individual entrepreneurs did find success.[29] An extra incentive for them was the fact that in 1813 the British government decided to open Java to free trade without restriction.[30] Raffles realised that to be successful in developing batik copies for export a thorough knowledge of the locally favoured colours and patterns was essential [31]. Crawfurd shared his vision:

> After a certain fineness is attained, the colours and patterns are of more consequence than the texture, cloths of approved patterns, often selling fifty percent higher than those that happen not to suit the native taste.[32]

In 1816, returning to Britain, Raffles brought twenty-two pieces of Javanese batiks as examples to show English manufacturers styles in the local taste.[33] Only a couple of textiles have survived from this collection. Most of them were given to British manufacturers to be copied for export, although to which companies is unknown.[34] It took several decades before a satisfying export trade was achieved with Britain becoming an important producer of imitation batik, but little is known of the companies involved at the beginning.[35]

The Netherlands before 1830

In 1815, under the terms of the Anglo-Dutch Treaty of 1814 following the end of the Napoleonic Wars, the island of Java was returned to the control of the Netherlands. During the Congress of Vienna (1814-1815) – organised to restore old boundaries and re-establish the main powers to guarantee European security – a new Kingdom of the Netherlands was created, the Verenigd Koninkrijk der Nederlanden (United Kingdom of the Netherlands), covering present day Belgium and the Netherlands. William I became the first king of the Netherlands.

His main interests were restoring economic growth and modernization. In the second half of the eighteenth century, the industry had stagnated, declined or disappeared altogether and this situation worsened during the Napoleonic Wars when French customs barriers had hindered trade and deprived the Dutch industry of access to a major part of the European market, which accelerated industrial collapse and unemployment.[36] In the northern provinces textile production had almost vanished putting the focus on trade and shipping. In 1813 only four printing workshops remained, largely old fashioned and not mechanised.[37] New printing techniques were known but little developed by the Dutch.[38]

1. Francois Joseph Navez, Portrait of Willem Frederik van Oranje-Nassau, King William I (1772-1843), 1823
This painting was given by the artist to J.-B. T. Prévinaire around 1830 and hung in the office of the company until its closure in 1917.
Private collection Marie Henriette del Court-Prévinaire,
Stichting van Pallandt, Velp
(The Netherlands)

Before the reunification in 1815 the situation was different for Belgium, where French occupation offered a new market without customs barriers and industrialisation proceeded rapidly. Assisted by mechanisation and local coal mines, a new textile industry was created. A significant role was played by Lieven Bauwens of Ghent, who was convinced that cotton manufacturing could be highly profitable with new technological innovations. Undeterred by the British ban on export of machinery, he started smuggling machine parts from Britain and constructed spinning mules and weaving looms with flying shuttles in the 1790s and early nineteenth century, thereby doubling productivity. Machine parts confiscated by British Customs were reproduced by Bauwens in a metal workshop in Ghent which he opened in 1798. He also introduced copper cylinders for mechanised printing of cloth. Belgian entrepreneurs quickly adopted these new technologies and by 1810, there were around thirty mechanised spinning mills in and around Ghent. By 1812, the Belgian cotton industry had attained the level of Britain in terms of technology and production.[39] But despite the important innovations, the first fifteen years of the nineteenth century were dominated by wartime turbulence, creating financial hardship for entrepreneurs who had invested heavily in modernisation.

King William was supportive and gave these entrepreneurs financial help by creating in 1821 a fund to encourage national industry (*Fonds ter Aanmoediging van Nationale Nijverheid*). He also initiated a trading company in 1824: the *Nederlandsche Handel-Maatschappij* (Dutch Trading Society) (hereafter NHM), aiming to promote trade between the Netherlands and its colonies. The NHM was set up as a private company with the goal of expanding trade by searching out new markets and developing finance and shipping. It would provide guaranteed orders to selected dyers and printers, mainly situated in the southern Netherlands, if price and quality were better than those of their competitors.[40] After the collapse of the Dutch East India Company in 1799, these measures can be seen as an attempt to reinvigorate trade with the Dutch East Indies. Its network could be found throughout South East Asia on the trade routes between the Netherlands and the Dutch East Indies.

To stimulate trade and end British dominance, the Netherlands introduced the Textile Ordinance of 1824, an import tariff of 25-35% on all textile goods imported to Indonesia via non-Dutch ships. Textiles produced in the Netherlands were exempt. While the British textiles imported to Java and Madura Island in 1823 represented 3 million out of a total 3.7 million guldens, by 1829 British imports were reduced to 30% of textiles sold in Indonesia.[41] Although the Dutch had not been able to force the British out, they managed to obtain the principal share of textile sales, supplied mainly by factories in Ghent.[42] Although most exports were organised by the government, local textile producers also exported at their own risk or in collaboration with merchants, for example the company *Société Anonyme Texas* of the Voortman family in Ghent. Another business method was the employment of representatives in special trading houses located in Amsterdam and Rotterdam. Voortman founded such a trading house in Amsterdam in 1826, which continued until 1842.[43] After the separation of Belgium from the Netherlands in 1830, its transactions represented more than half of the total sales by the company.[44] Overall, private initiatives represented only a small part of the export market, not only because of the risks involved, but also because much trade was in exchange for tropical produce, with which textile entrepreneurs were not familiar.[45]

Dutch interest in batik imitations

As set out above, Great Britain had already started exporting imitation batiks to Indonesia with mixed success. The Dutch interested in producing batik imitations faced the same problems as the English through lack of knowledge about desired patterns and colours.[46] To alleviate this problem, King William had samples collected of British imitation batik to show Dutch textile industrialists.[47] The Ministry of Colonial Affairs (*Departement van Koloniën*) compiled a pattern book of the best-selling designs. Information for this book probably came from a memorandum to provide information about cotton samples: the *Nota om te dienen tot inlichting van de Monsters der Lijwaten*, written in 1819 by C.F. Winter Sr, who worked for the colonial government in Indonesia. This included a collection of batik with detailed descriptions and explanatory notes to provide models.[48] Based on this information the Ministry prepared a sample card of the most sought after patterns.[49] In 1825, the NHM started collecting original batiks as examples for the various printing companies in the Netherlands.[50]

There is little information about the earliest production of imitation batik in the Netherlands. At an exhibition of products of the national industry in Ghent in August 1820, a gold medal was awarded to De Smet Frères of Ghent for their excellent imitations of Indian fabrics *destiné pour nos colonies* (destined for our colonies).[51] However, it is not known if these were versions of Indian cloth or whether they included batik. Voortman in Ghent, who began exporting to Java in 1823, received a silver medal.[52] Also mentioned are Jean Baptiste Theodore Prévinaire and Dieudonné Sény from Brussels, who received the bronze medal for their products. Five years later, at a similar event in Haarlem, they received a gold medal. Their Turkey red cottons were considered the best of Belgium and equal to those from Alsace.[53] Turkey reds were popular because they were supremely bright and colourfast, with the best qualities universally admired for their deep red colour. Although it is not known when they started printing imitation batik, other printers involved in this early period were *Non Plus Ultra* outside Rotterdam, and Sutorius, taken over in 1846 by P. F. Fentener van Vlissingen, in Helmond.[54] Mansvelt writes that the first consignments of the NHM in 1825 had more the character of experiments.[55] The competition, especially with the English, was fierce.[56]

A representative of the NHM in Batavia wrote on 15 June 1830:

> *Van de gedrukte Hoofddoeken en Sarongs is een gedeelte dadelijk alhier verkogt, echter trok de aankomst van eene partij engelsche Batticks van een nieuw patroon de kooplust geheel na zig toe, waardoor het overige gedeelte onverkogt bleef* (Some of the printed headscarves and sarongs were immediately sold here, but the arrival of a batch of English Batticks of a new pattern completely curbed the purchasing spirit, leaving the remainder unsold).[57]

Another report dated 25 June 1830 states that

de nagemaakte battiks worden weinig door den inlander gedragen, nu de echte zooveel in prijs verminderd zijn (the counterfeit batiks are rarely worn by the native now that the real ones have been reduced so much in price).[58]

Later that year a written report advises that given newly arrived batik imitations remained unsold and were sent to more distant markets for sale:

Wij betreuren dat de veranderlijkheid van den smaak der inlanders ons noodzaakt de aanmaak van eener soort van goederen afteraden (We regret that the variability of the tastes of the natives forces us to advise against the production of one class of goods).[59]

However, the somewhat lower technical capacity of the Dutch spinners resulted in an unexpected competitive advantage over the English, as Indonesians were willing to pay a premium for the coarser and more sturdy Dutch cottons. When the NHM eventually developed a greater knowledge of the market and found the necessary manufacturers to supply the desired cloth, the imitations, while not comparable in terms of quality to original batiks, quickly gained in sales because of their lower price.[60] The aim of the printing companies was to work as cheaply as possible to maximise profit and seek to produce a product for the masses.[61] The fact that specific cultural knowledge was required to produce marketable cloth was seen as a burden: Veth wrote about the *grillige eisen van de inlandsche smaak* (whimsical demands of the local tastes).[62] Voortman maintained that a profound knowledge of the local market was essential for success. The imitation prints should be as close as possible to the quality of the original batiks. The locals were aware of the inferiority of the imitations, but these were saleable if prices were kept low. Not until the 1850s was the desired commercial quality fully achieved.

Dutch batik production after the 1830 separation from Belgium

This technical and mercantile success reflected in medals, but the growing sales of the NHM did not last long. It collapsed in 1830 with the outbreak of the Belgian Revolution. Unemployment was high as was industrial unrest among the working classes, frustrated at their lack of influence in the politics of the United Kingdom of the Netherlands. Riots erupted, factories were occupied and machinery destroyed, especially that of the wealthiest entrepreneurs loyal to the king. It was not possible to preserve the union because the Belgian provinces were supported not only by France but also by Britain. The nine Belgian provinces separated from the Netherlands and created an independent country. And although in 1831 King Leopold I was installed as the new king of the Belgians, it was not until 1839 that King William accepted the independence of Belgium.

Until 1830 textiles from Ghent were the main export product to the colonies of the Netherlands and essential for the purchase of tropical goods. After 1830 the trade in Belgium suffered with the loss of its major buyer: the NHM. The Société Cotonnière de Gand, a merchant organisation, tried to maintain exports to the Dutch East Indies, but British competition and import tariffs of 50% imposed by the government of the Netherlands meant that the initiative failed.[63]

The collapse of the Belgian textile production allowed Britain, the principal victor in the Napoleonic wars, to quickly regain a dominant position in the Indonesian market despite the refusal of the Netherlands to modify or end the Textile Ordinance, introduced in 1824.[64]

Governor General Johannes van den Bosch suggested that King William I eliminate the input of the Belgian industry altogether and develop productivity in the Netherlands. He felt that companies should be invited to move to impoverished inner cities such as Haarlem and Leiden to reduce unemployment.[65] The NHM was clear as to its motivation:

La protection, que nous avions accordée à votre industrie, n'ayant point de rapport à nos intérêts personnels ou financiers, nous aimons à avouer que son but a été en grande partie de remédier au pauperisme toujours croissants de nos grandes villes et de mettre un grand nombre de nos compatriotes en état de gagner leur pain d'une manière honnête (The protection we had given to your industry had nothing to do with our personal or financial interest. We prefer to say that its purpose was largely to remedy the ever-increasing poverty of our big cities and to allow many of our compatriots to earn their bread in an honest way).[66]

King William I had little other alternative. Companies in the north were not prepared to service the NHM. Brabant in the south and Twente in the east were too far from the capital and their textile manufacturing not well developed. In Haarlem textile production was almost non-existant.[67] Unemployment was high among the local population, who were severely impoverished.

By contrast, in Belgium, important entrepreneurs with sometimes thousands of employees wished to safeguard their companies. Many of them belonged to the *orangistes,* strongly supporting King William I. In the first years after the separation, they actively worked as a counter movement, refusing to do business with the Belgian government, but their economic situation deteriorated.[68] The Dutch government, wishing to invigorate its backward textile industry, saw its best option to entice companies from the south with the promise of financial assistance and guaranteed orders. Several important textile producers eventually decided to move north, based on the royal promise of favourable trade conditions, and continuance of the NHM.[69] Attracting Belgian companies compensated for the loss of the region, and served to re-kindle the exports to Indonesia.[70]

Several important textile producers moved from Belgium to the Netherlands. Meanwhile, Belgium did little to stimulate export to boost its textile industry or protect against foreign, especially British, competition. Its entrepreneurs were mostly focused on production and not on the trade of their products, which had been mainly organised by the Dutch. Very quickly the cotton printers started to struggle to survive, unable to keep up with technological innovations. It took the remaining businesses in Belgium, mainly specialised in spinning and weaving, a long time to recover. By 1890, cotton printing was nearly non-existent.[71]

Charles de Maere, a Belgian textile printer, was the first to transfer his business in 1832. He moved from Sint Niklaas (St Nicolas) to Hengelo, a town in the east of the Netherlands, in exchange for guaranteed monthly deliveries to be taken by the NHM. He was one of many company directors who considered separation from the north commercial suicide for Belgium.[72] The next to follow was Thomas Wilson (1788-1867), a manufacturer from Lancashire who moved from Uccle, near Brussels, to Haarlem. He specialised in *imitation India cotton* for the Javanese market with the NHM as one of his main customers.[73] In 1833 Poelman and Vervaecke asked permission to transfer their spinning and weaving mills, called *The Phoenix*, from Ghent to Haarlem.

In 1834 a contract was signed with Prévinaire, who owned a major company that specialised in Turkey red, to move from Curinghem, near Brussels, to establish a company in Haarlem.[74] Frustrated at the lack of support from the Belgian government, this *fabricant d'indiennes* had made enough money with the export of printed and dyed cloth to Indonesia to buy the necessary land, built the company at his own cost and refused any loans. His was the last company to move to the north at this time as further approaches to transfer business were rejected.[75] The arrival of Prévinaire was for the NHM a major achievement. In a letter of 18 September 1830, Pierre Van Gobbelschroy, the Belgian Minister of the Interior, described Prévinaire to Prince Frederik, the son of King William I and in charge of the troops to suppress the rebellion in Brussels, as

l'un des fabricants les plus distingués du Royaume qui emploie même encore aujourd'hui 2500 ouvriers (one of the most distinguished manufacturers of the Kingdom, who even today employs 2,500 workers).[76]

Mansvelt called Prévinaire the father of the Dutch cotton industry and he soon became its most important textile manufacturer.[77] In 1835 Prévinaire installed a laboratory for chemical experimentation with colours, which may have been the first industrial laboratory in the Netherlands. His Turkey red products and his printed cottons enabled him to extend the factory and to export directly besides selling through the NHM.[78]

Lack of local skilled personnel obliged Prévinaire to employ foreign workers. Initially he recruited 54 people, but this number rose quickly to 242.[79] Prévinaire was outspoken in his negotiations with the NHM and soon became its main supplier.[80] A year after his arrival he employed 2,587 people, of whom 556 were in the Haarlem factory. He had several weaving mills in Twente and the province of Brabant as well as making use of the putting out system.[81]

The NHM not only exported printed cottons, but also more sophisticated fabrics, capturing a substantial market in South East Asia. Instead of ordering cloth directly the NHM left it to the various manufacturers to arrange them with orders. In 1835 the NHM agreed on the first contract to buy and export 3 million guilders of cotton cloth per annum, all made in the Netherlands. The Department of Colonies chose the producers, while the NHM management decided on price and quality. This policy was to ensure there was enough capacity to produce the desired quantity, but also that enough new employment was created. The decision to halt transfer of Belgian firms was reversed to create more jobs. De Heyder and Co, owned by the well-known Orangist Baron Van den Berghe, was invited to move from Lier to Leiden. The company was keen to move because of falling orders.[82] De Heyder and Co also brought their own skilled workers, as other companies had complained that while there were enough local workers available, candidates were lacking in physical and mental fitness.[83] The company continued to grow its workforce, and in 1877, when it changed its name to the *Leidsche Katoenmaatschappij voorheen De Heyder and Co,* it had a workforce of 1,200 people.[84]

Other companies that would become important printers of imitation batik in the Netherlands were *Van Vlissingen* in Helmond, *Non Plus Ultra,* a company in Kralingen, near Rotterdam and *Roessingh*, which started in 1804 in Enschede and moved in 1912 to Veenendaal.[85] Over the course of the nineteenth century several other Dutch companies printed imitation batik. *Arntzenius Jannink & Co* in Goor made printed imitation sarongs from around 1887 to 1912.[86] *C. T. Stork & Co* in Hengelo, *W. G. J. Ramaer and Co* and *Prinzen and Van*

Glabbeek in Helmond, *Ter Kuile-Morsman* and *J. F. Scholten and Son* also found success in this field.[87] Guaranteed sales by the NHM allowed them to expand and invest in new machinery and become internationally competitive.

Prévinaire – father, Jean Baptiste Theodore, and son, Marie Prosper Theodore

The most outstanding quality of imitation batiks was produced by Jean Baptiste Theodore Prévinaire (1783-1854) and later continued by his son Marie Prosper Theodore Prévinaire (1831-1900).

The elder Prévinaire fulfilled large orders for the NHM: in 1837 he sold goods worth ƒ747,640 and in 1838 sales reached ƒ862,320.[88] Orders for 1839 reached ƒ1,000,000.[89] More than half were for Turkey red products. Father and son Prévinaire did grow their own madder.[90] Until 1850 he was the main supplier of these products to the NHM and, although he was not the cheapest, his products were of the best quality and the name Prévinaire added prestige.

Not only had he been able to build a new company at his own cost, in 1840 he built a lavish residence, villa *Nijverveld* at the Zijlweg in Haarlem in neo-classical style with 25 rooms and a park.[91] Every room had its own function with opulent furniture and decorations. In the park were carriage houses, stables for several horses and seventeen dear.[92] Craandijk wrote in 1878:

> *Dat de nijverheid in haar priesters den zin voor het schooner, ook al is het improductief, niet behoeft uit te blusschen, ziet gij in den rijken bloemhof, het welig plantsoen en den hertenkamp bij het collosale huis van den eigenaar der fabriek, en dat de winsten ruim zijn, zouden wij haast aan den grootschen aanleg van den huize Nijverveld kunnen vermoeden* (That industry holds in its high priests a sense of the beautiful that will not be extinguished just because it is unproductive. You see it in the rich flower garden and the lush park wiith its deer park at the colossal house of the factory's owner. That profits are plentiful you can easily guess from the grandiose plan of the Nijverveld house).[93]

Prévinaire wanted to belong to the elite of Haarlem, but its upper class held manufacturing in disdain, preferring sea and land-based trade and agriculture. However, the esteem in which he was held in business was challenged in 1837.

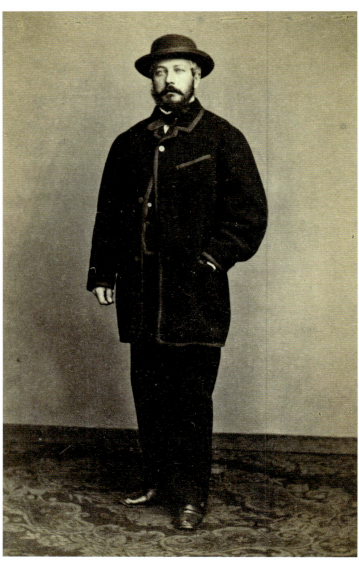

2. Charles Baugniet, portrait of Jean Baptiste Prévinaire (1783–1854), 1848
Noord-Hollands Archief, Haarlem, (the Netherlands), inv.no. 49814

3. Marie Prosper Theodore Prévinaire (1831-1900), photo by Ghémar Frères, Brussels 1870-1871
Collection Nationaal Archief, The Hague

4. Samples of imitation batik of Leidsche Katoen Maatschappij for NHM 1850
Contra stalen 1848–1854, p. 29-30, Inv. no. 9313.
Collectie De Lakenhal, Leiden

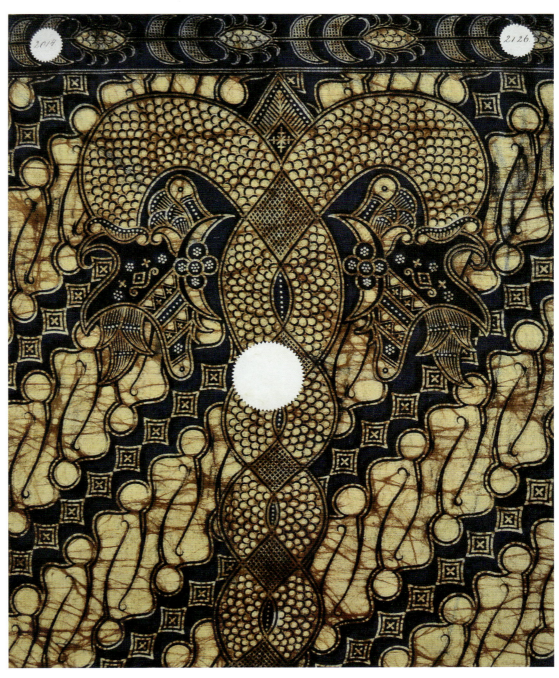

5. Sample Prévinaire Haarlemsche Katoen Maatschappij around 1880
HKM book 226, sample 2014
Vlisco Archive, @ Vlisco BV

Imitating Indonesian batik in Europe: the beginnings

Not able to produce the right quality of Turkey red required for the NHM, he began smuggling dyed cloth from his company in Belgium. When the NHM became aware of the illegal import, he declared himself to have terminated his interests in the Belgian company and to be unaware of how the cloth had come into the country. Given the importance of Prévinaire, the NHM decided not to pursue him or to revoke his contract, but stopped the monopoly he had had so far.[94] Less fortunate was *The Phoenix* from Poelman, Sons & Vervaecke, which ran into a conflict with the NHM in 1838 concerning cloth smuggled from Lancashire and sold as self-made products. *The Phoenix* did not get the support of the NHM and, notwithstanding major investments, it failed to make a profit and sold up to Prévinaire in 1842.[95] With this spinning and weaving mill, Prévinaire was finally able to produce the desired quality for his printed cloth, abandoning imported cloth.[96] He continued to search for improvements to his printing machinery. Already, before his departure to the Netherlands, he had purchased a *perrotine*, a block-printing machine developed in the same year by Louis Jérôme Perrot (1798-1878) in Rouen.

The economic crisis of 1840 led the government to discontinue its subsidy to the NHM. Now it had to operate on a fully commercial and competitive level, making sales to the NHM less profitable. Textile companies increasingly exported directly or through merchants, which gave them a better insight into their intended markets. Other markets in Asia and Africa were explored. Independent economic growth began, stimulated further by competition from English and Swiss companies. For Prévinaire, successful with his Turkey red products, he turned his attention to improving the quality of imitation batik. In a patent application in 1844, he wrote:

> *De bijzonderheid in fraaiheid der patronen, het grote vertier en de hoge prijs der in Oost Indië vervaardigde en aldaar algemeen gedragen wordende Batiks, hebben sedert geruime tijd de aandacht van Europese fabrikanten tot zich*

6. Previnaire's company in Haarlem around 1850
Noord-Hollands Archief Haarlem (The Netherlands), Inv.no. 45124

7. Prévinaire's Villa Nijverveld, Zijlweg Haarlem 1840, demolished in 1885
Collectie Vereniging Haerlem - Neg.no. KHIU: 9185; Kennemerland NL
HlmHA 5350076

getrokken. Bij de eerste blik op deze nagemaakte Batiks is het voor een fabrikant niet mogelijk de gelijkvormigheid te erkennen van de door de drukker regelmatig gestelde platen: ook zijn dezelve op de Indische markt zeer weinig gezocht en vinden slechts aftrek tot zeer lage en gedrukte prijzen (The special beauty of the patterns, the healthy trade and the high price fetched by the batiks manufactured in the East Indies and widely worn there, have attracted the attention of European manufacturers for some time now. At the first glance at these imitation batiks, it is not possible for a manufacturer to detect any similarity with the original patterns made by the printer: they are also very rarely sought after on the Indonesian market and are only found at very low and reduced prices).[97]

He was granted a patent for three machines, of which one was focused on improving the quality of the imitation batiks.[98] Cracks in the batik wax created *veins* which Indonesians tried to keep to a minimum, as a sign of the highest quality, but cheaper qualities would inevitably have some craquelure. European producers of imitation batik sometimes printed *craquelure* as patterns, overemphasising the cracks with a heavy and a systematic repeat rather than random natural cracking. In Europe, mixtures of wax with resin were used, but Prévinaire used more resin than wax, making the mixture stick better to the cloth using steam. After cooling, natural cracks would appear. He soda-washed the cloth so the wax could be removed, but not the resin. A second dye process would then dye the places where the wax had been removed, which added the much sought-after effect of *bleeding*.[99] In 1847, the works was equipped with a roller printing machine capable of printing five colours, and three years later a machine that could print six colours simultaneously. Almost annually father and son would buy new equipment in England and France.[100] To improve the quality of his imitations even further Prévinaire experimented successfully with adding a scent of wax, a characteristic much appreciated by the Indonesians, and before then a way to distinguish a real batik. He followed instructions provided by Edward Baudoin, an agent for the NHM on Java. Because of Prévinaire's close contacts with the NHM, he was often the first, and even the only one, to receive such information.[101]

Even with the NHM operating on a non-subsidised basis, Prévinaire's position remained dominant. The directors of the NHM, witnessing a decline in Indonesian sales against the rise of the Swiss production which was superior in colour, print and pattern, pleaded for more open competition, but under pressure from the King himself, Prévinaire was guaranteed a fixed number of orders, thereby reducing orders placed with other companies.[102]

Around 1850, Prévinaire and Son did have the largest machine printing company in the Netherlands. However, the high cost of investment in plant and relatively expensive products made for meagre profits, but father and son continued their pursuit of quality improvement.

On 22 April 1854, eight days before the death of his father, Prévinaire Jr filed a patent for a new machine, the *Javanaise*.[103] On 1 June 1854, a fifteen-year patent was granted. This would become the company's most important invention. By keeping precise details secret until around 1910, the company held an exclusive position in wax printing for more than fifty years.[104] The main innovation of the mechanised block printing of the *Javanaise* was its ability to print a warm wax-resin reserve on both sides of the cloth. Also, the print blocks used were larger than those of the *perrotine* giving greater freedom in design.[105] After the death of his father, Prévinaire Jr, then only 24 years old, took over the business, focussing on

8. Sample of Turkey red with printed label of Prévinaire's company 1873 LKM book 251, p. 85 Vlisco Archive, @ Vlisco BV

Imitating Indonesian batik in Europe: the beginnings

wax printing so that it became of equal importance to the company's Turkey red products.[106]

In 1854 Prévinaire Jr informed the NHM that he had four roller printing machines, two perrotines and three *Javanaises* for making batik imitations. This made his the largest and most modern textile company in the Netherlands at that time.[107] The firm, although over-equipped in terms of demand, was able to compete with English and Swiss companies. In contrast to other Dutch companies, his production had become exclusively for non-European markets such as Indonesia, India, China and Japan.[108] But despite all these efforts the company made scant profits.[109] The prices which the NHM offered barely covered the costs of production. Prévinaire Jr reminded the NHM that he had invested many years in improving his machinery and experimented to raise product quality, but the NHM refused to place big orders and only offered to sell products on a consignment basis, something which Prévinaire Jr reluctantly had to accept.[110] For a long time, the NHM was his only client, before he gradually managed to engage other mercantile clients.

While Prévinaire started regular production of his wax imitation batiks in the late 1850s, it was only at the beginning of the 1860s that growing demand in the East Indies brought financial relief after years of investment and development. Sales figures increased by 71% in this decade.[111] Clients appreciated the higher quality of Prévinaire imitation batiks and were willing to pay a higher price. For a short time, from 1863 to 1867, the company made huge profits, in part due to direct sales to merchants after the earlier dwindling of orders from the NHM. He worked with four merchants' firms, enabling production to be set a full year in advance. However, an offer by one of these to guarantee the sales for five years was rejected by Prévinaire.[112]

Prévinaire's success with wax printing resulted in the fact that other companies experimented with the technique in the 1860s. In the period between 1865-1867, De Heyder (LKM) managed to gain some insight into the recipes of Prévinaire as well as some idea of the method of printing with the *Javanaise,* but he was too slow in updating his process to eventually make a profit. The company struggled with finding a good recipe for a resist mixture.[113] Textile production historian Verbong found that Van Vlissingen managed in 1866 to make good quality *imitation* wax prints.[114] Wilson, the English manufacturer and one of the first to move from Belgium to Haarlem in 1833, showed some samples at the World Exhibition in Paris in 1867 securing orders for the NHM, but the volume remained low.[115] Despite mechanisation, making imitation batik with wax to the standards desired by Indonesian customers was still a costly, multi-stage, expertise-dependent, time-consuming process.[116]

The batik imitations of Switzerland

Mulhouse, until 1798 a Swiss enclave, developed a high standard of printing aided by excellent colourists. Already in 1746, the first cotton printing company, specialising in *indiennes*, was founded in Mulhouse by Samuel Koechlin (1719-1776), Jean-Henri Dollfus and Jean-Jacques Schmaltzer. Koechlin's grandson, Daniel Koechlin (1785-1871) studied chemistry in Paris and around 1815 he improved the technique of discharge printing Turkey red cloth, for which he received a medal at the 1819 *Exposition des produits de l'industrie française* in Paris.[117] Carlos Forel (1795-1872), who married into the Koechlin family, travelled in 1828 to India, Singapore and Indonesia to explore possibilities for production of textiles for export.[118] He assembled and brought home a collection of foreign cloth and European-made imitations.[119] But the Koechlin firm eventually decided to specialise in Turkey red products which fetched even higher prices than genuine batiks of the best quality.[120]

Around 1840, the province of Glarus became the main centre in Switzerland for printing batik imitations for the East Asian market. The province already had a significant textile production. Given the small size of its domestic market it mainly aimed at export to the Mediterranean area and the Middle East. As it was nearly impossible to compete with British mass production, the Swiss companies had already concentrated their attention on hand-printed specialties. The focus was imitation of cloth used for traditional folk costumes in France and Italy, but also printed cottons for India. Their printed imitations of complicated products were more affordable than the original models; moreover, they were able to adapt their production quickly to their clients' wishes. They also specialised in Turkey red products that were amongst the highest qualities in Europe.[121] Another commercial success was the production of handkerchiefs in various European tastes and headscarves for the Middle East, Syria, Iran and North Africa.[122] In 1860, twenty-two companies were printing cloth, making this province the most industrialised in Switzerland. Some Swiss companies sold to the NHM, others to agencies, so called commissionaires, who organised the sale to local traders in Indonesia.[123]

Trading in overseas markets was highly risky, especially for the Swiss who had no tradition of maritime transport and no navy for protection. A good knowledge of the markets was crucial. In 1840, Conrad Blumer, working for Blumer and Jenny in Schwanden, travelled to Java to study batik. Bringing back first-hand knowledge of the market, his father Peter Blumer, co-partner of the firm, began printing imitation batiks.[124]

Adolf Jenny-Trümpy, author of a comprehensive history of the trade and industry in Glarus published in 1898, explains that producing plain cloth or the so-called *indiennes*,

European copies of Indian print, for export to India was relatively easy. Developing imitation batik for export to Indonesia and South East Asia was much more demanding and initially not financially rewarding. The cloth needed to be printed on both sides and the patterns were too long for roller printing; cloth sizes and quality needed to be right.[125] As the English and Dutch had already experienced, a detailed knowledge of batik was essential for successful imitations. Development at Schwanden was initially slow because technical complexities that kept production relatively expensive needed to be resolved. The distance from the market was also a hindrance; Jenny-Trümpy emphasised that production was costly and clients far away.[126]

By 1860, Peter Blumer & Jenny had resolved these difficulties and began to enjoy success. In 1867, a new firm, Gebrüder Blumer & Cie, was founded to concentrate on batik only.[127] Other companies followed suit in making batik imitations of a relatively high quality, notably Bartholomé Jenny & Cie in Ennenda from around 1845 until 1860, and Egidius Trümpy in Glarus from 1852 onwards.[128] This last company managed in the 1860s to copy with success an artificial technique of Prévinaire to print the crackles of wax.[129] Companies outside Glarus ensued.[130] Notable firms are Greuter & Rieter in Islikon-Frauenfeld, the brothers Geilinger in Winterthur, and Ziegler & Cie in Richterwil.[131] Ziegler employed Conrad Herman Deutsch as technical director and in 1875 his son, previously at Van Vlissingen and Co in Helmond, was engaged as a colourist.[132]

Most patterns were derived from Indonesian batik originals. Initially, only large firms, like Bartholomé Jenny & Cie, could afford designers; the designer Niklaus Stäger-Heer (1820–1900) worked 58 years for the company.[133] However, by the middle of the nineteenth century about forty designers worked in the region's twenty-one factories, although many of these *designers* were probably pattern drawers, occupied with adapting existing designs or patterns from hand-printed originals to technical specifications. [134] The repeat size of patterns needed to be adjusted to the cloth width and roller-printed colours required modification to emulate the brightness achieved by hand-block printing. Combined techniques, adding block printed colours after machine printing, provided an alternative solution. What distinguished Swiss production was not only high-quality prints, but the creation of new designs and colour ranges. Their success was such that the Dutch started working in the same way, including Prévinaire.[135]

For their part, the Swiss manufacturers were impressed by the success of Prévinaire's wax-printed batik imitations. Swiss companies started to experiment with wax in the 1860s. The first was a colourist from Mulhouse, M. A. Schultz, who carried out experiments at Egidius Trümpy's company to make real wax prints around 1860.[136] Other companies followed their lead, but only for a very short time as the production was too complicated and the profits too low.[137]

Special effects for making imitation batik to give the cloth an authentic look, such as *craquelure* and *bleeding*, were introduced by the Swiss, resulting in attractive new products.[138] It was the colourist Jakob Elmer, working for E. Trümpy, who perfected this concept in 1863–1864.[139] It was an idea quickly imitated by the Dutch manufacturers.[140]

Decline of European imitation batik after 1867
After 1867, imitation batik export went into sharp decline, even though the demand for batik in Indonesia was quickly rising. The population increased because of better health care and the growth of trade and industry improved people's possibilities to purchase goods. By 1870, the opening of the Suez Canal and regular steamships service stimulated trade, and the construction of new roads and a rail network on Java made trade possible in hitherto isolated areas.[141] Nevertheless, the Europeans faced rising competition from the Indonesian batik industry which in the middle of the nineteenth century had introduced an innovation of its own – *batik cap,* a metal block for printing hot wax that did speed up the hand process considerably. Instead of lengthy hand-drawing, hot wax was printed from copper blocks for cheaper and faster production, a process aided by the European cottons which presented a more uniform surface.[142] For patterns traditionally drawn by hand with a canting, twelve to fifteen days were required to apply the wax, but with cap stamps up to twenty pieces could be completed in a day. The techniques could also be combined, for example outlines with caps and details drawn with canting.[143] The introduction of *batik cap* transformed Indonesian production of batik from an artisanal into an industrial business.

An extra hindrance to the export of imitation batik came in 1874 when the Dutch government abolished preferential rates for Dutch importers in Indonesia.[144] Only by supplying unprinted sarong lengths and bleached textiles for the Indonesian batik industry did these importers manage to maintain a significant proportion of Indonesian imports.[145] On the whole, European batik was considered a cheap surrogate and never received the esteem accorded to hand-made batik. Worn by the lower classes of Indonesian society, it was classed as *batik tiron* (imitation batik).[146] A fundamental problem with European imitations was that while the Indonesians tolerated fine cracks, the bolder cracking and bubbling effects of machine-made imitation batiks were not appreciated and considered a sign of inferior quality. Technically, the Europeans could have corrected this, but they chose quantity over quality. The machine-made product also had too much symmetry and systematic repeats. Moreover, the typical smell, appreciated by the Indonesians was lacking; only Prévinaire had experimented successfully with cloth odour.

The batik imitations did not change the customs in Indonesia, especially on Java, that chosen designs and colours were used to express social, religious and ethnic affiliations through dress.[147] People selected imitation batik by the same dress codes as if they were original batik.[148] Other cultural factors seemed difficult to comprehend for Western traders. Importantly, cloths were purchased only twice a year: after the harvest and after the period of Ramadan, in Indonesia called *Lebaran*. This made regular production and sales impossible. Correspondence of agents shows that Western producers were under the impression that the cloth was seen as a seasonally changing form of fashion as in Western Europe, but this was not the case.[149]

The decline of the market forced most of the manufacturers that worked with wax to stop producing wax batiks and to move to a cheaper form of imitation batiks, the so-called *non-wax fancy prints*.[150] In Switzerland most manufacturers abandoned the production of imitation batiks for the Dutch East Indies in the 1870s as their products could no longer compete with local Indonesian industry.

In the Netherlands De Heyder (LKM) had been too cautious and too late to innovate. By the time its version of the *Javanaise* was fully functional, the market had already collapsed. For Van Vlissingen, production was only carried out for a very short period – end of 1866, early 1867 – because it was not profitable enough to continue. Wilson died in 1867, and his company had overinvested; not able to keep up with modernisation, it was sold to Prévinaire in 1872. The only one who still believed in the future of this product was Prévinaire Jr. He was convinced his batik imitations were the best and that he was continually coming closer to original batiks. Highly innovative, he continued looking for new applications and further improvements, although batik imitations were a relatively small part of his total production.[151]

1 Wronska-Friend 2017, 49
2 These finds are today at the Ashmolean Museum in Oxford. Indian textiles came to Egypt on the maritime route via southern Arabia. For more information about these textiles, see Ruth Barnes, I*ndian Block-Printed Textiles in Egypt. The Newberry Collection in the Ashmolean Museum*, Oxford 1997. Philip Sykas suggests that in Xinijang (China) even earlier samples of wax resist have been found with an iconography that relates to the Kushan empire which continued approximately until 375 CE.
3 Guy, 61-62
4 Wisseman Christie, 192
5 This would later lead to the development of *isén* – the fine filling within a motif. McCabe Elliot, 36
6 Rouffaer and Juynboll 1899, 390-391
7 In the second half of the nineteenth century stamped batik or batik cap was also developed to shorten the manufacturing time. For this type a stamp tool of copper plates with a batik motif with wax instead of ink was used. This process needed a lot of experience. The process needed to be repeated depending on the numbers of color desired. All the motifs are the same, which makes this process less artistic, but also cheaper and quicker to produce. Later also *painted batik* or *batik lukis* became very popular, because it is affordable and follows a very creative manufacturing process. This type of batik can be used as decoration or clothing.
8 Wronska-Friend 2016, 19
9 Gittinger 1990, 16. In 1798 the VOC ceased to exist following bankruptcy. Its assets and debt passed on to the Dutch government.
10 It was purchased by George Day from a factory in Banten on Java and shipped on The Loyall Subject. India Office Records and Private Papers IOR/L/AG/1/1/4f.138(1), p. 183, British Library, London.
11 Veldhuisen 1993, 27-28. On page 29 he gives a detailed description of batik patterns that were in vogue around 1820.
12 Heringa 2010, 125
13 The British had seized the colony of Indonesia from the Dutch when the Netherlands had been under French control since 1795 because of the Napoleonic wars. The Batavian Republic, controlled by the French, was installed in 1806; later replaced by the Kingdom of Holland, in 1810 it was annexed into the French Empire.
14 Raffles 1817, 169-170. After Raffles it took many decades before studies appeared to describe batik and other forms of textile art in Indonesia in great detail. See, for example, G. P. Rouffaer and H. H. Juynboll, *De Batikkunst in Nederlandsch-Indië en haar Geschiedenis*, Haarlem 1899 and J. E. Jasper and Mas Pirngadie, *De Inlandsche kunstnijverneid in Nederlandsch Indië*, part two about weaving (The Hague 1912), and part three about batik (The Hague 1916).
15 For a detailed description and interpretation of these illustrations, see Natalie A. Mault, 'Java as a Western Construct: An Examination of Sir Thomas Stamford Raffles' *The History of Java*', PhD thesis, Louisiana State University, 2005.
16 These dolls are important because they represent the earliest set of batik designs known so far. See also Anthony Forge, 'Batik Patterns in the Early Nineteenth Century' in M. Gittinger (ed.), *To Speak with Cloth. Studies in Indonesian Textiles*, Museum of Cultural History, Los Angeles 1989, 91-105. The dolls and engravings are held at the British Museum in London.
17 The nephew and testament executor of Raffles after the death of his wife in 1858 first offered the collection to the British Museum for one thousand pounds, but the museum declined the offer. The collection was finally deposited at the museum on 3 September 1859, but the museum showed little interest at the time. In 1939, eighty years later, the Raffles descendants presented to the Museum some further objects that had been retained or overlooked since 1859, the so-called Drake collection. Forge, 91
18 Green, 27, 37
19 In 1795 the Dutch King William V was exiled to Britain. There he ordered all Dutch colonies to surrender their territories to the British, who then took advantage of the situation and introduced a naval blockade over Java.
20 Mault, 90-91. He was also convinced that, for Java to advance as a civilisation, the British should not have returned it after the Napoleonic wars. Davidson, 241

21 Apart from Pieter van der Burgh's general description of the batik technique, there are few earlier references. Van der Burgh wrote his book *Curieuse beschrijving van de gelegentheid, zeden, godsdienst, en ommegang van verscheyden Oost-Indische gewesten en machtige landschappen, en inzonderheit Golkonda en Pegu* under his initials P.V.D.B and published it in Rotterdam in 1677. He gives a description of batik on pages 103-104.
22 Legène and Waaldijk, 35-36. Crawfurd was appointed Resident Governor at the Court of Yogyakarta in November 1811.
23 Letter from Raffles to William Ramsay, Batavia, 8 January 1813, published in Sophia Raffles ,186. His policy was part of a conquest of world markets by the British from about 1780 with overall good quality and – thanks to growing mechanisation – falling prices. Kraan 1996, 42
24 He made an exception for the designs parang roosa and sawat which were reserved for the royal family. Kerlogue 2004, 20
25 Wang, 282
26 Letter Sir Thomas Raffles 12-1-1813, 206 in: British Library, India Office London: Factory records of East India Company Java 60 G/21/60
27 Advertisement for the sale in *Proclamations, Regulations, Advertisements and Orders, printed and published in the island of Java by the British Government*, vol 1 from September 1811 to September 1813, no 109, 46.
28 Raffles 1817 I, 216-217. For a detailed description of the measurements, colours and motifs of the different garments, see: Heringa 1989, 147-154
29 Wronska-Friend suggests that one of them might have been Raffles himself. Names of these individual entrepreneurs are not known. Wronska-Friend 2017, 51
30 Kraan, 44
31 For a long time, it was assumed that two pieces might have survived and are now in the collection of the British Museum, but the website of the museum indicates a different origin: http://www.britishmuseum.org/researchcollection_online/collection_object_details.aspx?objectId=558906&partId=1&searchText=raffles+batik&page=1, page visited 28 October 2018.
After another visit in 1822, he also brought back samples of Javanese fabrics, but they got lost in a fire on the ship sailing home. See Wronska-Friend 2017, 51.
32 Crawfurd 1820, 504
33 As recorded when released from excise in the London Dock Minute Book on 10 October 1816. Forge 91. Raffles also brought many other artefacts that were eventually donated to the British Museum in 1859. See Barley 11-15. Previously, two pieces of batik, donated to the British Museum in 1939, were thought to be the only survivors of this collection, but they have a different origin (As1939,04.119 and As1939,04.120). See Kerlogue 1999, 30-34.
34 Green, 115
35 Maria Wronska-Friend is researching the first British companies printing imitation batik for export and expects to publish her first results in 2025.
36 Griffiths 1979, 36. This in contrast to the Belgian cotton printers, see Sorber 1989.
37 Bijlsma and Rodenburg, 80
38 Significant industrial development in the Netherlands only occurred in the last decade of the nineteenth century. De Jonge 1976
39 Kraan, 48-49
40 Mansvelt 1924, 225
41 Brommer (2), 32
42 Kraan, 53
43 Voortman, 339; Paeye, 47
44 Scholliers, 120
45 Boot, 69
46 'Het resultaat der eerste in het jaar 1819-1820 aangewende pogingen, om de Nederlandsche katoene lijnwaden in onze Oostersche bezittingen een vertier te bezorgen, was wijnig aanmoedigend, door dien de bedoelde pogingen bijna mislukt waren, ten gevolge van begeerlijke vreemde medepogingen, en ook omdat men in die streken verkeerde begrippen wegens de Nederlandsche nijverheid had opgevat. Naderhand, Sire, en wel met 1821, werden de vorige reeds gedane, echter vruchteloos gebleven pogingen, met ijver en doelmatigheid hervat, en den gunstigen uitslag waarmeede zij bekroond werden, ging alle verwachtingen te boven' (The results of

the first attempts made in 1819-1920 to sell Dutch linen in our Eastern possessions were not very encouraging: attempts almost failed because of foreign competition and misconceptions of Dutch manufacturing. Then, Sire, in 1921 the same attempts which had failed previously were resumed with zeal and efficiency and the favourable results with which they were crowned exceeded all expectations). Algemeen Rijksarchief Den Haag, Ministerie van Binnenlandse Zaken: Nationale Nijverheid, exh. 17 september 1829 n°2, cited in Visser 1977, 187.
47 Brommer (2), 28
48 Van Hout 2017, 65; Rouffaer and Juynboll 1899, 139. The authors give a detailed description of the explanatory notes that were sent.
49 Mansvelt 1924, vol I, 152
50 Legene, 125
51 Voortman, 273
52 Voortman, 273-275 and Wronska-Friend 2017, 52. At a later stage this company also exported imitation batik to West Africa. It ceased its activities in 1890. See also Sorber, 1976 and Sorber 1989, 31-46. For photos of sample books of Voortman, see Debo 2005, 120-121. For a more detailed description of the company, see Interleaf Voortman.
53 See appendix about the life of Prévinaire in Belgium before he moved to the Netherlands in 1834 for more details.
54 For more detailed information about Non Plus Utra, see the appendix about the KKM (Kralingsche Katoen Maatschappij), for Sutorius, see Jacobs and Maas, 19.
55 Mansvelt 1924, vol. I, 152
56 Extract uit de aanteekingen omtrent de aangebragte ladingen en de in de pakhuizen zijnde goederen and report from Batavia d.d. 25 June 1830 in: Archief Nederlandse Handel-Maatschappij (NHM) in National Archives The Hague 2.20.01, iinv.no. 13095: no. 25 (not dated) and report from Batavia d.d. 25 June 1830.
57 Report 15 June 1830. Archive no 2.20.01, inventory no 13095 Ingekomen monsters van textielproducten, met aanbevelingen en curiosa, p. 2. Nationaal Archief The Hague, The Netherlands
58 Report 25 June 1830. Archive no 2.20.01, inventory no 13095 Ingekomen monsters van textielproducten, met aanbevelingen en curiosa, p. 2. Nationaal Archief The Hague, The Netherlands
59 Report 20 November 1830. Archive no 2.20.01, inventory no 13095 Ingekomen monsters van textielproducten, met aanbevelingen en curiosa, p. 2. Nationaal Archief The Hague, The Netherlands
60 Paeye, 44 and Griffiths 1979, 140
61 Voortman, 278
62 Veth 1875, vol 1, 541. For more information about Veth and his book, see chapter 4.
63 Paeye, 58
64 The Textile Ordinance stipulated that tariffs would be 25% directly from the United Kingdom, 35% from goods shipped via Calcutta or Singapore – most goods from the United Kingdom were shipped via this route – and only 6% from the Netherlands. Eng 2006, 4
65 Messing, 40. For more information about the social conditions in Haarlem at the beginning of the nineteenth century, see Doedens and Huygers 1983, 15-39.
66 Mansvelt, Eigen Haard 1924, 240
67 In their report for the year 1831, the Mayer and aldermen of Haarlem write to the Governor of the province of North Holland d.d. 29 December 1831: 'Allertreurigst zijn de narigten omtrent het fabrykwezen; de garentwijderijen staan geheel stil, de lintweeverijen gaan mede agteruit, de katoenspinnerijen en weeverijen hebben nog eenig vertier, doch de zijde- en builgaas-weeverijen zijn bijkans de eenigste, waarbij welvaart wordt waargenomen' (The situation in the factories is troublesome; yarn weaving mills are completely at a standstill, the ribbon weaving mills are also declining, the cotton spinning mills and weaving mills still have some business, but the silk and bolting cloth weaving mills are almost the only ones prospering). Mansvelt 1824, vol. I, 260
68 Prévinaire's company, for example, was looted in 1831 and 1834. The 'Orangistes, partisans of King Willem I, accused the temporary government in Belgium of not intervening. The city of Brussels and the community of Molenbeek were condemned and forced to pay indemnities'. Personal information, Jean Boterdael, president of the local history research group *Molenbecca,* 29 November 2018. It was only from 1834-35 that the Belgian government started to support them. Witte, 252-253

69 Witte, 256-259
70 Belgium did little to stimulate export to boost its textile industry or protect it against foreign competition. Entrepreneurs focussed on the production and on the trade of their products, which had previously been mainly organised by the Dutch. It took the businesses in Belgium, mainly spinning and weaving firms, a long time to recover. By 1890, cotton printing was nearly non-existent. Sorber 1989, 33, 43
71 Sorber 1989, 33, 43. Even one of the last printing manufacturers, the Société Anonyme Texas, previously called Voortman, in Ghent had to close its doors, see Sorber 1989, 44. The weaving companies had more success. King Leopold II stimulated Belgian export to Congo with special import conditions for the colony, see Brommer Zwolle 1991, 30.
72 Mansvelt 1924 ,vol I, 261
73 Wilbrenninck, 8. The cotton industry in Lancashire had been flourishing, but when the crisis hit, he moved around 1820 to Belgium. In Belgium he imported textile products from Britain and bought a factory for weaving, bleaching and printing of cotton materials. He produced imitation India cotton for the Javanese market. His business was very successful and employed hundreds of workers. In 1827 the factory produced a thousand pieces per week. Wilbrenninck suggests he was, alongside Prévinaire, one of the major production companies in this sector. Wilbrenninck, 9
74 For more information about Prévinaire's years in Belgium, see: 'Jean Baptiste Prévinaire'.
75 Mansvelt 1924, vol I, 282-284
76 Prévinaire had paid Van Gobbelschroy a visit to request the return of law and order in Brussels and the availability of the army to protect the citizens. He also promised Van Gobbelschroy he would support him where possible. Gerretson 1936, vol II, 16
77 Mansvelt 1924, vol I, 315
78 Mansvelt 1924, vol I, 314-315
79 Verbong 1994, 274. For more information about the foreign workers at Prévinaire's factory, see Huygers 1983, 57-58.
80 There is extensive correspondence between Prévinaire and the Nederlandse Handel Maatschappij (NHM) in the National Archives of the Netherlands, The Hague, over the time he did business with them.
81 Mansvelt 1924, vol I, 308, Brugmans, 57 and Kroese (2) 63.
82 The company changed its name in 1877 to Leidsche Katoen Maatschappij voorheen De Heyder and Co (Leiden Cotton Company, previously De Heyder and Co. For more information about the company, see the appendix about 'Leidsche Katoen Maatschappij'. The other companies were Couvreur, who installed weaving mills in Haarlem and the province of Brabant, and Bouquié and Van Eyck, who went to the east of the country. Mansvelt 1924, vol I, 288-297
83 Messing 1972, 43
84 For more information about this company, see the appendix about the LKM (Leidsche Katoen Maatschappij).
85 For more information about Van Vlissingen, see chapter V. For Non Plus Ultra see also chapter V and the appendix.
86 The company was founded by Engbert, Gerrit-Jan and Engbert Nicolaas Jannink in 1860. Another specialty of the company was the production of herring nets. https://iisg.nl/ondernemers/pdf/pers-0737-02.pdf, page visited 22 February 2023.
87 Personal communication Derk Jordaan, active for Archief Twentse Textielfamilies Enschede, 7 December 2022.
88 *f* stands for Dutch florins.
89 Kroese (2), 65. In 1840 Prévinaire turnover was *f*1,323,000 and from 1841 onwards an average of about half a million guilders. Griffiths 1974, 50
90 They held land in Zeeland and Zuid-Holland, two coastal provinces. In 1854 they bought land in the Haarlemmermeer polder. Prévinaire Jr. was also co-founder of the 'Noord-Hollandsche Maatschappij tot kultiveren en bereiden van meekrap' (the North-Holland Society of cultivating and preparing madder), which grew madder in several places in the country. Personal communication Dan van Lunsen 12 October 2023
91 The architect seems to be unknown. See Frits Niemeijer, 'Verdwenen buitenhuizen. Een schets aan de hand van Elsenburg bij Maarssen' in *Vitruvius* no. 53 (14) October 2020, 4-16.
92 Deed of notary De Booy 16 November 1859, made after the death of Prévinaire's wife, Johanna Maria van Wickevoort Crommelin in Vries, 77. Boudien de Vries is surprised that the Prévinaires, keen to impress for their social status, seem to have hardly any books in their house.

93 Craandijk, 329. He also had from 1873 until 1878 an eighteenth-century country house, Meer en Bosch, in Heemstede. https://ilibrariana.wordpress.com/2012/03/29/eigenaren-van-het-paradijsmeer-en-bosch/
94 Griffiths 1974, 42-43 and Wertz, 114. Prévinaire's partner Dieudonné Sény had continued business in Belgium. Prévinaire might have still had interest in the company, but I did not find any supporting evidence for this.
95 Mansvelt 1924, vol II, 107. Baars, 143-147. For further information, see appendix about Prévinaire and Griffiths 1974, 42-43.
96 Mansvelt 1924, vol I, 325 and Baars, 148. Prévinaire would continue weaving until 1886.
97 Request patent Prévinaire, approved 25 March 1844, National Archives, The Hague (The Netherlands) 1815-1848, inv. 4785
98 Verbong 1988, 147-148. For a complete overview of all the patents Prévinaire and his son applied for, see Doorman, *Het Nederlandsch Octrooiwezen en de techniek der 19e eeuw*, Le Hague 1947.
99 Verbong 1988, 190-191. For more information about this patent see Appendix 13, 347-349.
100 Baars, 150. The *Catalogus der Voortbrengselen van Inlandsche Nijverheid en Kunst ingezonden voor de Tentoonstelling te Utrecht*, Utrecht 1847 (no 152, p. 54-55) and the *Catalogus der Voorbrengselen van Inlandsche Nijverheid en Kunst voor de Provincien Zuid- en Noord-Holland te Delft*, Delft 1849 (no 154, p. 42-43) gives not only an overview of the product assortment including a large collection of imitation batik of Prévinaire, but also how these products were made. It gives an insight of the variety of equipment father and son Prévinaire had at their disposal.
101 Verbong 1988, 194-196. Rouffaer and Juynboll, 34
102 Griffits 1979, 173
103 See Register van octrooien 1839-1859. Binnenlandse zaken, afdeling nijverheid en voorgangers 1817-1877. Nationaal Archief The Hague (The Netherlands) Inv. 1239, 2.04.23.01. Prévinaire sr died in Brussels on 30 April 1854, aged 70 years old. He possibly died at the Rue Fossé aux Loups 54 in Brussels. The Noord Hollands Archief in Haarlem keeps an envelope, addressed to Prévinaire, with the year 1854. Box 663-2 Familie Prévinaire, Noord Hollands Archief Haarlem. Leon de Herckenrode suggests he died at Hotel de Belle Vue in Brussels. Report Baron Leon de Herckenrode, Brussels 25 January 1859 in Brussels, Noord-Hollands Archief in Haarlem (The Netherlands), file 3, page 27. He was buried at the cemetery of Laeken, a community of Brussels, in a special family tomb. The original request and approval are also kept at the National Archives, The Hague (The Netherlands). A copy and translation are in the Vlisco Archive, @ Vlisco BV.
104 For more information about the events after 1910, see chapter 5. Not even artist Anthon van Rappard, who in 1890 had received permission to make drawings and paintings in the factory, obtained access to the wax printing machines. Baars, 135. See also Brouwer, Siesling and Vis, 1974, 117-129 (nos. 219-260) Parts of this collection represent the best of his oeuvre but also give a rare insight of the Dutch industrial history of the nineteenth century. Both Van Rappard and Charles van de Poll, director of the company, were members of the Haarlem's Art club *Kunst zij Ons Doel*. Kuijl 1996
105 Verbong 1988, 190-193 and Kroese (2), 65-69
106 Verbong 1988, 147-149
107 Verbong 1988, 148
108 Verbong 1988, 180
109 Van Mansvelt, Eigen Haard 1988, 242
110 Verbong 1988, 194
111 *Catalogus der afdeeling Nederlandsche Koloniën van de internationale koloniale en uitvoerhandel tentoonstelling*, Amsterdam 1883, vol. 3, 86.
112 Verbong 1988, 180
113 Verbong 1988, 204, 207
114 Verbong 1988, 209. For an example of these wax prints by Van Vlissingen, see chapter 5.
115 Dutch imitations of Indonesian batiks were shown at the 1867 Paris exhibition, and British reviewers remarked on the imitations of Indonesian batiks: 'these as quite singular… remarkable in execution and interesting by its dissimilarity to anything else in the cotton trade'. J. O. Murray, Reports on the Paris Universal Exhibition, 1867-68 3968-I-IV, 20. It is not known if products of Prévinaire were shown as well.
116 Verbong 1988, 209-210
117 https://colorants.hypotheses.org/2476, page visited 22 February 2023
118 Wronska-Friend 2017, 54
119 This collection is now in the Musée de l'Impression sur Étoffes in Mulhouse. See for a description of this collection: Wronska-Friend 2017, 54-55
120 Wronska-Friend 2017, 55
121 Rast-Eicher 2014, 171
122 Wanner 1968, 61
123 Nabholz-Kartaschoff 2019, 205
124 Wanner 1968, 61
125 Jenny-Trümpy, Adolf, 'Handel und Industrie des Kantons Glarus. Geschichtlich dargestellt' in *Jahrbuch des Historischen Vereins des Kanton Glarus*, vol 33-34, 1898, 443
126 Rast-Eicher 2009, 32
127 Wanner 1968, 78
128 https://hls-dhs-dss.ch/de/articles/029305/2013-11-05/, page visited 8 March 2023
129 Nabholz-Kartaschoff 2017, 66
130 Verbong 1988, 210-211. For an overview of companies in Glarus in the eighteenth and nineteenth century, see Wanner 1968, 72-86.
131 Jenny-Trümpy, 457
132 Jenny-Trümpy, 483
133 Rast-Eicher 2009, 35
134 Gierberg, 95-96
135 Verbong 1988, 211
136 For a description of this technique, see Verbong 1988, 212. Interestingly the same Schultz describes in detail in the article 'Fabrication des Sarrongs Indiens Genre Batick' in *Le Moniteur Scientifique,* March 1877, 327-329, how he used a similar technique at Prévinaire's company: 'in Haarlem ou nous faisions beaucoup le genre Batick'. Schultz 328. However, he is not mentioned in Verbong's list of colourists that worked for the Prévinaire's Haarlemsche Katoen Maatschappij. Verbong 1988, 356, so he may not have worked there on a regular basis.
137 Verbong 1988, 211-212
138 Jenny-Trümpy, 450. See also Jenny-Trümpy, 645-646
139 Rast Eicher 2009, 41
140 Verbong 1988, 212-215
141 Veldhuisen 1996, 43
142 Veth 1875, 541. For more information about the introduction of the cap, see also Veldhuisen 1996, 42.
143 Nabholz-Kartaschoff, 68. For more information and description of combining the two techniques, see Annegret Haake and Hani Winotosastro, 'Batik or Plagiate? How to Distinguish Between Batik Tulis, Batik Cap and Direct Prints' in Marie-Louise Nabhold-Kartaschoff, Ruth Barnes and David Stuard Fox (eds), *Weaving Patterns of Life: Indonesian Textile Symposium 1991*, Museum der Kulturen Basel, 449-455
144 Jacobs and Maas, 25
145 Eng, 14
146 Heringa 1989, 142, Legene and Waaldijk, 41. For a detailed description of the use of batik imitations in the archipel by various groups, see Heringa 1989, 142-144
147 Heringa 1989, 141-142
148 Heringa 1989, 155
149 Veldhuisen 1996, 43
150 The export stagnation continued in the first quarter of the twenty-first century and only changed for the better in the 1930s. Lindblad 1994, 93-95
151 Prévinaire wrote: '*Nous n'avons maintenu sur un petit pied d'activité que l'impression des Batiks, parcequ'elle occupe beaucoup de bras*' (We have kept batik printing to the a minimum, because it is very labour intensive). Verbong 1988, 201

The process of wax printing

1.
The design is printed onto the fabric with molten wax (resin).

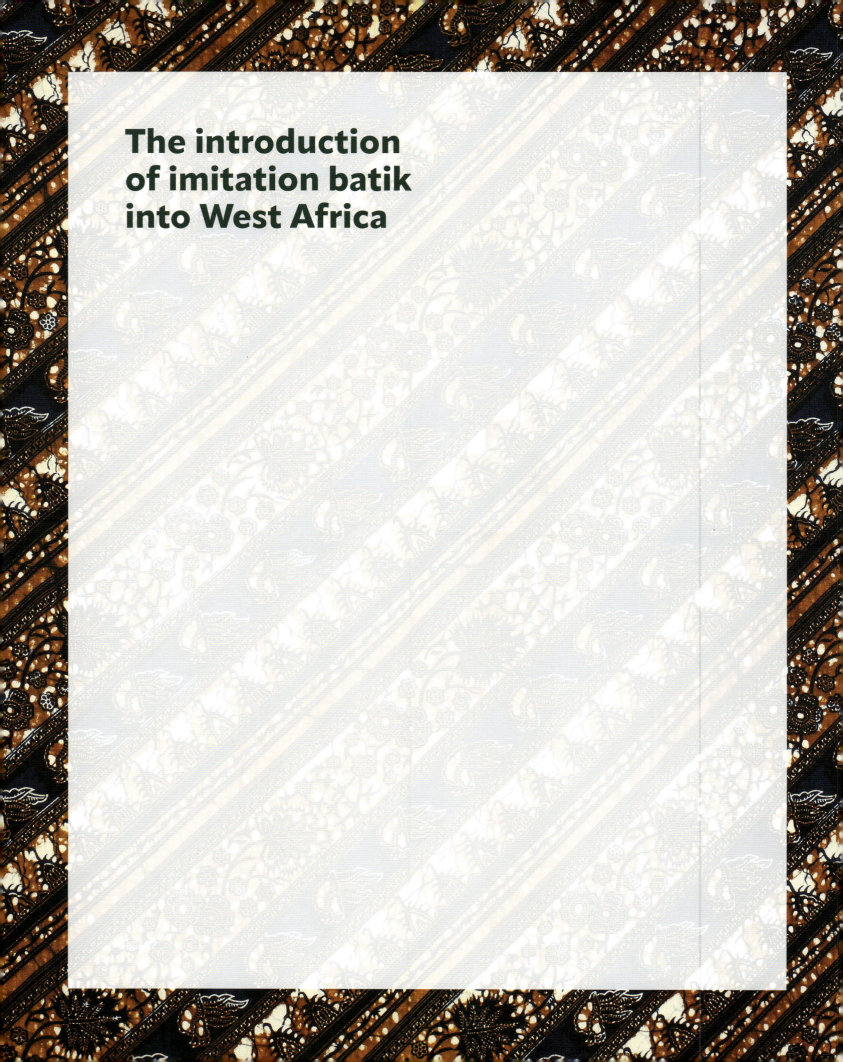

The introduction of imitation batik into West Africa

West Africans had been importing cloth from India and China centuries before the European trade in Indian textiles began in the fifteenth century. Abolition of the slave trade, widely legislated in European nations by 1815, meant a sharp drop in import of textiles, but by the end of the nineteenth century economic growth stimulated demand for luxury products, including high-quality cotton prints that appealed to wealthy African consumers. The non-European identity of imitation batik and its cracked wax imperfections suited tastes in the region. For Prévinaire, whose company was on the verge of closure, the African market meant a new lease of life.

Historically, the trade with West Africa was organised from the northeast of the continent by caravan route across the Sahara. Camels for long-distance transport were already introduced soon after the first century CE.[1] Muslim religious practice, which promoted the acquisition of literacy, spread in this area from the eighth century onwards. Caravaners relied on these literacy skills for administration, correspondence and legal agreements.[2] The period between the eleventh and fifteenth centuries is considered the *Golden Age* of trans-Saharan caravan trade.[3] West Africans needed salt, cereals and metals such as copper and brass for tool manufacture. Spices, shells, beads, pottery, glass and textiles including silks from China and South Asia, and woollen goods from Morocco and Tunisia, were in frequent demand. Already in the ninth century cloth from India arrived in Egypt for further transport.[4] Before the tenth century sub-Saharan Africans exported northwards gold (from Ghana), ivory and cowries; and later enslaved people. The Middle Niger River region became the centre of trans-Saharan traffic and cross-cultural exchange.[5] This trans-Saharan trade continued into the nineteenth century.

European commerce, initiated by the Portuguese in the fifteenth century, brought new goods that transformed consumption patterns and demand. Their ships enabled a greater variety of products to be traded at a lower price, without the middlemen of the trans-Saharan trade.[6] But caravans still transported goods from coastal ports into the hinterland. The Portuguese dominated the coastal trade from around 1470 to 1540. Portugal exchanged Dutch and English cloth for Moroccan cloth, which could then be sold for gold and slaves in West Africa. When the Portuguese opened navigation with Asia, Indian cloth came to be used as currency.[7] By the end of the 1500s, Indian chintz dominated West African harbours, a century before it gained a similar position in Europe.[8] India was the undisputed global centre of cotton growing and cotton textile manufacturing from the thirteenth to the start of the nineteenth centuries. Its cotton textiles were superior in quality and merchants in different parts of the world went to great lengths to acquire these utilitarian and spectacular commodities.

Apart from the Portuguese, not many Europeans had sailed to West Africa before 1500. Their initial interest was not actually the African continent, but pursuit of a seaway to India.[9] It was only during the sixteenth century that Spain, the Netherlands, Britain and France started sailing to India, the Far East and the Americas, assisted by new navigation technologies that enabled sailing the open ocean away from coastal waters.[10] During this period, they experienced national growth combined with expanding financial and military power.

Commercial prospects stimulated the nascent international trade. The Dutch and the English were interested in setting up a similar trade to the Portuguese in West Africa. The first English ship sailed to West Africa in 1553, and from 1598 the Dutch began trading on the coast, but it was only at the beginning of the seventeenth century that the Portuguese monopoly was broken, and both nations started building trade posts.[11] Trading stations were built on a coastal strip stretching 500km along the Gulf of Guinea. Most were sited on the Gold Coast (present day Ghana), which earned its name due to significant gold deposits. The largest and oldest, Elmina Castle, was built by the Portuguese in 1482. Later, British, Dutch and Danish traders built settlements to support their ships with secure harbours, but also to assemble captive Africans for the trans-Atlantic slave trade.[12] The fortress buildings had to defend against rival European traders and African adversaries. Goods were imported by governors of the local forts from friendly ships sailing along the coast or ordered from England and Holland in their own boats. European merchants had no authority outside their forts and trading posts. They traded with local chiefs and merchants, usually dependent on local brokers, mostly rich African middlemen who organised trade with the interior.

The Gold Coast became the focus of European trading companies. The Dutch founded the West India Company in 1621 as a counterpart to its East India Company (VOC). For a brief period from 1657 to 1666, the English East India

Company traded with the Guinea Coast, but the Royal African Company (RAC), established in 1660, was soon granted a monopoly of all English trade with Africa. East India Company cargoes were exchanged for gold and ivory then shipped to India to support the company's commercial operations.[13] But most trading companies took their profits in ivory and gold to Europe and slaves to colonies in the Caribbean.

Textiles represented half of the total import of goods in the seventeenth and eighteenth centuries including dozens of different types from Asia, Europe and Africa itself.[14] The Portuguese introduced Asian cottons at the beginning of the sixteenth century, the qualities of which varied from simple plain weaves to expensive chintzes. Popular were colourful woven check handkerchiefs produced by hand weavers in Madras. The designs were based on one square yard, but sold as eight-yard pieces which in Africa were worn uncut as a wrapped garment.[15] Striped and checked cloth, woven along the Coromandel coast of south-eastern India, appreciated for its intense blue dyes, came to be referred to as *Guinea cloth* because of its avid trade with coastal Guinea.[16] European cloths, predominantly wool or linen, were sold at lower prices than the Asian products, and only a small amount of trade cloth originated from Africa.[17] Accurate information about the exact demands of African patrons was crucial to sales.[18] Important were regional clothing styles, and variations related to class, age, gender, work, religion, etc.[19]

From the seventeenth century, growing interest in Africa was reflected in travel journals that describe local dress in detail, and its use to express wealth and power. In 1602, Pieter de Marees, a Dutch trader and explorer, published an extensive report of his trip to the Gold Coast. His *Description and history of the Gold Kingdom of Guinea otherwise called the Gold-Coast of Mina situated in a part of Africa (Beschrijvynge ende historische verhael van het Gout Koninckrijck van Gunea anders de Gout-Custe de Mina genaemt liggende in het deel van Africa)* was the first thorough description in Dutch, arousing interest in Africa within the Dutch republic.[20] This was followed by Olfert Dapper's *Accurate Description of the African Regions (Naukeurige beschrijvinge der Afrikaensche Gewesten)* published in 1668. An important description of the Gold Coast was published in 1704 by Willem Bosman, a merchant of the Dutch West India Company which operated from 1621 to 1674. In his *Accurate Description of the Guinean Gold-, Ivory- and Slave Coast (Nauwkeurige beschrijving van de Guinese Goud- Tand- en Slavekust)*, he describes in detail the fabrics and jewellery worn by men and women.

African traders knew the discerning taste of their customers and their preference for the finer cotton fabrics from India.[21] Some wealthy Africans also adopted European forms of dress: Isert describes them in 1788 as 'ordering cloths, like the Europeans'.[22] However, Africans

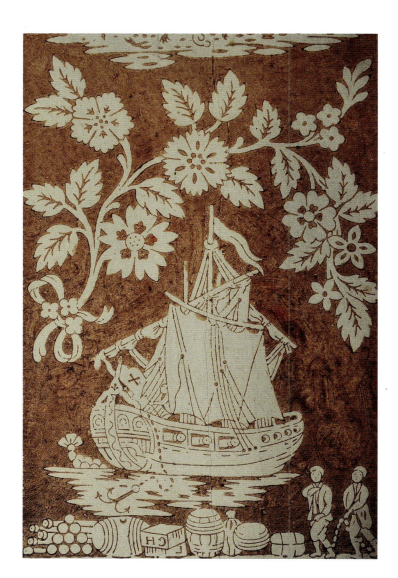

1. Block impression representing printed cotton sent for trade to 'Guinea' in 1787, from a sample book containing Flemish cloth alongside patterns of indiennes from Lenzburg (Switzerland) by the shippers Lacoudrais & Cie, Musée de la Marine, Honfleur (France) Inv. 39.2091

2. Map of the Guinea Coast in Africa, Olfert Dapper, *Accurate Description of the African Regions (Naukeurige beschrijvinge der Afrikaensche Gewesten)*, Amsterdam 1668 (first print), part II, p. 11
Vlisco Archive, @ Vlisco BV

3. Elmina Castle on the Guinea Coast in Africa, seventeenth century
Olfert Dapper, *Accurate Description of the African Regions (Naukeurige beschrijvinge der Afrikaensche Gewesten)*, Amsterdam 1668 (first print), part II, p. 68
Vlisco Archive, @ Vlisco BV

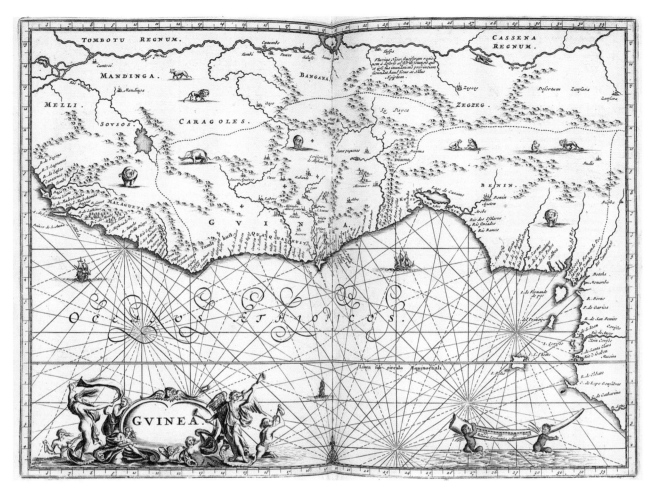

The introduction of imitation batik into West Africa

did not substantially alter their way of dress, which was allied to distinctive African ways of weaving, dyeing and decorating cloth—cloth produced with knowledge, skill and self-expression developed over centuries.[23] New ways of dressing were not a means of social differentiation but were blended into existing practices. Based on their own cultural perceptions, foreign items were appropriated in a purposeful manner and often in an act of creative transformation integrating the old and the new. Both men and women wore mainly untailored draped apparel in the form of lengths of cloth that were wrapped around the body, with the length and the way of shaping according to gender. Accessories and adornment, hairstyles, headgear and body decoration accentuated gender, status, occupation and wealth.[24]

European trade cloth supplemented rather than replaced existing cloth. From the beginning, attention to local tastes was required to send the right assortment of cloth.[25] Locally made cloth in traditional indigo, white and beige was worn with items from Europe and India, the imported along with local references enabling a distinctive, self-fashioned way of dress. Cloth, woven and dyed, had always been relatively expensive, which gave it prestige.[26]

West African traditional textiles

For weaving cotton yarns from West African production centres along the upper Niger, Gambia, Senegal and Hausa territory (from the fifteenth century also from the lower Niger region) were employed.[27] Asante and Ewe artisans in the region of modern-day Ghana incorporated the unravelled threads of imported silk in *kente* cloth.[28] It was woven in narrow strips and then sewn together to the garment size. Historically this type of cloth was worn only by royalty and the elite. The colour arrangements and motifs had specific symbolic meanings related to historical events, objects and sayings. Asante and Ewe *kente* are distinguished through pattern and yarns, with Asante favouring geometric patterns in silk or shiny fibres, and Ewe figurative motifs in a blend of cotton and silk. Raffia was also used by local artisans to weave cloth resembling satins and brocades. In places where raffia was not available bark was used to make cloth. Weavers were innovative in sourcing local raw materials as well as imported yarns.[29] The Yoruba in south-western Nigeria produced *aso-oke,* a cloth made from four-inch-wide woven strips stitched together. Locally sourced silk and cotton were hand-spun, dyed and woven to create this prestigious cloth. Varied by coloured stripes, beige, red or magenta; dark blue and white striped or checked patterns were also made. Ikat, a technique of patterning yarn by resist-dyeing prior to weaving was also employed.

The most common dye in West Africa was (and remains) indigo, holding positive significations like wealth and abundance. The Mandinka of Mali and the Yoruba of Nigeria are known for their expertise in indigo dyeing. Archaeological evidence of indigo resist dyeing from the eleventh to twelfth centuries was found in cave burials at Tellem in Mali.[30] Tie-dye, stitched and folded resist, but also wax and starch resist are all found among African resist dyeing methods to introduce patterns on woven cloth. Yoruba women produce *adire* cloth with distinctive indigo and white patterns, often carrying a specific meaning, and worn as wrapped or stitched garments. Three types are produced. *Adire alabere* uses folding and stitching as the resist method. *Adire eleko* is a time-consuming process in which patterns are hand-drawn or stencilled with cassava paste applied before dyeing, which enables complex figurative patterns.[31] *Adire oniko* uses raffia thread to create the pattern; before dyeing the cloth is manipulated by wrapping and gathering it tightly with raffia. Another resist technique characteristic of Mali is *bogolanfini*, which uses the local iron-rich mud as a mordant. The cloth is prepared with a tannin-containing vegetable dye leaving the cloth yellow. Abstract patterns are hand-painted or stencilled on with the mud solution, often in layers, reacting with the tannin to create different tones of brown and black.

From import to imposition: Euro-African trade in the early modern period

From the beginning of European trade until the start of the Industrial Revolution, textiles represented about half of the goods shipped to West Africa, making it the largest category of goods that were exported from Europe to the African continent. Ranging from cheap to expensive, light to heavy, plain and patterned, textiles imported from Europe were generally cheaper than those made locally; considered exotic, they took on associations of exclusivity and high status. Merchants brought European linens, woollens and worsteds, but also Indian textiles in qualities superior to European cloth. Only after the Industrial Revolution did Europe emerge as a major textile producer on the global stage.

Indian printed cottons enjoyed great esteem in Europe. France became the largest importer of Indian cottons until, in 1686, it was the first to ban both Indian and French-printed cottons due to protests from its own weaving industry. The Armenian community in Marseille created prints in the Indian manner from 1669, and production flourished there thanks to its special status as a free port.[32] The United Kingdom also saw the growth of imports from India as a challenge to silk and wool weaving, but restrictive measures against the import of plain and printed cottons and then the domestic sale of these, taken in 1701 and 1721, stimulated the process of import substitution.[33] The Netherlands also imported a substantial amount of Indian cloth. Due to greater demand than supply in Europe as a whole, an opportunity was available to improve their position in this lucrative textile trade. In 1678 the Dutch started making copies of Indian cotton and silk cloth with the help of Armenian technicians who had mastered the technique in India. The copies initially lacked the quality and refinement of the Indian originals, but gradually the quality improved, and by 1750 there were more than a hundred small factories all over the country.[34] By the end of the century printers had mastered the technique of applying warm mixtures of wax and resin resist before indigo dyeing, and developed cold-applied reserves containing gum that were easier to control.[35] Various technical improvements made close copies of Indian models possible, and mordant dyeing meant the work was colourfast.

In France the ban on printed cotton was lifted in 1759. In parts of Alsace not under French jurisdiction, cotton printing had already developed. Factories were also set up in Switzerland near the French border, so goods could be smuggled into France. Around 1720, textile printers began elsewhere in Switzerland, giving the Swiss a prominent position in the *indienne* business.[36] When the ban was lifted, the migration of Swiss and Alsatian expertise allowed printing companies in Marseille, Rouen, Nantes and Jouy-en-Josas quickly to compete with Swiss, English and Dutch printers.

In 1774, England's export of domestically produced cotton products expanded considerably when the ban on printing and selling pure cotton was lifted. Mechanisation of continuous printing by engraved cylinder was successful by the early 1790s and increased production rates significantly, while mechanical spinning enabled a cloth comparable in quality to original Indian product.[37] These Indian-style prints were not only for the home market, but also exported, curiously enough to India itself by the 1820s. English East India Company rule, and later the Raj, transformed India from a world-leading exporter to an importing country. The improved-quality British cottons were also exported to existing clients of Indian cloth in West Africa, where it was often used as *currency* for the slave trade.[38]

The trade in Indian cloth, and its copies made in European countries, was severely hit by the abolition of the British slave trade in 1807, which reduced the volume of trade to 80%, and it never returned to the original level.[39] This also resulted in a sharp decline of the influence of the English East India Company.[40] Private merchants, mostly based in London, Bristol and Liverpool remained, however, leading players in the palm oil trade, because of their experience and knowledge of West Africa. In West Africa, small-scale producers were now encouraged to grow for export, which in turn created buying power for themselves. This new form of trade resulted in economic growth. Initially the attractiveness of European cloth was its cheapness. Although cloth sales surged in the first half of the nineteenth century, this market was still relatively small for the British, representing only about 5 per cent of their total export.[41] But slowly the market started to improve and the demand for quality became increasingly important. A significant incentive for the textile industry was the variety of consumer choice wanted by West African patrons, differing from the novelty desired by English consumers.[42] Continued technical developments and mechanisation were important, but also the use of innovative marketing techniques such as the use of samples to assess and stimulate business. The structures of commerce under colonialism ensured that the Europeans would profit disproportionately from these developments.[43]

Developments in the nineteenth century

The nineteenth century saw developments in transport and communication that improved possibilities for exporting textiles to Africa. Around 1870, the *Scramble for Africa* had begun when several European nations started to compete for parts of the continent that were as yet uncolonised. Of Africa, 10 per cent was under European control in 1870; by 1914 this had increased to nearly 90 per cent. Colonisation offered Europeans opportunities for asymmetrical trade: buying cheap raw materials with limited competition. European industry expanded use of materials such as palm oil and groundnuts, copper, cotton, cocoa, rubber, tea and diamonds. The introduction of Western currencies further facilitated the trade.

European expansion was intertwined with new technology: railways, steamships and the telegraph. Territorial control paved the way for railway investments unlocking the export potential for the African interior. Steamships required coal stations and ports for maintenance. Speedy communication was needed to regulate markets. Guarded bases were needed for the protection of the sea routes and communication lines, and rapid-firing guns and battleships created an even greater power inequality between Europeans and Africans.[44]

Between the colonising European countries there was growing rivalry and competition. The British continued their colonisation of the Gold Coast and in 1872 forced the Dutch to cede their forts on the Coast to the United Kingdom. However, the Treaty of Elmina between Britain and the Netherlands exempted the latter from import duties for ever, so although exports from the Netherlands were low, they remained lucrative.[45] As the only power left on the Gold Coast, the British found local political institutions, infrastructure and industry an impediment to trade. Politically motivated to confirm British supremacy, they decided to extend their authority into the hinterland of West Africa by force. The established pattern of coastal trading was extended by opening an inland commercial network with new roads and railways. These were built connected by navigable rivers to natural harbours, where telegraph connections with Europe and colonial administrations were installed.[46] A British legal system was introduced. These developments supported a quick

The introduction of imitation batik into West Africa

increase in the volume of British trade to West Africa. Larger firms drove out smaller merchants without the capital to compete, and by the end of the century these firms often formed conglomerates or trade cartels.[47]

The Berlin Conference of 1884 marked the official beginning of colonialism in Africa, where the European powers took effective possession by laying down rules of competition. Signatories agreed on condemning slavery and the slave trade, which earlier in the nineteenth century had not been fully suppressed. The conference also stimulated the expansion of the missionary movement in Africa that had begun at the start of the century. A range of Christian churches, both Roman Catholic and Protestant (Anglicans, Methodists, Baptists and Presbyterians) got involved. Initially their messages were largely received with indifference, but in the coastal territories with European trading communities, they had some success. The interior was hardly known to Europeans before the last quarter of the nineteenth century. Missionaries were advised to respect the colonial authorities and not to meddle in their affairs. They were reliant on the goodwill and support of colonial administrators. Colonial powers appreciated the education and development efforts of the missionaries, especially if they organised such activities without requesting funds.[48] Their goals were different, but interdependent: the colonial powers pursued their national interests, the missionaries their educational and evangelical ones.

Although, especially in the beginning, there was a contrast between *settler* and *peasant* economies, increased trade led to rising standards of living and a new social order with various classes and levels of wealth. Showing wealth as a marker of well-being and success became significant to Africans, but within existing cultural structures.[49]

> Indigenous populations were drawn to imported goods not in some simple-minded childish way, as some contemporary Europeans thought; rather, they appropriated foreign items in a purposeful manner derived from their pre-existing cultural perceptions.[50]

The missionaries had their say in the way to dress with an influence that grew steadily. Clothes were an important tool to instil Christian values of simplicity, humility and modesty, but also to emphasise the hierarchy of the Christian community. In this way, missionaries created a route for European mores, in this case European styles of clothing, to spread globally.[51] The missionaries did not expect Africans to discard their ways of dressing but wanted to impose specific notions of acceptability and decency. They organised sewing classes to instruct in making an adapted European form of dress, more a fusion than real European style. Men adopted more relaxed European wear in the workplace, but women continued to wear African styles based on wrapped cloth on a daily basis. Anthropologist Phyllis M. Martin's interviews with African women found that 'people could read the value of a "pagne" or wrapper, which they could not with short dresses'.[52] Slowly, Africans, discerning and critical, adapted and transformed Western styles and absorbed them into local fashions.[53] A large and varied assortment of goods with a broad choice of different qualities and designs was required in the general stores run by traders: checks and stripes, fancy prints, chintz, silk, handkerchiefs, plain and printed muslins, woollen cloth in various qualities and patterns.[54] By 1900, Africans had begun to buy cloth for commissioning outfits from tailors and seamstresses, who themselves offered catalogues from which customers could select styles.

There was not a notion of Western fashion with the need to have the latest styles at the beginning of a new season, but rather inclinations towards popular styling communicated rapidly through daily interactions. Steiner noted that African consumers generated new trends so quickly and with so many regional varieties that European merchants struggled to follow. Instead of stereotypical visions of the 'primitiveness' of African taste and style that dominated European perceptions, merchants had to acknowledge the abundance and complexity of styles.[55] The stakes for a trader who wanted to be successful were high and required listening carefully to the demands of local market people.

Economic improvements had stimulated the development of luxury products such as high-quality cotton prints. However, improvements in manufacturing and technology enabled reproduction of previously costly textiles in large volumes. The seriality of mass production made these cloths more common and less interesting as a means for distinction for wealthier customers.[56] Social differentiation was best attained by rarity, and by the end of the nineteenth century there was a market for up-scale, exclusive cloth that would appeal to the taste of the wealthy African customer to show their wealth and power.

Preparing the context for batik in West Africa
Successful sales of European printed cottons in distant markets, such as imitation batiks for Indonesia, reinforced the understanding that accurate intelligence about market demands was needed to achieve the best results. Dutch operations were in general smaller than those of Manchester and served more specialised markets. Gathering information about the preferences of their customers was based on feedback from agents or traders stationed in port cities. This valuable feedback communicated through letters and samples was used to adapt colours, patterns and cloth qualities to the taste of non-European, *native* markets in the context of emerging colonialism. Even so, there were factors beyond their

control. As the Indonesian market for batik imitations went into decline at the end of the 1860s due to stronger competition from Indonesian makers, European producers sought other markets for these products. European merchants determined that West Africa could be a new market for the batik imitations they produced.[57] Around 1880 the market was still relatively small but began to expand rapidly taking advantage of a two-way trade, exporting finished goods in return for raw commodities: cacao, rubber, palm oil, ground nuts and raw cotton. In 1883 only 6 per cent of the cotton trade of the UK was with West Africa but held serious potential as an alternative to the declining Indian export market.[58]

In the UK the export trade was stratified to minimise the financial risks: textile printers controlled the production end including printing matrices and dyes; merchant converters provided cloth to be finished to their designs and specifications; and larger merchants and shippers took on the risk of granting credit and obtaining insurance. Shippers could also buy directly from printing companies, but the advantage of buying from merchant converters was their added expertise. They had specific knowledge of designs, production methods and cloth qualities to ensure printing to the customer's wishes.[59]

One of the most important British merchants was Swanzy. The elder James Swanzy had been trading with West Africa in the first half of the nineteenth century, but around 1850, his sons Francis (Frank) (1816-1851) and Andrew (1817-1880) founded the company F. & A. Swanzy, trading via agencies on the Gold Coast with a head office in London. Frank had developed a profound knowledge of the local culture and customs. Soon they had dozens of trading posts with sales managers along the coast to sell imported products and to handle larger public contracts for boats, kerosene etc.[60] In 1874, Andrew Swanzy wrote about the West African market for textiles:

> About sixty per cent of our shipments to the Coast consist of cotton manufactures, chiefly of Manchester make, but including some new fabrics from Switzerland and Belgium, of finer colour and quality.[61]

Around 1900 it was the largest trading company on the Gold Coast. Their shops had a high turnover, mainly selling textiles on credit. Arthur William London, chief agent of Swanzy in Kumasi (Ghana), handled sales of expensive garment fabrics. The ever-changing demand and fierce competition made it a lucrative but difficult market:

> The more one thinks one knows about cotton for West Africa, the more does everyone find out how very infinitesimal is one's real knowledge.[62]

A well-known merchant-converter was Paterson Zochonis in Manchester. George Henry Paterson and George Basil Zochonis had been trading in Sierra Leone in the 1870s before setting up a business first in Liverpool in 1884, and two years later in Manchester. They had an intimate knowledge of the West African market and a large network of trading contacts. They were known for the high quality of their goods, which they commissioned with their own designs and branded with their own trademarks.[63] Manchester-based textile printers that produced work for them were R. Brotherton and F. W. Ashton & Co., amongst others, mainly supplying imitation batik and, later, wax prints.[64] Also of importance in the early days were the shipping merchants G. B. Ollivant & Company Limited of Manchester, founded in 1858; and Israel Werner of London, who took over the business from John Hall in 1874.[65]

The dominance of Manchester in the textile trade attracted many foreign merchants to the city. By the end of the nineteenth century up to one hundred and fifty Greek and Syrian merchants could be found (Syria included present-day Lebanon until 1918). The troublesome situation under Ottoman rule made many willing to become naturalised British citizens. They organised the export of goods largely through Constantinople (present-day Istanbul) and to third countries in which they had trading connections, often linked to their ethnicity.[66] From 1880 Lebanese traders started settling in West Africa. The late economic historian Laurens Van der Laan suggests that they were a small part of the Lebanese who had wanted to emigrate to North and South America, but by accident or lack of money had come to West Africa.[67] Although the Lebanese were not numerous – initially only a few, later about a thousand in the various countries in West Africa – their position as traders was very strong given the low level of international commerce in that region.[68] Lebanese traders were often the middlemen between Europeans and Africans, well placed as cultural intermediaries. Missionaries and merchants would ask them about African customs and traditions if they sensed discontent. The Africans appreciated the fact that the Lebanese were in-between, not paid by Europeans.[69]

In the Netherlands, two companies specialised in trading with the West African market. Kerdijk & Pincoffs were active only for a relatively short period; in 1857 they founded an import and export company for the African market and managed dozens of trading posts in West Africa and the Congo. In 1868 the business decided to change its status into a limited company: the Afrikaansche Handelsvereeniging; it was dissolved in 1879.[70] Another important shipper was Hendrik Muller. He started his career as a textile merchant in Amsterdam in 1839, but in 1850 he set up a partnership with his later brother-in-law Huibert van Rijckevorsel. Following his partner's retirement in 1863 he continued the business under

The introduction of imitation batik into West Africa

the name Hendrik Muller & Co. His son, also named Hendrik, eventually took over the business.[71]

A recurring question is how European merchants discovered the potential for sale of imitation batik in West Africa. An oft-touted explanation for their popularity is based on the so-called *Belanda Hitam* (Black Dutchmen). About 3,000 soldiers from Elmina (Ghana), who served in the Dutch army in Indonesia between 1831 and 1872, are said to have brought back Javanese batik and batik imitations as gifts and merchandise upon their return to Java Hill in Elmina, where they received housing to retire. First put forward in an article by Mansvelt in 1924, this theory of the source of the taste for batik styles on the Gold Coast has proved surprisingly resilient.[72] Ingenbleek suggests it was most probably voiced by the personnel of the Haarlemsche Katoen Maatschappij that closed only a few years before the article was published.[73] After the Second World War, the theory returned in Van Vlissingen & Co.'s centenary publication, their *Gedenkboek* (1946) and in an article by G. H. Rodenburg, who also contributed to the *Gedenkboek*.[74] But most influential were the publications of W. T. Kroese, who even went to Java Hill to interview residents to support the theory.[75] Cees Krantz, head of design at Vlisco from 1952 until 1985, thought Kroese's findings exaggerated.[76] Ingenbleek had doubts as well,[77] although he mentions the delivery of one bale of batik cloth (*één baal batikdoeken*) to Elmina by the Dutch trading firm Van Rijckevorsel & Co. in Rotterdam as early as 1857.[78] But this unsubstantiated idea was repeated over the years in many publications and academic studies, even recently by John Picton and Chris Spring.[79] Ineke van Kessel claims that there is no evidence for the idea and calls this explanation a *tenacious historical myth*.[80] Many of the soldiers did not come back but stayed in Indonesia or came to the Netherlands. As they only got paid upon their return to Ghana, it is questionable whether they had the means to buy batik. The few soldiers who did come back, sometimes married to Indonesian women, would probably have brought the cheap imitations, not the real batik cloth, as that would have been far too expensive. Any small quantity of batik and batik imitations is unlikely to have influenced the West African market greatly.[81]

A more likely explanation is that at least some batik imitation producers were already familiar with the West African market, even before their product was introduced there. It is known that in the seventeenth century blue and white checked *Guinea cloth*, manufactured in India, was sold in Senegambia.[82] When the Europeans started copying Indian cloth it is likely they copied this cloth as well and sold it in West Africa. In the second half of the nineteenth century European printers made trips to the west coast to purchase indigenous cloth with the aim of making copies.[83] Samples were collected as examples for production.[84] Factories such as Voortman in Ghent were already selling products to places like Accra and Elmina catering for an established taste preference for this type of cloth.[85]

Copies of authentic West African cloth proved to be saleable in woven, printed, tie-dye and resist dyed types.[86] The Tissage de Bornhem near Antwerp specialised in mechanical imitations of African textiles like strip-woven cloth using crammed warps every 10-15 cm to look like strip cloth sewn together, then decorated with geometric motifs.[87] They also specialised in imitations of *kente* for the Asante in Ghana. Locally made, these cloths were expensive and were held in high esteem.[88] The production of the Tissage de Bornhem, consisting of good-quality copies specifically made for various tribes, was entirely focused on the export to West and East Africa.[89] Factory printed copies of *kente,* made in Europe, were an affordable alternative.[90] Such European trading companies and merchants might have proposed to their West African clientele the same batik imitations which by then they were starting to struggle to sell in Indonesia.

Another possibility is that original batik might have been sold on its way from Indonesia to Europe, or the copies from Europe on their way to Indonesia, as ships made their necessary stops. Officers on the ship were allowed to carry small quantities of saleable goods to sell for their own profit.[91] The result of these opportunistic sales might have been convincing enough to explore market potential further. Kessel suggests that at least in Ghana batik cloth was already known as a luxury item. In 1832, the Asantehene, monarch of the Asante empire, ordered from the Dutch goverment in Elmina *beste oude Oostindische chitzen (*best old East Indian chintz). In 1836 Jan Verveer went to Kumasi on the orders of King William I to conclude a treaty with the Asantehene for the supply of recruits for the colonial army and regularly gave batiks as a presents.[92] Finally, missionaries of the Basel Mission Trading Company (BMTC) in West Africa imported imitation batiks from Swiss cotton printers in Glarus.[93] Initially only cotton cloth from Manchester was sold by the organisation, but the founder of the BMTC, Ulrich Zellweger, insisted on the sale of Swiss cloth, because he had found out that the local population had a refined taste and with an increased budget sales could grow.[94] Exports to West Africa may well have started early in the 1860s, but even in the 1870s sales were very low. Only around 1900 was a satisfactory level of sales reached.[95] Ankersmit suggests that Swanzy was also importing imitation batik at an early stage, but the sales volume was also marginal.[96] It is therefore difficult to estimate the influence the import of these imitation batiks might have had.

Cloth imported from India was a much-appreciated addition to locally made cloth without being competitive.

It was seen as luxurious, and its possession carried status. If batik imitations were seen from this perspective, it could have been the *exotic* designs that appealed to African consumers.[97] This can be compared with the taste for the exotic in Europe in the eighteenth century, which could be found everywhere: furniture, porcelain, paintings, clothing and accessories were influenced by the art of China, Japan, India and other Asian countries.

For West Africans, the distinctive non-European identity of the designs might have added to their appreciation.[98] This did not mean that Africans were aware of the symbolic or religious meaning which the various motifs had in Indonesian culture; they just loved the beauty of them and assigned new cultural meanings.

Another factor Africans appreciated was that imitation batiks were by nature *imperfect*. In general Indonesians tried to limit the irregularities as much as possible, not really accepting them as an unavoidable technical constraint and almost inherent signature of the technique. The Africans embraced and admired just this very aspect. Every single yard was different.[99] This gave the cloth the authenticity and desired exclusiveness that mass-produced Manchester cloth, although technically perfect, could never offer. Africans were familiar with the resist printing technique which they used themselves to add patterns to cloth before dyeing and also via the Indian fabrics, which had been traded for centuries in Africa.

4. Dutch printed cloth for export to the Coast of Guinea 1852
Sample book LKM 259 1846-1858, p. 66
Vlisco Archive, @ Vlisco BV

The situation of the Haarlemsche Katoen Maatschappij

By the time the export of imitation batiks from Europe to West Africa started, the situation of Prévinaire's company was precarious. The production of his Turkey red dyed products was still successful because of their high quality, even when synthetic alizarine began to replace madder in 1868. This made it possible to keep the company going, helped by extension of exports of Turkey red yarns to markets in Rangoon and Singapore, both British colonies. His dyed and printed cloth was sold to the NHM, but also to individual merchants, destined for the South Asian market.[100] Prévinaire wax prints were considered the best on the market, but production was limited.[101] In 1875 Prévinaire Jr changed the name of the company to the Haarlemsche Katoen Maatschappij (Haarlem Cotton Company Ltd, or HKM).[102]

While HKM survived the 1870s due to an increased demand for Turkey red products, in the 1880s the market situation further deteriorated. In 1881 the Chamber of Commerce concluded that the company was no longer able to compete with other domestic and English companies. Despite the difficult situation the company faced, Prévinaire Jr continued to have faith in the success of his wax batiks. Around 1883, he managed to print his wax batiks on both sides of the cloth on a roller printing machine instead of on the *Javanaise*, obtaining satisfactory results that enabled a significant increase in productivity. Now he could print 150-200 twenty-two metre pieces per day instead of twelve pieces with the *Javanaise*. He also replaced expensive wax with cheaper resin, attaining a better result. This technique was called *lijmdruk*, translating as *glue print*. After dyeing and removing the resin, further patterning in additional colours was printed by hand. Competitors quickly implemented similar improvements, but were unable to produce an equivalent, let alone surpass Prévinaire's results, despite the fact that M. A. Schultz, an old staff member of Prévinaire, had published detailed descriptions of the recipes in 1877 in *Le Moniteur Scientifique*. Apparently, this information was not picked up then.[103]

In 1886, Marie Prosper Theodore Prévinaire retired at the age of 55. The previous year his only son, Theodore, an avid jockey, was thrown from a horse and died at the age of 29, leaving no immediate business successor.[104]

Charles van de Poll (1855-1936), Prévinaire's son-in-law, would take over the company. Despite the hurdles Prévinaire had faced and the fact his company was struggling at the time of his retirement, he could look back on a prosperous career during which he accumulated an impressive fortune. In 1875 he had bought the estate *Heerlijkheid Callantsoog*, an area of more than 730 acres of meadows, arable land, dunes and two lakes, extending over twelve miles along the sea between Den Helder and Petten. In 1883, on the outskirts of the village of Callantsoog, he built a flamboyant villa with medieval battlements where he retired until his death in 1900 at the age of 78.[105] With four storeys, it was the tallest building in the area, higher than the local church. From the roof, the residents had a panoramic view of the surroundings.[106] He also built two smaller villas opposite as a summer residence for his daughters. Fiercely private, Prévinaire did not tolerate anyone other than family and friends using the land. He enjoyed hunting with sons-in-law Charles van de Poll and Aalbrecht (Albert) Del Court van Krimpen (1856-1924). On these occasions, from the slow train from Haarlem that would bring them to Callantsoog, they would shoot out of the window at every station *pour dire que nous arrivons* (to say that we are coming). Del Court van Krimpen would install a golf course behind the Grand Villa, where his son Gerard and Andre van de Poll, son of Charles, would become avid players.[107] In 1885, Prévinaire demolished the villa *Nijverveld* at Zijlweg in Haarlem, where he had lived since 1840, and built on the same plot a smaller one, *Rosenhaghe*, for Van de Poll.[108]

Prévinaire had also invested in land. In the 1880s he had already acquired nearly 200 acres. By 1890, he held over 4000 acres, making him one of the largest landowners

---

5. Marie Prosper Theodore Prévinaire with his son Theodore Prévinaire (1854-1885)
Photo Ghemar Frères, Brussels 1884, Collection Nationaal Archief The Hague

6. Charles van de Poll ca 1880
Photo De Lavieter & Co., The Hague, Noord-Hollands Archief Haarlem, Inv.no. 33879

7. Anthon van Rappard, interior of HKM, 1891
Van Rappard (1858-1892) was a friend of Charles van de Poll and of Vincent van Gogh, with whom he corresponded extensively. Private collection Willem Ankersmit, The Hague, long term loan Museum Helmond (The Netherlands)

in North Holland. In the nineteenth century, investing money in land was symbolically important for nouveau riche families wishing to gain aristocratic status. In pursuit of a title of nobility, in 1859 Prévinaire had his lineage verified with the assistance of the leading genealogist and heraldist in nineteenth-century Belgium, Leon Baron de Herckenrode.[109] Noble titles were still given, but less frequently, and conferred no special privileges.[110] Despite these efforts, Prévinaire did not manage to obtain the title. Another Belgian entrepreneur, Charles de Maere (1802-1885), who came after the independence to the Netherlands to establish a company in Enschede, became *jonkheer* (squire) in 1842. Possibly Prévinaire did apply too late.[111] However, in 1874 he was conferred the title *Ridder in de Orde van de Nederlandsche Leeuw* (Knight in the Order of the Lion of the Netherlands), founded by King William I in 1815 and given to individuals from all walks of life. His father had received the same knighthood in 1843.[112]

Prévinaire's successor in 1886, Charles van de Poll, had received his training at the military academy in Breda and was a lieutenant in the 3rd Regiment of Hussars of the Royal Forces.[113] G. S. de Clerq describes him as the prototype of an *English gentleman*. He turned out to be a determined and dynamic businessman, and from 1902 until 1914 he was president of the Dutch Society for Industry and Trade (*De Nederlandsche Maatschappij voor Nijverheid en Handel*) and the Association for Exhibition Matters (*Vereeniging voor Tentoonstellingsbelangen*).[114] He was also a member of *Kunst zij ons Doel* (Art Be Our Goal), an art society in Haarlem.[115]

Confronted with the critical situation of the company, he felt drastic action was needed for it to have any chance of survival. One of his first decisions was to close the weaving mill The Phoenix in 1887.[116] There was more than enough printing cloth of good quality on the market at competitive prices, which he could purchase from companies in Twente in the Netherlands and from the United Kingdom.[117] He stopped the Turkey red dye works, using the space gained for wax printing, which was the only profitable part of the company, even though the export of imitation batiks to Indonesia was at a low level.[118] Of the 800 people employed in 1860, only 157 were left in 1894.[119] Van de Poll must have realised that despite the outstanding quality of his wax print, continuing to print a limited and repetitive variety of designs for a declining market would not enable the company to survive. At this crucial moment a collaboration with Ebenezer Brown Fleming, proposing sales in West Africa, would offer an unexpected solution.

The introduction of imitation batik into West Africa

1 Lydon, 9
2 Lydon, 5, 11
3 Lydon, 50
4 Guy 1998, 39
5 Lydon, 59
6 Kessel 2018, 103
7 Davidson 2012, 9
8 Krantz 1985, 5
9 Crowley, 34
10 Davidson 1998, 197
11 Reikat 1997, 78
12 See for example Albert van Dantzig, Forts and Castles of Ghana, Accra 1980 and a more recent publication of John Kwadwo Osei-Tutu (ed.), Forts, Castles and Society in West Africa. Gold Coast and Dahomey 1450-1960, Leiden/Boston 2019.
13 https://blogs.bl.uk/untoldlives/2016/01/east-india-company-trade-in-west-africa.html, last accessed 15/02/2023
14 An interesting insight gives the The Dutch Textile Trade Project, presented by Carrie Anderson and Marsely Kehoe. This project aims to understand the circulation of textiles on Dutch ships around the world in the seventeenth and eighteenth centuries. https://dutchtextiletrade.org/textiles/slaaplakens-bed-sheets/. Last accessed 21/12/2023.
15 Laurens van der Laan, 287
16 For a detailed description of local dress in West Africa in this period, see Duplessis, 33-40.
17 Den Heijer mentions Qua Qua Cleetjes from the Ivory Coast and Benijnse Paden from Nigeria.
Den Heijer, 1997, 116-118
18 Benjamin, 60
19 Benjamin, 273
20 See description of clothing in Benjamin, 30-34.
21 Peck, 284
22 Isert 1788, 173-174
23 Reikat, 193
24 Duplessis, 36
25 Benjamin, 58
26 Bender, 160
27 Duplessis, 35
28 Duplessis, 239 and Meij, 10. For more information about African textiles, see for example John Gillow, African Textiles, London 2016; John Picton, The Art of African Textiles. Technology, Tradition and Lurex, London 1995; and Chris Spring, African Textiles Today, London 2012.
29 Davidson 2012, 10
30 For more information about these finds, see Rita Bolland (ed), Tellem Textiles. Archaeological finds from burial caves in Mali's Bandiagara Cliff, Amsterdam 1991.
31 For more information and a list of literature on adire, visit https://www.adireafricantextiles.com/textiles-resources-sub-saharan-africa/some-major-west-african-textile-traditions/adire-cloth-of-the-yorubas/. Last visited 2 March 2021.
32 Gril-Mariotte, 25
33 In the United Kingdom the import and use of Indian cloth was prohibited, but selling on to other countries was allowed, especially to the Dutch, who had a more liberal attitude. Hartkamp-Jonxis 1978, 34
34 Weel, 45-46. In 1678 two textile merchants from Amsterdam, Jacob ter Gou and Hendrik Popta, started a printing company in Amersfoort. Not enough research has been done on what exactly was sold. An interesting article on this subject is by Beatrice Veyrassat, 'Schweizer Erbe des Kolonialismus. Konsum, Kattunproduktion und Sklavenhandel im 18. Jahrhundert. Wo steht die Geschichte der schweizerischen Tuch-Industrie heute?' in Glarner Tuch Gespräche. Kunst und geschichte des Glarner und europäischen Zeugdrucks, Glarus (Switzerland) 2017, 40-48.
35 Verbong 1988, 189 citing Smit 1928, 82.
36 Holenstein, 42
37 Hartkamp-Jonxis 1978, 37
38 See for example George Unwin, Samuel Oldknow and the Arkwrights: The Industrial Revolution at Stockport. The Industrial Revolution at Stockport and Marple, Manchester/London 1924.
39 Kobayashi, 166-167
40 The East India Company's monopoly ended in 1813 with the Charter Act, when individual merchants were also allowed to do trade with India. Kobayashi, 174

41 Kobayashi, 54 (fig. 2.5), 199-200
42 Peck 2013, 283
43 Duplessis, 242-243
44 Bayly, 2004, 230-231
45 Meij, 15. The Dutch continued to enjoy this privilege right up to the Independence of Ghana in 1957. Ingenbleek 1998, 275
46 Laurens van der Laan 1981, 554
47 Launert, 165-166
48 Schmid, 10-11
49 Sill, 314-315
50 Martin, 404
51 Ross, 84
52 Martin, 419
53 Sylvanus 2016, 68-69. Gott stipulates that some elements of dress which ceased to be used in Europe, are still worn today. See Gott 2010, 90
54 Launert, 164
55 Steiner, 97, Sylvanus, 68-69
56 Sylvanus, 57
57 Sykas 2005, 27, Brommer 1989, 13 and Krantz 1989, 115.
58 Sykas 2005, 27
59 Ibidem
60 Swanzy 1956, 113, 116
61 Swanzy (1874) 482. For more information about the Swanzy family, see Henry Swanzy, 'A Trading Family in the Nineteenth Century Gold Coast' in Transactions of the Gold Coast & Togoland Historical Society, vol 2 no 2 (1956), 87-120.
62 E. A. Shaw, Swanzy's London to Arthur William London, Chief agent of Swanzy in Kumasi from 1907-1920, 25 July 1912, London Papers, Unilever Art, Archives and Record Management, Port Sunlight (UK). Dorward, 64
63 Archival material including fabric samples, registered design samples and certificates, shipping labels, photographs, hand printing blocks etc are kept at the Science Museum in Manchester: https://discovery.nationalarchives.gov.uk/details/c/F218284, last visited 22 February 2023
64 https://www.gracesguide.co.uk/Paterson_Zochonis, page visited 16 October 2022. For more information about the company, see the appendix.
65 In the United Africa Company archive, part of the Unilever Archives in Port Sunlight (UK) photos are kept of various trading companies, for example a warehouse in Manchester of G. B. Ollivant, filled with cloth and wax prints for export. https://transnationalarchitecture.group/2021/11/09/the-united-africa-company-uac-archive-october-updates/comment-page-1/?unapproved=2581&moderation-hash=5550285e68526be0af50576220e594fc#comment-2581, page visited 16 October 2022. For more information about Israel Werner, see the appendix.
66 Halliday 160-161
67 Van der Laan 1975, 1
68 Halliday, 171
69 Van der Laan 1975, 317
70 Joosse, 3
71 Ankersmit 2007, 20-21, 34-35
72 Mansvelt, Eigen Haard, 1924, 243
73 Ingenbleek 1998, 78
74 Bijlsma, 36-38 and Rodenburg, 18-51
75 See W. T. Kroese, The Origin of the Wax Block Prints on the Coast of West Africa, Smit van 1876, Hengelo 1976. Also published with the title 'De oorsprong van wasdruktextiel op de kust van West-Afrika' in Textielhistorische Bijdragen 17 (1976), 22-89.
76 Unpublished document of C. Krantz, September 1985. Vlisco Archive, @ Vlisco BV.
77 Ingenbleek 1998, 79
78 This firm had contacts in the East Indies and in West Africa. His research shows that Elmina was the only place that got this batik cloth. Ingenbleek suggest that this demand was not present in other places in West Africa at that time. He pleads that more research is necessary to see what happened between 1857 and around 1890 with deliveries of batik cloth to this region. Ingenbleek 1996, 16. For more information about the company of Van Rijckevorsel, see Ankersmit 2007, 20.
79 Picton, 26 and Spring, 77. Grossfilley presents it as the official legend without giving any other explanation or documentation. Grosfilley 2024, 84. See Ineke van Kessel, 'Wax Prints in West Africa: Unravelling the Myth of Dutch Colonial Soldiers as Cultural Brokers' in Osei-Tutu J. W. (ed)

Forts, castles and society in West Africa; Gold Coast and Dahomey, 1450-1960, African History no. 7, Brill Leiden 2019, 92-118

80   See Ineke van Kessel, 'The Black Dutchmen: African soldiers in the Netherlands East Indies' in Ineke van Kessel (ed), *Merchants, Missionaries & Migrants. 300 years of Dutch-Ghanaian Relations*, Amsterdam 2002, 133-43. See also from Van Kessel *Zwarte Hollanders: Afrikaanse soldaten in Nederlands-Indie*, Amsterdam 2005 and 'Wax prints in West Africa: unravelling the myth of Dutch colonial soldiers as cultural brokers' in Osei-Tutu J. W. (ed) *Forts, castles and society in West Africa; Gold Coast and Dahomey, 1450-1960*, African History no. 7, Brill Leiden 2019, 92-118

81   See also Ankersmit 2009, 46.

82   Perani and Wolff, 97. Senegambia encompassed nowadays Senegal, The Gambia, Guinea-Bissau and parts of Mauritania, Mali and Guinea.

83   See for example the Charles A. Beving Collection at the British Museum in London. Beving was a partner of the printing company Blakeley and Beving in Manchester.

84   See book of the LKM 27(250) on page 67: samples d.d. 28 August 1852.

85   Ingenbleek 1996, 14

86   For more information about Voortman, see the appendix. Samples of this type of cloth can be found in the collection of the Momu in Antwerp (Belgium). See, for example, T3792, T3793, T3806, T4495 and V92TD.

87   The company was founded in 1830 and closed in 1962. Boecke and Janssen (Brommer 1991), 91-92. For more information about the weaving techniques, see Daniël de Jonghe 1991, 95-100.

88   See Braeckel (Brommer 1991), 101-127. The remaining samples of the company are kept at the Momu in Antwerp.

89   Braeckel 1991, 101-127 and De Boecke and Jansen (Brommer 1991), 91. For a detailed description of the weaving techniques at Bornhem, see De Jonge (Brommer 1991), 94-100.

90   In a book of the Leidsche Katoen Maatschappij (LKM) 27(259) several samples of Voortman from 1852 and 1856 can be found. Vlisco Archive, @ Vlisco BV.

91   Personal communication Philip Sykas 4 October 2023. See also Verbong 1988, 221 and Arts, 30

92   Kessel 2005, 194

93   Wanner 1959, 575, Nielsen 470, Ankersmit 2009, 55

94   Wanner 1959, 176

95   Wanner-Jean Richard, 49

96   Ankersmit 2009, 55

97   Interestingly enough these designs had little or no appeal to European clients in the nineteenth century. There was hardly a market for them. Henry van de Velde was one of the few to use batik in his interior designs. See Maria Wronksa-Friend, 'Fernöstliche Faszination: Henry van de Velde und die javanische Batik' in Thomas Föhl and Antje Neumann (eds), *Raumkunst und Kunsthandwerk/Interior Design and Decorative Arts,* Band II Textilien, Weimar 2014, 369-398

98   Wronska-Friend 2016, 113

99   Cousin, 19

100   Apparently, he only sold to a total of four merchants. Verbong 1988, 180

101   See samples in a report of Louis Pierre Bienfait (1855-1944), 'Aanteekeningen gemaakt bij de Heeren P. F. van Vlissingen & Co.', 1876. A photocopy of this report is in the Vlisco Archives, Helmond (The Netherlands), the original still in hands of members of the Van Vlissingen family. He received his training in 1876 at Van Vlissingen & Co. in Helmond. He would marry in 1916 Julia Catharina Fentener van Vlissingen, the sister of Pieter van Vlissingen III. In his report he exclusively shows examples of wax prints of Prévinaire. The samples in the report of 1876 could have been in the missing books of the collection sample books of the HKM in the Vlisco Archives, but are like the wax prints in the first books kept – nos. 213, 226 etc. For more information about Louis Pierre Bienfait, see https://www.dbnl.org/tekst/gene002cmve01_01/gene002cmve01_01_0278.php, last visited 4 January 1998.

102   Van Mansvelt, Eigen Haard, 1924, 243

103   M. A. Schultz, 'Fabrication des sarrongs indiens, genre batick', *Le Moniteur Scientifique*, [t.7 ser. III] 19 (423), mars 1877, pp. 327-239. Evidence that a prominent producer of imitation batik like Voortman was not aware of the article by Schultz is given by Verbong: Voortman visited the factory of Prévinaire at the beginning of the 1880s and saw the rouleau printing with a reserve that did not spill. Voortman assumed that the reserve was applied warm, but Prévinaire kept the procedure secret. Verbong 1988, 221

104   Weekblad van Haarlemmermeer 19 december 1885, 3. Prévinaire was left with his three daughters, Elisabeth Aldegonde (1853-1915), Marie Henriëtte (1856-1918) and Eugénie (1858-1912). Marie Prosper Theodore Prévinaire was buried next to his son, Theodore Prévinaire, at the Algemene Begraafplaats (general cemetery) Kleverlaan in Haarlem.

105   For more information, see Kees Zwaan, 'Van Heerlijkheid tot badplaats. De ontwikkeling van Callantsoog tot badplaats van 1876-1940', MA 2023 Open University: https://research.ou.nl/ws/portalfiles/portal/61451661/Masterscriptie_Van_Heerlijkheid_tot_badplaats.pdf

106   The villa would later be occupied by his son-in-law Charles van de Poll and after his death in 1936 transformed in a hotel. Like the rest of the village, it was demolished by the German occupiers during the Second World War.

107   https://historiek.net/van-lichtgeraakte-fabrieksdirecteur-tot-grootgrondbezitter/130697/. This was the first golf course in the Netherlands. Del Court van Krimpen is seen as the person who introduced the game in the country.

108   See Frits Niemeijer, 'Verdwenen buitenhuizen. Een schets aan de hand van Elsenburg bij Maarssen' in *Vitruvius*, no. 53 (14) October 2020, 7-8.

109   It is not known whether it was only his initiative or in collaboration with other family members. Another well-known Previnaire, his brother-in-law Eugène Marie Ignace Prévinaire (1805-1877), married to his sister Séraphine, was chef-de-bureau of the Belgian Home Office and later governor of the National Bank. The dossier, presented on 25 January 1859 in Brussels, with the necessary correspondence and book with the complete genealogy of the Prévinaire family is kept at the Noord-Hollands Archief in Haarlem (The Netherlands), files 1-3, access number 663. The actual request to get a noble title has not been found. De Herckenrode also made suggestions for a family crest with shearing scissors and a *chevron d'or* with three merlettes.

110   Moes 158-159

111   See https://www.derkjordaan.com/de-vlaamse-sporen-van-jhr-charles-karel-de-maere-1802-1885/, last accessed 7 March 2024.

112   Personal information Esther Tak, Kanselarij der Nederlandse Orden 20 February 2024.

113   A *carte de visite* with his portrait is kept at the National Militair Museum in Soest (The Netherlands), object number 00161808.

114   This association was focused on interest of exhibitions In and outside the Netherlands to promote the Dutch industry. Van de Poll was for example member of the Dutch jury for the World Exhibition in Brussels in 1897 and Paris in 1900. De Clerq 1936, 15

115   Through this association he became friends with Anton van Rappard, a friend of Vincent van Gogh and an important artist. Van Rappard was a member from 1899 until his death in 1892. He was like Vincent van Gogh, interested in working class subjects and made 50 drawings, watercolours and oil paintings of the HKM, that represent one-sixth of his whole oeuvre. Most of them are kept at the Rijksmuseum in Amsterdam. They are also interesting, because it provides insight in nineteenth century Dutch industry, especially the retardation of mechanisation.
For more information, see Jaap W. Brouwer, Jan Laurens Siesling and Jacques Vis, *Anthon van Rappard. Companion and correspondent of Vincent van Gogh. His life and all his works*. Exhibition Catalogue Vincent van Gogh Museum Amsterdam, 1974. See also Aart van der Kuijl, *Kunst Zij Ons Doel. 175 jaar wel en wee van een Haarlemse kunstenaarsvereniging*, Haarlem 1996, 40

116   Messing, 57. In 1876 Prévinaire had already sold his weaving mill in Eisinghen close to Halle in Belgium, which he had opened in 1844 with his nephew Frédéric Fortamps. It was bought by Edouard Van Ham, who named his limited company, the Cotonnière de Buysinghen, which was operational until the outbreak of the First World War.

117   Baars, 148

118   Verbong 1988, 180

119   Ibidem

The process of wax printing

2.
The wax printed fabric is dipped into a bath of indigo dye.
The resin resists the indigo dye to penetrate the cloth.

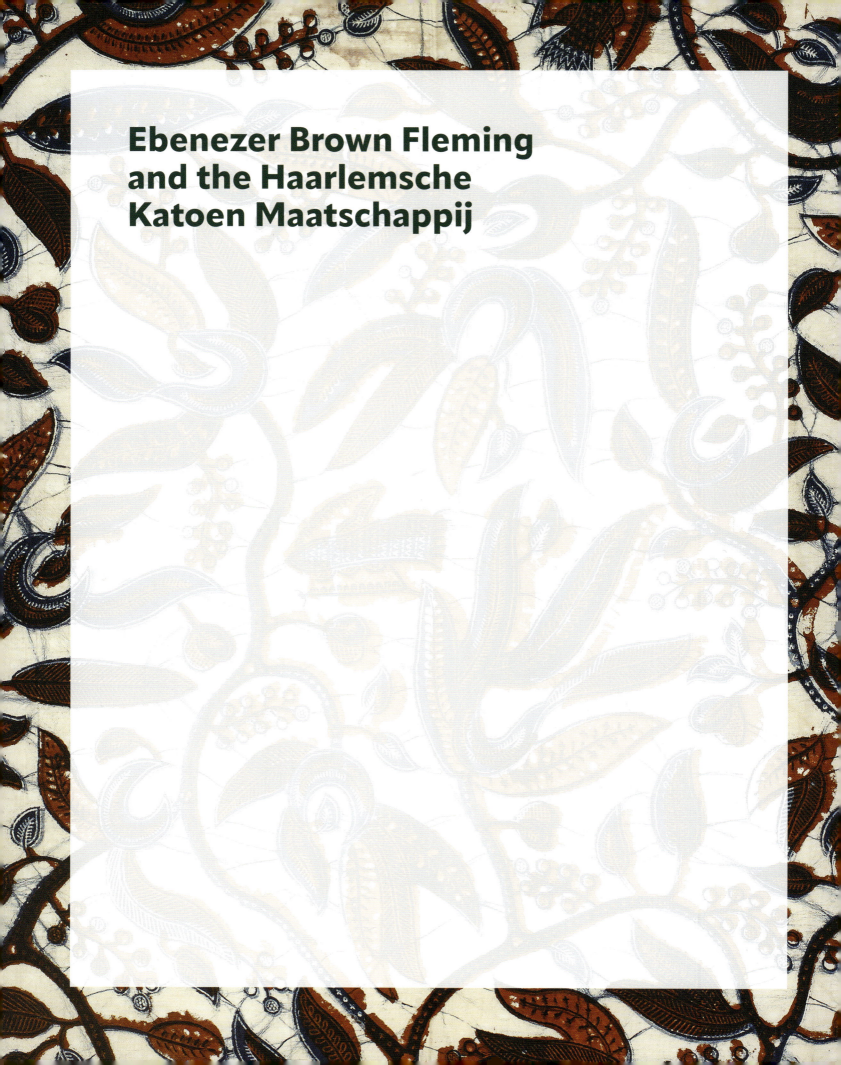

Ebenezer Brown Fleming and the Haarlemsche Katoen Maatschappij

Towards the end of the nineteenth century the market for high-quality and exclusive cloth was increasing in West Africa. Manchester exporters were focused on prints for mass consumption leaving a niche market that needed special expertise and flexibility. A collaboration between Ebenezer Brown Fleming of Glasgow and Charles van de Poll of the HKM, sole producer of the most accomplished wax prints, opened the door to success. Not only was the quality of HKM's prints outstanding, but also the expertise of its designers. Brown Fleming, for his part, had excellent local knowledge and loyal trade connections that enabled him to become a market specialist capable of instructing the HKM with precision on catering for West African markets.

Brown Fleming and Prévinaire: a propitious collaboration

During the last quarter of the nineteenth century Great Britain, the last European power on the Gold Coast, had tightened its grip on the area, politically and economically. Colonisation meant that inhabitants could be paid in Western currency, which stimulated the inland market. European companies now had direct access to markets behind the coast, which made them less dependent on indigenous traders.[1] Many new traders came to West Africa, making competition stiff and entry for newcomers challenging. Manchester cotton exports dominated the market, and business in African trade affairs was largely determined in London and Liverpool, where the dominant Elder Dempster shipping company, established in 1868, was based.[2]

There was a demand for more prestigious and higher-quality cloth from Europe. Machine-printed batik imitations, although only single-sided, found sales, but there was potential to excite wealthier customers with the more richly coloured, double-sided batik imitations, printed with wax, at Prévinaire's HKM. The HKM was the only producer of this type on the Continent; all other European firms had stopped producing them altogether in the 1860s or early 1870s, having been making them often only for a very short period of time. In any case, nobody else had been able to achieve the quality of Prévinaire and the details of his production methods remained secret. Wax print was the only product of the company that held this exclusivity and, if a profitable market could be established, would secure its future.

This relatively niche market needed a merchant promoter with the necessary expertise and flexibility. Most Manchester merchants had grown too much by the end of the nineteenth century. In Scotland, the city of Glasgow was developing quickly and by the 1880s was notable for its expansion of trade, industry and transportation, supported by its churches and missionaries.[3] The city quickly urbanised with half a million inhabitants in 1871, reaching a million in 1914, and its economy became dependent on overseas markets.[4] In shipping it developed as the third city after London and Liverpool, and between 1885 and 1914 it was at its peak of power. It is interesting to observe that by setting up their empire globally, the United Kingdom, in this case Scotland, made use of a continental company, in this case a Dutch one, to cater for its more specialised markets. It is precisely in this period that the Scottish merchant Ebenezer Brown Fleming (1858-1912) was able to build up his business.

At the beginning of the 1880s Ebenezer Brown Fleming is mentioned in Glasgow directories as a salesman for Turkey red dyed products.[5] He worked as the Scottish representative for F. Steiner and Company of Church Bank near Accrington, one of the major Turkey red printers and known for its excellent quality of cloth and designs.[6] When Brown Fleming married in 1883, he was registered as an *East India Merchant*. He must have been familiar with the trade of the United Kingdom with overseas territories in Asia, Africa and the Far East and might already have been marketing Turkey red cloth in Africa. A collaboration with Charles Van de Poll, who became director of the HKM in 1886, became a pathway to business success.

Kroese describes Brown Fleming as an 'extrovert personality with flair and considerable acumen [and] a much-travelled trader'.[7] Van de Poll and Brown Fleming met on a regular basis to keep the business running and enjoyed each other's hospitality.[8] According to Kroese, Brown Fleming entertained Van de Poll on a regular basis several times a year at his second home in the Scottish countryside. It is likely that Van de Poll entertained him at his seaside estate in the Netherlands as well.[9]

It is unclear when and where the men met for the first time. It is likely that they knew each other as business colleagues, because both were specialists in the field of Turkey red dyed yarn and cloth. For both men the collaboration could have been essential. Brown Fleming as a merchant on the West African market faced new competitors on the coast, all trying to get control of the

market. New products might safeguard his position and Meeles suggests that Brown Fleming had already been informing the HKM about the exports of English cloth to West Africa.[10] He must have known the wax prints of the HKM, the most refined of all imitation batiks, and probably realised their potential within the West African market. Sales of these exclusive prints produced by the best wax printing company in Europe could make his business flourish. For Van de Poll their collaboration offered the opportunity to reinvigorate his company. Both men would profit from this joint business venture that was to make them very wealthy by the end of their careers.[11]

Brown Fleming must have realised that, facing a relatively new market, it was crucial first to find out what would appeal to customers in order to compile a successful sales offering. He ran his business from Glasgow and did not have an office on the coast of West Africa, but managed to get the essential feedback from wholesale customers there through one or more shippers, which was not unusual practice at the time.[12] The wholesale merchants had hundreds of local traders as clients, nearly all of them women. Being close to the consumer, they were a crucial element in the supply chain, holding knowledge that allowed them to supply information on desired patterns and colourings.

Incorporating wax prints into West African culture

Ethnographic accounts reveal the importance of local trading women in the sale of wax prints. These women not only retailed the goods but gave them names which added to their value. It is thought that this system of trading evolved alongside the sale of European prints and was already in place in Brown Fleming's time. Europeans had little influence on this aspect of sales. The habit of giving names and symbolic meanings to cloth was centuries old (applied to *kente* and *adinkra*). It was a way of marketing tied to the local culture and social structure and remains prevalent today.[13] Naming was part of designs gaining *classic* status and remaining popular for decades, and wax prints, with their high-quality status and durability, warranted naming. Not all wax-prints have names and not all named patterns are popular, but all popular wax-prints have names. A pattern may undergo a series of name changes before one is retained.[14] There need be no self-evident relation between the forms in the pattern and its name. Patterns deemed classics are re-issued on a regular basis, adding to their cultural value and

---

1. Ebenezer Brown Fleming ca 1905
Photo collection Malcolm Fleming, Porton (UK)

2. Wim ter Reehorst, Charles van de Poll 1905
Collection Hofje van Noblet, Haarlem
Collection RKD Netherlands Institute for Art History, The Hague

competing with new patterns through the prestige of longstanding use.[15] This custom is most common in Ghana and Togo, where classic designs can count on the greatest longevity, especially in the countryside. Creating new classics takes time.[16]

A West-African proverb says: *A person without clothes is a person without language.*[17] Clothing patterns can have a particularly expressive function. Especially where culture is passed down through oral tradition, the spoken word must be treated with care. Wearing clothes with a specific pattern can work as a messenger. An example is *The Eye** or the *Bull's Eye* pattern as it is called in Ivory Coast. A woman can wear this to show a man she desires him, enabling the wearer of a specific pattern to express thoughts without speaking directly.[18] Marital issues can also be addressed. Wearing patterns with names like *My husband is able*, *The eye of my rival*, *I can run faster than my rival*, and, *If you go out, I go out as well*, send out clear messages.

The choice of colours is also important, and this varies from region to region for the traditional designs. In neighbouring areas, the same colours may be liked or disliked. It is said that in Ghana, people prefer traditional batik designs without indigo, but red, yellow and turquoise and a strong effect of spots from resin resist. The Igbo in Nigeria like yellow and red, or yellow and blue, without the effect of the bubbles.[19] In Congo, indigo with small accents in yellow and red is popular. In Ivory Coast neat all-over designs in indigo with yellow are prevalent.[20] The choice of colours may also vary with the season.[21]

West African women have collected dress lengths of classics and other prestigious wax prints (called *pagnes* in French speaking Africa). Given or bought for special occasions, these become an investment. Often wax print classics are seen as a safer investment than money in the bank. At the time of a woman's death, the wax prints would be shown as a reflection of her life and wealth.[22] Inheriting wax prints from one's mother or grandmother is also a way to maintain and memorialise those precious relationships.

Local knowledge, accumulated by Brown Fleming as he developed his West African market specialism, was crucial for reaching customers at the right time with the patterns, colours and cloth qualities desired. A close study of the first years of his enterprise show that Brown Fleming was carefully exploring his new market before expanding the business.

A first indication of the collaboration with the HKM can be traced in fifty-nine designs from the Dutch company, submitted to the British Patent Office in London for design registration on 12 February 1889, only three years after Van de Poll became director.[23] Design registration was at that time customarily organised by the producer, who controlled to which merchant a pattern might be exclusively engaged. But registration by merchants was possible when they supplied the designs or held ownership of printing blocks or rollers.[24] These first registered designs

for the HKM were mostly Turkey red patterns created by discharge dyeing techniques, a style familiar to Brown Fleming from his time as a representative for Steiner. A third of the designs are imitation batik prints for sarongs. Only one of the registered samples is printed with wax using hand-blocks; this pictures a steamship flying the nautical flag *India,* which means coming into port, and a large triangular pennant above a descate flag.[25] On the ship's side is the name *Slamat*, possibly short for *selamat*, an Indonesian greeting.[26]

This was the first time that the HKM registered designs in the United Kingdom.[27] It may indicate that Brown Fleming had already started exporting cloth printed by the HKM to West Africa and, given the fierce competition in this market, the HKM felt the need to *protect* them. Complaints about piracy of designs were frequent.

---

3. *Let Glasgow Flourish*. HKM book 309, no. 8636 Ebenezer Brown Fleming ca 1905, registered at the Design Registry of the Board of Trade (BT) in the United Kingdom as no. 6840, 5 October 1908
Vlisco Archive, @ Vlisco BV

Registering designs in the United Kingdom

In Britain, copyright of designs became possible in 1787 with the *Designing and Printing of Linen Act*, although it only gave limited protection of two months. In 1794, this was extended to three months. Heated debates preceded the introduction of the *Copyright and Designs Act* in 1839. Questions were raised about what constituted an original design and how to define the difference between a genuine original design and plagiarism. The new Act required the *proprietor* or owner of a design, mostly the manufacturer or merchant converter, to submit at least two identical samples, described as *representations* to the Designs Registry. Each *representation* was stamped with a registered design number. The registry and the owner each kept a copy of the representation. The Designs Registry would also keep a separate register, which recorded the specific design number, name and address of the owner and the date of registration. No longer could only cottons, linens, calicos and muslins be protected, but any type of fabric or wallpaper.

The Act of 1839 was three years later replaced by the *Ornamental Designs Act*. Designs for mass-produced objects covering all areas of the decorative arts could now be registered for copyright protection. The articles of manufacture were divided into classes with different periods of protection for each class, ranging from nine months to three years. One year of protection was provided for textile designs. Other important Acts for the registering of fabrics were the *Patents, Designs and Trade Mark Act* of 1883 which united the three Acts and protected via registration in thirteen different classes; and the Patents and Designs Act of 1907, where designs for textiles needed to show the entire pattern and part of the repeat and for which a period of five years' protection, renewable twice, could be granted.[28]

The batik imitations originated for the purpose of substituting for original batiks, not for Indian prints imported to Europe and re-exported. They were destined for the markets batiks came from to sell at lower prices than the originals. This changed when imitation batik started being exported to West Africa. Brown Fleming registered copies of original Indonesian designs that were already in the HKM portfolio before he became a client. Several of those became classics, e.g. *Snail** and *Tree of Life**.[29] According to the Patents, Designs and Trade Mark Act of 1883, designs had to be new or original.[30] These designs were certainly not new to the world, but they were so within the confines of legislative jurisdiction. Intellectual property rights could only be granted to designs registered in Britain, although foreigners were allowed to register designs, in practice extending rights to a few firms in Western Europe. Eurocentrism blinded Europeans to the irony of their own copyrighting of copies of patterns from India, Indonesia and other non-European countries, or else they saw these as timeless patterns that were part of global culture (within the developing Orientalist viewpoint of the West). For merchants like Brown Fleming, the crucial point was to be able to protect the designs he was selling from British pirating, even when designs already existed. In tandem, he also introduced patterns based on traditional African cloth, like printed versions of woven cloth and tie-dye motifs.

From 1895 onwards he started ordering his own collection for export to West Afirca with a much broader range of qualities and motifs, adapted to and at the request of his African clientele. This meant that he had to invest much more on designs that required printing in the highest quality of wax prints available. In a fast-changing and highly competitive market, Brown Fleming must have clearly felt it was important to register such designs because registering designs was a time-consuming and costly exercise for the owner.

Brown Fleming would go on to register about 250 designs under his name between 1895 and 1912. He did not register only wax prints produced by the HKM, but other different varieties and qualities of printed cloth and, from 1903 onwards, a series of designs likely of his own production.[31] As far as the HKM designs are concerned, it is not clear why he registered some and not others. Some that were registered became classics, but many did not. Similarly, many that achieved the status of classics were never registered. Designs sometimes appeared in the HKM books years before they were registered, possibly so successful that Brown Fleming was convinced to take out protection.[32] Registration was a claim of ownership and originality, but the reasoning behind decisions to register a design are otherwise inconsistent.

The collection Brown Fleming developed from 1895 drew upon not only Indonesian batik but also traditional African cloth, proverbs and archetypal symbols and even European and other influences. Beyond mere imitation, imagination and even innovation became important. Brown Fleming would send instructions for new designs to Haarlem, where the designers developed the patterns and sent them back to Glasgow for approval, a process that could be completed in a matter of weeks.[33]

Designing batik imitations required good drawing skills. The HKM stood out from its competitors for the high quality of drawing. Employers were concerned that successful in-house designers might leave or be poached by other companies if their work became more widely known. This might explain why few names of individual designers from the nineteenth and beginning of the twentieth centuries have come down to us, and little is generally known about them. In practice, much studio work was collaborative with several hands contributing according to their particular expertise.

4. Wax print HKM of steamship Slamat, BT no. 123514, 16 April 1889 as no. 123514
The National Archives, Kew (UK)

From the HKM only one name is known and this by chance: C. Prins, who paid a visit to Van Vlissingen on 7 October 1955.[34] From Van Vlissingen the names of several people who worked around 1900 are known, but unfortunately little more than the names. Artist and designer Johan Jacobs is one exception.[35] Typically, names only became known to the public when designers were successful as independent artists, outside the manufacturer's studio.

Design Education

The quality of the designs of the HKM strongly suggests that their designers had a formal drawing training.[36] The city of Haarlem had a long tradition of special training for artists and artisans working in industry. Already in 1796, a *Teekencollegie* (Drawing College) had been founded in Haarlem. Only working members had access to the evening classes where live models were used, but plaster casts were inherited from the *Teekenacademie* (Drawing Academy). In 1809 the name of the school was changed to *Kunstmin en Vlijt* (Love of Art and Diligence), surviving until 1821. Probably out of frustration several members split away in 1820 to open a new drawing school *Kunst Zij Ons Doel* (Art is our Goal). Its members were mainly working artists. The association is the oldest in the country still in existence.[37] In 1879 the *Teekenschool voor de kunstnijverheid* (Drawing School for the Arts and Crafts) was founded in Haarlem in *Paviljoen Welgelegen*.[38]

In 1871 the *Maatschappij ter bevordering van Nijverheid en Handel* (Society for the Promotion of Industry and Trade) was accommodated in the same location as the *Koloniaal Museum* (Colonial Museum) (1871-1923) and the *Museum van Kunstnijverheid* (Museum of Arts and Crafts) (1877-1926), both with their own libraries. In the carriage house, the *School voor Bouwkunde, Versierende Kunsten en Kunstambachten* (School for Engineering and Decorative Arts and Crafts) was housed in 1879. The school initially offered only evening classes, but director Eduard von Saher, appointed in 1880, decided to provide day classes. He was also curator of the *Museum van Kunstnijverheid*. The collection was important for the school. Students made copies of items from the museum in historical styles to develop their own style and were encouraged to explore museums and in 1889 even taken to the *Exposition Universelle* in Paris.[39]

What made it the most progressive school in the country was that at a very early stage the study of nature itself was seen as paramount.[40] Supervised by T. K. L. Sluyterman (1863-1931), students were invited to make drawings in the dunes between Haarlem and Zandvoort. Flower growers in the area opened their gardens and offered flowers for study.[41] One of the teachers, who assisted Sluyterman,

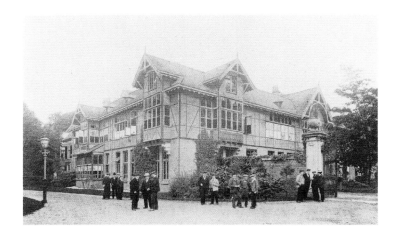

was Michel Duco Crop (1886-1901).[42] Inspired by the Arts and Crafts Movement, he wanted to design beautiful but affordable products for ordinary people. Important for him was the idea of *vlakornament*, flat designed ornament based on geometrical grids of straight lines and triangles with a perfect repeat. In this way ornaments were transformed into intricate designs. It was a way of designing that was popular within the *Nieuwe Kunst* (New Art), comparable to Art Nouveau, especially applied to organic forms like flowers and foliage.[43]

The study and creation of batik in Europe

To produce saleable copies, the designers of imitation batik in Haarlem and elsewhere could rely on the batik collection which the NHM had started in 1825 to provide study material for the various companies. Batiks were also sent by clients, often with a specific request for copies, or donated by travellers and ethnographic collectors. In the Vlisco archives, sample books of the Leidsche Katoen Maatschappij are kept, often with handwritten notes of requests and comments on imitations by competitors.[44] Occasional study trips to Indonesia were made; Felix Driessen, director of the LKM went to Indonesia in 1878 and 1892, where he collected batiks and assessed samples from other companies.[45]

Designers also consulted publications focused on their interests. The designers in Haarlem, for example, used publications by the British Museum.[46] Moreover, they could visit a growing number of public collections. The most important collection of original Indonesian objects, including batiks, was held by the *Koloniaal Museum* (Colonial Museum) in Haarlem, founded in 1864 and officially opened in 1871 by Frederik Willem van Eeden. This museum, the first of its kind, was a private institution owned by the Nederlandsche Maatschappij voor Nijverheid en Handel (Dutch Society for Industry and Trade).[47] Van Eeden was not interested in assembling a cabinet of curiosities in which to display the marvels of the world, but wanted the collections to stimulate trade and disseminate knowledge about the colonies. He installed a laboratory for scientific research where dyestuffs and batik techniques were investigated.[48] There was now, too, a growing trend for studying arts and crafts as practised in the colony. The core function of the museum was to gather this 'colonial wealth', as examples of craftsmanship to be admired and preserved, especially as an impetus to improve design.

A second museum dedicated to ethnography, founded in 1838 by the Royal Zoological Society Natura Artis Magistra and housed in Amsterdam since 1858, focussed on presenting this aspect of the Dutch colonial territories.[49] In 1910 the *Vereeniging Koloniaal Instituut* (Colonial Institute Association) in Amsterdam was established, to which the Colonial Museum in Haarlem was annexed. In 1926, these three institutions were united in a single new building.[50]

Since 1864, Leiden has had an ethnographic museum. In the years 1891 and 1892, Dr J. Groneman, who worked as a private doctor for the sultan of Jogyakarta, donated an important collection of 118 pieces of batik, with representative motifs ordered by him and made in Jogjakarta.[51] In Rotterdam the *Museum voor Land- en Volkenkunde* (Museum of Geography and Ethnology) was housed in the building previously occupied by the Royal Yacht Association, opened in 1852 by King William III. Especially noteworthy was a donation of batik cloth collected between 1872 and 1877 on Java by the scientist Elie van Rijckevorsel (1845-1928).[52]

The first important research on the arts and crafts of Indonesia published in the Netherlands appeared in 1899, by G. P. Rouffaer and H. H. Juynboll: *Het batikwerk in Nederlands Oost-Indië en haar geschiedenis* (Batik in the Dutch East Indies and its History). This was translated into German the following year. Haarlem, where these books were published, was a hub where aesthetic appreciation of batik took hold, and artists started drawing inspiration from authentic batik. Stimulated by the opening of museums, the organisation of exhibitions and the publication of research, interest began to grow. Many were not only motivated to study the art as practised in Indonesia, but to apply it; interest was aroused among Belgian and French, as well as Dutch artists.[53]

The first European artist to experiment with the batik technique was Carel Lion Cachet in 1891. With Gerrit Willem Dijsselhof and Theo Nieuwenhuis, he worked for the Van Wisselingh gallery in Amsterdam. Chris Lebeau,

---

5. *Teekenschool voor de Kunstnijverheid* (Drawing School for the Arts and Crafts) Haarlem 1900
Noord-Hollands archief Haarlem, Inv.no. 32690

Jan Thorn Prikker and Henri van de Velde used the batik technique not for clothing but for their luxurious domestic interiors.[54] Their aim was not to re-create traditional batiks, but to apply the technique to their own stylised use of natural forms.

In 1898 the various batik imitation companies were able to organise a special exhibition with their own batiks at the Colonial Museum in Haarlem. This event was supported by the Nederlandse Maatschappij ter Bevordering van de Nijverheid (Dutch Society for the Promotion of Industry), of whose board Van de Poll, director of the HKM, was a member.[55] Van de Poll allowed Rouffaer and Juynboll to study the whole collection of batiks from Java at the company headquarters in Haarlem and to borrow the necessary samples for reproduction for their book.[56] The Leidsche Katoen Maatschappij had a collection of original batik dating back to 1835, and a library for design inspiration and support. Unfortunately, this collection was destroyed by fire in 1898. Van Vlissingen and Co. in Helmond had a smaller collection dating from 1856,[57] but in 1876 it also suffered a fire, and an even larger one in 1883, when this collection was destroyed. Only the samples which 'Uncle Frits', a member of the Van Vlissingen family, had sent from Indonesia around 1850 were saved.[58] In 1899, Rouffaer and Juynboll concluded that compared to the LKM and HKM, Van Vlissingen had only a modest collection of batiks.[59]

With the opening of public collections of batik, designers could benefit from studying a greater variety of examples and develop a broader cultural understanding. Van Vlissingen, for instance, signed up for a membership of the Vereeniging Koloniaal Instituut in Amsterdam in 1913 to give its designers the opportunity to study the collection and copy original batiks. The developing market in West Africa opened up even greater possibilities, for which a wide range of new designs could be deployed. The new learning facilities were beneficial. Ways of designing *vlakornament* (ornament with flat colour) were incorporated that resulted in surprisingly new, but clearly batik-related motifs that turned out to be commercially successful.

Designers in the United Kingdom and Switzerland must have relied solely on batik samples sent to them for inspiration, because museums did not hold many examples of batik in the early 1900s. In the British Museum, two major collections related to batik were donated only in the 1930s. Most famous is that of Thomas Stamford Raffles, who collected objects from 1811 until 1816 to support his contention that the Javanese were an *advanced* civilisation by European standards and therefore the island should have been retained as a colony by the British.[60] The British Museum received a part in 1859, but a second part with textiles and batik-related puppets only in 1939. The other collection of about 500 pieces of African and Indonesian textiles came from the estate of Charles Beving (1858-1913) in 1934. Before becoming a partner in the company Blakeley & Beving in Manchester, he was a merchant in the cotton trade, working in Africa a few months every other year. He was listed in the 1891 Manchester census as *Africa Merchant* and in 1901 as *merchant and calico printer*. Later he owned his own company Beving & Co. He had a large collection of Indonesian and African textiles as inspiration for his own production for export to Africa.[61]

While he probably collected the African fabrics during his trips to Africa, he may well have purchased the Indonesian batiks from dealers in Asian decorative arts. One sample in the British Museum has a tag of *Van Veen & Co. Import China, Japan. Amsterdam*. Their main business was the importation of tea, but they also sold fabric and art from Southeast Asia.[62] Platt Hall, a branch of Manchester Art Gallery, also received a small portion of African cloth from the Beving collection in 1934.[63] About one hundred pieces of nineteenth-century batik in the Victoria and Albert Museum (V&A) were donated in the twentieth century. As to Swiss collections, the Textilmuseum in Sankt Gallen has a small collection of original batiks with some fragments coming from the industrial collection of Jenny-Trümpy.[64] The Museum der Kulturen in Basel holds batik samples mainly from the 1920s and 1940s. We can see that Dutch designers enjoyed an advantage in their greater access to a wide range of batik examples.

Trade connections of Brown Fleming

On 1 January 1895, Brown Fleming began to register designs under his own name: *Brown Fleming and Company, 205 Buchanan Street Glasgow, manufacturers, and merchants*.[65] This is a measure of his growing confidence in his understanding of the West African market. A comparison of the HKM sample books containing design and roller numbers from the 1880s with those from the first half of the 1890s shows that the variety of printed designs had increased enormously with wholly new styles introduced. The expanding range indicates that HKM's director, Van De Poll, had found clients for his wax prints, most importantly clients like Brown Fleming who served new markets. But for the HKM, business remained an up-hill struggle. In 1860 the company had about 800 workers, but with a stagnating market and the closure of its weaving mill in 1887, only 157 employees were left in 1894. The new sales initiatives took time to make strides, but resulted in the employment of 305 people by the turn of the century. The HKM was well equipped; mechanisation of production was among the most innovative in the country, and Verbong confirms the company closely followed English technical advances.[66]

Brown Fleming was to become the main client of the company, even receiving exclusive rights to sell wax prints.[67] He appears to have used various shippers according to differing markets. Kroese writes that he had good contacts with John Holt.[68] Holt was an English merchant who founded a shipping line in 1868, operating between Liverpool and West Africa for importing ivory, palm oil and rubber, and exporting foodstuffs, alcohol, textiles and firearms. Between 1869 and 1897 he opened several trading posts on the West and Central African coastline and at key centres inland. Nigeria was his largest and most important market. His extensive sales and distribution network, with a quarter of the trade passing through company shops and the rest through middlemen, taught him the importance of high-quality cloth, variety in designs, and novelty for the West African market. Sourcing good assortments was the main problem, with intense competition between merchants looking for similar small and diverse assortments. Manchester manufacturers were more focused on cost-effective larger volume sales. Brown Fleming with his quality range, presented in smaller quantities would have been an attractive client for Holt.[69]

Another important shipper or consignor for Brown Fleming was London-based Israel Werner. He did not have his own ships but had organised the import and export of goods to West Africa and India since 1870.[70] For transport, Werner used the British and African Steam Navigation Company, taken over in 1891 by Elder Dempster and Co. with headquarters in Liverpool.[71] From 1890, a regular service of steamboats and the newly opened telegraph with West Africa enabled rapid connection with European markets.[72] The Basler Mission Handlungs Gesellschaft (Basel Mission Trading Company), hereafter BMTC, was a major client of Werner's since 1874, which he represented in England.

Brown Fleming sold to merchants like Alexandre Dumas, Swanzy and Co. and Martin Hertz & Co. of Manchester. Dumas is often considered as a pioneer in the sale of wax prints, although it is not known when he started selling cloth from Brown Fleming.[73] He worked initially for the French army in Indochina, but settled in Ada Foah, Ghana and became a merchant for rum, salt and textiles.[74] He must have been a successful trader because his name is still used today in Ghana for superior quality cloth, including wax prints.[75]

Swanzy, around 1900 the largest trading company on the Gold Coast, had been trading batik imitations from Dutch, Belgian and Swiss printers in West Africa.[76] Verbong suggests that around 1900 Swanzy was selling the wax prints of the HKM via Brown Fleming, which shows that he had managed to create a new market, but, as mentioned earlier, sales were still relatively modest.[77] Dorward describes the African textile market as extremely fluid due to prestige competition and ever-changing fashions. Trade in expensive garments was profitable, but the risk of overstocking when placing advance orders in England was great. For this reason Swanzy maintained a cautious approach to stock.[78]

6. Wholesale Basel Mission
in Akuse, Ghana, date unknown
Basel Mission Archives/Mission 21
Basel, ref. no. QU-30.003.0293

Meeles mentions M. Hertz & Co. as a client of Brown Fleming.[79] Known as manufacturers and traders of all cotton goods, Hertz focused on trade with East and West Africa.[80] The company was founded in 1846 in Bradford by Martin Hertz (1821-1885), originally from Hamburg. In 1883, his sons William Martin Hertz (1846-1912) and Frederick Moxon Hertz (1858-1918) opened a branch in Manchester to focus on the cotton trade. The Bradford branch closed in 1894 due to a decline in demand for woollen cloth for the continental market, whilst the Manchester branch was flourishing thanks to the expansion of Asian and African demand for Lancashire textiles.[81]

Although no sales figures are known, it is safe to say that the BMTC would become a major client for Brown Fleming, whose Scottish Presbyterian family contacts might have helped establish this business relationship. The BMTC probably started buying HKM-printed patterns at the beginning of the 1890s via Brown Fleming through their connection with Werner. The BMTC could no longer obtain wax prints from Swiss printers because they had ceased production in the 1870s, but non-wax imitation batiks may have been available from Swiss printers in Glarus, thereby preparing the West African market for wax prints.[82] Brown Fleming's cloth, printed in Haarlem, was sent to Glasgow where it was cut to size and sorted into bales, then wrapped in jute for shipping.[83] Werner also arranged with Fleming to make up bales with a selection of cloth in four-yard lengths instead of the usual six yards for specific destinations.[84] The BMTC requested labels with the name of the distributor on the imported prints.[85] In later years, printed labels about the size of a postcard with the name of the company and texts like *Real Dutch Block Garments* or *Real Dutch Wax Block Prints* were attached to each piece. The HKM was not mentioned.[86] Sometimes shippers marked the cloth with their name instead of the merchant's.[87] In shops, pieces of cloth were displayed in such a way that identifying stamps and labels were prominent. Visually recognisable branding was of key significance in non-European markets and often heraldic imagery was employed.[88]

Unfortunately, no early examples of Brown Fleming branding remain, but in 1920 an open hand with coins was registered in the Netherlands as the company trademark, and it is likely this had prior associations with the firm. Many colonial textile exporting companies developed colourful, visually appealing labels to distinguish their products. For the purchaser, the mark stood for a quality known in that marketplace; the design itself was less relevant. Between 1830 and 1870, such marks had become a permanent feature in markets where people were not necessarily familiar with European writing. Trademark registration, introduced in Britain in 1876, enabled producers retrospectively to register their traditional marks, as well as new ones going forward.[89] Prévinaire was one of the first to take advantage of registered trademarks. Cited as the manager of the HKM, 'dyers of red cotton yarn', he applied for registration in March 1876, granted under nos 3308 and 3309 for *Prime Turkey red* and *Dyed Yarns*. The application makes clear that these marks had been in use for at least six years.[90]

7. Sewing class in Mangamba, Cameroon around 1910
Basel Mission Archives/Mission 21
Basel BM ref. QE-30.012.0124

Ebenezer Brown Fleming and the Haarlemsche Katoen Maatschappij

The BMTC was part of the Swiss Basel Mission, a successful missionary organisation still active in several places in the world. Their first mission was established in 1828 in Christiansborg on the Gold Coast (now Accra, Ghana). The founders were a small group of bourgeois Protestant families of Basel. The Mission operated as a pietistic organisation not just by preaching the gospel but by living a Christian way of life. One of the first activities of the Basel Mission on their arrival on the Gold Coast was to encourage agriculture to supplant the transatlantic slave trade. Rulers and traders were encouraged to develop plantations to supply commodities for local and overseas markets, although initially less profitable. Other partners were invited to take part in this production of legitimate goods which was felt would give local people access to education and train them in all areas of work to sustain themselves.[91] Female converts were given training in cooking, baking, housekeeping and sewing.

Males could work in the missionary workshops to become artisans, for example in the fields of carpentry and masonry. Some were employed as apprentices in the missionary trading stores. The mission trading company had an objective of encouraging the consumption of European goods as a mark of 'civilisation'. Firearms, ammunition and alcohol were not sold, and Mission shippers were not allowed to transport these for other clients on the same vessel. The interest in African cultures was mainly limited to the needs of supporting Mission activities.

8. Fante women, Ghana, 1904
Postcard collection Duncan Clarke, Adire Textiles London

Missionaries had their own interests foremost; imperial officials had their political and economic goals. In general missionaries were respected for their activities if they did not hinder the colonial authorities and did not get involved in their affairs. They could rely on mutual support, because of shared links to the home country and the country where they were resident. The situation for the members of the Basel Mission was different because Switzerland was not a colonial power; they were more dependent on the colonial authorities, a situation which sometimes led to a difficult balancing act: opposing official policies while still relying on officialdom.[92]

An important part of living a *Christian* way of life were conventions of dress signifying true moral behaviour, according to Mission beliefs and their interpretation of Christian tradition. This resulted in the spread of European styles of dress.[93] Missionaries did not insist on exact copies of European dress, but the body had to be 'decently' covered, including women's breasts. This entailed a change of dress; whereas clothing was traditionally made of straight pieces of cloth, draped or tied, now shaped clothes made by cutting and sewing were introduced. The form of dress introduced - not only in Africa, but in other parts of the world where missionaries were active – was loose, uncomplicated to make and could be worn for a long time, even if the body changed shape. In general, six-yard pieces were used: four yards for the dress and two for accessories, like headcloth or wrapper. In practice, people wore European dress in church and school, but local dress for daily life.[94]

Girls could learn sewing as part of the promotion of civil life, which meant living like Europeans.[95] The teaching was done initially by missionaries' wives in the extended households that served as the missionaries' earliest educational settings. Soon it became part of the basic education programme of schools, and from the 1880s sewing was part of the curriculum in girls' boarding schools.[96] In a culture where women had a tradition of independent economic activity, the goal of the missionaries was to enable schoolgirls to become dressmakers to earn a living.[97] The schools made clothing an all-female domain and an exception in the otherwise male-centred missionary organisation.[98]

Once the BMTC was established in Christiansborg in 1859, it imported the necessary commodities from Europe, not only for the missionaries themselves but also for African followers, as well as to provide material support for educational and mission activities.[99] This business allowed the organisation to expand activities at its own pace without being dependent on donations from Swiss supporters. All kinds of commodities were imported, from building materials to household articles, speciality foods, etc., but cloth had a unique place: European-manufactured cotton, wool, silk and velvet. Most important was cotton fabric, largely sourced from Lancashire. From 1861, cottons from Switzerland were also imported, but sales were hindered by Swiss producers' lack of knowledge of the requirements of the African market, but they quickly learned that the Africans would reject any cloth that did not suit their taste.[100]

One of their salesmen, Ernst Preiswerk, observed in 1879 that local people, when they really liked a piece of cloth, were willing to pay any price, but when they did not like the article, it was not possible to sell it, even as a bargain.[101] It was also crucial not to have too much stock and to sell quickly to avoid accumulation of goods difficult to sell. It was better to have 'novelties' on a regular basis to keep the clientele interested.[102] With staple articles, the Mission had a more conservative and uniform pricing policy.[103]

In a report of the BMTC in Accra, the need to adapt the selection of goods to the local markets was emphasised. Tastes varied from one region to another, and mapping these required close communication with the main office. Rather than impose a choice of patterns, Werner, for example, would delay negotiations by several weeks to obtain correct information.[104]

Binhammers correspondence provides an insight into the textile trade. Binhammer, working as a trader for the BMTC, mentioned in a letter of 8 August 1897, that the trade with individual women was difficult. He described them as dishonest and, despite agreements to work exclusively for the BMTC, still working for various merchants and with their shops dirty and not secure, resulting in a lot of theft. He therefore started financing shops directly and employing people trained by the Mission, who were able to do bookkeeping but also to sleep on the premises.[105] He set out clear rules about how to run a shop and how to do business. One had to be aware of the stock in the warehouse before placing orders, to keep in touch with other trade companies of the Mission, inform each other about saleability and, where worthwhile, exchange goods, to cater for the taste of the local clientele.[106] Werner sent Binhammer samples of prints on a regular basis.[107] Important was a good assortment of designs, without too many of the same design. Names of manufacturers are not often mentioned by Binhammer, apart from Brown Fleming (called *Fleming*) and F. W. Grafton.[108] F. W. Grafton and Company at Broad Oak Works in Accrington were calico printers who started producing wax prints in 1907. It is likely that Brown Fleming also sold fabric to Scottish missionaries in West Africa. The United Presbyterian Church of Scotland, formed in 1847, had a mission in Old Calabar, Nigeria and started to expand around the 1880s. The Hope Waddell Training Institute in Calabar organised sewing and tailoring classes for girls and women as part of their curriculum and they may have bought cloth from Brown Fleming.[109]

A smaller and less known but nevertheless significant market for Brown Fleming was Surinam, which was, from 1667 until 1954, a colony of the Netherlands.[110] When slavery was abolished by law in 1863, indentured servants from British India were employed on the plantations, but this depended on the good will of the British. From 1890 until about 1930, the Dutch government contracted with more than 30,000 people from Indonesia, mainly from Java, to work there. These workers largely retained their own culture, religion and traditions. People from Surinam of African and Asian origins were purchasers of imitation batik.[111]

No sales figures have survived so it is difficult to determine which clients of Brown Fleming were most important, but it is safe to say that the BMTC was a major one. His clientele would prove to be crucial in the successful sales of the sought after wax prints of the HKM. To achieve this, the right choice of designs would be essential.

1. Ingenbleek 1996, 14
2. Another important shipping company, based in Hamburg, was the Woermann Linie from 1885 until 1942.
3. For more information, see Breitenbach, Esther, 'Scots Churches and Missions' in Mackenzie, John M. and Devine, T.M., *Scotland and the British Empire*, Oxford University Press 2011, 196-226.
4. Mackenzie and Devine, 234
5. For more details and references, see the appendix about Brown Fleming.
6. Frederick Steiner (1787-1869) joined the Broad Oak in Accrington in 1817 as a colourist, moving from Ribeauvillé in the Alsace in France. Steiner would eventually start a partnership with James Haworth and Joseph Barnes, working on further improvements in dyeing techniques and making them more economical. In 1836 he established himself as a dyer. He took over the works at Church Bank from Robert Peel in 1841. In the same year he also entered into a partnership with Frederick Gatty (1820-1888), also from the Alsace, where he had also been working on improvements on Turkey red dyeing. In 1843 they took out a patent for a new method of dyeing using garancine, made of the roots of madder, which would prove to be very profitable. In the 1850s he expanded into printing and formed F. Steiner & Company. When Frederick Steiner died in 1869, Gatty continued to run the business. The company was successful until the 1950s when it went into liquidation. https://amazingaccrington.co.uk/flippingbook/26-27/#zoom=z, last accessed 15 March 2023
7. Kroese (1), 53
8. Kroese suggests that Van de Poll visited Brown Fleming on various occasions in Scotland. Kroese (1), 53. Brown Fleming left in his will a portrait of Van de Poll to his son William Elphinstone Fleming. Legal Records Wills and Testaments Reference Sc51/32/65 Dunoon Sheriff Court Wills, National Records of Scotland, p. 151. Verbong cites a note from the HKM about an upcoming visit of Brown Fleming to Haarlem. Verbong 1988, 238
9. Initially Brown Fleming had a second home in Lochanbrae in Mambeg, Garelochhead, Argyllshire. In 1906 he bought also a country house in Kilchoan, Loch Melfort, also in Argyllshire. Kroese (1) 1976, 53 and Kroese (2) 22. As son-in-law of Prévinaire, in 1900 Van de Poll had inherited with his wife, her two sisters and brothers-in-law the estate *Heerlijkheid Callantsoog*, a beach resort north of Amsterdam. Niemeijer 6-7 and Lunsen, De Previnaires. For more information, see chapter 2.
10. Meeles I, 35
11. For Brown Fleming, see the appendix about him, for Van de Poll see for example https://historiek.net/de-moeilijke-relatie-tussen-familie-van-de-poll-Prévinaire-en-badplaats-callantsoog/142873/, last accessed 28 October 2021.
12. My research did not uncover any visit to Africa nor was his great grandson, Malcolm Fleming, aware of any visit to the continent. Personal information Malcolm Fleming d.d. 16 November 2016. An important merchant like Haijkens, another very successful trader on the West African market for more than forty years, also never travelled to Africa himself. For more information, see the appendix about Haijkens.
13. Ingenbleek 1998/2, 97. For the explanation of the names assigned the pattern, see Marie-Cecile Zinsou (ed.), *Wax Stories*, Fondation Zinsou 2023 Ouidah, Benin. https://www.fondation-zinsou.org/en/_files/ugd/c712ca_73ecff6a4f2c4efa9909f7d12a901c49.pdf and https://www.vlisco.com/fabric-stories, last accessed 15 March 2023.
14. Bickford Berzock, 73
15. For Vlisco this *oldtimeren* – reprint in new colour ranges of old designs – which was done approximately every five years became a conscious policy. It kept the interest in these designs alive and limited the number of engravings, which was cost efficient and attracted a good level of sales each time. See also chapter 5, Vlisco.
16. Cortenbach, 15-16
17. Kriger 2006
18. Cortenbach, 33-35
19. Cortenbach, 9
20. Personal communication Frans van Rood, 3 September 2023
21. Tabiou, 361
22. Krantz 1985, 4. For more information see also Koyo Kouoh, *Hollandaise. A journey into an iconic fabric*, Stedelijk Museum Bureau Amsterdam, Newsletter 130, Amsterdam 2012
23. Samples of these design registrations can be found at The National Archives, Kew (UK):
BT 51/53
p. 373 No 119506-16 HKM 12 February 1889 (see BT50/114) Note: BT 119507-11 Certificates not issued: See Correspondence 9298 – see BT 50-115
p. 373 No 119517-38 HKM 12 February 1889 – see BT 50/114
BT 51/54
p. 202 No No 121628-32 HKM 19 March 1889 Class 13 – see BT 50/115
p. 202 No 121633-9 HKM 19 March 1889 Class 14 – see BT 50/115
p. 545 No 123514-16 HKM 16 April 1889 Class 14 – see BT 50/117
BT 51/55
p. 121 No 124666-7 HKM 4 May 1889 Class 14 – see BT 50/118
BT 51/56
p. 2 No 127679-82 HKM 25 June 1889 Class 14 – see BT 50/120
p. 234 No 129785-90 HKM 29 July 1889 Clas 14 – see BT 50/122
p. 291 No 130329-33 HKM 4 August 1889 Class 14 – see BT 50/123
24. Launert. 188
25. The triangular flag shows plain, striped and checked stripes; and the descate flag features flowered, waved and geometric stripes, possibly representing the major divisions of woven and printed patterns. This design was still exported by F. W. Grafton in Accrington (UK) to Zaire in the 1950s and 1960s. Samples are in the Brunnschweiler Archive, held at the Whitworth Art Gallery, University of Manchester (UK). The design appears for the first time approximately at the beginning of the 1880s as no. 2941 in the books with only roller numbers. This design (no 3860) and other registered designs can also be found in sample book 214 of the HKM in the Vlisco Archives in Helmond (The Netherlands).
26. *Slamat* might be short for *Selamat*, a form of greeting one could use when wishing somebody well or good. Personal communication Itie van Hout 22 November 2023. It is not legible on the sample at The National Archives, Kew, because it appears upside down in the sample book, but is visible on other samples.
27. These registered designs can also be found in book 214 (1888-1889) of the HKM sample book collection in the Vlisco archives. For a description of the sample books of the HKM, see appendix.
28. Carter-Silk, 34. For a detailed description of the various acts in history, see Alexander Carter-Silk and Michelle Lewiston, *The Development of Design Law. Past and Future. From History to Policy*, independent report commissioned by the Intellectual Property Office (IPO) 2022. The obligation to show at least the entire pattern and part of the repeat was especially useful in the study of Dutch wax prints because the designs are in general covering the whole width of the cloth.
29. He registered *Snail**, which appears as design 3837, 3840 and 4017 (book 248) in the HKM sample books under no. 292268 on the twentieth of January 1897. *Tree of Life** can be found in book 248 (3910, 4140) and book 228 (4285). It was registered under no. 292267 on 20 January 1897.
30. The Patents, Designs, and Trademarks Act, 1883 (46 & 47 Vict. C. 57), part III, 1 (p. 73)
31. For more details, see chapter 4 and the appendix with Brown Fleming's biography.
32. An interesting example is *Snail**. It was registered under no. 292268 on 20 January 1897, but appears already as numbers 2935 and 3023 in the sample books with only roller numbers nos. 3837 and 3840 in book 214 (1889), no. 4018 (book 248) and 5134 (255).
33. Krantz 1985, 6. A little note in an order book of the HKM 1904-1906 reveals that a design, that had to be redrawn, was received in Haarlem on 17 October 1907, and was sent back to him on 16 and 17 November with the original. On 21 November the HKM received the approval of Brown Fleming to engrave the new design. Notes of some dates on designs, that would later be registered, in the sample books of the HKM reveal that time to register a design in the United Kingdom after being engraved and printed in Haarlem was about six to eight weeks. See for example book 309 of the HKM in the Vlisco archives. However, in some cases Brown Fleming took months before registering, for unknown reasons.
34. Vollaard, 3. Vollaard suggest that a report of this visit was made and kept at the Export Department of Vlisco, but it was impossible to

find it in the archives of Vlisco. Lists of pupils of the *Teekenschool voor de kunstnijverheid* (drawing school for arts and crafts, founded in 1879 in Haarlem), were consulted: in 1894 a A. P. Prins (male) is mentioned, in 1900 J. Prins (female), but no C. Prins was found. It is, of course, possible that he received his training elsewhere. Enschede, 93, 100

35   Verschueren, 67. For more information about Johan Jacobs, see chapter 5.

36   For more information about education for artisans in the eighteenth century, see the appendix about The Teekenschool.

37   See Aart van der Kuijl, *Kunst zij ons doel, 175 jaar wel & wee van een Haarlemse kunstenaarsvereniging. Van teekencollegie, teekengenootschap tot beroepsvereniging*, Haarlem 1996 and https://www.kzod.nl/. Charles van de Poll was also a member of *Kunst zij ons Doel* in Haarlem. See chapter 2.

38   This manor house, built in 1789 by the American banker Henry Hope, in 1838 passed to the Dutch government and was used as a museum.

39   Sluyterman 89

40   Kuijl, van der, 47

41   Simon Thomas 1988, 49

42   In 1894 he would make about 25 designs for Van Vlissingen in Helmond. https://www.kunstbus.nl/design/michel+duco+crop.html, last accessed 15 September 2022.

43   For a detailed description of the vlakornament, see Simon Thomas 1998, 38-84.

44   See for example book 27 (259) 'Java' 1846-1858.

45   Stichting Erfgoed Leiden, archief LKM, Inv. no. 8

46   See chapter 4 for more details of Egyptian motifs for cloth after 1906.

47   Bergvelt and Elands, 86. See also *Gids voor de bezoekers van het Koloniaal Museum te Haarlem*, Amsterdam 1902. The collection was eventually transferred to the Koloniaal Instituut, later Royal Tropical Institute and Tropenmuseum in Amsterdam, opened in 1926. The Tropenmuseum is today part of the National Museum of World Cultures. For more information, see Daan van Dartel, 'Het Tropenmuseum and Trade: product and source' in *Journal of Museum Ethnography*, 20(2008) 82-93. C.F. van de Poll, director of the HKM, was president of this association from 1902 until 1914. De Clerq 1936, 17

48   For details, see Herman A. J. Baanders, 'Over nieuwe proeven van batik-techniek in Nederland' in *Bulletin Koloniaal Museum Haarlem*, Amsterdam 1901.

49   The idea behind it was based on Linnaeus' effort to comprehend the Creation as a ladder of development, where the human being represented the top rung. Collecting not only animals, but also minerals and objects created by humans made sense to him.

50   In 2014 the Tropenmuseum (Tropical Museum) became in part of the Stichting Nationaal Museum van Wereldculturen (Foundation National Museum of World Cultures) and has a collection of 3000 pieces of batik, the oldest dating back to 1840.

51   This collection formed the basis of the important study of batik by Rouffaer and Juynboll, *Het batikwerk in Nederlands Oost-Indië en haar geschiedenis*, 1899.

52   Simon Thomas 1998, 157

53   Wronska-Friend 2001, 117, 121

54   Bergvelt and Elands, 84-85. See also J. M. Joosten, 'De batik en de vernieuwing van de nijverheidskunst in Nederland 1892-1905' in *Nederlands Kunsthistorisch jaarboek* 23(1972) 407-429.

55   Rouffaer and Juynboll, VII-VIII

56   Rouffaer and Juynboll, VIII

57   Rouffaer mentioned a visit to the youngest of the four main printers in the Netherlands, the Kralingsche Katoenmaatschappij in Rotterdam, but not the presence of a batik collection. Rouffaer and Juynboll, IX

58   Bijlsma and Rodenburg, 31-32 and Personal communication Ruud Sanders, Vlisco Helmond, 13 October 2022

59   Rouffaer and Juynboll, IX

60   https://www.britishmuseum.org/about-us/british-museum-story/people-behind-collection/sir-thomas-stamford-raffles, last accessed 14 April 2023. His goal was to establish a free-trade port in Southeast Asia. Java's location was ideal for this purpose. He eventually made of Singapore a British port in 1819. https://www.britishmuseum.org/blog/sir-stamford-raffles-collecting-southeast-asia, last accessed 14 April 2023

61   https://www.britishmuseum.org/collection/term/AUTH235390, last accessed 17 March 2023. The company registered many of its designs, now kept at The National Archives Kew, London (UK). For more information, see J. Halls and A Martino, 'Cloth Copyright and Cultural Exchange: Textile Designs for Export to Africa at The National Archives of the UK', *Journal of Design History* 31, 3, September 2018, 236-254.

62   On 19 November 1907 the Dutch newspaper *De Eemlander* reported of an exhibition of old Japanese artworks (1500-1865) in the Vereniging Voor de Kunst in Utrecht. Another newspaper, the *Haarlems Dagblad*, reported on 7 February 1914 the sale of various exotic cloths and kimonos.

63   https://archiveshub.jisc.ac.uk/search/archives/9f4dd31f-c141-3120-952d-15a6e194ec39, last accessed 28 August 2023

64   Excerpt of database listing the objects connected to the term batik Textil Museum Sankt Gallen, 13 May 2023. For more information about the museum: https://www.artemorbida.com/textilmuseum-st-gallen/?lang=en, page visited 17 May 2023

65   See BT 51/79 247016 1 January 1895 p. 537 National Archives, Kew (UK)

66   Verbong 1988, 180

67   Meeles 1972, Kroese (1), Verbong 1988, Ingenbleek 1998

68   Kroese (3), 21

69   Launert, 197-200

70   For more information, see the appendix about Israel Werner.

71   See for example in the archives of the Basel Mission shipping documents of Werner with detailed lists of packages for example the steamship The Calabar, dated 28 January 1892: 10748 UTC: Korrespondenz Basel Kassa Herr Muller 1892-1898. On other lists dates are missing or illegible.

72   'Der neu mit Westafrika eröffnete Telegraf ermöglicht eine und damit die Fuhlungnahme mit den Europäische Märkten'. Bericht über das Geschäftjahr 1890 in 4255 UTC: B.H.G. 1859-1934 in Archives of the Basel Mission, Basel (Switzerland).

73   Frensel, 10

74   He died in 1919, leaving large warehouses behind. His family continued his business. Auzias and Labourdette, 2014

75   Ingenbleek 1998/2, 91 and Auzias, 136. There are so far no proven links between the writer Alexandre Dumas and the textile merchant. Alexandre Dumas, the writer, did have a son Alexandre born in 1824, but he seems to have been a writer as well and died in 1875. https://gw.geneanet.org/garric?lang=fr&p=alexandre&n=dumas&oc=2 last accessed 14 april 2021. He could be related to Manufacture Paul Dumas at Montreuil-dur-Bois (1906-1978), producer of wallpaper and textiles, who developed the surface roller technique in the early 1900s. Personal communication Philip Sykas 15 November 2023.

76   Verbong 1988, 222

77   Verbong 1988, 223

78   Dorward, 63

79   https://www.gracesguide.co.uk/M._Hertz_and_Co, last accessed 6 March 2022

80   Meeles I, 21

81   Hurst, 206. See also http://www.davenportstation.org.uk/reinbek.html, last accessed 6 March 2022. Hertz from Manchester should not be confused with Joseph Hertz in Amsterdam, who was an agent of imitation batik for Indonesia and Southeast Asia. Wanner-Jean Richard, 78

82   Ankersmit, 55

83   One bale would typically contain 5 lumps, which is 10 pieces of cloth of 22-30 yards. Personal information Philip Sykas 19 October 2018. Today Vlisco packs 120 pieces of 6 yards per bale of jute (80-85kg) and send the bales to distributors in Ghana, Togo, Benin or Congo. Personal communication Ruud Sanders, Vlisco Helmond, 11 May 2023.

84   Werner mentions this in a letter with Cameroon as example. See letter by I. P. Werner d.d. 17 July 1909 in 4263 UTC: Ausgewahlte Korr. Basel – Werner London 1905-1909 in Basel Mission Archives, Basel (Switzerland).

85   Werner even suggested to have more 'sophisticated', better looking stickers printed. See letter 10 September 1897 in 4267 UTC: Ausgewählte Korrespondenz Zusammenfassung – I. P. Werner London 1874-1914 in Basel Mission Archives, Basel (Switzerland)

86 Meeles I, 34-35
87 John Holt, for example, had the habit to mark with his own trademark and name. Launert, 198
88 Launert, 203
89 Zangger, 767
90 Email correspondence with Philip Sykas 19 December 2013. Possibly, there was a more immediate need to protect his Turkey red products than his batik imitations.
91 Oppong-Boateng, 3-4
92 Miller, 19
93 Ross, 85
94 Sill, 316-318
95 Oppong-Boateng, 59-60
96 Gott 2010, 21
97 Jenkins, 93. Suzanne Gott suggests that the missionaries' sewing teachings might have resulted in the current Ghanaian fashion industry. Gott 1994, 120
98 Sill, 319
99 There were other missionary societies that organised economic activities to fund their work like the Bremen Missionary Society and the Wesleyan Mission, but the BMTC was particularly well organized. Oppong-Boateng 9, 55, Reynolds, 148-150. In 1921 it would change its name into Union Trade Company (UTC) International
100 Wanner 1959, 175
101 Wanner 1959, 176-177
102 Letter from Ch. Leger of the BMTC Winnebah to M. Binhammer in Accra, 9 April 1906. 4004 UTC:M Binnhammer Korrespondenz 1901-06 in 1914 in Basel Mission Archives, Basel (Switzerland).
103 4004 UTC:M Binnhammer Korrespondenz 1901-06 Gewinn- und Verlust Konto 1899-1900 in Basel Mission Archives, Basel (Switzerland).
104 Report BMTC Accra 24 October 1912 in: 4412 UTC: Westafrika Generalagent 1912-1914 in Basel Mission Archives, Basel (Switzerland).
105 Binhammers' frustration makes an interesting read: '*Das seitherige System die Waaren durch Commissions Weiber zu verkaufen, hatte nicht mehr Zug genug und daneben ging durch die Gleichgiltigkeit der Weiber und die schmutzigen kleinen locale, worin die Waaren zum 'Verkauf untergebracht sind, sehr viel zu Grunde. Auch war mir das ein Dorn im Auge, dass die Weiber meistens fur mehrere Hauser zugleich verkauften entegegen aller Verbote und Drohungen. Diese com. Weiber sind ein eigenartiges Volk, voller Ranke und Hinterlist. Vor dem Schuldenmachen und den Betrugereien will ich gar nicht reden, denn die sind einmal jeden Neger und jeder Negerin eingefleischt und ohne Verluste ist bei aller Vorsicht nicht durchzukommen.*' (The previous system of selling the goods through commission women no longer had enough traction, and in addition, a great deal perished due to the indifference of the women and the dirty little premises in which the goods for sale were kept. It was also a thorn in my side the fact that the women usually sold goods for several companies at the same time, despite all the prohibitions and threats. This com. women are a peculiar race, full of tendril and deceit. I don't even want to talk about the debts and the scams, they are ingrained in every Negro and every Negress and no matter how careful you are, you can't get through it without a loss), p. 16 of letter M. Binhammer aan BMTC Aburi 8 September 1897 in: 4035 UTC: Historisches M. Binhammer 1 January 1895-July 1901 Basel Mission Archives, Basel (Switzerland)
106 Instructions for trade – document without date- part 2, article 1 in 4004 UTC M. Binhammer Korrespondenz 1901-1906 in: Basel Mission Archives, Basel (Switzerland).
107 See for example a letter of Werner to M. Binhammer of 30 June 1904 sent with three packages of cloth to order from with interestingly number 3092 and 3099 that could refer to the range of prints of Brown Fleming, although I was not able to find these specific numbers. See 4267 UTC: Ausgewahlte Korr. Zusammenfassung, I. P. Werner London 1874-1914 in Basel Mission Archives, Basel (Switzerland). In another letter from Werner to M. Binhammer d.d. 29 November 1904 he mentions even more numbers but suggests he has his own numbers for specific designs and not those of the producers. See 4004 UTC: M. Binhammer Korrespondenz 1901-1906 in Basel Mission Archives, Basel (Switzerland).
108 Letter Werner to Binhammer d.d. 21 May 1908 in: 4005 UTC: M. Binhammer Korrespondenz 1907-08 in Basel Mission Archives, Basel (Switzerland).
109 See also William H. Taylor, *Mission to Educate. A History of the Educational Work of the Scottish Presbyterian Mission in East Nigeria 1846-1960*, Brill Leiden, 1996, 17, 129 and 139
110 On a sample in the HKM books - design 6183 (book 245) – is a sticker, mentioning 'Surinaam doeken. Ellemaat. Flemming'.
111 Email correspondence with Christine van Russel-Henar, Paramaribo (Surinam) 4 August 2023. For further details, see chapter 4.

The process of wax printing

3.
The fabric is creased by a machine that creates lateral cracks to the wax.

The creation of the Haarlem Collection by Brown Fleming 1895–1912

The title Haarlem Collection is given within the wax print industry to the set of designs issued by Brown Fleming between 1895 and 1912 that were printed by the HKM. Their patterns and motifs were to become classics which formed the core references for companies that started wax printing after 1910. Versions of most of these designs are still in print today.

Brown Fleming introduced most of these designs during a relatively short period from 1895 until 1906. In the latter year when his son William Elphinstone Fleming and son-in-law Ronald Richmond Herbertson joined the business, the core of the Haarlem Collection had already been created, and Brown Fleming's reputation established. Alongside these wax prints, the firm sold a wide variety of cloth aimed mainly at West African, but also East African markets.

In this chapter selected designs from the Collection are discussed. When a design belongs to the Haarlem Collection, an asterisk (*) is added after its name. Where there is a reference to the HKM sample books, it is to the specific group of records with design and roller numbers, unless otherwise specified. In 1939 the Calico Printers' Association Ltd (CPA) acquired Brown Flemings Ltd with the intention of printing Brown Fleming patterns at its branch, F. W. Ashton and Co in Hyde.[1] To abide by the terms of the royalty agreement, a list was made of designs for which royalties were due, along with photographs.[2] The presence of a design on this list is also indicated, when necessary, as BF photo number. The importance of the photo numbers is limited because only fragmentary sales figures linked to the numbers are known. The quantities of forty-eight patterns sold from 1937 until 1939 were compiled by Philip Sykas from a surviving album. This provides an indication of the best sellers at that time, but no details of the remaining patterns.[3]

For Brown Fleming to submit British design registrations starting 1 January 1895, he must have been convinced of their sales potential in West Africa, and the presence of competitors willing to copy successful patterns. Selling the high-quality wax prints of the HKM, for which demand was small but growing, gave him an enviable position as an early entrant into the West African market. For the financially struggling HKM, Van de Poll must have had faith in the expertise of Brown Fleming as a merchant for his most prestigious products. He agreed to give Brown Fleming the exclusive rights for the sale of the wax prints, which Brown Fleming could register under his own name.[4] As was usual business practice for commission printing, Brown Fleming presented the products of the HKM as his own.[5] This meant that even important clients such as Swanzy had to buy from Brown Fleming and could not purchase directly from the HKM.[6]

Brown Fleming introduced a broad range of motifs, adapted to the taste and requirements of the West African clientele, but he did not limit himself to HKM production. He registered about 250 designs in total of which about a fifth were from the HKM. This obscures the relative sales value of prints from Haarlem versus those of others.

In 1881, the census returns show the young Brown Fleming as a Turkey red salesman. According to Kroese, he represented the Lancashire firm of Steiner for the Scottish market. But Scotland at the time already had ample home production of Turkey reds, and it is therefore likely that he was also involved in export markets. From 1886, Glasgow directories list Brown Fleming as a commission merchant, in which role he would have gained further experience of non-European markets, possibly in West Africa. By 1893, directories indicate that he had set up his own company Brown Fleming and Co., dyers, printers and cloth factors, and in 1897, the description had changed to dyers and printers of African specialities, indicating a commitment to the African market. From 1903 he sold his own production of Turkey red cloth. Brown Fleming had this prepared, states Kroese, at Springfield Dye Works in Dalmarnock, an industrial area in east Glasgow; Glasgow directories show Springfield Works under Brown Fleming's management by 1906. As Kroese notes, the block prints produced at Springfield were probably *chintz block prints* rather than wax prints.[7] According to Kroese, he employed at least one designer. This person most probably did not originate designs but was responsible for preparing designs that had been acquired for printing.[8] In November 1902 Brown Fleming sent the substantial amount of thirty designs for registration for all-over designs and square pieces of cloth.[9] In May 1903 he registered another seventeen designs for Turkey red prints.[10]

Brown Fleming also operated in markets other than South East Asia and West Africa. He sold *kangas*, pieces of cloth of Indian influence, for the East African market, possibly via merchants such as Hertz & Co. and Swanzy. A *kanga* is a printed cloth with a length of about two yards, often containing a pair of bordered squares. It was mostly printed in only one or two colours, relatively cheap to print, sold in pairs and could be used as skirt, head-wrap, apron and much more. From the early 1900s proverbs, sayings, and slogans were often added to the design. Several companies did print kangas by the end of the nineteenth century. Because the designs had cross borders, few printers had the specialised machinery to print these by roller. Even with the introduction of the so-called *sarrie machine* to print cross borders, hand block printing remained more economically viable due to small print runs and the desirability of deep dye penetration.

In 1902 Brown Fleming registered a series of nine designs on cloth with a grid woven into it, that were most probably not printed by the HKM.[11] It is unlikely that he sold kangas of the HKM, because the kangas in the sample books are annotated with the initials of the client, and his initials are not present. The HKM had clients besides Brown Fleming, although he was to become the most important one, selling the expensive wax prints.

Clients of the HKM

Over the years kangas gradually assumed a more prominent place for HKM than batik imitations, by the start of the twentieth century representing the majority of HKM production with numbers of clients indicated by initial(s) in the sample books.[12] From 1905 no more than 10 per cent were orders for new batik imitations for anyone other than Brown Fleming. His orders for new engraving of batik imitations were less than 2 per cent, wax prints excluded, which were no more than about 5 new engravings per year. Clients are difficult to identify by initials alone and often just a single letter is shown on the sample ticket. Clients of batik imitations can sometimes be traced by their initials or their name.[13] The German company Hansing & Co. had experimented in the West African trade in the 1840s and began a regular shipping line from Hamburg in 1852.[14] Maintz, a merchant of Amsterdam, was a longstanding client of the HKM.[15] George Wehry & Co., a merchant established in Amsterdam in 1867, traded in textiles with the Indonesian archipelago.[16] Together with Borneo Sumatra Handelsmaatschappij, and Hagemeyer, Wehry was among the major trading houses in Indonesia.[17] Another merchant is referred to as *Veth*.[18] This might be (Se)Bastian Veth (1860-1922), who after working for the trading firm J. F. van Leeuwen in Makassar, founded in 1886 with his father, shipper Jan Veth, and brother Franz Herman, a company shipping colonial goods to the Netherlands and imitation batik to Indonesia. In 1891 he returned to the Netherlands, having made his fortune, but continued trading.[19] Another sample was sent to Katz Brothers, a limited trading company in Singapore.[20] The name Sutorius is also found.[21] In 1843 Peter Antonius Sutorius (1804-1886), owner of a small printing company that produced batik imitations, started collaborating with Pieter Fentener van Vlissingen, leading to van Vlissingen's acquisition of the company in 1846.

To be successful on the West African market Brown Fleming had to rely on people who had made a conscious effort to grasp the intricacies of African cultures and understand the African way of thinking. Africans were clearly not interested in indiscriminate imitations of African symbols or motifs from African arts and crafts, but wanted designs that related to their own interests.[22] Many traditions preserved for centuries were transmitted orally and embodied within material culture such as textiles. Where words could or would not be used, cloth could help by providing symbolic meaning. Specific motifs were used to represent concepts of family and marriage, but also power, force, jealousy and protection, sometimes acting as the visualisation of proverbs[23]. This might explain why a range of motifs in the Brown Fleming collection quickly became successful: they could be adapted to African cultures, as understood or interpreted by Africans themselves. The human eye motif prominent in Brown Fleming's pattern *The Eye**, issued in 1902, appeared at a much earlier stage for African export. In a book of Favre Petitpierre & Cie in Nantes, dated 1800-1825, Chonja Lee found a design with eyes destined for export to Africa.[24] It is possible that such motifs were in constant demand.

Halls and Martino suggested that some motifs might be related to *fraternal orders* that became active across the British colonial territories in the nineteenth century, including the Grand United Order of the Oddfellows and the Orange Order.[25] The last Order was founded in West Africa by Protestant Ulster-Scots missionaries at the beginning of the twentieth century. It is feasible that motifs like *Shaking Hands* are related to such sources, but fraternal orders adopted symbols common across many religions and institutions (the heart, the star, etc.).[26] There is so far no direct evidence proving a specific relationship.

Designs served as a facilitator of the (un)spoken word in a similar way in Indonesia as in West Africa, although on a different basis. In Indonesia this was more class related: the type of fabric and its patterns conveyed messages about the wearer's personal status, ethnic identity and social position. In traditional batik about forty to sixty principal motifs can be distinguished with many variants, resulting in hundreds of different designs, most with a specific symbolic meaning that can vary from region to region and across time. The name of a motif can be descriptive with no relation to meaning, or names can encapsulate the significance accorded to the design. When these principal motifs were copied in Europe and transmitted

1. *Banana Boarder**. Not registered design. Brown Fleming, production HKM ca 1900 Brunnschweiler Archive, held at the Whitworth Art Gallery, University of Manchester (UK)

2. Woman, wearing her child in cloth with design *Banana Boarder** Benin 2010, Archives Missions Africaines, Rome

to the African market, West Africans adopted some of them for the beauty of the design and assigned to them their own cultural meanings. Indonesian elements were shown in a new setting, retaining an Indonesian feel but not in compliance with authentic Indonesian batik.[27] One example is *Banana Border**, a non-registered design with stylised banana leaves and the wing of the *garuda* bird (*lar*) as principal motifs, but not arranged in an Indonesian manner.[28]

The designs of Indonesian batik were welcomed in West Africa because they were not only different, perceived as exotic and prestigious, but invited the assignment of meanings. In contrast to the taste of Indonesians, who disliked the irregularities of imitation batiks, people in West Africa loved their *perfect imperfection*, a consequence of the wax resist technique. Manufacturers, cognisant of African taste, developed imperfections into a signature feature of the cloth. One way to do so was on purpose not to remove all remaining resin after indigo dyeing, leaving *spots* that resisted successive dye colours, which gave the cloth *sparkle*. The characteristic *veining* associated with African wax print was also not in line with Indonesian taste but developed in conjunction with African preferences. The wax was deliberately cracked prior to immersion in dye. Prévinaire even directly printed artificial veining to imitate the effect that was normally caused accidentally during the process. The designer can incorporate crackles in the design itself by drawing lines that look like veining but are

The creation of the Haarlem Collection by Brown Fleming 1895–1912

in fact printed on both sides of the cloth, but these will of course be repeated at intervals. Initially, printed veining was a solution to avoid excess wax usage, although the non-repeating veining patterns engineered by the deliberate vertical and horizontal breaking of the wax gave the most appreciated effect. Soon it became a signature and is still in use today as part of the typical wax print iconography.[29] Adding extra colours with wooden blocks by hand lent even more unpredictability to the finished result.

Another much appreciated aspect that added to the typical *Haarlem* signature was a special *touché* effect along indigo dyed lines with wax pastels in a lighter shade of indigo, which would give a smooth, veiled shadow effect.[30] Today companies such as Vlisco still apply this technique, which is now called the *halftone effect* or the *Haarlem gravure*. It is created through the imprint of unequally engraved rollers on the front and the back of the cloth.[31]

A fourth effect that became a characteristic of wax prints was *bleeding*, which means the running of one colour from a dyed spot into a section next to it. This can happen accidently when washing cloth with colours that have not been properly fixed or washed before use, but can also be done on purpose to achieve the desired effect.

Prévinaire would print on specific sections with a mixture of resin and real wax. Washing the dyed cloth with sulphuric acid would remove the resin, but not the wax. A second dye would give the effect of bleeding, but on purpose.[32] The effect can also be created by mechanised printing.[33] The Swiss would eventually be able to create the best effects with this technique.

3. Example of printed crackle. Detail of the design *The Eye*,
BT reg.no. 387613, 13 December 1901
Brunnschweiler Archive, held at the Whitworth Art Gallery,
University of Manchester (UK)

4. Touché effect. Detail of the design *The Peacock*,
BT reg.no. 482072, 6 June 1906
Brunnschweiler Archive, held at the Whitworth Art Gallery,
University of Manchester (UK)

The collection of the HKM before 1895

A better understanding of the prints made in this period and thereafter for export to Indonesia and South East Asia, can be obtained from a collection of about sixty sample books of the HKM in the archives of Vlisco in Helmond. Most important are twenty-four books that include roller and design numbers.[34] The original collection must have comprised thirty-two, possibly thirty-three books in total.[35] These books reflect the production of the HKM after 1875 until its closure with the last order despatched from the company on 27 August 1917.

The first six books of the group with roller and design numbers are missing, but the following volumes produced in the 1880s contain many variations of imitations of traditional batik. Most are just printed on one side without wax, some with wax in the traditional colours dark blue or brown. There are also some striking examples of the double-sided wax print that clearly show the skill and quality of Prévinaire's output.[36] It is only in the second half of the 1880s that red was used to print the design, or colours like red and yellow were added by hand on indigo dyed cloth.

The first indication that Brown Fleming was a client of the HKM can be found in sample book 214 (nos 3560-3857) from around 1890. Above sample 3645, which is a typical Indonesian design that would also become a classic in West Africa, the abbreviation *Flg* (Fleming) is written.[37] The same book shows a large collection of Turkey red cloth, which the HKM registered in the UK, probably by or on behalf of Brown Fleming.[38] The next three HKM sample books are nos 248, 228 and 210, covering the period 1890 to 1895. The numbering of the books itself is random. Most of the books were rebound in the 1960s by the Vlisco Company without paying attention to their sequence and content. Fortunately, the design numbers are continuous, so the books can easily be put in the right order. Looking through these books, new designs appear which Brown Fleming may have suggested, because they differ from imitation batik in the previous HKM sample books. It is quite likely that designs were not only ordered by Brown Fleming but also by other new clients of the HKM. Van de Poll was actively seeking more clients given the difficult situation of the HKM. But many can be attributed to Brown Fleming because of their specific styles that re-appear in his later, registered collections.

5. Printed version of patola (double ikat) from the Patan region of Gujarat in India, Haarlemsche Katoen Maatschappij, sample book 248, design no. 3887, ca 1890
Vlisco Archive, @ Vlisco BV

6. Patola imitation. BT reg.no. 263771, 15 October 1889
Brunnschweiler Archive, held at the Whitworth Art Gallery, University of Manchester (UK)

The creation of the Haarlem Collection by Brown Fleming 1895–1912

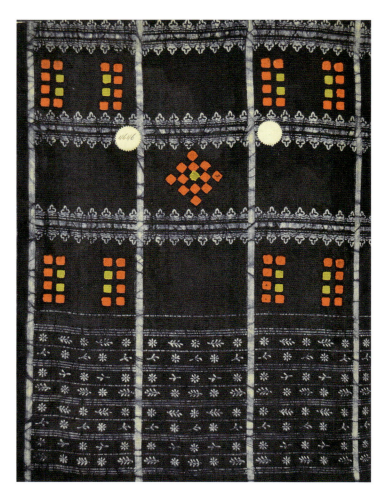

72 — 73

One of the *novelties* are the first examples, introduced around 1889, of printed versions of sought-after *patola* (double ikat) from the Patan region of Gujarat in India.[39] Similar examples can be found as registered designs in the Brown Fleming collection after 1895.

The original cloth was made using silk threads resist dyed with natural colours and woven together to create intricate patterns and designs. It was worn for special occasions in India, but also in the Indonesian archipelago, where it had already been introduced in the thirteenth or fourteenth century.[40] The printed version was obviously much more affordable, but when seen from a distance gave a similar effect. Brown Fleming registered three such designs in 1895, 1897 and 1902.[41] It is interesting to observe that printed imitations of woven cloth, although successful with other firms like Turnbull and Stockdale in the UK and Voortman in Belgium, did not become an important part of the Brown Fleming collection. No more than three were eventually registered. Also related to India is a series of motifs that look as if painted with a brush like Indian *kalamkari* cloth.[42] These are also found in books after 1895 with initials of clients other than Brown Fleming, but do not seem to have been a success.

In the same book covering 1889-1890, original batik designs that would later become Dutch wax classics are gradually introduced. The first versions of *Snail** and *Tree of Life** can be found.[43] In this book appear for the first time also several versions of a later classic *Canoe Peak** or *Tortoise Shell*.[44] Book 210, covering about 1894 to 1895, shows the first example of a printed version of *tie-dye* (nos 4649-50) and other designs inspired by traditional African textiles.[45]

Although the name of the client is not indicated on the designs, it is likely to have been Brown Fleming. The same applies to several designs that are built up with horizontal and vertical stripes created with wax resist.[46] He would later use similar designs with and without the added print-ons like designs 4270-3 in book 228 and 4721 in book 210.

The HKM started producing roller-printed *kangas* in this period. Because of the special patterns that cover the entire length of the cloth (66 inches) they had been hand printed. Machine-printing was theoretically possible from 1871 when a machine to print cross borders was patented, but this was not economical for small quantities, and the HKM waited for

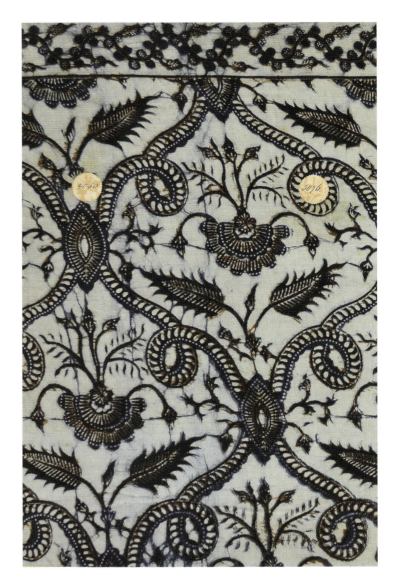

---

7. Design 4646, HKM book 210, around 1895
Built up with horizontal and vertical stripes created with wax resist, indigo dyed and added yellow and red decorations
Vlisco Archive, @ Vlisco BV

8. *Allemansdoek*, registered by Brown Fleming BT reg.no. 263770, 15 October 1895. Design 4903, HKM book 224
Vlisco Archive, @ Vlisco BV

9. *Snake Pattern*. BT reg.no. 387659, 24 February 1902
Vlisco Archive, @ Vlisco BV

10. *Loop Trail*. Design 4050, HKM book 248
Vlisco Archive, @ Vlisco BV

11. Women with European umbrellas. The second woman from the right is wearing cloth with *Loop Trail* design, place unknown, around 1910
Basel Mission Archives/Mission 21 Basel QD-30.019.0005

The creation of the Haarlem Collection by Brown Fleming 1895–1912

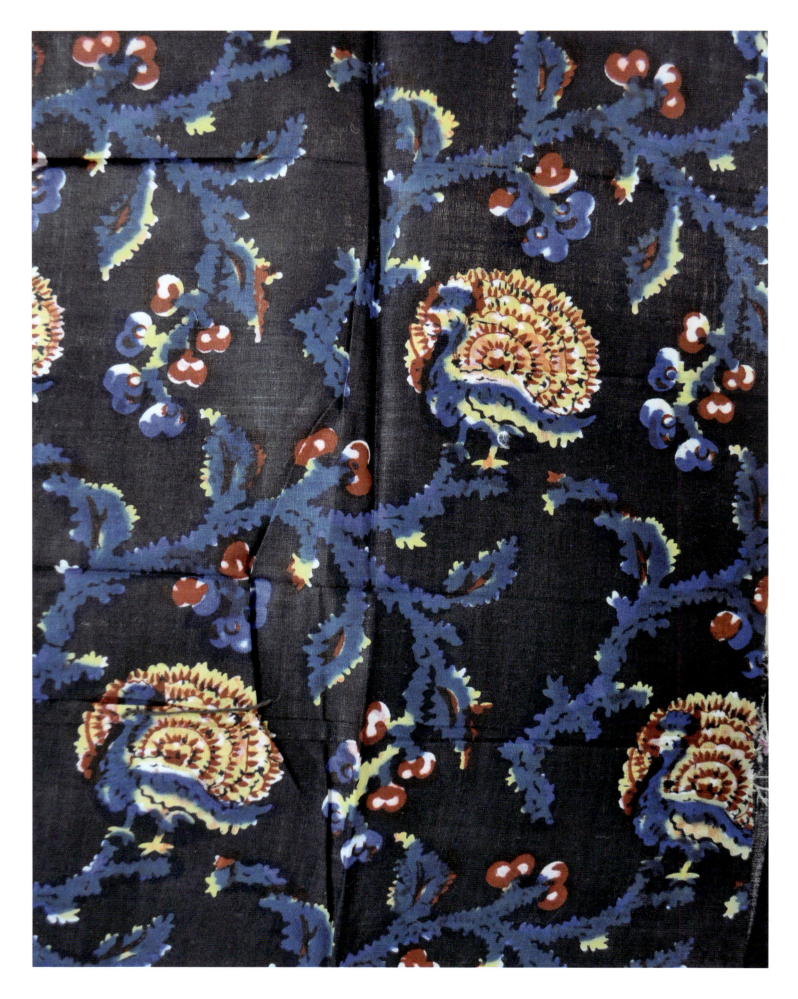

extra-large 21-inch diameter rollers to print kanga patterns with a single revolution.[47] In book 248 (around 1890) there are two identical designs called *Halve maan* (Half-moon) for kangas (4118 and 4119) with a handwritten note that these are the first *kangas* produced on a roller printing machine around 1890: *Met dit patroon zijn de eerste Kanga's aan de rol ingevoerd* (The first *kangas* were introduced on the roll with this pattern).[48] Very soon the roller-printed cloth sample books are more than half filled with *kanga* designs, suggesting it must have been a lucrative business for the HKM. There is no indication for which client(s) these were printed, but Brown Fleming would sell *kangas* himself in later years.[49]

A very popular item, not related to imitation batik but inspired rather by *indiennes*, and already exported to West Africa at an early stage was the *Allemans Doek* (Everyman's cloth), which could be worn on or around the neck, shoulders or head. Around 1875, this type of cloth was among the earliest exports to West Africa for Van Vlissingen in Helmond.[50] In the books around 1890 samples can be found like no 4398 (book 228). Brown Fleming would order them in later years from the HKM in many designs and many colours.

The handkerchief-like patterns are all built up in the same way: around a central area, plain or with diapered motifs and sometimes a central decoration like a medallion, all surrounded by a symmetrical border. This border consists of tendrils, garlands, flowers, paisley or geometric motifs. Most motifs come from fabrics that were imported to Europe from the East such as India, China and Iran. They became popular in Europe, and many other countries.[51]

The Brown Fleming Haarlem Collection, 1895-1912

By the time Brown Fleming started registering designs under his own name, on 1 January 1895, he had already developed a good idea of the West African market. The collection he introduced can be roughly divided into four categories:

- copies of, or designs inspired by, traditional Indonesian batik motifs;
- designs based on traditional African fabric;
- designs based on archetypes, proverbs and elements of African cultures;
- designs based on European culture and other influences.[52]

In each category, designs from the *Haarlem Collection* became classics. Although wax prints were a prominent part of this collection, regular prints also played an important role. Those designs are in general less outspoken and more *mainstream*. In this period, Brown Fleming also ordered a broad assortment of fancy prints of 36-inch width, and one-yard squares. About thirty designs are based on Indonesian batik, and over fifty designs are from other categories, many European in style. Some of those, but not many, were registered, such as no. 387659, registered on 24 February 1902. It is an original Indonesian design of a bird surrounded by a snake, but with borders imitating lace.[53] The registered pattern is an all-over version without the lace-like borders.

Copied many times is the motif of a clock, registered in 1897, embedded in the design *Loop Trail*, that appeared in earlier books of the HKM around 1890.[54] A design with peacocks, that forms part of a series incorporating similar floral motifs like cherries and berries, has a hand-painted effect.[55]

When choosing fancy prints from the HKM that were already sold to other merchants, Brown Fleming gave these an extra touch and added lines, dots, smudges or dapples for a less neat impression. Clearly this was done to make them more appealing to a specific market.

Batiks for Indonesian dress

The most important pieces of garments for which batik was used were a *kain sarong* (a sewn up tubular skirt), a *kain panjang* (wrap around skirt), a *kain dodot* (like a *kain panjang* but for royalty), a *slendang*, worn around the shoulders or to carry a baby, and the *iket* or headscarf. The designs for a *sarong* were the most complicated: on a piece of cloth of 1 x 2 m, a third or a quarter was covered with the *kepala* or heading, the main field or *badan* having a continuous motif surrounded by a border. The *kepala* often consists of a vertical border (*papan*) with two rows of facing isosceles triangles called *tumpal*. The *tumpal* design may sometimes appear at each end of the cloth. The *tumpal* section of a sarong was in general worn in front by women and in the back by men, but this could vary. The *kain panjang* was slightly larger – 1 x 2.5 m – with an all-over design or one big design in the middle. Sometimes a different design can be chosen on each half of the cloth. The division may be vertical or diagonal. This contrasting design is referred to as *Night and Day* or *pagi-sore* (*pagi* means day, *sore* evening, or night) cloth. While the *sarong* may be regarded as everyday wear for the less affluent part of society, the *kain panjang* was worn on more formal occasions by the middle and upper classes.[56] A *kemben* was a piece of cloth that covers the chest, wrapped around the torso of a woman. It could have a plain field in the middle in a rectangular or diamond shape. A *slendang* was about 2.5 x 0.5 m, draped around the head in a variety of ways. It could also be used to carry food, a baby or personal objects. An *iket* or *iket kepala* was a head-cloth for men, consisting in general of a 36-inch square with an all-over design, sometimes with a rectangular or lozenge-shaped central area. Right-angled border patterns, sometimes with series of vertical lines imitating a fringe, could be added. The designs were in general printed on cloth with a width of 36 inches that could be cut into pieces for head cloths, worn in specific regions, where this was customary, as in Suriname.

12. Design with peacocks BT reg.no. 274699, 21 April 1896
Brunnschweiler Archive, held at the Whitworth Art Gallery, University of Manchester (UK)

Copies of or inspired by traditional Indonesian batik

The first imitation batiks for West-African markets were the same as the copies for Indonesia and South East Asia. Gradually the designs started to be adapted to the cultural and aesthetic expectations of the local consumer. Where in original Javanese batik detailed drawing, precision and control are dominant, the African consumer preferred larger designs, an expanded colour range and less detailed, often simplified and even isolated patterns. The slight irregularities of machine production, especially its craquelure, were enhanced and accentuated. Sometimes effects like dots and stripes were layered on top of an original design. Despite such adaptations, the Javanese origins of these designs are clearly discernible, although adaptations for the African market would no longer be saleable on the Indonesian market.[57] The sizes of the cloth were adapted as well. In general, pieces of cloth were sold in lengths of 6 or 12 yards.

Designs for batik can be separated into geometric and non-geometric (*semen*) designs. An important series of designs consist of *ceplokan*, symmetrical motifs in the form of stars, crosses, lozenges, rosettes and polygons. These can be single motifs or pairs, spaced at regular intervals over the surface of the cloth, but also in more complex patterns where design elements coalesce into different patterns. The entire design can be aligned on a horizontal or diagonal axis or in a symmetrical arrangement. Variations in colour intensity can enhance illusions of depth or multiple layers. The design *Key Square* is an example after this traditional type.

Batik *tambal* features small motifs enclosed in a grid. *Tambal* means 'to patch' referring to the way in which the motifs resemble patches sewn onto a piece of fabric. Patchwork garments were associated with Buddhist priests in old Java as part of their vow of poverty. One example *of tambal* uses a small animal like a shrimp as motif, repeating within squares or lozenges aligned diagonally across the material.[58] Brown Fleming had various versions in his collection of which two became best-sellers: *Shrimp Check** and another design, also with shrimps.

Leidsche Ruit* or *Lino** (short for linoleum in English) is a well-known design and an example of a *tambal batik* consisting of ornamented squares arranged in a diagonal grid or trellis. The varying distribution of the ornamental elements, coupled with the contrasts between density of pattern and colour, gives a strong suggestion of patchwork.

13. *Key Square*, not registered
Brunnschweiler Archive, held at the Whitworth Art Gallery, University of Manchester (UK)

14. *Shrimp Check**, not registered
Brunnschweiler Archive, held at the Whitworth Art Gallery, University of Manchester (UK)

15. Batik tambal with shrimp motif, BT reg.no. 405016, 11 February 1902
Brunnschweiler Archive, held at the Whitworth Art Gallery, University of Manchester (UK)

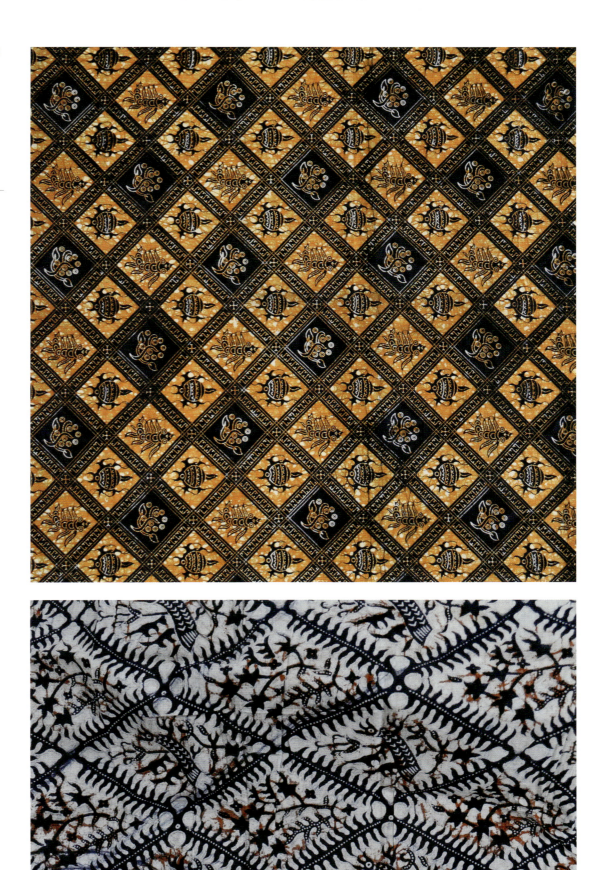

The creation of the Haarlem Collection by Brown Fleming 1895–1912

16. *Leidsche Ruit** or *Lino**, not registered.
Brunnschweiler Archive, held at the Whitworth Art Gallery,
University of Manchester (UK)

17. Example of *Garis Miring**, not registered, design 4922, HKM book 224, around 1895
Vlisco Archive, @ Vlisco BV

18. *Garis Miring**, not registered, design 5084, HKM book 255, around 1897 with added blue dot with tie-dye effect, adapted for West-African market
Vlisco Archive, @ Vlisco BV

19. *Udan Liris**, not registered, sample in Brunnschweiler Archive, held at the Whitworth Art Gallery, University of Manchester (UK)

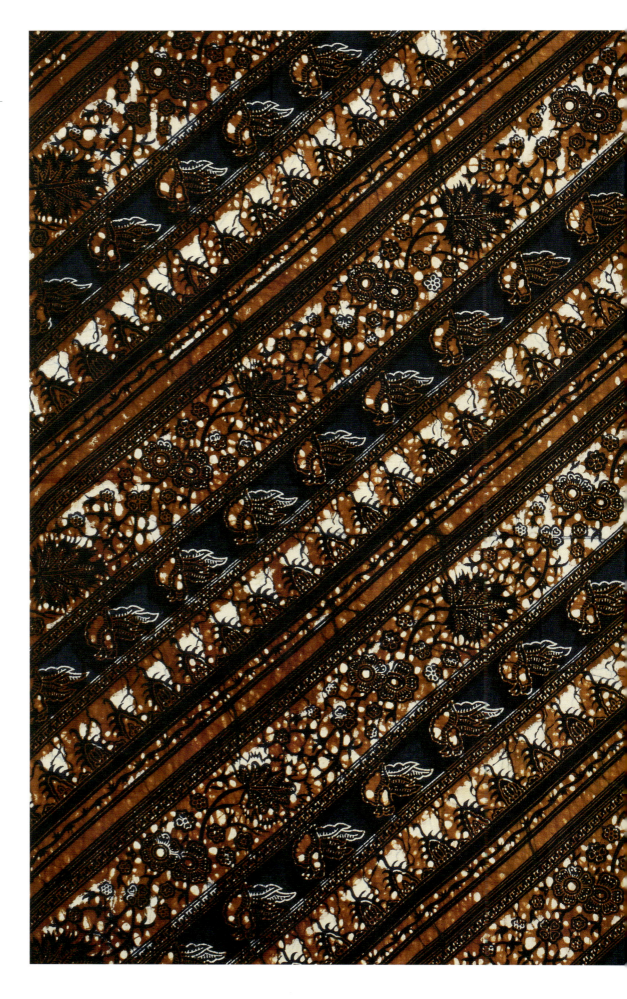

The creation of the Haarlem Collection by Brown Fleming 1895–1912

20. *Hindoo*, not registered
Brunnschweiler Archive, held at the Whitworth Art Gallery, University of Manchester (UK)

21. *New Fine Trail**, example of *Lung-Lungan* – plants that spread
Not registered, HKM around 1900
Brunnschweiler Archive, held at the Whitworth Art Gallery, University of Manchester (UK)

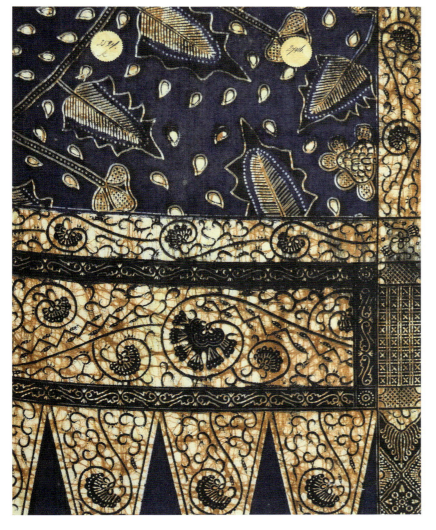

22. Design with branches, example of *Lung-Lungan*,
BT reg.no. 420628, 2 November 1903
Brunnschweiler Archive, held at the Whitworth Art Gallery,
University of Manchester (UK)

23. Imitation batik for sarong design 3524, HKM book 233,
around 1888
Vlisco Archive, @ Vlisco BV

24. Design 3645, HKM book 214, around 1889
Vlisco Archive, @ Vlisco BV

The creation of the Haarlem Collection by Brown Fleming 1895–1912

25. *Tree of life**, BT reg.no. 292267, 20 January 1897 Brunnschweiler Archive, held at the Whitworth Art Gallery, University of Manchester (UK)

26. Batik of nutmeg tree by Carolina Josephina von Franquemont, c. 1840-1867 Wereldmuseum Amsterdam, inv.no. TM-1585-4

This design was never registered but appears at least six times in the HKM sample books, which means that at each time a new roller had to be engraved – an indication that it must have sold very well. It also appears in the list of designs made in 1939 and is still in print today.[59]

Garis miring* is another type of a visually striking batik design with diagonal stripes or lines. Two versions appear among the designs photographed in 1939. The first one appears as sample 4922 in book 224 of the HKM but was sold later with added dark spots for the West African market. The second one is an example of *udan liris** meaning light rain *(BF photo 80*, Vlisco 14/1003). It consists of row upon row of diagonal bands featuring well-known classical batik figured stripes on a light ground.

Hindoo* (*BF photo 80*, Vlisco 13/0094) is also a design with figured bands but not in the Indonesian manner, apart from the traditional colours of blue and dark brown. Especially designed for the African market, the bands run across the width of the fabric in varying sizes. This pattern sold well.[60]

Non-geometric designs, known as *semen* can be imaginative and ornamental designs usually composed of three aspects representing: land (plants and four-legged animals), water (fish, snakes) and air (birds, clouds). Forms from nature, human and animal, are not represented in a realistic manner, respecting the religious restrictions of Islam for the Muslim population in Indonesia. Instead, the designer focuses on one or more key elements such as a bud, a leaf or a feather and through styling and embellishment develops it into a pattern.

Some *semen* designs consist entirely of flower and leaf motifs. Designs focusing on climbing plants and vines are often referred to as *lung-lungan*, which means the plants that spread. Successful examples are *New Fine Trail**. For Indonesians it had the symbolic meaning that the wearer would have a life that continues to grow and be successful. Several similar designs of trailing plants, sometimes with flowers, can be found in the Brown Fleming collection.[61]

The sample books of the HKM, prior to Brown Fleming, show field patterns surrounded by borders for sarongs

The creation of the Haarlem Collection by Brown Fleming 1895–1912

27. Design 3910, HKM book 248, 1896
Vlisco Archive, @ Vlisco BV

28. Design 4140, HKM book 248, 1896
Vlisco Archive, @ Vlisco BV

29. Design 4285, HKM book 228, 1896
Vlisco Archive, @ Vlisco BV

intended for the Indonesian market. Later the same main field patterns or *badan* were printed without borders for the African market, as in the example shown in photo 24.[62]

Featuring a central tree with an abundance of smaller motifs filling the whole width of the cloth is the design *Tree of life**, registered in 1897 under number 292267. This design clearly has Indian influence, which was noticeable in nineteenth-century batiks. For both Indians and Indonesians, the tree holds an important place in their philosophical tradition.[63] Hindus have great reverence for nature and view trees as a symbol of life. Their sprouting, growth and decline, the elasticity of their branches, their marks of ageing and their recovery from injury have all been interpreted as powerful symbols of the life process. The tree is an emblem of longevity and divine creation. However, the design shown here is not in the traditional style. Batik specialist Itie van Hout has identified this is as an example of a nutmeg tree with mature fruits bursting. Nutmeg is not a common motif in textiles. Closer investigation showed that the design is a copy of an original batik by Carolina Josephina von Franquemont, who worked in Indonesia between 1840 and 1867. Since 1942, this batik has been in the collection of The Tropenmuseum, now the Wereldmuseum, in Amsterdam.[64] It must have been a special opportunity for the designers of the HKM to be able to copy this design, because exceptionally not one but three slightly different versions were engraved of which number 4140 was registered in 1897.[65] Two variations were issued: one dyed with indigo only and one with additional colours.

Batik designs were originally meant for various elements of clothing. Sometimes the design for a specific piece of cloth can still be recognised, like this design for a sarong, registered in 1897, but would be presented in a not always authentic, adapted way for its new market. Although this design contains authentic Indonesian elements, this version would not be saleable in Indonesia, because it has an oversized

The creation of the Haarlem Collection by Brown Fleming 1895–1912

tumpal. *Tumpal* or triangular border designs, consisting of a row of isosceles triangles, are a popular pattern element in Indonesian batik and often used as a border at one narrow end of the piece in the case of a sarong. The decoration on the main field or *badan* of the sarong is not authentic either, because it is an imitation of woven cloth and not of batik.[66]

Tumpal can also be used at both ends of the cloth for a *slendang*. Samples in the Brown Fleming collection show designs based on these elements, but in a way only applicable to the West African market, like *Capella**.

A design of a square with lozenges in the traditional colours of blue and brown, clearly created for the African market, was called *Slendang** within the wax print industry. For Indonesians it would refer to a rectangular piece of cloth to be used as a headcloth or to carry objects, but this is a *kemben*, a piece of cloth that covers the chest of a woman.[67] The motif used in this design is rare in Indonesian batik, but popular in West Africa and still in print today called *Canoe Peak** or in French *Dos de tortue* (tortoise shell), although it is not easy to recognise as such. It appears on a regular basis in the HKM sample books and Brown Fleming registered the design in 1906.[68]

30. Imitation batik for sarong, BT reg.no. 301998, 23 July 1897
Collection The National Archives, Kew (UK)

31. *Capella**, not registered. Imitation batik with double border and row of tumpals at each side of the border
Brunnschweiler Archive, held at the Whitworth Art Gallery, University of Manchester (UK)

Designs covering the whole width of the cloth were also sought after. Well known is *Night and Day**, or *pagi-sore*, which Brown Fleming registered in 1902 a traditional Indonesian pattern arrangement with adjacent light and dark triangles making a square. He also registered a variant of two light and two dark blocks in a square three years later.[69] The photos of the Brown Fleming collection of 1939 show another related square design with a light lozenge in the centre of a dark surrounding band, completed with four light triangles at the corners (BF photo 179). The design was initially used on a *kain panjang*, where each half of the cloth would have a different design. A square version was registered in the same year and clearly made up with Indonesian elements like the *tumpal* for export to Africa.[70]

88 — 89

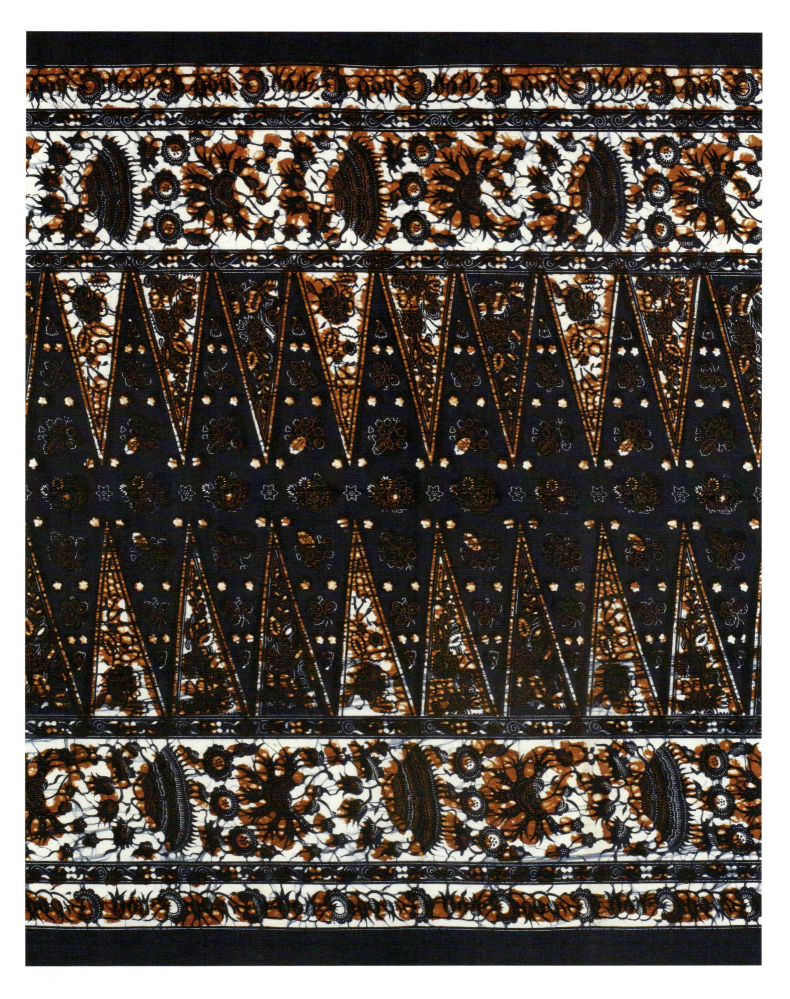

The creation of the Haarlem Collection by Brown Fleming 1895–1912

Molatto Stripe Pattern* or *Watercress**, registered in 1897, is also a design that covers the whole width of the cloth.[71] The motifs are taken from Indonesian batik but given a completely new setting. The design is dominated by three main stripes. The middle one is on a light background, the lines at the left and right on a darker background. In the middle stripe is a square with flattened corners and at either side two horizontal diamonds. The surface of all three stripes is filled with trailing vines and a total of fifteen six-pointed stars per repeat with the word *Allah* written in the middle. This motif can be found in batiks for an Islamic market but also incorporated within a more complex design. In this design, which is not an original batik but recreated with *batik style* motifs, the star takes an important place. Before the star became the colonial symbol for Nigeria in 1914, it was already a major symbol for Igbo culture; it figures prominently as a motif on the regalia of clan and even tribal chiefs, among others. This might explain the choice of the star as dominant motif, reflecting its desirability for the West African clientele.[72] There is also a square version of this design, called *Capella Square*.

Square pieces of cloth were sought after because they could not only serve as a headcloth but also for many other purposes. For export to West Africa, they were not always cut into pieces, but left in the desired length so they could also be worn as cloth, wrapped around the body. *Good Husband**, especially popular and still in print, is designed in

---

32. *Canoe Peak** or *Tortoise Shell**, traditional Indonesian motif. Woodblocks for hand printing, used at W. Ashton and Co. of Newton Bank printworks in Hyde near Manchester, various periods
Donation Brunnschweiler Archives/ABC Hyde, Collection Science and Industry Museum, Manchester

33. *Canoe Peak** or *Tortoise Shell** design in Slendang, 90x90cm, adapted for African market, BT reg.no. 36177, 25 July 1912
Collection The National Archives, Kew (UK)

The creation of the Haarlem Collection by Brown Fleming 1895–1912

34. *Day and Night**, traditional Indonesian design, BT reg.no. 427678, 27 February 1904
Brunnschweiler Archive, held at the Whitworth Art Gallery, University of Manchester (UK)

35. Dancer, wearing design *Day and Night**. Photo Maudry, Ghana around 1920
Basel Mission Archives/Mission 21 Basel QD-30.103.0018

36. *Watercress**, design BT reg.no. 309473, 20 November 1897
Vlisco Archive, @ Vlisco BV

37. King and his bride from Christiansborg (Accra, Ghana), photo c. 1900
Basel Mission Archives/Mission 21 Basel QW-30-11.0030

38. *Good Husband**, BT reg.no. 402351 , 17 December 1902
Brunnschweiler Archive, held at the Whitworth Art Gallery, University of Manchester (UK)

The creation of the Haarlem Collection by Brown Fleming 1895–1912

39. *Star** or *Table Cover**. Not registered
Brunnschweiler Archive, held at the Whitworth Art Gallery,
University of Manchester (UK)

40. *Pineapple Square**. Not registered
Brunnschweiler Archive, held at the Whitworth Art Gallery, University of Manchester (UK)

The creation of the Haarlem Collection by Brown Fleming 1895–1912

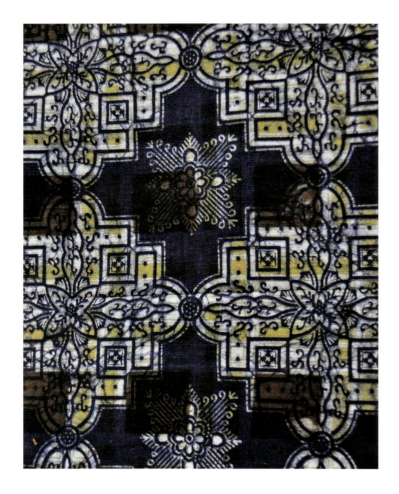

41. Imitation batik with strong effect of veining. BT reg.no. 251961, 24 March 1895
Brunnschweiler Archive, held at the Whitworth Art Gallery, University of Manchester (UK)

42. Batik motif *Lar* (wing of the *garuda* bird, venerated in Indonesia) in continuous pattern. BT reg.no. 263778, 15 October 1895

43. *Pisan(g) Bali*, traditional Indonesian batik motif of stylized banana leaves and flowers
Design 3872, HKM book 248, around 1890
Vlisco Archive, @ Vlisco BV

44. *Pisan(g) Bali* design, HKM production, not registered
Brunnschweiler Archive, held at the Whitworth Art Gallery, University of Manchester (UK)

The creation of the Haarlem Collection by Brown Fleming 1895–1912

45. BT reg.no. 292266, 2 January 1897. The veining of the wax print gives the cloth the desired effect for the African market
Brunnschweiler Archive, held at the Whitworth Art Gallery, University of Manchester (UK)

46. *Sawat**, BT reg.no. 292264, 20 January 1897, with stylised large wings of the Garuda bird
Brunnschweiler Archive, held at the Whitworth Art Gallery, University of Manchester (UK)

47. Stylised wings of the Garuda bird, adapted for the West African market, BT reg.no. 303041, 10 August 1897
Brunnschweiler Archive, held at the Whitworth Art Gallery, University of Manchester (UK)

48. *Bunch of bananas**. BT reg.no. 256955, 26 June 1895
Brunnschweiler Archive, held at the Whitworth Art Gallery, University of Manchester (UK)

The creation of the Haarlem Collection by Brown Fleming 1895–1912

49. *Snail**, BT reg.no. 292268, 20 January 1897
Brunnschweiler Archive, held at the Whitworth Art Gallery, University of Manchester (UK)

50. Nurse-girl in Christiansborg (Accra, Ghana), wearing dress with design *Snail**
Photo Max Otto Schultze 1901-1904
Basel Mission Archives D-30.03.007

The creation of the Haarlem Collection by Brown Fleming 1895–1912

51. Fragment of sarong with peacock pattern
Brunnschweiler Archive, held at the Whitworth Art Gallery, University of Manchester (UK)

52. Sample of imitation batik, design 3342, HKM book 233, around 1887
Vlisco Archive, @ Vlisco BV

a similar way with elements of traditional batik re-arranged. It illustrates how original batik ideas were adapted for export to Africa.[73] Other examples of designs for cloth square, which in the engraving books are called *Star* or Table Cover** and *Pineapple Square**, were also created for export.[74]

More complex designs based on traditional batik are also found in the collection. The design of the next pattern (photo 41) with alternating stars and medallions is recognisably Indonesian, but the emphasis on veining is an adaptation for the African market. Brown Fleming registered this as one of his first designs in 1895.[75] Still Indonesian but also with an accent on veining is another early registration using as its principal motif the *lar*, a wing of the venerated *garuda* bird.[76]

An original and very old Indonesian design, which has been found in stone carvings on Java from the ninth century, appears in the early sample books of the HKM. *Pisan(g) Bali** is a design of stylised banana leaves and flowers that came to be much appreciated in West Africa.[77]

Many designs are no longer related to traditional clothing, taken out of their context and used as elements to make an

---

53. *Peacock design**. BT reg.no. 253268, 17 April 1895
Brunnschweiler Archive, held at the Whitworth
Art Gallery, University of Manchester (UK)

54. Women from Benin, one wearing *Peacock* design*
Photo 'Photohom' Lagos, dated 20 October 1906
Collection Duncan Clarke London

The creation of the Haarlem Collection by Brown Fleming 1895–1912

appealing pattern. An example is a design with elements that look like butterflies and insects on a background of fine lines, was registered in 1897 and has become a classic in wax prints. It appears already in an early HKM book from around 1885.[78]

*Sawat**, a registered design with a similar lay-out, is also a typical adaptation for West African export.[79] An important place is reserved for the *garuda* bird, highly venerated and associated with power and success. The *garuda* has become the national symbol of Indonesia. In batik it can appear as an entire bird or as just the wing (singly or paired), called a *lar*. An example with paired *garuda* wings adapted to the African taste is the design seen in photo 47.[80]

Another motif with a single wing of the Garuda bird is *Bunch of Bananas** where it is shown against a typical Javanese background. The incongruous title comes from Ghana where the wing was seen as a bunch of bananas. In Togo, it was interpreted as a snail coming out of its shell. Brown Fleming had two versions registered in 1895, one on a background of coloured stripes and another with indigo only.[81] The motif, still widely used today, also became popular in combination with other motifs.

Another important design with animals, possibly depicting a sea slug, is called *Snail**. Still in print today, it appears in early books of the HKM for the Indonesian market, and Brown Fleming registered it in 1897.[82]

The peacock, popular in Indian and Chinese mythology, also appears in Indonesian batik and its imitations.[83] In the Brunnschweiler Archive is a fragment of an Indonesian batik of a woman's sarong with a design of peacocks with tail feathers fanned.[84] Renderings appear in the HKM sample books, and in 1895 Brown Fleming registered a non-wax print version that gained wide popularity.[85] Although designs that become classics are in general of the best quality cloth and print, this design was not a wax print, but did become a classic, an indication of the popularity of the motif. In a sample book of around 1902–1903 from the Manchester merchant Edwin Goodwin, an identical pattern can be found next to samples of a chinoiserie pattern known to have been printed in the Netherlands by the KKM.[86] It gives an indication of the tight competition at the time.

The peacock motif was also popular in locally made *adire* cloth where individual cotton seeds were tied into the cloth in a fan shape and then dyed with indigo to suggest the beautiful *eyes* of peacock tail feathers.[87]

Peacocks appear in two more related designs. The first has a striped arrangement with the birds in a central position on a lighter background and the second is presented as a square with the birds in the middle, known as *Batik Ancienne**.[88]

Other animal motifs also appear. The lion, although not indigenous to the archipelago, is a prevalent motif in batik. Most probably it has its origin in Chinese imagery. The design *Java Lion** or *Little Lion* sold very well in West Africa.[89]

A group of imitation batiks, called *Batik Tulisan Arab* or *Besurek Batik*, is an illustration of Muslim influence on batik, using Islamic calligraphy developed initially on the north-eastern coast of Java and in Sumatra, where Islam was introduced in the eleventh century. This type of cloth was initiated by Arab traders in Indian manufactures in the seventeenth century in Benkulu, Sumatra. It often comes as a square for a head cloth worn during prayers and rituals, or in large rectangular cloths as for a *kain* (skirt). Most of them are dyed indigo blue, occasionally intense red with waxed elements in white or cream. The calligraphy is in Arabic script, sometimes contorted into the shape of zoomorphic figures as the *Quau* bird motif, a symbol of the relationship between humans, nature and their creator. As Islamic art does not allow the realistic depiction of humans or animals, stylised birds were often used as a symbol for Allah.[90] The texts are Arabic formulae, taken from the Qur'an, and would give the cloth powerful protective properties. They could have been used as a garment or to cover the Qur'an.[91] The batik imitations, made in Haarlem most probably by designers unfamiliar with Islamic calligraphy, are at times difficult to decipher. Kerlogue points out that this is not in itself a problem. Calligraphy was the most tangible visualisation of the Word of Allah. Those who cannot read the verses are still able to recognise the presence of Allah and see it as a symbolic affirmation of allegiance to the faith. It was more the Arabic script than the literal meaning of the words that had significance. This could also be the case with the presence of numbers. In many motifs the meanings are encoded with numbers representing letters or vice versa.[92] The cloths are more a symbolic testimony to the faith of both their makers and their users and attest to the importance of Islam, first in Indonesia, later in West Africa.[93] Early examples can be found in HKM book 233, dated around 1888.[94]

Significant is a sample with the label *Surinaam doeken. Ellemaat. Flemming*.[95] This cloth might have been destined for Suriname, where people from Indonesia but also Creole people of African (European) origin wore (imitation) batik.[96] The usual female dress was a type originated by slave owners to encourage modesty in apparel. It consists of a *koto* (skirt), *jaki* (jacket) and *angisa* (headscarf). The Javanese and Creole peoples wore the skirt in *sarong* style but wrapped slightly differently.[97] The *angisa* (headscarf) could be chosen from machine-printed patterns. The cloth was heavily starched and folded in various shapes reflecting the mood of the wearer, or a special occasion. This way of communicating feeling through dress is associated with the Asante, who from 1730 until 1780 represented the largest contingent of slaves in Suriname.[98] Brown Fleming, as probably also other merchants, exported batik imitations to Suriname, known there as *yampanesi* (Javanese).[99]

55. *Batik Ancienne**. BT reg.no. 517088, 5 December 1907
Brunnschweiler Archive, held at the Whitworth Art Gallery,
University of Manchester (UK)

56. *Little Lion** or *Java Lion**. First example: design 1770,
HKM book 213, around 1880
Vlisco Archive, @ Vlisco BV

57. Example of *Batik Tulisan Arab* or *Besurek Batik*, example of zoomorphic calligraphy with a bird as symbol for Allah
Design 4101, HKM book 248
Vlisco Archive, @ Vlisco BV

58. *Surinaam doek*, batik imitation or yampanesi for export to Suriname, 1897
Design no. 6091, HKM book 247
Vlisco Archive, @ Vlisco BV

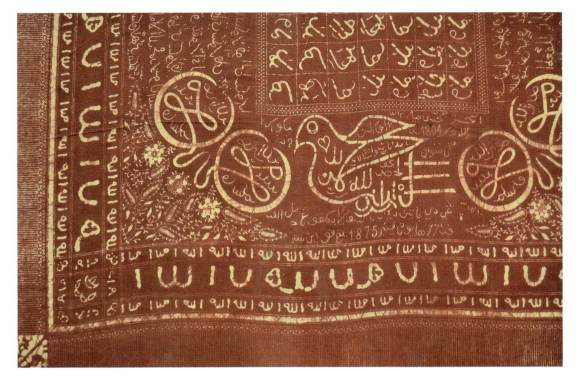

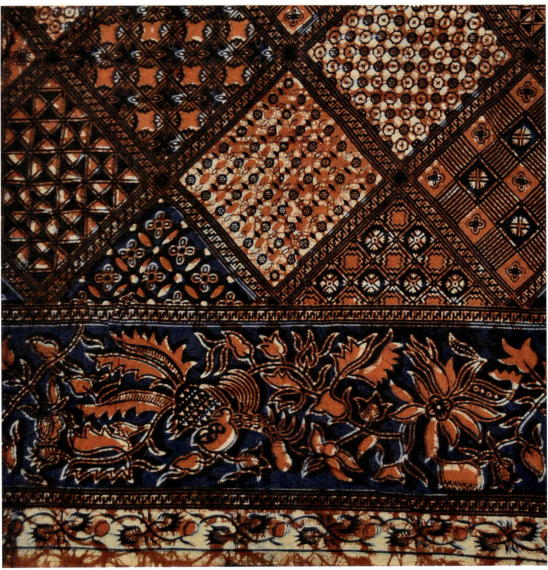

The creation of the Haarlem Collection by Brown Fleming 1895–1912

Designs based on traditional African fabric

Among the very first designs which Brown Fleming registered in 1895, soon after starting his own business, was an important range of designs inspired by traditional African fabric. A significant number can be found in the HKM sample books from the same year. Copies of African fabric had already been sold with success on the West African market in the nineteenth century by companies like Voortman in Gent and Turnbull and Stockdale in Ramsbottom (UK).[100] He must have been aware of the potential of this type of design and, after having explored the possibilities of the market, felt confident enough to introduce his own collection. All are indigo dyed and adapted from African wax print and tie-dye effects.[101] The selection presented here gives an impression of the many variations he sold from 1895 onwards. One of the first was an indigo dyed pattern with a simple repeat of two different tie-dye motifs, registered as no. 250492 on 1 March 1895. A similar design was created by squares formed by four marbled lines alternated with small circles.[102] A more complex pattern of a rectangle outlined by triplet stripes, enclosing nine *tie-dye* rings, formed by tying knots, called *Tie-up and Fishbone**, is still in print today.[103]

Fir-Tree is an imitation of a very time-consuming technique, *adire eleso*, produced by folding a slight tuck into the material, rolling a ridge of fabric over the tucked area and finally sewing a whip stitch over the design with raffia thread before dipping it into the dye. In another example, registered in 1902, the tie-dye effect of a circle dominates with multiple stripes, created by stitching, marking the edges of the square.[104]

Often wax designs are printed on weave-patterned cloth or on cloth already printed with a pattern to give the fabric extra 'depth'. Africans appreciated this double decoration for the layering effect. This technique was already in use before the arrival of the Brown Fleming collection on the Gold Coast. Nowadays it is called at Vlisco the *Emily Jagge* procedure.[105] Parts of a piece of European printed cloth were prepared with wax or by tying up so the dye could not penetrate. After the wax and/or the tying up was removed, the initial design of the printed cloth would still be visible on the prepared parts. Brown Fleming preferred to use his own version of printed cloth with special designs before applying a second design with wax.

It is worth emphasising that the effect of this design is thus the result of a double printing procedure. The design which has been used for the first print can be found in an earlier HKM sample book from around 1895 and has been used as a base for various wax print designs.[106] The combination shows skilful drawing enhanced by the randomisation of wax printing.

59. Indigo dyed pattern with a simple repeat of two different tie-dye motifs, BT reg.no. 250492, 1 March 1895
Brunnschweiler Archive, held at the Whitworth Art Gallery, University of Manchester (UK)

60. *Tie-up and Fishbone**. BT reg.no. 253267, 17 April 1897
Brunnschweiler Archive, held at the Whitworth Art Gallery, University of Manchester (UK)

61. *Fir-Tree*. Sample of design not registered, design 4720, HKM book 210, around 1895
Brunnschweiler Archive, held at the Whitworth Art Gallery, University of Manchester (UK)

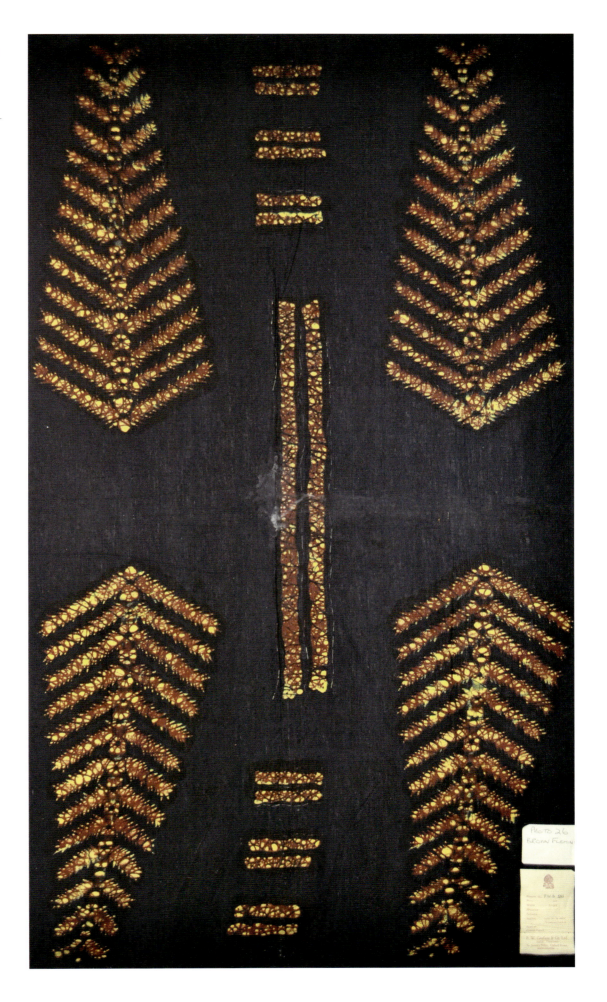

The creation of the Haarlem Collection by Brown Fleming 1895–1912

62. Design with tie-dye effects, BT reg.no. 402047, 11 December 1902
Brunnschweiler Archive, held at the Whitworth Art Gallery,
University of Manchester (UK)

63. Tie-dye effect of horizontal and vertical stripes on a background of already printed and dyed cloth, BT reg.no. 298263, 4 May 1897
Brunnschweiler Archive, held at the Whitworth Art Gallery,
University of Manchester (UK)

64. Design used for printing base pattern before printing final design
Design 4484, HKM book 210, 1895
Vlisco Archive, @ Vlisco BV

65. *The Wheel**. BT reg.no. 300707, 24 June 1897
Brunnschweiler Archive, held at the Whitworth Art Gallery,
University of Manchester (UK)

The creation of the Haarlem Collection by Brown Fleming 1895–1912

66. *Shaking Hands**. BT reg.no. 307892, 23 October 1897.
Brunnschweiler Archive, held at the Whitworth Art Gallery,
University of Manchester (UK)

67. *Fishes**, BT reg.no. 307893, 23 October 1897
Brunnschweiler Archive, held at the Whitworth Art Gallery, University of Manchester (UK)

The creation of the Haarlem Collection by Brown Fleming 1895–1912

68. *Target**, design not registered.
Design 6251, HKM book 245,
Brown Fleming collection, 1897
Vlisco Archive, © Vlisco BV

A design that uses the same base pattern of wavy white and yellow lines and stylised leaves is *The Wheel**, registered under no. 300707 on 24 June 1897.

The central motif of the design *Shaking Hands* is a pair of black and white hands that shake each other, possibly as a symbol of interracial cooperation and equality. The handshake within a reserved heart-shaped surround is overprinted in indigo. The top border shows a straight chain pierced by spears, and the bottom border a continuous swagged chain with pendant hearts.[107] It is not known who ordered this motif. It was not re-engraved by the HKM, but Haijkens would sell a similar version not long after.[108] The motif of shaking hands on its own became a classic. *Fishes** is a design that has been printed over the base pattern and that displays seaweed, crabs and fish.[109]

Two famous patterns, *Target** (or *Sunray*) and *Grammophone**, both classics, are most probably also derived from tie-dye effects. *Target** was not registered and appeared for the first time in the HKM sample books around 1902.[110] The design is built up with horizontal yellow and white lines, overprinted with a network of red lines and indigo dots arranged in concentric circles.[111]

*Grammophone** was registered in 1903.[112] Here, stylised African tie-dye motifs are arranged on a ground pattern typical of Indonesia. The ground employs an element from traditional batik *isen*, patterns of simple repetitive design elements based on dots, lines, squares, crosses, foliage and flowers. In this case it is covered with little hooks or *ukel*. Vlisco still uses these *isen* to give wax prints its signature look.

69. *Grammophone**. BT reg.no. 419879, 22 October 1903
Collection The National Archives Kew, London (UK)

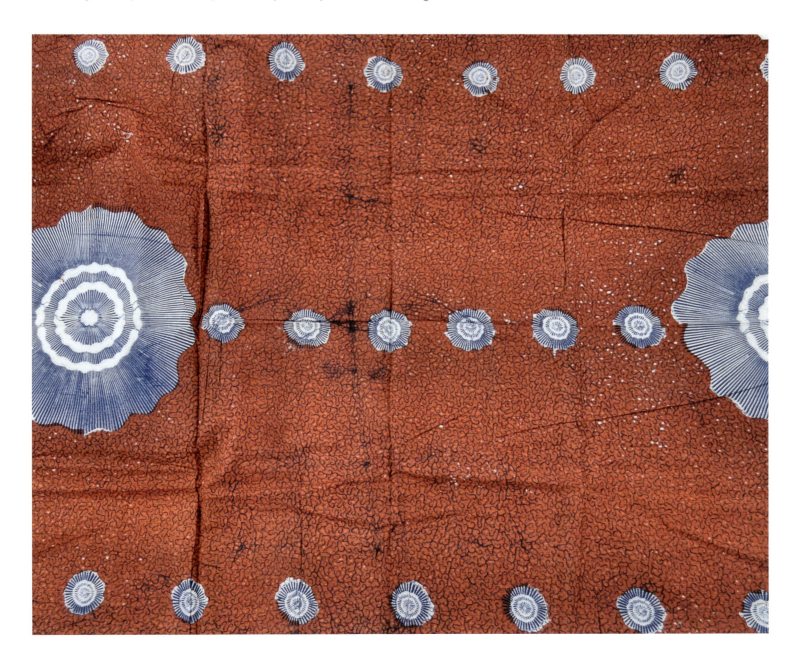

The creation of the Haarlem Collection by Brown Fleming 1895–1912

70. *Hand and fingers**. BT reg.no. 260844, 31 August 1895
Brunnschweiler Archive, held at the Whitworth Art Gallery, University of Manchester (UK)

71. *Staff of Kingship**.
Not registered design
Brunnschweiler Archive, held at the Whitworth Art Gallery, University of Manchester (UK)

Designs based on proverbs, archetypes and other elements of African cultures

Proverbs are important in traditional Africa, mostly preserved by oral tradition. A famous saying among the Yoruba is:

> Owe lesin oro, oro lesin owe: ti oro ba sonu owe la fin nwa (A proverb is a guide to a word and a word is a guide to a proverb: when a word is lost, a proverb is used to find it).[113]

As collections of wisdom they are intimately related to the culture of a people and carry authority in respect of social relationships.

Based on an African proverb: *the palm of the hand is sweeter than the back of the hand* (because the palm holds the money, so we hope to receive good fortune) is the design *Hand and fingers**. It was one of the very first designs Brown Fleming registered.[114] The motif consists of a hand with coins and individual fingers forming a border on each side of the cloth. In the hand are twelve coins, twelve pence that make one English shilling. According to John Picton it is a key element in the visual culture of the Twi-speaking people in Southern and Central Ghana. Twi is one of the four major dialects of Akan, the principal lan guage of Ghana.[115]
An earlier printed handkerchief from 1884 by Moir & Co., active in Glasgow and Manchester, bears a similar motif of black and white hands. The white hands with the back of

72. *Staff of Kingship**, worn by man (pointed at by the arrow) in Aburi, Ghana 1909
Basel Mission Archives/Mission 21 Basel QW-30.006.0022

73. *The Eye**. BT reg.no. 387613, 22 February 1902
Brunnschweiler Archive, held at the Whitworth Art Gallery, University of Manchester (UK)

The creation of the Haarlem Collection by Brown Fleming 1895–1912

74. *Staircase**. Not registered. Design 6436, HKM book 262, around 1902
Brunnschweiler Archive, held at the Whitworth Art Gallery,
University of Manchester (UK)
75. Ghanaian men wearing wax cloth: left and right design *Staircase**,
in the middle *Day and Night**, c. 1920
Basel Mission Archives/Mission 21 Basel QD-30.107.0074

76. *Skin**. BT reg.no. 250494, 1 March 1895. Sample 4842, HKM Book 224 Collection The National Archives Kew, London (UK)

hand visible touch money, but the black hands hold coins in the palm of their hands.[116] Given the fact that the design refers to an African proverb, one can assume it was destined for export to Africa.

Picton identified another design as a celebration of Akan culture and values in the face of colonial rule: *Staff of Kingship**. The design was not registered, but appears in the HKM sample books around 1902.[117] It is the first example in which the main motif was inspired by an actual African object. Picton suggests the principal motif is based upon an Asante ceremonial sword held in the British Museum since 1896.

It was bought from William Owen Wolseley, who was part of the Second Ashanti Expedition' (1895-1896) to the Gold Coast, when this sword and other objects were confiscated following the defeat of the Asante by the British. Their king, Asantehene Prempeh I, was consigned by the colonial government to exile in the Seychelles.[118] This war was the fourth in a series of five conflicts between the Asante Empire and the invading British Empire between 1824 and 1901. The Asante refused to become a British colony, but despite sending a delegation to London offering concessions, the British chose military force. In 1897 the Asante territory became a British protectorate.[119] The Asante sword, an *afanatene,* was a symbol of power and authority for the Asante people, and offering this pattern was not just responding to local demands, but providing the Ghanaians with a means to subvert colonial rule.[120]

A classic symbol, the *Eye**, was introduced in 1902.[121] It can be seen as the *All Seeing Eye* or *God's Eye*, applied in many cultures. In this context it is related to an African proverb that says that when the eyes are looking, the mouth does not speak. It invites to wisdom, patience and discretion before taking action. A famous but unregistered design is *Staircase** for which the first sample can be seen in the HKM sample books.[122] It can be interpreted as a symbol of the possibility of rising up the social ladder or as the strength of one who builds a house with multiple storeys.

*Skin** is a design imitating the skin of a snake. It was registered in 1895 in Brown Fleming's first group of registrations, and quickly became a classic through its lasting popularity.[123] The outlines of the pattern have also been used for printing over other patterns to provide layered depth and make them more attractive for the African market.[124]

The popularity of this design may be related to special leadership attire through emphasis on 'bigness', which can be achieved in various ways. Leadership dress in Africa can be layered and appear bulky using heavy fabric. The body, enveloped, draped and wrapped in large quantities of cloth, expresses the authority and dignity of a ruler. Elements of elephants, lions and leopards can enhance this. Metaphorically the skin of powerful animals like in this case the skin of a snake can also be used.[125]

The creation of the Haarlem Collection by Brown Fleming 1895–1912

Designs based on European culture and other influences

In this category very different elements form the base for a specific design. Some relate directly to the colonial relation of the United Kingdom with the West African countries like *Postal Pattern** and *Nigerian Railway**. Although it is not known who ordered these designs, both were clearly successful. *ABC**, a motive ordered by the missionaries, was initially not a success. Many others were simply decorative and appreciated in their own right.

*Postal Pattern**, issued in 1906, is arranged in a square format with the British Crown as central motif, surrounded by ten hearts, each bearing the name of one of the ten towns on the Gold Coast (now Ghana) and a square in each corner with the silhouette of the flag of the Gold Coast. From 1877 to 1957, the flag had a blue field with the British Union Jack in the top left corner and the badge of the Gold Coast in the opposite corner.[126] This design reflects the fact that the British colonial settlers set up a mail service *Ghana Post*, starting in 1853 and issuing the first stamps with the portrait of Queen Victoria in 1875. It might have been

77. *Postal Pattern**. Not registered, around 1906
Brunnschweiler Archive, held at the Whitworth Art Gallery, University of Manchester (UK)

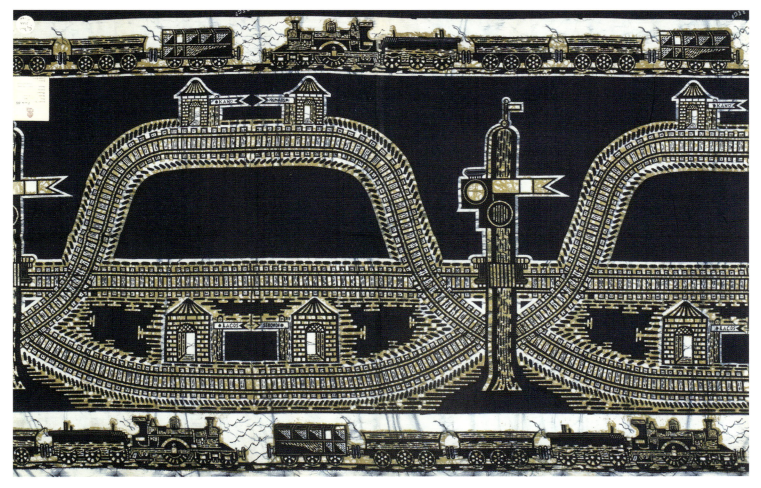

78. *Nigerian Railway**. BT reg.no. 3222, 5 June 1908
Brunnschweiler Archive, held at the Whitworth Art Gallery, University of Manchester (UK)

79. Man in Grand-Bassam (Ivory Coast) wearing design *Nigerian Railway**, c. 1915
The man on the left is also wearing a wax print from the Brown Fleming collection. Not registered, no. 17 in the Ashton collection
Photo L. Météyer, Grand-Bassam. Collection Duncan Clarke, London

The creation of the Haarlem Collection by Brown Fleming 1895–1912

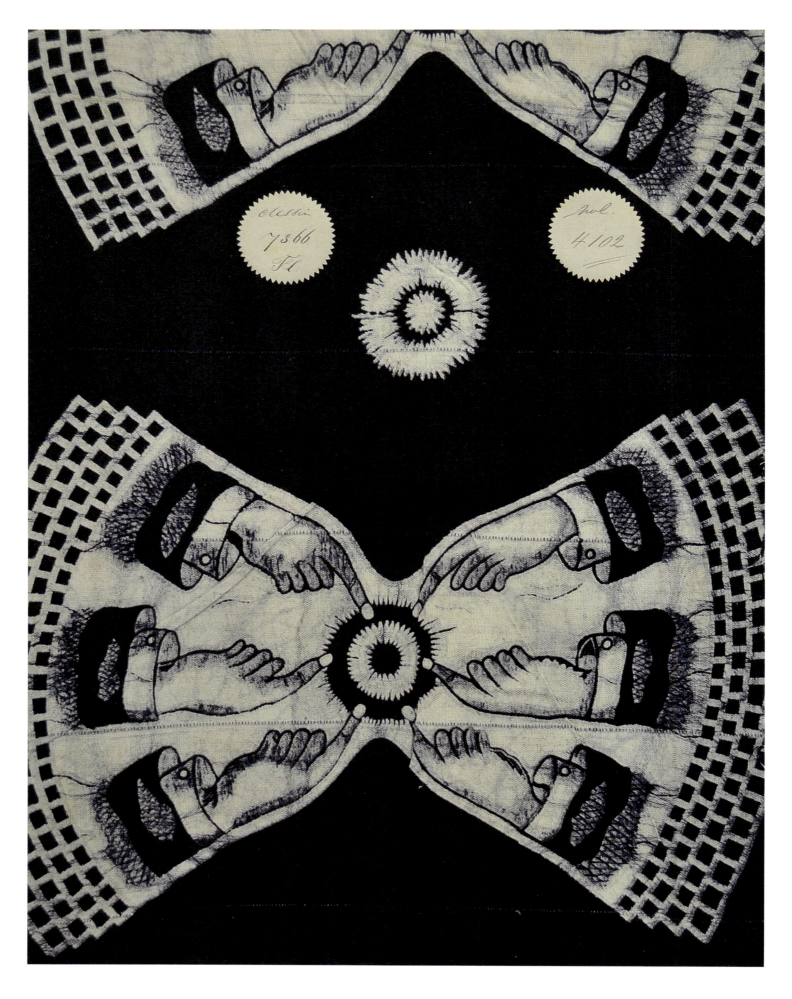

80. *Pointing Fingers**, Not registered, design 7366, HKM book 310, around 1902
Vlisco Archive, @ Vlisco BV

81. *Sibi Saba**. BT reg.no. 468211, 1 November 1905
Sample printed by Roessingh in Veenendaal (The Netherlands)
c. 1920-1930
Brunnschweiler Archive, held at the Whitworth Art Gallery, University of Manchester (UK)

82. *ABC**. Design 7591, HKM book 311, 1903-04
Vlisco Archive, @ Vlisco BV

The creation of the Haarlem Collection by Brown Fleming 1895–1912

released to celebrate the opening of the tenth post office in the country.[127] On the registration samples the places where text should be printed have been left blank, which left the possibility that the design could eventually also be used for other countries or purposes.

Nigerian Railway is a design depicting a railroad with four stations, Lagos, Sekondi, Kano and Kumasi, conceived simultaneously in plan and elevation to form a decorative garland.[128] The borders are decorated with a steam locomotive and four waggons. Construction of railroads in Nigeria was started in 1898 by the British colonial government to facilitate the transportation of agricultural commodities to the ports for export to Europe. Registered in 1908, this pattern may commemorate the railway's first decade.

Pointing Fingers*, a design of six white hands pointing to a target, was introduced in 1903 and has been printed afterwards by many other companies.[129] The gesture is universal, when people want to draw attention to something, they instinctively extend an index finger. In this case it seems towards a kind of target. It could refer to the fact that the United Kingdom added in 1903 six provinces to the country of Nigeria after the conquest of Sokoto, making a total of seventeen. This was the final act in setting the boundaries of the British Protectorates of Northern and Southern Nigeria. In 1914 both protectorates would be amalgamated into a single Nigerian nation.

Sibi Saba* was introduced in 1905, registered as number 468211, and in later years issued in different versions.[130] In Yoruba the name of the design has the possible meaning of *Get used to it*. It is laid out in a 1 yard (90x90cm) square divided into four square compartments containing drawings of a vulva and a fantasy floral design in the top row, facing peacocks and a hand with pointing index finger downwards in the bottom row.[131] The particular motifs seem to relate to female and male sexuality and beauty. The idea behind the form of the design is possibly connected to handkerchiefs which the Portuguese imported to Africa. Local people would sew them together to use as cloth. This printed version imitates that effect.

Not registered, but one of the best known classics is *The Alphabet** or *ABC**, introduced in 1905 upon request of the Basel Mission.[132] Apparently, its initial success was short-lived:

Wir haben es seinerzeit selbst auf der Goldküste eingeführt, doch hat es sich längst überlebt und wird nicht mehr gefragt. (We introduced it to the Gold Coast ourselves at the time, but it has long outlived its usefulness and is no longer asked for).[133]

It was only in 1921 when Swanzy in London, client of Ankersmit, asked to re-engrave the design that it soon became one of the best-sellers for the company. To help Ankersmit with the right engraving, the BMTC provided an original sample. The first production was shipped from Liverpool in August 1921 for Calabar and Opobo.[134] Perhaps the design was now less associated with the missionaries

---

83. Two men from Winneba in wax print cloths with *ABC** design, 1910?
Photo Erick R. Lutterodt, Accra (Ghana)
Collection Duncan Clarke, London

84. Women from Lome (Togo), wearing skirts with *ABC** design
Postcard around 1910.
Collection Duncan Clarke, London

and more with the meaning it was given: the importance of good education and the willingness to pay for it and support it.

A classic, first seen as number 6240 (245) in the HKM sample books, is *Dice**. At the time of its first sampling, the pattern had a border, but in later versions it is printed as an all-over design without a border.[135] This pattern was widely used by European missionaries, possibly attracted by its modest checkered character and unaware of the African interpretation as the popular gambling object. After 1910, other companies would print similar designs with, for example, little hearts.

One design that became a classic received its actual name, *Congres**, much later in 1947 on the occasion of the first congress of the Democratic Party in Ivory Coast. It could be a simplified version of a European-style design arranged in an ogee grid known as *Loop Trail*. This was registered on 1 March 1895 and appears in an HKM sample book of around 1890.[136]

It is not clear whether the design *Dutch Landscape* found successful sales in West Africa, but it was registered in 1904, and still on the list for Ashton in 1939. One may well ask why it is called *Dutch*, because it depicts a hilly landscape with a bridge and some trees rather than the flat terrain of Holland. The land is filled with a fish-scale ground also seen in some Indonesian batik, called *isen*.[137]

A subject that proved popular is a parasol or umbrella, often seen in grouped arrangements. In Africa, the umbrella usually carries a meaning of protection. In later years other companies would issue various interpretations of the object.[138]

---

85. *Dice**. Design 6240, HKM book 245, around 1900
Vlisco Archive, © Vlisco BV

86. *Congres**. Design 4968, HKM book 224, no. 4968, around 1895
Vlisco Archive, © Vlisco BV

The creation of the Haarlem Collection by Brown Fleming 1895–1912

87. *Dutch Landscape*. BT reg.no. 443630,
20 October 1904
Brunnschweiler Archive, held at the Whitworth Art Gallery,
University of Manchester (UK)

88. Umbrella*. Design 6570, HKM book 262, around 1900
Vlisco Archive, @ Vlisco BV

89. Design with shells. BT reg.no. 414967, 4 August 1903
Brunnschweiler Archive, held at the Whitworth Art Gallery,
University of Manchester (UK)

90. Man, wearing design with shells, from Drewin, Ivory Coast.
Photo Eug. Aubert, Marseille. Collection Duncan Clarke, London

The collection of Brown Fleming also contains wax prints with a multitude of subjects from birds' nests to beehives, palm trees, bars of music, domino, smoking pipes, wooden planks, mushrooms and shells.[139] Even a sport such as cricket, introduced by the English to West Africa, was once a wax print motif.[140] Rather an exception are publicity motifs, like a design with thread spools and sewing machines for Clark & Co.[141] The Clark Thread Company was originally a Scottish firm that manufactured embroidery and sewing thread, established in the 1750s in Paisley. The company introduced in 1812 a cotton thread that was similar in appearance and strength to that of the silk formerly used by the Paisley weavers.[142] This thread might have been used by the missionaries, who organised sewing classes in their West African congregations.

Another such design is for the African Association Limited, a trading organisation founded in 1889 in Liverpool.[143] It was established as an amalgamation of English firms and companies trading in the Oil Rivers,

The creation of the Haarlem Collection by Brown Fleming 1895–1912

known as the Southern Nigeria Protectorate. Since its foundation it extended its operation in Nigeria and opened businesses in the leading towns of the Gold Coast.[144] In 1919 it changed its name to the African and Eastern Trade Corporation.[145]

Changes in the collection from 1906

Although no comprehensive sales figures are known from this period, evidence points to sales of the best sellers continuing to provide a comfortable base for Brown Fleming. The HKM sample books support this with mention of several re-engravings of successful designs. But from 1906, a fundamental change can be observed, with existing motifs presented in a new way and new motifs introduced. Motifs based on or inspired by traditional Indonesian batik were no longer introduced. The number of registered designs decreased to less than half compared to the previous years with an average of 6-7 per year. This could be related to the fact that Brown Fleming's son and son-in-law joined the business in 1906. In the same year he changed the name of the company to *Brown Flemings Ltd*.

In the period 1906 to 1912, about sixty designs were registered of which fifteen designs were for square formats of 36 inches, all fancy prints in varied styles.[146] The other registrations were for wax prints in a style departing from the past. The pre-1906 arrangement whereby Brown Fleming would provide suggestions, but designs were drawn in Haarlem, may no longer apply.[147] The subjects of some designs require a detailed understanding of African or colonial culture, which would likely be provided by the client. The visual interpretation might have needed more precise instructions or illustrated reference books on specific subjects. The divide between initial suggestions and the ultimate design is less clear.

One explanation might be that Brown Fleming himself was increasingly relying on his son and son-in-law and not investing as much time and energy in the business as in previous years. His son had just turned 21 the year before he joined and must have been relatively young and inexperienced, compared to his father who was already 37 when he started his business in 1895 and already had 15 years of prior experience. His wife Alice Spence had suffered for a long time with ill health and her condition was deteriorating. She eventually died in 1908. By that time, Brown Fleming had reached the age of fifty. It is said that Brown Fleming himself also suffered from chronic health problems, but his physical vitality was sufficient to take care of his property *Kilchoan* at Loch Melfort and to allow him to participate in local activities. It seems that increasingly he left the running of the business in the hands of his partners. As the company had to obtain feedback from African clientele through its shippers, it is unclear who the source of ideas for motifs was, as they would need precise information and an excellent knowledge of specific consumers. It is unlikely that the ideas came from the HKM. Unlike the pre-1906 patterns that went on to become classics, many of the designs introduced in this period did not survive the second decade of the twentieth century. Only some like *Osiris* stayed in print until the 1950s or even the 1960s.[148]

Designs with composite elements from before 1906

Starting in 1906, Brown Flemings Ltd created designs composed of elements introduced in previous decades. Many of the motifs had become popular in West Africa in a relatively short time and these composite designs would also become popular. Variations were formed by printing composite designs in square formats, and by reproducing the main motifs on different ground patterns.[149]

The younger partners were perhaps more conscious than Brown Fleming himself of the sales potential of re-introducing these by now well-known and appreciated motifs.

A striking example depicts a peacock spreading its feathers revealing ten small rectangles showing popular motifs like *Staircase*, the *Hand* and *Staff of Kingship*. The company first registered an indigo version in 1906, and later that year it also registered a coloured version with red and yellow added.[150]
Peacock feathers also feature in later designs and could indicate trade opening with the Congo where there is a native species of peafowl. One pattern shows a band of a dozen peacock feathers on an indigo ground alternating with narrower bands with butterflies.[151] Another design introduced in 1911 uses the peacock feathers in geometrical grids of straight lines and triangles with a mirror repeat.[152]

Issued in 1908, another design reviving multiple previously successful motifs is *Let Glasgow Flourish*. On the registered design the place for the text has been left blank, so it could be used in the future for not one, but also other texts featuring the coat of arms of the city of Glasgow where Brown Fleming lived and worked.[153] The motto is a shortened version of the phrase *Lord, let Glasgow flourish by the preaching of the word*, part of a sermon preached by Saint Mungo, the founder and patron saint of Glasgow. Motifs of a bird, a tree, a bell and a fish on the armorial shield refer to the legend of Saint Mungo. Above the coat of arms are vertical strips with classic Brown Fleming motifs, and below are represented bales of cloth. This design is clearly to honour the success of his trade, possibly in connection with the Franco-British Exhibition held in White City, London.

A later design contains six elements such as *Tree with bird and bell* and the Glasgow coat of arms.[154] They are presented in a quadrillage format of two rows and three columns. This way of combining motifs was employed in *Sixteen Objects*, registered in 1909, as well as *Key* featuring Adinkra-inspired motifs.[155]

Three Bells* was released in November 1912, seven months after Ebenezer Brown Fleming's death; the three bells probably refer to the passing bell, death knell and funeral toll rung to mark the end of life. The pattern is built up in the same way as the previous designs with three rows and three columns, showing three bells in the centre surrounded by eight heraldic shields. A tree with fish, bird and a bell probably refers to the city of Glasgow (in the middle at the bottom); the triple-towered castle topped with three flags and a portcullis on a rock is the coat of arms of the city of Edinburgh (top row, right). The others are difficult to identify as official coats of arms. The one in the middle row on the left with the chevron and three barrels could refer to his love of whisky. The design at the bottom left with the cross and two eyes could refer to one of his famous wax designs. The design opposite bottom right with the three diamonds could refer to the armorial bearings of the Van de Poll family. Others might be related to more personal interests and matters connected to Brown Fleming.[156]

Popular wax-print designs were also united in patchwork styles to feature multiple designs on a single cloth. The first example is a collage of favourite motifs, arranged randomly, that was registered on 18 July 1913.[157]

In later years not only Brown Flemings Ltd but many other companies would print patchwork-style designs to pay homage to classic wax-print patterns. In Ivory Coast these are called *nzassa*, in Ghana *nsaasaawa*.[158] This was the original mode of patchwork wrappers made at the turn of the century, sewn from strips of wax and fancy prints. This could be done for the sake of economy but could also hint at potential wealth, because others could not know where the strips of cloth came from. Even when the garment was not valuable, it could be meaningful for the wearer, made from cloth that had been personally collected, evoking memories of the past.

In the 1940s, the Portuguese trader Antonio Nogueira, working for Haijkens as a merchant in Congo and client of Vlisco, came up with a variety for a *zoba zoba* or patchwork, in which several different motifs and ground patterns are combined, and the central motif is emphasised by a ranking of the several elements. This pattern turned out to be a real success for the company and has been produced in many versions.[159] Today textile manufacturers produce cloth printed to look like patchwork designs that are used in the collections of fashion designers. From a humble start, such cloth now appears on the catwalk.[160]

Also, a complex collage of well-known designs presented in an elaborate structure is a design registered just weeks after the first patchwork pattern, on 9 August 1913 under number 90669. The lower part is decorated with figured lozenges identical to *Leidsche Ruit** or Lino*. The upper part of the cloth along the selvedge holds rectangles with dots terminated left and right by squares showing paired animals in a roofed structure. The central panel is built up with classical Doric columns enclosing chained hearts, eyes, Arabic text, peacocks and the *Postal* pattern. Left and right from the columns are unfolding pieces of cloth with the *Hand* and *Lamp* patterns.

Introduction of Egyptian and other motifs

Egyptian and Egyptian-style motifs were introduced for the very first time between 1906 and 1913.[161] In Europe and West Africa, they had already been adopted earlier throughout visual culture including clothing, jewellery, decorative arts, interior design and architecture. This renewed interest had been seen in many places and at many times in history with some noteworthy peaks. It is tempting to speculate what could have caused this sudden interest in Egyptian culture in West Africa. It seems that colonialists left about 140 Egyptian artefacts behind, which are now in the National Museum of Accra, but it is not known in what year and at which location. They were probably only accessible to the general public after the opening of the museum in 1957.[162] If this was not the stimulus, perhaps it simply indicates a similar taste for exoticism that intrigued the western European cultures in this period, but it might also be related to a section of the Egyptian Free Masonry or the Rite of *Memphis-Misraïm*. This Masonic rite was formed by merging the two rites of *Memphis* and *Misraïm* in 1881. Both combined elements of Templarism with Egyptian and alchemical mythology. The rite was particularly active around 1900, mainly in the UK.

The textile designs of Brown Flemings Ltd contain images of real hieroglyphs and Old Egyptian motifs as well as fantasised shapes. The designers could have seen original artefacts at the Museum voor Oudheden (Archeological Museum) in Leiden (The Netherlands), but it is obvious that its employees also used illustrated publications about Egyptian art. The copied hieroglyphs are often readable, sometimes distorted but still decipherable. In several cases they dominate the entire design, and in other examples they are mixed with Muslim, traditional West African and other elements known from prior designs.

Egyptologist Rene van Walsem of Leiden University recognised that the designers must have referred to illustrations in the books of Ernest A. T. Wallis Budge (1857-1934). Budge worked for the British Museum from 1883 until

The creation of the Haarlem Collection by Brown Fleming 1895–1912

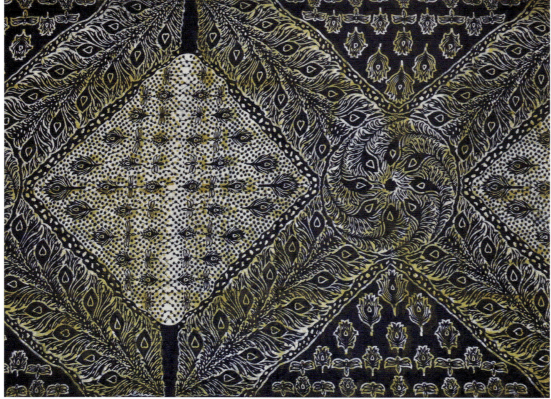

91. *Peacock*, BT reg.no. 482072, 6 June 1906 with on its feathers eleven of the most famous symbols in wax print, introduced by Brown Fleming since 1895
Brunnschweiler Archive, held at the Whitworth Art Gallery, University of Manchester (UK)

92. *Peacock feathers*. BT reg.no. 40820, 15 August 1911
Brunnschweiler Archive, held at the Whitworth Art Gallery, University of Manchester (UK)

93. *Let Glasgow Flourish*, BT reg.no. 6840, 5 October 1908
Brunnschweiler Archive, held at the Whitworth Art Gallery, University of Manchester (UK)

The creation of the Haarlem Collection by Brown Fleming 1895–1912

94. *Sixteen Objects*. BT reg.no. 12593, 28 August 1909
Brunnschweiler Archive, held at the Whitworth Art Gallery, University of Manchester (UK)

95. *Three Bells**. BT reg.no. 12593, 28 August 1909
Brunnschweiler Archive, held at the Whitworth Art Gallery, University of Manchester (UK)

96. *Patchwork Pattern*. BT reg.no. 88682, 18 July 1913
Brunnschweiler Archive, held at the Whitworth Art Gallery, University of Manchester (UK)

97. Untitled. BT reg.no. 90669, 9 August 1913
Brunnschweiler Archive, held at the Whitworth Art Gallery, University of Manchester (UK)

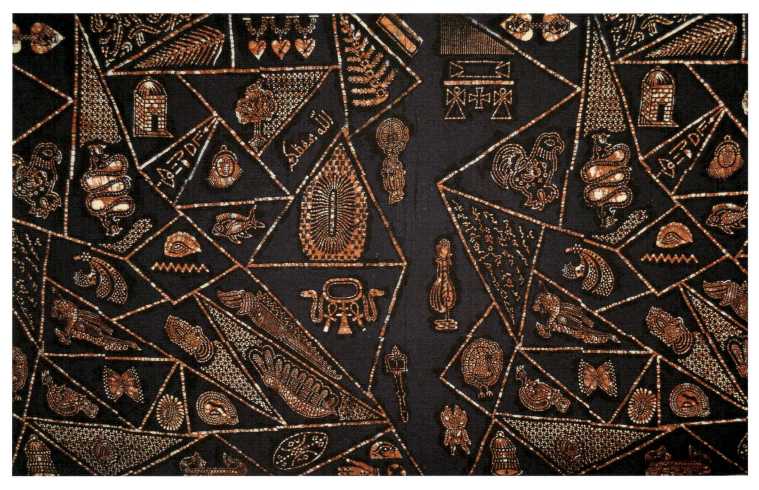

The creation of the Haarlem Collection by Brown Fleming 1895–1912

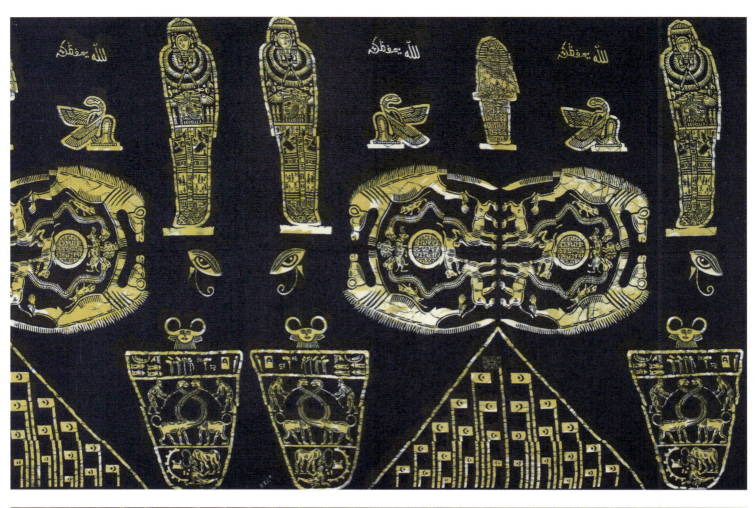

98. Wax print with Egyptian motifs. BT reg.no. 60396, 8 June 1912
Brunnschweiler Archive, held at the Whitworth Art Gallery, University of Manchester (UK)

99. Temple of Solomon? BT reg.no. 54764, 8 June 1912
Brunnschweiler Archive, held at the Whitworth Art Gallery, University of Manchester (UK)

100. *Osiris*. Not registered, but in Ashton list figuring under nos. 53 and 122
Brunnschweiler Archive, held at the Whitworth Art Gallery, University of Manchester (UK)

The creation of the Haarlem Collection by Brown Fleming 1895–1912

1924, building its collection of ancient Egyptian and Near Eastern manuscripts, and publishing numerous works for a wide audience. A book the designers certainly consulted is Budge's *Guide to the first and second Egyptian rooms, predynastic antiquities, mummies, mummy-cases, and other objects connected with the funeral rites of the ancient Egyptians*, published in London in 1904. His 1893 work, *The mummy: a handbook of Egyptian funerary archaeology* appears also to have been accessed in Haarlem.[163]

One design with Egyptian motifs, registered in 1923 (number 60396), depicts a pyramid of flags with star and crescent, often the symbol of Islam, but at the apex the Union Jack. The remaining motifs can be seen in illustrations from plates seen in Budge's 1904 *Guide*. Flanking the pyramid is an interpretation of one side of the Narmer palette in the Egyptian Museum at Cairo.[164] The central piece is a stylised version of the prehistoric Dog Palette from the Ashmolean Museum in Oxford.[165] Above are mummies taken from the painted case of an unknown female priest.[166]

Another significant example shows a building within a domed building flanked by torsadé Doric columns. Gauntlet-like raised hands spring from the dome. At the right and left are birds on a pedestal with wings spread like the *hudhud*, a holy bird of Islam. The scene, surrounded by palm trees, may be a reimagining of the Mount, location of the Temple originally built by Solomon, considered a site of holy worship in Islam. At the bottom of the design is a plinth with oval cartouches holding Egyptian hieroglyphs with the names of several pharaohs of Egypt.[167]

A design called *Osiris* was not registered but figured on the list for Ashton under both number 53 and 122. The name is of the god of fertility in ancient Egyptian religion. A picture of Osiris seems to be at the centre of the upper band of the design with above two wide open eyes and surrounded by various motifs. This design was in print at ABC for a relatively long time until at least 1955.[168]

Egyptian motifs were sometimes mixed with African imagery as in a design called *Ju-Ju* (full moon).[169] Ju-Ju is a spiritual belief system in West Africa in which objects from religious practices are used as part of witchcraft for both benign and malicious purposes, especially in Nigeria. The central motif at the base resembles Benin ancestral altars, such as the early twentieth-century Palace Altar to Oba Eweka II. To left and right of the altar are the bronze masks with elephant tusks specific to royal altars and royal stools. Through honouring the deceased and worship at these altars, ancestral kings were asked to provide protection and prosperity to the community. Here, at the centre of focus above the altar, is a raised arm holding in its palm coins as in Brown Fleming's *Hand and Fingers* (1895). This is probably a misinterpretation of the *altar of the hand* celebrating manual skill as the source of wealth and success.

Supporting the arm is a fan-like ornament holding the cross of the Royal Victorian Order. The Egyptian motifs that fill the upper part of the composition are copied from extant hieroglyphs.[170] The British royal insignia also became more prominent in this period, spreading, through cloth, images and messages of colonial power in West Africa, as seen for example in registration number 517089, 5 December 1907 (BF photo 61).

Only one design refers to French colonial power in West Africa, with its federation of eight colonial territories: Mauritania, Senegal, French Sudan (now Mali), Guinea, Ivory Coast, Upper Volta (now Burkina Faso), Dahomey (now Benin) and Niger.[171] In the centre are four pavilions linked to an axial arch structure, topped with the French tricolour and surrounded by six raised arms with open hands.[172] At the top, the five-armed Cross of the French Legion of Honour is suspended at each side of the flag. Centrally below is a ropework device enclosing an Ottoman flag with star and crescent moon, more generally symbolising Islam.

A true homage to Brown Fleming was issued on 5 June 1912, two months after his death.[173] Called *Exhibition*, the design assembles the most famous motifs he had introduced over the years. Two peacocks holding in their beaks a piece of cloth exhibiting the motifs are overlooked by two winged cobras in Egyptian style.[174]

On 20 May 1912, about a month after Brown Fleming's death, HKM sold off several printing rollers. When expectation of sales of specific designs became limited, keeping value tied up in copper rollers was no longer viable.[175]

However, still another eight designs were registered. Like many post-1906 patterns, these combined past motifs with those of Egyptian origin, not adding new visual material. The final registration of Brown Flemings Ltd was on 2 December 1913, with a motif of a large scarab, surrounded by other small insects and Egyptian elements. For the Egyptians the scarab is the emblem of the highest sun god.[176]

Conclusion

Brown Fleming's collection of designs introduced between 1895 and his death in 1912 shows clearly that two categories formed the base of his success: copies of and designs inspired by traditional Indonesian batik; and designs based on archetypes, proverbs and elements of West African culture. Only a few designs based on traditional West African fabric, most notably *Target** and *Grammophone**, withstood time. Those based on European and North African (notably Egyptian) influences sold only for a limited period. Only those motifs that were related to traditional African cultures or were interpreted by Africans themselves ultimately became classics like the original Indonesian motifs.

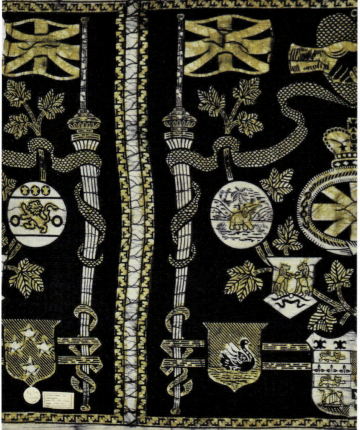

Initially perceived as exotic, wax prints were adapted and incorporated by Africans into their own culture, often accompanied by renaming (whereby a wing becomes a bunch of bananas, for example). Brown Fleming succeeded in catering to West African culture and its visual thinking in the library of patterns that formed the Haarlem collection, classics in print for more than a century.

101. *Ju-Ju*. BT reg.no. 27019, 11 January 1911
Brunnschweiler Archive, held at the Whitworth Art Gallery, University of Manchester (UK)

102. Untitled. BT reg.no. 517089, 5 December 1907
Brunnschweiler Archive, held at the Whitworth Art Gallery, University of Manchester (UK)

The creation of the Haarlem Collection by Brown Fleming 1895–1912

103. Design with French flags. BT reg.no. 494677, 24 January 1907
Brunnschweiler Archive, held at the Whitworth Art Gallery,
University of Manchester (UK)

104. *Scarab*. BT reg.no. 96756, BT reg.no. 494677, 2 December 1913
Brunnschweiler Archive, held at the Whitworth Art Gallery,
University of Manchester (UK)

The creation of the Haarlem Collection by Brown Fleming 1895–1912

1   Although the conglomerated companies of the Calico Printers' Association were run relatively independently in day-to-day matters, they were jointly governed. Major decisions such as acquisitions were taken by the CPA.
2   Samples arriving in Manchester from Glasgow were photographed and numbered in random order. Sometimes the same sample was photographed twice.
3   There also survives a group of invoices from April 1935 to March 1936 that detail patterns commission printed by the CPA for CFAO, sometimes named and numbered.
4   From 1 January 1895 most wax prints in the HKM books are recognisable as being for Brown Fleming, because they are registered by Brown Fleming. The others are classical batik imitations and could also be for him or for existing clients. In 1896 the HKM started putting the initials of the merchant on specific designs. Initially this was done occasionally, but from design 5590 (book 246) it was done systematically. Because there is a difference in time between producing a design at the HKM and registering in the UK, which could vary according to the wishes of the merchant, an exact date is difficult to determine. Normally a design would be registered within two weeks.
5   Meeles I, 35. This was entirely normal business practice in the eighteenth and nineteenth centuries. The manufacturer's name was not revealed, and the product rebranded by the merchant. Both manufacturer and merchant were complicit in the agreement to conceal the origins. Personal communication Philip Sykas 9 December 2023.
6   Verbong 1988, 222
7   Kroese (1), 53
8   Kroese (3), 22. Information based on interview with Ethel Spence Wylie, daughter of Brown Fleming, on 1 December 1975 Helensburg, Dunbartonshire. For Brown Fleming there was no need to compete with the wax prints of the HKM. In a letter to D. van Lookeren of Vlisco Helmond from the UAC 14 September 1976 about Kroese's mention of a designer, the writer is adamant that based on conversations with Jock Campbell of UTR and Edwards, Haykens' agent in the UK, Brown Fleming never had his own designer, possibly only someone to adapt designs. Vlisco Archive, @ Vlisco BV.
9   Between 1895 and 1912 he would register about 250 designs in total, so an amount of 47 of Turkey red designs is relatively substantial. On 11 November 1902 he registered BT reg.nos. 400539-43, on 12 November 1902 BT reg.nos. 400592-99, on 13 November 1902 BT reg.nos. 400696-703 and on 17 November 1902 BT reg.nos. 400830-37. See BT 51/113 13 September 1902 – 3 December 1902 The National Archives Kew (UK). All are very well drawn.
10   He registered BT reg.nos. 410149-72 on 16 May 1903, but for the BT reg nos. 410151, 410156, 410162, 410169, 410171 and 410172 the certificates were not issued.
11   The designs he registered on 15 March 1902 for kangas, 60x90cm, BT reg. nos. 388579-87, are not in the sample books of the HKM.
12   In book 228 (early 1890s) of the HKM sample books over twenty different designs for kangas are added and in book 210 (early 1890s-1895?) even more. Especially in the books after 1895 they do take up a large part of the designs, probably for multiple merchants given the various initials that are on the samples. The motifs that are used are graphic or influenced by Indian textiles. There is also an interesting variety of figurative motifs like a jumping horse (6014), the front of a mansion (6015), an elephant (6321), a camel (6963), the Statue of Liberty (6495) and the Eiffel Tower (6497).
13   Examples of names that could not be traced are Van Horsten, Kauman, Thomas, Bonstead, Puttforeken, Leon Maskens, Sutor and Merens.
14   Modi, Salazar and Venkatachalam, 55
15   Numbers 3982-3985 (book 248) come with notes, stating that the designs were send to Maintz. The archive of the NV Handelsvennootschap Maintz & Co. in Amsterdam (1874-1970) is in The National Archives The Hague, no. 2.20.06.01. Rouffaer and Juynboll mention in their book Batikkunst that the HKM on 12 December 1871 received a Javanese headcloth from Maintz & Co. in Batavia. See p. 88.
16   See designs 4022 and 4023 (book 248). For more information about Georges Wehry, see https://iisg.nl/ondernemers/pdf/pers-1606-01.pdf, last accessed 17 May 2023.

17   https://www.indischhistorisch.nl/tweede/familieverhalen/familieverhalen-armeniers-in-indie-deel-2-het-verhaal-van-varsenike-knape-elisha-1/, last accessed 17 May 2023
18   His name is mentioned on the stickers of designs 5673, 6220, 6432 and 6433.
19   https://www.hansvervoort.nl/Artikelen/article/102/Bastiaan-Bas-Veth-1860-%E2%80%93-1922-, last accessed 20 May 2023. Sebastian Veth is better known as the author of Het leven in Nederlandsch-Indië (1900), in which he expresses a dislike of life in Indonesia.
20   Sticker on sample 3635 in HKM book 214 (3560-3857, sent under no 3548). Vlisco Archive, @ Vlisco BV.
21   See design 7408 and 7410 (book 310).
22   Jacobs and Maas, 76-77
23   Clear examples in the field of African textiles are the Fante flags, that combine proverbial, visual and political elements.
24   Lee, 74
25   Halls and Martino, 14-15. David Quinn, Grand Secretary of the Grand Lodge of Glasgow, insists that none of the motifs are Masonic, but could refer to other fraternal orders that used to exist. Personal communication 2 December 2023
26   For a description of the design Shaking Hands, see under Based on archetypes, proverbs, and elements of African cultures.
27   I have not systematically added the meaning of a specific design, because they often vary from region to region and can change over time.
28   Personal communication Itie van Hout 22 November 2023. This design can be found in the HKM sample books under number 6993 (232) and was listed as BF photo 109. The actual Vlisco number is 14/2205.
29   Interview Gerhard Frensel, Milsbeek (The Netherlands) 4 May 2022
30   Frensel, Gerhard, Real Dutch Wax Block Print, Milsbeek (The Netherlands) 1980, unpublished document, 141
31   Personal communication Ruud Sanders, Vlisco 15 November and 24 December 2023.
32   Verbong 1988, 191
33   For more information, see the explanation of bleeding in the glossary.
34   When not mentioned otherwise, I refer to these twenty-four books with roller and design numbers.
35   See appendix for a detailed list of the sample books of the HKM.
36   See book 226, design number 1970. See also in book 226 the numbers 2013, 2014 and 2027.
37   Written at the top of the page is Dit patroon bestaat nu vóór Batiksche ellemaat Flg (This pattern exists now for batik ellemaat Flg [measurement hand to elbow 68-70cm] – design 3645, book 214 of HKM sample books. Vlisco Archive, @ Vlisco BV.
38   See chapter 2.
39   See nos. 3884-6, book 248.
40   Gillow and Barnard, 100
41   The design for the central part was also used in two other registered designs by Brown Fleming: the design with a black boarder was registered under BT reg.no. 263771 dd 15 October 1895. The version with a white lozenge in the middle was registered under BT reg.no. 397536 dd 19 September 1902. Another design, copies from original woven cloth, is BT reg.no. 30706, 24 June 1897 in only a brown colour on a white background.
42   They do appear on a regular basis: book 248:3986-88, 4087-90 and 4137-9, book 228: 4184 and book 210: 4471, 4585-6 and 4712.
43   Snail* can be found under number 4018 and Tree of Life* under number 4140 in book 248. For further descriptions of these designs, see chapter 3.
44   Book 228, numbers 4173, 4174 and 4270
45   See the tie-dye sample in book 210 number 4649. A later variety was registered under BT reg.no. 250492, 1 March 1895. The other samples are 4561, 4625-8, 4645-48 and 4720-21 in the same book.
46   See 3893 and 3895 (book 248), 4270-4273 (book 228), 4561 and 4721 (book 210).
47   Krantz 1989, 115. It is not possible to find out if the HKM also printed kangas by hand, because there are no such sample books left.
48   In the earlier sample books of the HKM kept at the Vlisco archives I did not find examples of kangas.
49   Brown Fleming registered nine designs on 15 March 1902. See

50   BT reg.nos. 388579-87. Kangas represent a large majority with various initials in the sample books of the HKM, but none of them with those of Brown Fleming.

50   An example is shown in a report of 1876 of Bienfait during an internship at Van Vlissingen in Helmond as sample for the West African market. L. P. Bienfait, *Aanteekeningen gemaakt bij de Heeren P. F. van Vlissingen & Co. 1876*. A photocopy of this report is in the Vlisco Archive, @ Vlisco BV. The original is still in the hands of members of the Van Vlissingen family.

51   Vlisco has continued printing these types of scarves until the 1980s according the *Aliemans procédé* (Everyman's procedure). Personal communication Ruud Sanders, Vlisco 30 November 2023.

52   Various criteria can be used to classify designs, but the aim is to keep it relatively straightforward. Other ways have been explored. See for example Nielsen 1979, 484-494.

53   In the Ashton list as BF photo number 114 an all-over design version without the lace imitation borders can be found. Other designs also got a lace border. See for example design 7022 in book 232 with a classical batik imitation between the two borders.

54   The first, European looking design appeared in the HKM sample books 224 as number 4968. It was registered as BT reg.no. 311578 on 31 December 1897.

55   It was registered on 21 April 1896 as BT reg.no. 274699.

56   As the imitations were made for the poorer people it is no surprise that especially in the early books of the HKM samples of sarongs dominate. Personal communication Maria Wronska-Friend 28 April 2014.

57   Good illustrations are the designs BT reg.nos. 263772-3 and BT reg. nos. 263775-6, registered on 15 October 1895.

58   *Shrimp Check* was not registered but can be found on the Ashton list as BF photo 110. The second example was registered twice, first as BT reg.no. 263773 on 15 October 1895 and a second time as BT reg. no. 405016 on 11 February 1903 (BF photo 64). The first registration has blue dots added to make it more attractive for the West African market. It is still sold by Vlisco as number 14/0812.

59   The design appears as no. 2621 (book 211), 3242, (266), 4013 (248), 4897 (224), 5202 (255), 6413 (262) and the last time in 1915 as 9481 in book 212. In the list of 1939, it has number 105. In the Vlisco collection it has number 14/0014.

60   The design is not registered but on the list for Ashton in 1939 as BF photo number 126.

61   Other examples are a design of branches with BT reg.no. 420628 (2 November 1903) and a design with branches and flowers, registered as BT reg.no. 426747 on 16 February 1904.

62   See for example design 3524 in the HKM sample book 233, used as the continuous motif of a traditional sarong. Design 3645 in book 214 is almost identical to BF Photo 24.

63   Veldhuisen 1993, 30, Gittinger 131

64   Personal communication Itie van Hout 22 November 2023. The batik by Von Franquemont is registered at the Wereldmuseum Amsterdam as TM-1585-4 and donated by P. H. Q. Bouman in 1942. Personal communication Daan van Dartel Wereldmuseum Amsterdam 12 February 2024.

65   It appears in the HKM sample books as number 3910 and 4140 (248) and 4285 (228). Numbers 4219 (228), 4520 and 4521 (210) have a similar design as 3910 (248) but are presented with a boarder. It was registered under BT reg.no. 292267 on 20 January 1897 and listed as BF photo number 72 in 1939 for Ashton. The registration sample is missing in the books at The National Archives, but is present in the Brunnschweiler Archive, held at the Whitworth Art Gallery, University of Manchester (UK). In the Vlisco collection is has number 14/0741. One other, similar example of a unique and outstanding batik, that was the model for an imitation batik is in the Beving collection. For a description, see chapter 6.

66   This design, BT reg.no. 301998, was registered on 23 July 1897.

67   Personal communication Itie van Hout 22 November 2023. *Slendang* was registered under number 361775 on 5 June 1911 (BF photo 116). Another variety with the design *Canoe Peak** are the almost identical nos. 480431 (7 June 1906) and 482073 (6 July 1906), presented in a square design with a lozenge of plain blue in the middle (BF photo 116).

68   Numbers 4173 and 4174 (228), like reg. no. 480431, 4472 (210), 6183 and 6184 (245). A square version (90x90cm) with a lozenge in the middle was registered under number 480431 on 7 June 1906. It appears as BF photo number 117 in the list of 1939 for Ashton. In the Vlisco collection it has number 14/0022.

69   The original *Night and Day* was registered under BT reg.no. 427678 on 27 February 1904. It also appears in the HKM sample books: 5216, 5217 and 5262(255) and on the list, made up for Ashton in 1939 as BF photo 115. The copyright was extended multiple times. The last time was on 1 August 1912. In the actual Vlisco collection it has number 14/0022. The second registration was also on 27 February 1904 under BT reg.no. 427679 and is BF photo 132 number on the list for Ashton.

70   This design BT reg. no. 301272 was registered on 9 July 1897 and can be found as number 5195 in the HKM sample books. It was also listed as BF photo 135.

71   The design was registered on 20 November 1897 under BT reg. no. 309473. In the HKM sample books it can be found as number 5195 (255) and it was listed for Ashton in 1939 as BF photo 77. BF photo 46 is a variant with a circle in the middle. In the Vlisco collection the design has number 14/0636.

72   In a picture of the king of Benin Oba Ovonrramwen Nogbaisi, stars can be seen on his hat: https://www.metmuseum.org/art/collection/search/320791. See also https://www.crwflags.com/fotw/flags/ng-gb.html, both accessed 22 December 2023.

73   *Good Husband** was registered on 17 December 1902 under BT reg.no. 402351 and listed as BF photo number 113 for Ashton. In the Vlisco collection is has the number 14/0052.

74   *Star* or *Table Cover* is still in the actual Vlisco collection as 13/0066. *Pineapple Square** was not registered, but in the list for Ashton as BF photo number 57. In the Ankersmit collection it had no. 8250 and in the Vlisco collection it has no. 13/0002. Other pieces of square cloth with traditional looking designs are BT reg.no. 387612 (12-12-1901) with a sticker with the date 29-6-88. It might have been registered later because of its success, 292262 (20 January 1897), BT reg.no. 475189 (6 March 1906), BT reg.no. 476385 (28 March 1906) and BT reg.no. 480430 (7 June 1906).

75   He registered this design under BT reg.no. 251961 on 24 April 1895. It can be found in the HKM sample books under number 4865 and in the list for Ashton as BF photo umber 137.

76   This design, BT reg.no. 263778, was registered on 15 October 1895 and can also be found in the HKM sample books no. 4820 (224). It is BF photo number 22 on the list for Ashton.

77   The design can be found in book 248 as number 3872 and appears on the Ashton list as BF photo number 52.

78   This design was registered as BT reg.no. 292266 on 2 January 1897 and later listed as BR photo number 148 for Ashton. It can be found in HKM book 211 as number 2386.

79   The design was registered under BT reg.no. 292264 on 20 January 1897.

80   This design was registered as BT reg.no. 303041 (10 August 1897) (BF photo 76).

81   The first registration was on 21 May 1895 under BT reg.no. 255141, the second on 26 June 1895 with BT reg.no. 256955. The design is on the Ashton list as BF photo number 112. In the Vlisco collection it has number 14/0012.

82   This design, *Snail**, can be found in book 214, no. 3837. It was registered on 20 January 1897 under BT reg.no. 292268. BF Photo number 23. In the Vlisco collection it has number 14/1027.

83   The CPA had a collective library of books and samples originating from the various companies. It is not known from which company this sample came.

84   https://collections.vam.ac.uk/item/O454067/fragment-unknown/, last accessed 26 August 2023

85   See nos. 1970 (226) and 3342-44 and 3407 (233) in the HKM sample books in the Vlisco Archive, @ Vlisco BV. On 17 April 1895 he registered under BT reg.no. 253268 a design of peacocks on a green background on the border of the cloth, flowers on a white background covering the rest. On 21 August 1895 he registered under BT reg.no. 260847 a square cloth with a peacock in the middle on a white background, in every corner a peacock on a green background and a border with flowers and under number 260864 the same peacock in three rows on a blue background.

86   See the appendix about the Kralingsche Katoen Maatschappij (KKM).

The creation of the Haarlem Collection by Brown Fleming 1895–1912

87 Renne, 61

88 The first one was registered on 5 December 1907 as BT reg.no. 517088 (BF photo 102), the second one was registered on 18 January 1909 with BT reg.no. 8651 (BF photo 20 and 102).

89 A first example can be found as number 1770 (213) in the HKM sample books. It was listed as *Java Lion* or *Little Lion* as BF photo number 33 in 1939 for Ashton. In the Vlisco collection it has number 14/0511.

90 Birds were often a symbol for Allah. For more information, see https://www.modemuze.nl/blog/arabische-kalligrafie-de-nederlandse-streekdracht, last accessed 12 July 2023. Design 3542 contains a drawing of a pigeon, a design that will be re-used later (book 248, design number 4101). An exact copy of this design is depicted in *Batikpatterns*, edited by Pepin van Rooyen (2002: 91). A similar design was registered as BT 52/60 1440 on 13 March 1908 TNA by Brown Fleming.

91 Suggestions that it could also have been used to kneel on during prayers are contradicted by Kerlogue, because the inscriptions often surround the entire cloth, which makes that one had to kneel on the word of God. Kerlogue 2001, 124

92 Kerlogue 2004, 78

93 Kerlogue 2001, 135

94 See book 233, design numbers 3368-3369, 337, 3378, 3379, 3542 and 5343.

95 Ellemaat was a length size of 69 cm. On design 6183 (book 245) is mentioned *ellemaat 35x35*. The size would be in inches, which is the usual size for this type of headcloth. In the sample books there are more designs with the mention *ellemaat* like 6098, but this is the only one where Suriname is mentioned.

96 Personal communication Christine van Russel-Henar, Paramaribo (Suriname) 4 August 2023. Zie ook Sylvia Gooswit, 'Gebruik van Javaans goed onder creolen 1900-2023' in *De Ware Tijd*, 2 August 2023, A10 and the article of Hariëtte Mingoen and Patmo Shoehirman, 'Javanen hebben betaald voor afschaffing slavernij in Suriname en Caraïbisch-Nederland' in *De Ware Tijd,* 19 January 2023.

97 Personal communication Christine van Russel-Henar, Paramaribo (Suriname) 4 August 2023.

98 Yampanesi, information on: https://collectie.wereldculturen.nl/#/query/97792c06-54a9-4ba9-bf1a-34755deaa17e, last accessed 13 June 2023.

99 Personal communication Daan van Dartel, curator Wereldmuseum Amsterdam, 13 June 2023.

100 For more information, see chapter 2.

101 See for example in the HKM sample books nos 4625-28, 4645-4650, 4747-50 and 4765.

102 This design was registered as BT reg.no. 246016 on the first of January 1895 and in the HKM sample books as nos. 4474 (210) and 4818 (224) (identical).

103 The first samples can be found in the HKM sample books under number 4819 and 4867 (224). BF photo 74. The number in the actual Vlisco collection is 14/1087. See also illustration in chapter 7.

104 This design was registered under BT reg.no. 402047 on 11 December 1902.

105 Emily Jiagge (1913-2003) was the first wife of Nii Amaa Ollennu, a lawyer and in 1970 for a short period of time president of Ghana. She should have approached Vlisco in the 1950s or 60s to re-develop the technique. Personal communication Joop Martens 8 May 2024.

106 See design 4484 (book 210). BF photo 141. Designs 4482, 4483 and 4485 (book 210) are similar black and white designs, developed for the same method, but with stripes and waves as design.

107 Registered under BT reg.no. 307892, 23 October 1897 and photographed for the Ashton list as BF photo number 71. This is the only sample left. The counter piece for registration has not been found at the Brunnschweiler Archives.

108 See chapter 6, illustration 3.

109 The registration number of *Fishes** is BT reg.no. 307893 (23 October 1897), no. 5342 (255) in the HKM sample books. Another design, also related to the sea is *Anchor and Shell*, designed in a square format with shells, an anchor in each corner and a chain border, registered under BT reg.no. 307893 on 23 October 1897.

110 *Target** or *Sunray** can be found in the HKM sample books under number 6251 (245) and in a green version on a white background as number 7488 (310). It is on the list for Ashton as BF photo number 92. In the Vlisco collection it has number 14/0633.

111 The same effect has been used on BT reg.no. 419328 (13 October 1903), see description design *Skin**.

112 Registered on 22 October 1902 under BT reg.no. 419879 and on the Ashton list as BF photo number 73. The number in the Vlisco collection is 14/40850.

113 Familusi 2012, 301

114 He registered this design on 31 August 1895 under BT reg.no. 260844. It can be found in the HKM sample books under number 4960 (224). On the Ashton list it has BF photo number 90. In the actual Vlisco collection is has number H816. Design BT reg.no. 468212 (1 November 1905) and HKM sample book no. 8059(312) is a derivative: a strip in the middle separates the cloth in two with on both sides two rows of loose fingers. This design is on the Ashton list under BF photo number 40.

115 Picton 2017, 20. Brown Fleming would add in 1905 a motif with just loose fingers: the fingers are in two rows on the left and right in the length of the cloth on an indigo fond, separated by a red band in the middle (BT reg.no. 468212, registered on 1 November 1905).

116 Sykas 2005, 147.

117 Design 6438 (book 262), BF photo 118 and Vlisco collection 14/0578.

118 Phillips, 434. For details on the sword, see https://www.britishmuseum.org/collection/object/E_Af1896-0519-4.

119 https://en.wikipedia.org/wiki/Anglo-Ashanti_wars last accessed 14 August 2023

120 Picton 2017, 20

121 It was registered on 22 February 1902 with number 387613. The sample at The National Archives is missing, but traces of the piece of cloth left on the paper are clear enough to recognise it. In the actual Vlisco collection it has number 14/0760. Another design, BT reg. no. 397408 (18 September 1902) and HKM book 7216 (310) consists of wavey lines that intersect with a dot in the middle and gives the illusion of an eye.

122 See number 6676 (244). The motif is also on the list for Ashton, as BF photo 123 and in the actual Vlisco collection number 14/0024.

123 Registered on 1 March 1895. A sample of this version can also be seen in the HKM sample books under number 4842 (224). Other versions can be found under number 5032 (224), 6114 (247), and 6613(262). On the Ashton list it has BF photo number 35.

124 See for example BT reg. no. 263772 (15 October 1895) and BT reg. no. 419328 (13 October 1903). In the actual Vlisco collection it has number 14/40850. Brown Fleming also registered another imitation of an animal skin, BT reg.no. 18577 on 21 June 1911, but this design did not become a classic.

125 Perani and Wolff, 89-94

126 The names are Accra, Cape Coast, Sekondi, Saltpond, Keta and Winneba on the coast and Kumasi, Nkawkaw, Koforicua and Ksawam in the hinterland. The design can be found under number 8174 (220) in the HKM sample books, as BF photo 136 and in the Vlisco collection as number 14/2747.

127 https://www.accraarchive.com/blog/the-accra-post-office, page visited 23 December 2023.

128 The design BT reg.no. 3222 was registered on 5 June 1908. BF photo 85 and in the Vlisco collection H171.

129 The design was not registered but can been seen as number 7366 in book 310. Its number in the actual Vlisco collection is 14/41850.

130 The first registered version of *Sibi Saba** is BT reg.no. 468211 (1 November 1905), HKM sample books no. 8060 (312). It appears on the Ashton list under BF photo number 111.

131 The European ornamental design, potentially related to *Congres**, can be seen in the HKM sample books as number 4958 (224) and 4050 (248).

132 The design can be found as number 7591 in book 311 of the HKM sample books. Its number in the actual Vlisco collection is 14/0017.

133 Citation from a letter from the Basel Missionaries in 1913 to Ankersmit. Meeles I, 109

134 Ankersmit descriptions of designs 1912-1930. Vlisco Archive, @ Vlisco BV.

135 The later version can be found as number 6366 (245) in the HKM sample books. In the actual Vlisco collection it has number 14/0575.

136 The first European-looking design appeared in the HKM sample books under number 4968 (224) and 4050 (248) and BF photo 9. The *simplified* version was registered under BT reg.no. 250493 (1 March 1895), HKM sample book 4822 (224). In the actual Vlisco collection it has number 14/1070.
137 BT reg. no. 443630 (20 October 1904), HKM book 7757 (311) and BF photo 30. A sample of a variant with a palmtree and several animals added (BF photo 34) can be found in the Brunnschweiler Archive held at the Whitworth Art Gallery, University of Manchester.
138 A first version is number 6570 (262), a second version 6770 (244). On the Ashton list it has BF photo number 91. Ankersmit would introduce a similar version under number 11500. Another version, also similar, is in print by Vlisco: 14/0029.
139 Birds' nests with eggs can be seen on cloth, registered under BT reg.no. 419330 (13 October 1903) and HKM 7552 (311), swarms of bees BT reg.no. 419329 (13 October 1902) and *Beehives*, the identical design twice registered BT reg.no. 388035 (4 March 1902) and BT reg.no. 394628 (30 July 1902). Palm trees were registered on 27 February 1904 as BT reg. no. 427676. The music bars are registered under BT reg.no. 419331 (12 October 1903), the smoking pipes BT reg.no. 356288 (21 April 1900) and the mushrooms BT reg.no. 432290 (13 May 1904) – BF photo 130.
140 Registered under BT reg.no. 468210 (1 November 1905), HKM sample books no. 8011 (312).
141 The design can be found in the HKM sample books no. 7653 (311). A more recent, comparable image of thread spools and sewing machines *Six bobines* can be found in Gott and Loughran, ill. 37, 44.
142 https://trc-leiden.nl/trc-needles/organisations-and-movements/companies/clark-thread-company, last accessed 3 August 2023. Clark & Co. amalgamated with J. and P. Coats Ltd in 1896.
143 The design can be found in the HKM sample books no. 7893 (312).
144 https://www.angelfire.com/pr/perfinsoc/abstracts/1962.pdf, page visited 4 August 2023.
145 See chapter 6.
146 Registered were in 1906 the BT reg.nos. 475189, 4768885, 480430, 480431, 482073 – the last two with the motif *Canoe Peak** or *Dos de tortue** (back of a turtle), BT reg.no. 4826645, BT reg.no. 486074 and in 1907 BT reg.no. 498743 and BT reg.no. 509884.
147 Krantz 1985, 6
148 For a description of this design, see further in this chapter.
149 Vollaard, 55
150 The indigo version was registered under BT reg.no. 482072 (6 June 1906), the coloured version under number BT reg.no. 489319 (15 October 1906). Both designs can also be found in the HKM sample books, nos. 8249 (220) (indigo) and 8326 (220) (coloured). On the Ashton list it can be found under BF photo number 42.
151 This design is registered as BT reg.no. 513190 on 5 October 1907.
152 The design was registered on 15 August 1911 as BT reg.no. 40820 and figures on the list of Ashton as BF photo number 2.
153 This design BT reg.no. 6840 was registered on 5 October 1908. In the HKM sample books it can be found as number 8636 (309). It was on the list for Ashton as BF photo number 139. In the Vlisco archives is a sample of the design with the specific text Let Glasgow Flourish (inv.no. S487/154) and in HKM book 309, design no. 863. See also chapter 3, photo 1.
154 This design, BT reg.no. 12593, was registered on 28 August 1909.
155 *Sixteen Objects* was registered under BT reg.no. 12593 (28 August 1909) and renewed on 25 July 1912, in HKM sample book no. 9483 (212) and BF photo 84. The design is divided in four rows, each with four squares. Its number in the actual Vlisco collection is H904. *Key* is mentioned on the list for Ashton as BF photo number 94.
156 This design, BT reg.no. 73290, was registered on 11 November 1912 and figures on the Ashton list under number 6.
157 This design BT reg.no. 88682, registered on 18 July 1913, was still on the list for Ashton in 1939, BF photo number 39.
158 Bickford Berzock, 78
159 Gerards and Suze May Sho, 253
160 Boatema Boateng, 158
161 The first one was registered on 20 August 1906 as BT reg.no. 485228.
162 Morfini describes boxes in the basement of the museum with about 140 objects like vases, palettes, mummified bodies and animals and amulets from the Predynastic times to the Greco-Roman period. The highlight is a stela from Deil el-Medina See Irene Morfini, 'An Egyptian collection held in the National Museum in Accra' in *Göttinger Miszellen* 249: 125–29 (2016).
163 The first edition was printed in 1893, a second in 1894 and a revised and expanded edition in 1925. It figures on the Ashton list as BF photo number 63. Personal communication 1 November 2023
164 See Budge 1904, 40, 42 and 43.
165 See Budge 1904, 44 and 46.
166 See Budge 1904, plate XXVII.
167 Rene van Walsem refers to Shosh(enk), of which minimal five individuals have governed between 950-820 BC, king Pianchi around 750 BC. The cartouches are linked with each other by the words *Son of Re*, which is a permanent part of the name and royal title. Personal communication 1 November 2023. The design is registered under BT reg.no. 54764 and on the Ashton list as BF photo number 38.
168 Stalenboek X3601-4800 Asthon, Brunnschweiler Archive, held at the Whitworth Art Gallery, University of Manchester (UK).
169 This design was registered on 11 January 1911 under BT reg.no. 27019 and figures on the Ashton list of 1939 as BF photo numbers 27 and 54. The name of the design is written on the sticker on the sample in the HKM book 309, number 8775.
170 Personal communication Rene van Walsem 1 November 2023
171 This design, BT reg.no. 494677, was registered on 24 January 1907 and can be found in the HKM books under number 8460. BF photo 147. On the Ashton list it can be found under BF photo number 147. The year 1907 marked the start of the French conquest of Morocco.
172 Other designs with a raised hand are BT reg.no. 13492 (8 October 1909) and BT reg.no. 54764 (8 March 1912).
173 It was registered on 5 June 1911 under BT reg.no. 36176 and can also be found in the HKM sample books under number 8791 (309). On the Ashton list it is BF photo number 101.
174 For a photo of the design and a further description, see the epilogue.
175 Examples are design 6672 and 6732 (HKM book 244), 7467 (HKM book 310) – registered under BT reg.no. 407447 d.d. 27 March 1903 – and 8351 (HKM book 220) – registered under BT reg.no. 486074 on 30 August 1906.
176 Registered under BT reg.no. 96756 on 2 December 1913, on the Ashton list as BF photo number 44.

The process of wax printing

4.
A first wash of the cloth removes some of the wax, leaving small and large spots of wax, a process known as marbling.

The rise of Brown Fleming's competitors in wax printing

Until around 1910 Brown Fleming dominated the market for imitation batiks on the West African Coast. Increasing demand, in combination with limited production, led to frustration on the part of traders in Africa. However, while several attempts had been made to gain an insight into Prévinaire's production process, it was only in the years directly leading up to 1910 that a few other companies in the Netherlands, the United Kingdom and Switzerland managed to produce a quality of wax print that compared to that of Prévinaire and could capture sales on the African markets.

Developments from around 1906 until the start of the First World War

At the start of the twentieth century, barely a dozen companies situated in the Netherlands, the United Kingdom and Switzerland, produced batik-style prints for the West African market. They printed simulations and variations of Indonesian designs and motifs, almost all using methods without wax. Towards the end of the first decade and during the second decade of the twentieth century these companies also printed imitations of the famous wax prints of Brown Fleming, but still without wax. It was also in this period that some began with wax printing and apart from Prévinaire, introducing African-oriented motifs inspired by Brown Fleming's patterns.

Brown Fleming had monopolised the market for wax prints on the West African coast. By controlling the number of designs and the amount of cloth sold, he kept prices high and turnover rapid.[1] While demand was growing quickly, Prévinaire's printing process was time consuming, restricting the production output. A wall of secrecy surrounded the process of wax printing, protecting Prévinaire's dominant market position. In contrast to other processes such as Turkey red, which was by then supported by extensive literature, few colourists possessed details of wax printing. Even when companies were able to hire colourists from the HKM, their knowledge regarding the technique of making wax prints was incomplete and insufficient. Copies of his famous wax prints were made, but they were of course less profitable.

At the time various companies started experimenting with the wax printing process, the technical literature started to show more interest in what was described as the *peculiar kind of 'resist work' known as 'Battick printing'*.[2] Elbers describes in 1909 improvements in copies of batik obtained by developing better equipped machines.[3] Knecht and Fothergrill also describe the improvements thanks to more specialised machinery and the amelioration of the quality of dyes and the way of dyeing the cloth.[4]

It was a fact that continued developments in synthetic dyes had changed the field of textile colouration in the last quarter of the nineteenth century. Colourists could now attend technical schools in place of traditional on-the-job training. The latest technical developments became available through trade journals and expanding chemical literature, through which colourists and managers could inform themselves. This resulted in a more systematic and analytical approach to dyeing and textile printing. But wax printing was about complex manipulation more than chemistry. Prévinaire did not change his colouration methods or his way of training colourists, focusing his innovations on perfecting mechanical processes. Conquering mechanical hurdles, Prévinaire's wax prints improved, staying ahead of the competition during the first decade of the twentieth century.[5] It was only at the end of the decade, hastened by industrial espionage alongside applied experiments, that several companies in the Netherlands and the United Kingdom managed to produce a quality of wax print that could compare to that of the HKM. These firms, in turn, guarded their wax printing processes from competitors. Until the Second World War, HKM production retained its supremacy in the African market. Clients preferred the HKM wax prints because of the quality of the cloth, the beauty of its colours, the mode of craquelure (even printing crackle patterns directly on the cloth) and special effects like *bleeding* of the printed motif, and a *touché* effect.[6] In addition, an evolution in the layering of colour and texture gave patterns an attractive density and depth. This is not to deny that others achieved considerable commercial success in wax printing, but it often involved prioritising quantity over quality.[7]

In the Netherlands, in addition to the HKM, there were five established companies able to print with wax for the African market by around 1910. The first to produce an acceptable quality of wax prints was the Deventer Katoen Maatschappij (formerly Ankersmit & Co., hereafter Ankersmit). Ankersmit was fortunate to hire Jean Jacques Jr, son of the chief colourist at the HKM (of the same name). The company knew the Basle Mission Trading Company (BMTC) was looking to increase their sales but was also interested in cheaper alternatives so it could bypass Brown Fleming. With helpful instructions from the BMTC, Ankersmit started wax printing by the end of 1911, emulating the most successful designs of Brown Fleming. P. F. Fentener van Vlissingen in Helmond had its first duplex roller resin-printing machine installed in 1906, but it was only around 1910 that it could make satisfactory wax prints. From 1899 until 1910 the company had the services of the colourist Charles Henri Jacques, the second son of Jean Jacques. As with Ankersmit, the wax was applied by roller, but the remaining colours were applied by hand-block printing. The irregularities that resulted from this process gave the wax prints their uniqueness. The other three Dutch firms had smaller operations, and slightly later entry into the wax printing market, as discussed later in this chapter.

In the United Kingdom calico printers were focused principally on a wide export trade. Of those printing for the West African market, it may have been Horridge & Cornall that produced the first wax print; this was in 1908 for the merchant firm Logan Muckelt.[8] But F. W. Grafton and Co. at Broad Oak works in Accrington were ready at almost the same time. In 1907 the company obtained the help of Carlos Casanovas, a colourist who had previously worked for the Leidsche Katoen Maatschappij.[9] F. W. Ashton and Co. of Newton Bank printworks in Hyde near Manchester began full production of duplex machine-printed wax styles in 1909 after a period of trials. The work was of high quality and Ashton quickly became one of the most important wax printers in the United Kingdom.

Most manufacturers in Switzerland had ceased production of imitation batiks in the 1870s. An exception was the company Hösly and Leuzinger in Glarus which restarted production of good-quality wax prints in 1878.[10] Although the company had difficulty competing with cheap English prints and high-quality Dutch imitation batiks, it was successful, notably because its aesthetically interesting *bleed* effects pleased consumers. The company saw its export to Indonesia slowly growing to a peak in 1891 but with a drastic decline thereafter along with their English and Dutch counterparts. It was able to continue by extending its exports to other markets in South East Asia.[11] For other Swiss companies, wax printing resumed only after the First World War.[12]

The Netherlands

Deventer Katoen Maatschappij, formerly Ankersmit & Co.
The first company in the Netherlands that successfully copied Brown Fleming's wax prints was the *Deventer Katoen Maatschappij voorheen Ankersmit & Co.* (Deventer Cotton Company formerly Ankersmit & Co.), known as Ankersmit. In 1798, Hendrik Jan Ankersmit founded a handweaving and indigo dyeing business in Deventer. His son, Hendrik Jan Jr, replaced hand weaving by steam-driven cotton manufacturing in 1865. Plain-weave products like *blue baftas* – an indigo dyed cloth – and *sucretons* (a type of cretonne) were exported to the Dutch East Indies and West Africa.[13] The firm began printing in 1890 but stopped before 1900 because it was not profitable. However, when Hendrik Jan of the fourth generation Ankersmit, with his doctorate in organic chemistry from the University of Bern, took the reins in 1899, he was convinced that the company should move to cotton printing as its main business. It was also Hendrik Jan who instituted the name change to Deventer Cotton Company in 1902, but it is unclear what other changes began in the early 1900s.[14]

In 1907, a collaborative venture with the HKM for indigo dyeing led to a successful development.[15] At a meeting of the *Nederlandse Maatschappij ter bevordering van Nijverheid en Handel* (Dutch Company for the Promotion of Industry and Trade), Van de Poll of the HKM arranged with Ankersmit to dye mastic-printed cloth for the HKM to satisfy increasing demand on the Gold Coast.[16] The first order came on 11 February 1908 and by November of that year almost 460,000 yards had been dyed. Over the summer the HKM also sent wax prints for dyeing.[17] However, on 24 October the HKM suddenly terminated the agreement, Van de Poll claiming a shortage of unprinted English cloth due to a strike.[18] Nonetheless, Ankersmit's offer to supply the cloth was rejected by the HKM, and Hendrik Jan Ankersmit surmised that the HKM suspected his company had kept samples of wax prints to obtain printing secrets. This he denied, but later admitted buying HKM samples via Haijkens, their agent in Hamburg, maintaining that the purpose was for comparison of cloth quality before sending out samples.[19]

On 16 April 1910, Hendrik Jan Ankersmit convinced his co-directors and shareholders to invest the necessary funds to set up wax printing. Careful market research had been carried out in 1909, including discussions with the BMTC, keen to have an additional provider to Brown Fleming. Able to sell more cloth in Africa, the BMTC was willing to help Ankersmit by providing crucial information about the quality and selection of designs for wax printing.[20] In addition to current provision of indigo dyed cloth to the BMTC, discussions in July 1910 led to an agreement that gave the BMTC favoured status for purchase of Deventer wax prints. Prior to this, Haijkens had shown interest in getting sales rights, and Ankersmit gave him in total confidentiality a sample to show to a specific client. However, Haijkens also showed it to the BMTC, who were annoyed and consequently demanded sole rights to Ankersmit's wax prints.[21]

BMTC's problem was a lack of stock, which it signalled at an early stage, as confirmed by letters in the Basel

Mission archives.[22] It was Brown Fleming's policy, known to the BMTC, to keep stocks low to keep prices high.[23] Martin Binhammer of the BMTC wrote to Israel Werner, the sales agent of Brown Fleming, in an attempt to resolve the problem, but to no avail.[24] A personal visit to Brown Fleming from Binhammer and Alfred Opferkuch, general agent of the BMTC in Accra, apparently also came to nothing.[25] Brown Fleming himself blamed the situation in Lancashire and the United States as the cause of higher prices.[26] But frustration within the BMTC grew. The trading post in Akuse even decided to become *Flemming frei* (Fleming-free) and was looking for another provider.[27] Such business decisions probably reflect the reorganisation of the BMTC around 1910 so that commercial logic could prevail over religious influence.[28]

A letter from Brown Fleming's son and son-in-law, written after his death on 16 April 1912, suggests that they were aware of the frustrations of the BMTC. They wrote to the BMTC that they planned large extensions to their plant with the intention of enabling small print runs for greater variety in their assortments.[29] But the BMTC decided that it would cease business with Brown Fleming altogether once a cheaper alternative was found by working directly with a wax print manufacturer. On 27 December 1912, Opferkuch, wrote to his head office:

> *So sehr ich wünschte, wir könnten die ganze Produktion abnehmen, so sehr muss ich davon abraten. Wir dürfen nicht vergessen, dass Fleming seine Ware dadurch eingeführt hat, dass er die Küste an Ware knapp hielt. Hätte er sie überschemmt, er hätte nie das Geschäft gemacht. So es auch mit der Deventer-Ware werden, sonst bekommen die Leute bald über. Er wäre ein grösser Fehler von Deventer, wenn diese Leute darauf dringen würden, die Westküste mit ihrer Ware zu überfluten. Sie müssen langsam mit der Produktion voranmachen*. (As much as I wish we could take care of the entire production, I must advise against it. We must not forget that Fleming introduced his ware by keeping the coasts short of goods. Had he swamped them, he would never have been so successful. The same will be true of the Deventer goods, otherwise people will soon get swamped. It would be a great mistake for Deventer if they insisted on flooding the West Coast with their wares. They need to slowly get the production going).[30]

The BMTC had learned a lesson from Brown Fleming. It was in their interest to control supplies to the West African market, with careful consideration of the optimal quantities.[31] For a certain period, cloth would be bought from both Brown Fleming and Ankersmit to allow the company in Deventer to develop the necessary assortment of designs.[32] Meanwhile, discussions with other possible partners took place. The BMTC contacted William Ewart Clucas of M. Hertz & Co., a Manchester merchant firm exporting textiles to East and West Africa from a range of suppliers.[33] He proposed to help Ankersmit with samples, provision of white cloth and drawings for new designs, but insisted that Hertz finish the products. However, Ankersmit felt his company would become too dependent and was not happy to give a monopoly of production to Hertz.[34]

Ankersmit had begun setting up the new printing department and preparation for wax print production. The wax print technique needed to be tested and refined to reach a quality comparable to Brown Fleming's. The BMTC selected samples from which Ankersmit chose the pattern *Leidsche Ruit**, a trellised arrangement with a relatively small repeat, for their first number: 5000.[35] Not without problems with printing blocks and rollers, Ankersmit was able to produce its first wax print on 5 July 1911.[36] Printing machines had been ordered and installed by Voss and Delius from Manchester.[37] The technique maintained from day one until the closure of the company in 1965 paralleled other companies using duplex roller printing with wax. Initially the rollers were engraved by hand, which gave the desired effect of irregularity.[38] Further colours were added by hand block.[39] On 7 December, the BMTC placed the first order for wax prints: 2,400 pieces of 12 yards of *Leidsche Ruit** and 1,000 pieces of 12 yards of the *Pelican* design.[40]

An experienced colourist was essential for any printing company,[41] but for knowledge of wax printing, specialised experience was necessary. Here, the company was fortunate in hiring, on 1 April 1910, Jean Jacques, son of Joseph Jacques and grandson of Jean Joseph Jacques, colourists at the HKM. Jean Jacques (known as Jean Jacques jr. or Jean Jacques) duly received his training there along with his brother Charles Henri, but had the advantage of inheriting the family recipe book.[42]

Company historian G. J. Meeles claims that Jean Jacques kept his laboratory experiments completely secret. When a duplex printing machine was installed in the second quarter of 1911 he required a wooden barrier around it, only accessible by himself and his assistants. Ankersmit tolerated this behaviour because Jacques was considered indispensable, but eventually fired him in April 1915.[43] From then onwards, Ankersmit relied on *Badische Anilin- und Soda Fabrik* (BASF) for colour advice. Producers of chemical dyes like BASF and the Swiss company *Ciba Geigy* took over some of the technical advisory role of colourists at the beginning of the twentieth century as part of servicing and marketing their products. However, the in-house colourist was not superseded in practical day-to-day matters. Ankersmit consequently hired Jean Disch, a colourist from the HKM when it closed in 1918. Although already of retirement age on his arrival, Disch continued to work until 1930.[44]

The rise of Brown Fleming's competitors in wax printing

On the non-technical side, the most pressing question was how to assemble a collection of designs attractive to existing clients. For creation of new patterns, the company of Hendrik Gerrit Bokhorst, founded in 1830 in Deventer, was contacted. This firm was active in both home decoration and applied art. Meeles stipulated the designer R. J. Zeeman as a contributor from 1911 to 1912. Also drawing new designs were H. Bon Jr from Haarlem and W. Kuit from the Koninkijke Deventer Tapijfabrieken.[45] It is notable that both Bokhorst and Kuit attended the same school in Deventer.[46] The Deventer *Maatschappij tot Nut van 't Algemeen* (Society for the Benefit of the General Public) opened in 1800, a *Teekenschool* (drawing school) aimed at low-income artisans and anybody (women included) interested in improving their drawing skills; it offered evening classes.[47] The school attracted people from beyond Deventer, and many artists and designers for local industry were taught at this school. When King William I issued a royal decree in 1817 that every town needed a drawing academy, the town of Deventer decided to subsidise the school and re-named it the *Teeken-Academieschool* (Drawing Academy).[48] Members of different generations of the Bokhorst family attended.[49] Zeeman was eventually recruited from the Bokhorst studio as Ankersmit's full-time in-house designer from 1 January 1913.[50]

For Ankersmit, it was important that a design was not too closely related to existing ones on the market to prevent copyright disputes with fellow textile printers. Given the limited number of existing designs, finding new motifs was not as difficult as meeting expectations for colour and character of rendering. The idea was to create an initial portfolio of twelve designs representative of the future Ankersmit offering. The company, which was not familiar with wax printing but had already heavily invested in its production, was dependent on information given by the BMTC, who were keen to extend their business with their new supplier. The BMTC's suggestions were mainly based on best sellers from Brown Fleming, designs they knew would sell. So some designs created in Ankersmit's studio were based on elements taken from existing designs.[51] Even though Ankersmit wanted the firm to start with its own signature designs, half the designs from the first collection were in reality similar to existing ones. The others were a mixture of ideas from the BMTC and the designers of Bokhorst. A document that describes the source of designs relates how eventually design ideas originated with requests from merchants.[52]

Although the collaboration with the BMTC was fruitful, Hendrik Jan Ankersmit felt the need to personally investigate the situation in West Africa and spent time in Accra and Akuse in January 1912. He wanted to understand how the prints found their way to clients after arrival and

1. Photo taken during the trip of Hendrik Jan Ankersmit to the Gold Coast in 1912 of people wearing examples of the first wax prints from Ankersmit: *Leidsche Ruit** (no. 5000) (third person from the left), *Pelican* (no. 5025) (second person from the left) and *Phoenix* (no. 5050) (left and right) NL-DvCO, Collectie Overijssel locatie Deventer, ID 0895, Ankersmit's Textielfabrieken NV - Deventer Wax Beheer B.V., inv.no. NL-DvCO_0895_219

to get an idea of what these clients really wanted. He took with him samples of the three first designs, 5000, 5035 and 5050, and drawings of new designs for feedback.[53] Agents of the BMTC were so used to the smooth sale of Brown Fleming's output that they were apprehensive about offering Ankersmit prints at the same time; clients knew perfectly well how to tell the difference and always preferred the Brown Fleming prints. Critical aspects were colour, especially white and indigo, cracks in the wax and the width of the selvedge.[54] As with Brown Fleming, the BMTC wanted their mark – a sailing ship with rowers – on every piece of cloth. Clients appreciated a clear brand.[55] The stamp was soon replaced with paper labels, considered more attractive by buyers.[56] The choice of a four-digit number for the designs imitated Brown Fleming, who also used the same system, with which the local population had become familiar.[57]

The first experiments started on 5 July 1911, but it took the company another three months before it could send samples for approval to Basel.[58] By 1912, the company had developed a regular production of about 600 pieces of 12-yards length per week, based on the most successful designs of Brown Fleming.[59] In the first year of production the BMTC ordered an average of 1,800 pieces of all twelve designs, implicitly taking a certain risk, because the company knew that when too many pieces of cloth with the same design were offered, sales could stagnate. To help Ankersmit, the BMTC asked Werner to sell the cloth in other parts of West Africa where they did not yet sell themselves, but this did not improve sales sufficiently, so other merchants were approached.[60] Initially Ankersmit had agreed not to offer any of its products to other merchants and although the BMTC was informed, this created frictions, leaving the BMTC concerned that their sales interests on the Gold Coast would be put at risk.[61] Ankersmit promised to give the BMTC exclusive rights at a special price for the Coast. Outside the Coast, merchants could obtain the monopoly for specific regions, controlled by adding the initials of these merchants before the serial number of a design. Despite these initiatives, sales figures in Meeles's study show that revenues outside of the Coast were marginal.[62]

By the beginning of 1913, Ankersmit's production had dropped to about 500 pieces a week, not enough to keep the printing business profitable in the long run. The BMTC did not just want to increase sales of existing designs but

suggested adding new designs that 'would correspond completely to the taste of the negroes'.[63] Another dozen designs were developed: three derived from Brown Fleming patterns, six based on BMTC instructions and three created in-house.[64] Production increased to 800 pieces a week, but for the BMTC this was still too low. The BMTC looked to cessation of business with Brown Fleming by the end of 1913, with Ankersmit becoming their sole wax print supplier. To accelerate their attempt to side-line Brown Fleming, the BMTC asked Werner to order comparable prints produced by Grafton and Welch *die Fl[eming] schlagen sollten'* ('that would hit Fleming').[65] The choice of these companies was shrewd. F. W. Grafton was probably the first in the UK to print wax prints of a quality comparable to Brown Fleming.[66] Thomas Welch, who had registered designs for the African market since 1885, occasionally imitated tie-dye fabrics and patterns from African cloth.[67] However, this initiative was unsuccessful. Firstly, it resulted in over-delivery of wax prints from orders already placed with Brown Fleming, Ankersmit, Grafton and Welch.[68] Secondly, the different trading posts of the BMTC were not impressed with the prints of the last two companies and considered the whole delivery from the

The rise of Brown Fleming's competitors in wax printing

UK a failure: *Leider war ja auch alles was in Imitation von England kam misraten* (Unfortunately, all the imitations that came from England failed). Fortunately, the designs printed by Ankersmit were deemed a great success.[69]

During the first six months of 1914, another dozen designs were added, giving a collection of thirty-six designs, while sales of both existing and new designs improved.[70] Until then, prints were on cloth finished at 36 inches wide, but on 12 March 1914, the first order for wax prints 48 inches wide was placed.[71] Wider prints necessitated new printing machines, which was a considerable investment. Business was going well. Sales figures show that especially the copies or interpretations of Brown Fleming designs sold very well, but all trading focused on export markets was to be seriously disrupted by the outbreak of war.[72]

P. F. van Vlissingen

The company P. F. van Vlissingen was owned by members of the Fentener van Vlissingen family. It was founded in 1846, and became a limited partnership (*commanditaire vennootschap*)[73] in 1883, and a limited company in 1916: P. F. van Vlissingen & Co.'s Katoenfabrieken N.V.[74] It was renamed Naamlooze Vennootschap P. F. van Vlissingen & Co. Katoenfabrieken in 1934 (*NV* or *Naamloze Vennootschap* is Dutch for limited company).[75] In 1965, the name Vlisco, a contraction of Van Vlissingen & Co., was adopted. For four generations, a descendant with the same name would be the Director or one of the Directors of the company: Pieter Fentener van Vlissingen I (1794-1844), Pieter Fentener van Vlissingen II (1826-1868), Pieter Fentener van Vlissingen III (1853-1927) and Pieter Fentener van Vlissingen IV (1890-1962). For the reader's ease, they will be referred to hereafter as Pieter I, Pieter II, Pieter III and Pieter IV.

In 1843 Pieter I, a merchant from Amsterdam, started a collaboration with Peter Antonius Sutorius (1804-1886). Sutorius was since 1834 owner of a small textile printing company in Helmond founded in 1802 by his father producing cloth for the domestic market and batik imitations for export.[76] During the 1830s, Sutorius already supplied well-known Amsterdam merchants, such as Marsais, Sinkel, Kersents and Clasing.[77] He ran into financial difficulties around 1840, when the NHM was no longer subsidised by the government and became more commercially rigorous. Pieter I was already exporting to Indonesia, where two of his brothers were trading, and he agreed with Sutorius to share ownership of the firm, with the possibility of assuming total control. To this end, he arranged for his son Pieter II to start training at the company. In 1846, Pieter II acquired the company, two years after the death of his father, when it was renamed P. F. van Vlissingen & Co.[78] In 1852 he joined forces with Frederik Jacob Matthijsen. Most of the printing was done by hand, but a perrotine was purchased in 1846 and a roller printing machine in 1853. Alongside printing for the local market Van Vlissingen continued to print for the colonies the imitation batiks that Sutorius had been printing before the takeover. Pieter II's uncle Frederik Hendrik van Vlissingen (1803-1862), known as Uncle Frits, a sugar producer in Indonesia, took original batiks to Helmond in 1852 with the request to make copies to be sold in Indonesia exclusively by himself. The arrangement between Uncle Frits and Pieter II was called the *Batick Associatie* (or Batik Coalition) formalising the aim to expand in the export market. Initially, only batiks from Solo in Java were used as models, but soon experiments with handkerchiefs and sarongs from other regions were carried out. The first delivery to Indonesia was well received, but the Batik Coalition deal was not working satisfactorily for either party. The design suggestions proved successful, but because Uncle Frits was the sole trader, marketing was limited. Other Indonesian merchants sold imitation batik printed by Sutorius, but they were interested to sell the Coalition patterns as well. When Uncle Frits fell ill in 1853, the Coalition started selling the reserved designs to others. Uncle Frits eventually died in 1862, when his business interests were taken over by Simon Paulus Fentener van Vlissingen until 1876.[79] The company hence continued its policy of dealing with private merchants rather than be restricted by the monopolistic practices of the NHM.[80]

The huge success of Prévinaire's wax prints from 1863 until 1867 attracted other companies to experiment with the technique. In 1866 Van Vlissingen managed to make good quality *imitation* batiks although, like other companies, only for a short time. The costs of development and production were too high.[81] Rivalry and frustration at competition come to the surface in a note accompanying a Van Vlissingen sample:

> [...] *monsters [...] perfect geïmiteerd, v. Vlissingen. Dat is geen aangenaam gevoel voor u nog mij. Daarop zijn door [...] [Prévinaire] schatten op verdient. Ge hebt het niet gewild.* [Our] samples [...] perfectly imitated [by] v. Vlissingen. That is not a pleasant feeling neither for you nor for me. [...] [Prévinaire] has earned fortunes on this. You did not want this.[82]

Pieter II was involved in developing new designs, and engravings based on his ideas were introduced. Continual offering of new patterns, with variations and multiple colourings, were demanded by customers. Until 1878 samples were sent to Indonesia for approval, but thereafter drawings were sent and only upon approval were designs engraved.[83] Over time, the company employed several colourists. Jacques Braun from Mulhouse started around

2. Van Vlissingen's first wax print 1866 LKM book 19, p. 1006
Vlisco Archive, @ Vlisco BV

1849 and was replaced in 1861 by Antoine Lejeune from Paris, who continued until 1868. The sons of the two partners were still young, so Pieter III and Jan Matthijsen Jr were sent to Zurich to study at the Polytechnische Schule from 1869 to 1873. And in the meantime Swiss colourists Friedrich Hayder and Conrad Hermann Deutsch were employed. After completing their studies, the two young men were taken on as colourists and directors of the company. Deutsch left in 1874 and Hayder died in 1881.[84]

The company's products sold well in Indonesia until the end of the 1860s when the trade in European-made batik imitations stagnated. New markets were sought, and, starting in 1875, several trips to East Africa resulted in requests for the printing of kangas. Orders were received from German traders in Mombasa, Dar Es Salaam and Zanzibar, but it was only around the end of the century that a regular export trade was secured.[85] When export to West Africa started is uncertain. A report made by L. P. Bienfait during his training in 1876 reveals that at that time Van Vlissingen was already exporting to West Africa, but quantities were small. The report shows samples for the West African market such as European-style shawls, but not imitation batik.[86] For the market in Zanzibar, two Indonesian-style prints were shown, but only single colour patterns. Local historian J. M. T. Verschueren suggests it was in 1878 that Pieter III first approached merchants for the East and West African markets in London and Manchester.[87] However, according to G. E. Rodenburg, co-author of the company's centenary history, shipping of imitation batik started only in 1893. Because Van Vlissingen wax prints followed Brown Fleming's opening of the market, it can be posited that Brown Fleming started shipping HKM wax prints earlier, around 1890, an observation with which Krantz, head of the Vlisco collections from 1952 until 1985, agrees.[88] Fancy prints and imitation batik were exported and sold as *Java Prints* or *Java Garments*, but initially the market was small.[89] For Van Vlissingen, the domestic market in the Netherlands and Belgium was still its most important customer in the last quarter of the nineteenth century. Besides Africa, attempts to increase exports were focused

The rise of Brown Fleming's competitors in wax printing

on European-style printed furnishings and chintz, sent to Japan from 1885; prints for the Balkan area; and imitation batiks for Burma, Thailand and Singapore.[90]

Like his father, Pieter III was also responsible for the design department and was active as a designer himself. Designs were initially acquired for the home market, often in Paris, while for the export market, they were usually based on Indonesian batik motifs. In-house designers mainly adapted designs for printing requirements. Pieter III wanted to end buying and copying designs and create a proper in-house studio, which he finally achieved in 1894,[91] furthered in 1897 with the separation of design and engraving studios. In Pieter III's desire to create a more artistic environment, he invited Michel Duco Crop in 1895 to make designs for printed furnishings, such as *cretonnes* and velvet curtains, tablecloths and bedcovers. The connection was established a year earlier by Jan Veth, an artist, art historian, writer and member of the family of one of the directors.[92] Duco Crop was one of the first Dutch industrial designers, greatly influenced by the English *Arts and Crafts* Movement.[93] Between 1894 and 1900, Crop made about twenty-five designs, some for roller-printing, others for hand-block printing. On the domestic market they were not successful, perhaps due to relatively high prices. Van Vlissingen exported them mainly to England until 1912 when high production prices made their sales no longer profitable.[94] While Duco Crop's curtain fabrics for Van Vlissingen may not have been a commercial success, they were probably the earliest examples in the Netherlands of an intentional collaboration between an artist and a manufacturer.[95] It added to the prestige of the company and later resulted in similar collaborations.

In 1900, Johan Jacobs (1881-1955) became head of the design department.[96] He had begun to work for the company at the age of fourteen in 1895, but when Pieter III discovered his talent for drawing, he insisted that he attend the *Teekenschool* in Helmond. Because the company supported the school, there was an important textile design section.[97] At this school, Jacobs followed a four-year course in drawing and textile design. *Art Nouveau* and *Arts and Crafts* were important influences on textile design at the school, but crucial was the notion of non-naturalistic *vlakornament,* flat-designed ornament built upon geometric frameworks.[98] In 1896, Jacobs became the assistant of Duco Crop. Although it is not certain how long this apprenticeship

3. Design department at Van Vlissingen with Johan Jacobs standing, 1921
Vlisco Archive, @ Vlisco BV

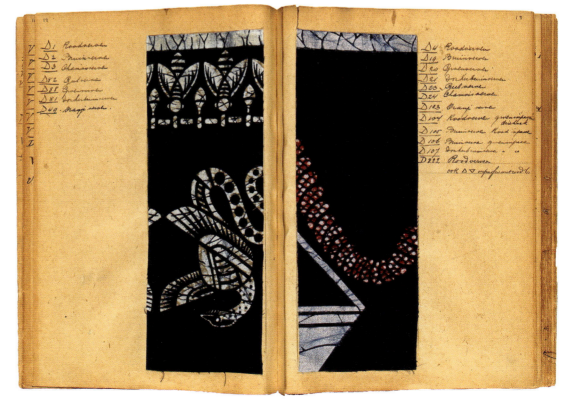

4. Experiments with wax prints at Van Vlissingen, Helmond around 1910
Sample book S. W. Lijndruk.
Kantoor A. P. M. pp. 28-29
Vlisco Archive, @ Vlisco BV

5. Experiments with wax prints at Van Vlissingen, Helmond around 1910
Sample book S. W. Lijndruk.
Kantoor A. P. M. pp. 12-13
Vlisco Archive, @ Vlisco BV

The rise of Brown Fleming's competitors in wax printing

lasted, Duco Crop had a great influence on his later work. Five years after becoming head of the design studio, Jacobs became an assistant at the *Teekenschool* in Helmond, where, in 1914, he was appointed a teacher. He carried on both design and teaching roles until his retirement in 1951.[99] For Van Vlissingen he turned out to be a prolific designer and an inspiring leader of his team.

Several designers who worked for the company in the 1900s are known by little more than their names.[100] Beginners started with work more on the technical drawing side, but over time their creative input became more relevant. In the 1910s, Pieter III and Jacobs were joined by Frans Jacobs – Jacobs's brother (1900), Bert Visser (1906), P. L. Snel (1909), Frans L. J. Beekhuizen (1914) and Johan Schuring (1919).[101] In the 1920s, Dries van de Ven (1924), Antoon van Dupper, Harry Sanders, Jack Bombeek (1925) and Hein Bullens (1927) joined the team.[102] Jacobs took them on regular outings to beautiful nature spots or museums. His preferences were ethnographic and historical museums.[103]

From 1912, the designers for wax print had their own space, under the instruction and leadership of Pieter III.[104] He discussed his ideas for potential new designs with European traders, who were well informed by African market women in the various centres. Many designs of the HKM were revisited.[105] In 1913 Pieter III arranged membership of the *Vereeniging Koloniaal Instituut* in Amsterdam to inspire his designers.[106] This gave them the opportunity to study the collection and copy original batik.[107] When his son Pieter IV became director in 1921, he shared the same passion for design, but Pieter III retained responsibility for the business until his death in 1927.[108]

Pieter III was aware of the export potential of the more exclusive, high-calibre wax prints and was keen to produce a quality that attracted good sales. Since 1899 he had the services of one of the best colourists, Charles Henri Jacques, brother of Jean Jacques of the family of colourists that worked at the HKM.[109] In 1906, two duplex roller printing machines capable of printing melted resists were installed for experimentation with wax prints. In 1911, the same year as Ankersmit, a satisfactory quality of print was achieved under the supervision of Jacques. The resist was no longer wax but resin that had more the resemblance of glue and was printed on the cloth with deeply engraved rollers (*lijmdruk*).[110] A sample book thought to have been made around 1910 shows the earliest wax prints at Van Vlissingen.[111] The letters A. P. M. in the book's title refer to the company director Alexander (Lex) Pieter Mathijssen, active from 1864 until 1919. He apparently kept this book in his own office, reflecting the importance of resist print for the company.[112] The designs are clearly inspired by Brown Fleming's collection from that time, but not closely imitative as in the Ankersmit collection, albeit they adopt similar themes and treatments.

It is thought that Van Vlissingen probably started exporting wax prints to West Africa around the start of the First World War. The first evidence is found in invoices to the London agents F. & A. Swanzy for bales of block-printed wax garments for Accra, starting 16 October 1914. By the end of the year, a total of 125 of 448 bales for West Africa had been dispatched to Accra, making it the largest market.[113] Swanzy had about thirty trading stations in West Africa and sold to African merchants on a monthly credit basis.[114] The outbreak of the War quickly meant a shortage of materials to print, and wax printing had to stop in 1917. Like Ankersmit, very limited to no exports to West Africa meant that stocks built up.[115]

Other companies that entered the Dutch wax printing market

In the Netherlands, three other well-established companies printed imitation batik around 1910: *the Leidsche Katoen Maatschappij* (Leiden Cotton Company) (LKM), the *Kralingsche Katoen Maatschappij* (Kralingen Cotton Company) (KKM), and the *Maatschappij voor Textiel Industrie, voorheen C. Roessingh & Zoon* in Veenendaal (Roessingh).[116]

Leidsche Katoen Maatschappij

The history of this company goes back to 1757, when De Heyder started manufacturing woven and printed cloth in Lier. After the separation of Belgium from the Netherlands in 1830, the company struggled due to a lack of orders. In 1835, the owner, the well-known *Orangist*, Baron F. Van den Berghe decided to move to Leiden, where the company began printing imitation batiks. It made good profit from deliveries to the NHM, but this activity went into rapid decline after 1840. In 1846 Heinrich Driessen became the new owner. The NHM remained a client, but private merchants were also approached. When exports stagnated at the end of the 1860s, the company ran into serious problems. Efforts to specialise in making wax prints were too slow and their block-prints were mediocre. In 1877, Driessen changed the name of the company to *Leidsche Katoenmaatschappij voorheen De Heyder and Co.* (hereafter LKM).

As Van Vlissingen, the LKM now began printing and exporting kangas to East Africa. Interest in the West African market arose only around 1910 with renewed production of imitation batik prints. To assist with wax prints, the colourist Alfred Kunig, who had previously worked for Roessingh in Veenendaal, was hired from 1911 until 1913. A wax printing machine from the HKM was bought, installed and made operational, but the printing process could not be satisfactorily developed A shortage of funds hindered expansion of wax printing.[117]

Kralingsche Katoen Maatschappij

The precursor of the KKM was established in 1701, beginning with imitations of Indian chintz. Later, evidenced by orders from the NHM, batik imitations for export to Indonesia were added. In 1836, the company had to close because of a lack of orders for export, but in 1839, with Dutch government subsidies, it was acquired as a going concern by G. van Sillevoldt, who developed it as a successful producer of imitation batik. In 1864 the company was renamed *Rotterdamsche Katoendrukkerij*. When the company suffered a reduction in sales of imitation batiks after 1867, it was taken over by van Sillevoldt's son. Its product range was comparable to the LKM and Van Vlissingen, but quality lagged behind. In 1882, the company was renamed *NV Kralingsche Katoen Maatschappij*. Exports were mainly to Asia, but sales to West Africa began slowly with imitation batiks, although production of wax prints was extremely low.[118]

Maatschappij voor Textiel Industrie, formerly C. Roessingh & Son

This company was founded in Enschede in 1804 by Carel Roessingh. Part of its production was imitation batik, but it is uncertain when this started. In 1898, Carel's three sons, who had become partners, set up a limited company *Maatschappij voor Textiel Industrie voorheen C. Roessingh & Zoon* (hereafter Roessingh). It moved to Veenendaal in 1912, where it carried out linen and cotton weaving, as well as perrotine and roller printing. Their wax prints competed with Ankersmit and Van Vlissingen. After the closure of the HKM in 1917, Brown Fleming had cloth printed at Roessingh. The company had the advantage that its production was already up and running while Ankersmit and Van Vlissingen were still developing their own.

United Kingdom
F. W. Ashton and Co. of Newton Bank Print Works

Benjamin Ashton (1718-1791), a farmer, was the first member of the Ashton family to show interest in textile manufacturing by distributing yarns to local hand-loom weavers and selling the finished goods in Manchester. His son Samuel continued and expanded the business. He began spinning in 1800 or 1802 in a small building at Godley Brook in Hyde. Because he saw better prospects in factory-based production, he and his children established several factories for cotton spinning and weaving in and around Hyde. At Newton Bank, from 1812 his sons Joseph and Benjamin acquired steam engines and roller printing machines to establish a print works. Joseph had studied chemistry in Jena (Germany) and became the colourist. Printing started in 1816 and in 1834 or 1835 they produced just under three million yards annually.[119] Benjamin died unmarried in 1835, and Joseph in 1856 without issue. Francis William Tinker, a nephew who inherited the company in 1856, started trading as F. W. Ashton, referring to his mother's maiden name. His son James, who had studied at the École de Chimie in Mulhouse, took over the technical management and established a laboratory for experiments. He developed complicated printing styles that gave the company a reputation for technical innovation.

In 1899, with fifteen roller printing machines, it was one of 46 textile printers and 13 merchants (representing 85 per cent of the British calico printing industry), that formed the conglomerate the Calico Printers' Association (CPA). Although the textile industry had prospered in the second half of the nineteenth century, by the 1890s fierce competition led to a decline in quality and profits. The goal of the CPA was to preserve the competitiveness of calico printing by making savings on bulk purchases and rationalising production; output was geared towards middle-range textiles of a standard achievable for mass-market prices.[120]

Around 1903 Frank Ashton started experimenting with wax printing by hand with wax resin applied by hand block on both sides of the cloth. The company was already printing cloth for export to Africa, indigo dyed to imitate tie-dye and paste resist styles. But gradually other styles were added, some exclusively for Africa: imitation wax, African fancy, tie-dye, madder prints and green grounds. The move to wax prints was a natural progression. An unpublished history of the *Newton Bank Printworks* written in 2007 suggests that the first wax design printed by hand was *Window Frame*.[121]

Because printing by hand block was slow, wax machine print trials started in 1906. Laborious attempts were made with rollers, but initially this proved a disaster. The distance between the printing rollers was too great, and the first wax layer had already contracted before the reverse side could be printed. Placing the rollers within inches of each other solved the problem. Experiments were also carried out using synthetic indigo. After three years of trials, full production of machine-printed duplex wax styles began in 1909.[122] The duplex machine was in operation at the nearby site of Godley Mill, presumably separated from the block printing for secrecy.[123] The titles of various designs like *Staircase*, *Peacock*, *Egyptian* and *Fern Leaf* suggest that these were imitating successful Brown Fleming prints.[124] The work was of high quality and Ashton quickly became one of the most important wax printers in the United Kingdom.

From 1905, designers worked in company studios situated at the main office of the CPA in Manchester. They typically worked based on suggestions or sketches from agents in Africa or from cuttings or images supplied by customers. Existing designs from earlier collections with proven success

The rise of Brown Fleming's competitors in wax printing

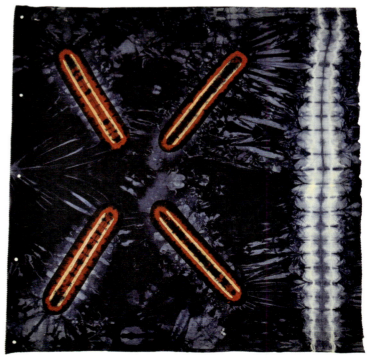

6. Newton Bank, design printed with machine and hand-block, 1911
Brunnschweiler Archive, held at the Whitworth Art Gallery, University of Manchester (UK)

7. Newton Bank design printed with hand-block, 1909
Brunnschweiler Archive, held at the Whitworth Art Gallery, University of Manchester (UK)

8. Newton Bank design, created with hand tye-dye and block print, 1908
Brunnschweiler Archive, held at the Whitworth Art Gallery, University of Manchester (UK)

were re-worked and, to a lesser extent, designs were acquired from commercial studios. The studio also made use of published design and natural history reference material.

F. W. Grafton and Co. at Broad Oak Print Works

F. W. Grafton and Company at *Broad Oak Works* in Accrington was the largest calico print works in that town. The company was among the first to successfully produce wax prints in England. Founded as a bleachworks in 1782, Broad Oak began printing in 1792. In 1812 the company was taken over by Thomas Hargreaves, a former manager, and Adam Dugdale.[125] When Dugdale retired in 1836, the firm became Hargreaves, Brothers & Co., carrying on until the death of Robert Hargreaves in 1854. In 1855, Frederick William Grafton (1817-1890) leased the works in partnership with his brother John Grafton and the colourist Thomas Lightfoot.[126] In 1880, Grafton was able to purchase the works. About 1,000 people were employed at that time. In 1899 the company became part of the Calico Printers' Association with Grafton as the first chairman. Grafton and Co. was renamed Broad Oak Print Works in 1923.

The works expanded substantially after 1816 when steam power was introduced. One of their specialities was Turkey red discharge, introduced by Frederick Steiner (1787-1869), who joined the company in 1817 as a colourist, arriving from Ribeauvillé in Alsace. He only stayed for two years before going to James Thomson at Primrose Works in Clitheroe. Afterwards he formed a partnership with James Haworth and Joseph Barnes as manufacturing chemists, working on further improvements in dyeing techniques. In 1836, he began his own printing firm at Church Bank near Accrington.[127] When Steiner left Broad Oak, he chose John Emmanuel Lightfoot (1802-1893) as his successor. Lightfoot was helped by John Hargreaves, son of the director, who had studied chemistry. Lightfoot was first of a family of colourists at the works, in succession Thomas Lightfoot (1811-1866), John Lightfoot (1832-1872) and Thomas E. Lightfoot; the latter was directly involved with the development of wax printing at the works.[128]

In 1902, the company began experiments applying wax resin by hand block on two sides of the cloth. Soft wax was used to obtain clear, clean white surfaces, brittle wax for a crackle effect. Although technical progress was made in the first years, production capacity was limited because all the colours applied to the basic indigo design were blocked by hand. In 1907 Carlos Casanovas, a colourist who had worked for the Leidsche Katoen Maatschappij in Leiden from 1889 to 1898, joined the company.[129] He had finished his studies at the *École municipale de chimie industrielle* in Mulhouse in 1879, as had Felix Driessen, director of the LKM, who finished in 1875. Casanovas came to Broad Oak to help with batik printing and although he had not been active for the last twelve years, he was able to give useful advice.[130] The earliest surviving engraving records for duplex wax printing at Broad Oak are from November 1909. Large samples have not been kept, but the titles of designs in the engraving book suggest some originality; a greater number that may be based on Brown Fleming models.[131] In 1918, Broad Oak employed 115 hand blockers of whom 90 were engaged for wax prints.[132] In the same year the last Lightfoot retired and George Walker became a colourist from 1918 until 1967. Apart from personal knowledge, he was able to draw information from the Lightfoot manuscripts.

Switzerland

Swiss manufacturers had largely ceased production of imitation batiks and wax prints in the 1870s. Some companies, such as *Blumer & Cie* and *Trümpy, Schäppi & Cie* in Mitlödi, still exported imitation batiks to South East Asia, but sales volumes were low. Hösli and Leuzinger in Hohlenstein started around 1878[133] with a limited production of wax prints, but developed in 1881 a simpler and cheaper method with very satisfactory results, especially beautiful imitations of Prévinaire wax prints.[134] Around 1890 the batik imitation printing for export to Asia had more or less ceased.

9. ABC design as square cloth 90x90cm Daniel Jenny & Cie Ennenda, Switzerland, copperplate print 1905
Print Pattern Collection of Adolf Jenny-Trümpy DMS XV Koll. J (1905), Private archive R. D. Jenny

Export of batik imitatons to West Africa might have started as early as the beginning of the 1860s by the BMTC. Initially they only exported Manchester cloth to the region, but started around 1860 to export Swiss cotton products. Not only printed cloth but also other types of cloth were exported, such as Indian-style Madras checks by Fröhlich, Brunnschweiler & Cie in Ennenda from 1872 onwards.[135] Initially it was difficult to find out which styles the local clientele appreciated and even in the 1870s sales were at very low volumes.[136] It would take until 1900 before a satisfactory level of exports was attained.

This might be the reason that Ernst Segemann, a German agent in Bremen, approached Daniel Jenny & Cie in Ennenda in 1903 to start the production of textiles for West Africa in close collaboration with his clients. For Gerard Howe not only imitation batik was printed, but also series of *native* prints developed, based on popular designs of Brown Fleming like the ABC motif and a motif with musical bars with notes. Howe wanted prints that were identical on both sides, most probably in an attempt to imitate a real wax print, but Daniel Jenny explains in his correspondence that with his roller printing technique the details will only be perfect on one side of the cloth. The samples were printed on a stiff, but also a smoother quality of cloth.[137] Finding designs and the quality of cloth that pleased traders for their West African clientele proved to be difficult and time consuming. The orders were too small to be commercially viable, so the company decided to cease the printing of batik imitations in 1906.

At the start of the First World War the BMTC was forced by the United Kingdom to halt all trading. In 1918, the Colonial Office went even further and ordered the expulsion of the Basel missionaries and the seizure of all BMTC properties on the Gold Coast. The British had become less willing to accept trusteeships and became increasingly reluctant to tolerate non-British activities on the Gold Coast. The Commonwealth Trust Ltd was formed to manage the resources of the Basel Mission and the BMTC with the promise to provide some of its profits to philanthropic activities for the native population. This turned out to be an empty promise because of financial difficulties encountered.[138] In 1919, the British government still refused the BMTC permission to resume trading on the West Coast of Africa. When Ankersmit started selling to Swanzy in 1919 the BMTC was left without a provider of wax prints. Attempts to obtain wax prints for trade via the UAC were unsuccessful.[139]

Conclusion

In the decade leading up to the start of the First World War, the HKM was still the leading force in the development of semi-mechanised wax printed cottons, not only in technical matters but also in design. Combined with Brown Fleming's powerful merchanting force it was able to keep its monopoly, but this was about to change. A handful of rivals did emerge: in the Netherlands Ankersmit, aided by the ambitions of the BMTC to shed its dependence on Brown Fleming and Van Vlissingen, had developed comparable products. In the Lancashire region of the United Kingdom, F. W. Ashton and F. W. Grafton had begun commercial production of duplex wax prints by 1909. The beginnings of wax print at both firms trace a lineage involving Dutch colourists with technical knowledge deriving from the HKM. Swiss companies had capabilities and knowledge of production, but wax printing for West Africa was not yet seen as a potentially lucrative business. All the players in the market were still closely following the quality of print and cloth of the HKM and the design lead of Brown Fleming for the West African market.

1 Letter Alfred Opferkuch, General agent of Basel Mission Trading Company, Accra, to Head Office, Basel, 27 December 1912. Basel Mission Archives, 4412 UTC: West Afrika, General agent 1912-1914.
2 J. B. Fothergill and E. Knecht, *The Principles and Practice of Textile Printing*, London, 1912, 491-492. Earlier mentions, like Joseph Depierre who describes already in 1879 the original but also successful imitation batik in the Netherlands and Switzerland, were rare. See Joseph Dépierre's 'Notes sur la fabrication des battiks' in : The Bulletin de la Société Industrielle de Rouen (v.4, juillet 1879, 260-265 and his notes *Sur les industries de l'impression et de la teinture à l'Exposition universelle de 1878*, 1880, 69-73
3 W. Elbers, *Die Bedienung der Arbeitsmaschinen sur Herstellung bedruckter Baumwollstoffe*, Vieweg, 1909, 96.
4 Knecht and Fothergill, 491-492
5 Verbong 1988, 225
6 Krantz 1985, 9
7 Sykas 2005, 29
8 *History of wax printing in the UK for the West African market*, unpublished document 1 August 1977 Brunnschweiler Archive, held at the Whitworth Art Gallery, University of Manchester (UK).
9 Sykas, 2005, 28
10 Heinrich Blumer founded with Johann Heinrich Tschudi the company Blumer & Tschudi in Glarus. The two sons of Blumer, Heinrich Leuzinger and Rudolf Hösly took over the company. When the Blumer brothers left the company in 1872 it was called Hösley & Leuzinger. Wanner 1968, 73
11 Jenny-Trümpy, 648-549
12 Nabholz-Karaschoff, 207
13 Touaregs were especially keen on this fabric for the care that had been taken to dye the cloth so that the deep surface layer of indigo would rub off on the wearer, which gave the desired copper sheen to the skin. Pedler, 243
14 Ankersmit 2009, 57
15 Gerrit Jan Meeles started working for Ankersmit when he was 15 years old in 1905 and retired in 1957. After his retirement the company asked him to write a detailed document about the beginning of wax printing at Ankersmit. The original study is in the Vlisco Archive. A published version with a limited number of copies was released as *Wasdruk: de door G. J. Meeles geschreven geschiedenis van het wasdrukartikel van Ankersmit's textielfabrieken N.V*, Helmond: Gamma Holding, 1972.
16 A first try was unsatisfactory and the HKM suggested sending one of their dyers to advise. Initially rejected by Ankersmit, after several attempts the offer was finally accepted and results became satisfactory for the HKM.
17 Verbong 1988, 229
18 The strike began on 21 September 1908, with about 150,000 operatives locked out and 140 mills closed; it ended on 7 November 1908. Notes attached to letter of A. Ankersmit to T. Booth Esq. of the United Africa Company Ltd in London, Deventer 22 February 1996. Ankersmit holdings in the Vlisco Archive.
19 He wrote this letter to Driessen, Director of the LKM, because he feared that this misunderstanding would lead Van de Poll of the HKM to refuse to buy Ankersmit's machinery after the closure of the company. Letter H. J. Ankersmit to Felix Driessen, Leidsche Katoen Maatschappij in Leiden, dated 24 July 1918, in Meeles I, 10.
20 Meeles I, 18-19
21 Meeles I, 23
22 In a letter from Werner to M. Binhammer of 21 May 1908 he stipulates that certain prints from Brown Fleming will be only available by the end of 1909 or even at the beginning of 1910. See 4005 UTC: M. Binhammer Korrespondenz 1907-08 in Basel Mission Archives. See also letter 5 October 1910 from BMTC to Werner about frustration of lack in stock in 4263 UTC: Ausgewählte Korr. Basel – Werner London 1905-1909 in Basel Mission Archives.
23 Report from Mr Opferkuch head of BMTC Accra 27 December 1912 in UTC 4412: West Afrika Generalagent 1912-1914 in Basel Mission Archives.
24 See M. Binhammer to I. Werner 5 October 1910 in 4267 UTC: Ausgewählte Korrespondenz Zusammenfassung – I. P. Werner London 1874-1914 in Basel Mission Archives.
25 See letter of 19 May 1911 in 4263 UTC: Ausgewählte Korr. Basel – Werner London 1905-1909 in Basel Mission Archives.

26 Letter from Brown Fleming, Glasgow 29 September 1910, in 4267 UTC: Ausgewählte Korrespondenz Zusammenfassung – I. P. Werner London 1874-1914 in Basel Mission Archives. Demand for cotton from Lancashire and the US, especially Massachusetts, in this period was huge. Leaders of industry were not always willing to pursue increased efficiency through new inventions and novel processes if these resulted in delivery problems. They were not flexible enough to adapt in a rapidly changing economic reality. Higher prices were also caused by the provision of better working conditions, the reduction of the number of working hours on a weekly basis and, of course, higher wages. For more information, see Lars Sandberg. *Lancashire in Decline. A Study in Entrepreneurship, Technology and International Trade*, Ohio State University Press 1974.
27 Report BMTC, Akuse, 25 May 1914 in UTC: Westafrika Generalafgent 1912-1914 in Basel Mission Archives.
28 https://www.stsa.swiss/know/basler-mission-handlungs-gesellschaft-utc-international, last accessed 16 February 2022.
29 Meeles I, 95
30 Letter Alfred Opferkuch, General agent of Basel Missionary Trading Company, Accra to head office in Basel 27 December 1912 in UTC 4412: West Afrika Generalagent 1912-1914 in Basel Mission Archives.
31 Report from BMTC Accra 27 December 1912 in UTC 4412: West Afrika Generalagent 1912-1914 in Basel Mission Archives.
32 Meeles I, 95
33 For more information about William Ewart Clucas, see http://www.davenportstation.org.uk/reinbek.html, last accessed 7 May 2022.
34 Meeles I, 21
35 Meeles I, 59-60
36 A detailed description of the various printing issues are described in Meeles, part I, chapter 9: 'Problemen met de drukwalsen' (Problems with rollers), 64-72; and chapter 10: 'Problemen met de drukplaat' (Problems with the printing plates), 73-80.
37 For a detailed description, inventory and financial report of the extension of Ankersmit 1910-1912, see Meeles I, 40-49.
38 For a detailed description of the procedure, see Gerhard Frensel, 'Real Dutch Wax Block Print', Milsbeek (The Netherlands) 1980, unpublished document, 141. This technique was also used in later years, but just to create the effect of being hand made.
39 Janszen and De Visser, 43
40 Letter Anton Ankersmit to T. Booth, United Africa Company, London 22 February 1966, Vlisco Archive.
41 For more information about colourists and particulary the family of Jean Jacques see Appendix.
42 Verschueren, 56
43 Meeles I, 51-52
44 Disch was born in 1851, so already 67 years of age on his arrival. He died in 1934. Meeles I, 54-55
45 For more information about W. Kuit, see Mienke Simon Thomas, 'KVT' in *Industrie en Vormgeving 1850-1950*, Amsterdam 1985, 94-97; and Titus M. Eliëns, *Frans Leidelmeijer and Marjan Groot. Kunstnijverheid in Nederland 1880-1940*, Bussum 1996, 224-225.
46 For more information, see Korteling, H. D. 'De vroegere avondtekenschool te Deventer' in G. J. Lugard Jr. (ed.), *Overijssel: Jaarboek voor cultuur en historie,* Zwolle 1955, 96-105.
47 For more information, see the appendix 'Origins of the Teekenschool in the Netherlands in the nineteenth century'.
48 Herweijer and De Visser, 146
49 H. D. Korteling, 'De vroegere avondtekenschool te Deventer' in G. J. Lugard Jr. (ed.), *Overijssel: Jaarboek voor cultuur en historie,* Zwolle 1955, 96-105; and https://www.canonvannederland.nl/nl/overijssel/salland/deventer/teeken-academie-school, last accessed 17 March 2022. For more information about the Bokhorst family, see Roel Smit-Muller, *De familie Bokhorst. Verrassend veelzijdig*, Zwolle: Waanders 2014; and an extra document complementing this publication: https://docplayer.nl/68549025-Bijlage-fouten-en-verbeteringen-m-b-t-waanders-publicatie-48.html, last accessed 7 March 2022. See also http://deventer-bokhorstkunst.nl/pages/home/
50 He would work for Ankersmit until his death on 5 April 1940. Meeles I, 59-60
51 Design descriptions start with the first design number 5000 (1911) until design number 44555 (1948). The document is part of the

Ankersmit holdings, kept at the Vlisco Archive, @ Vlisco BV.

52   Meeles I, 59-60. The twelve designs were numbered 500-5275. Nos 500, 5025, 5075, 5100, 5150 and 5175 were based on classics from the Brown Fleming collection. Numbers 5050, 5125, 5200, 5225, 5250 and 5275 were new designs. Meeles I, 61. The Ankersmit holdings, kept at the Vlisco Archive, contain a register with all design numbers and the year they entered the collection from 1911/1912 (no. 5000) until 1964 (no 72950).

53   For a detailed report of this trip, see Meeles I, 88-89.

54   Meeles I, 92-94

55   Letter dated 6 December 1912 from BMTC, Accra, p. 16 in 4412 UTC West-Afrika Generalagent Korrespondenzen in Basel Mission Archives. Meeles indicates that local clients appreciated a clear brand name on the cloth. Meeles I, 90

56   Meeles I, 90

57   Meeles I, 90-92. He also gives a lengthy explanation about the numbering of the various designs.

58   Verbong 1988, 231

59   Meeles I, 57 and 98

60   Meeles mentions the Compagnie Générale de l'Afrique Française, based in Bordeaux, selling on the Ivory Coast; Bödecker, Meyer of Hamburg selling in Togo; Victor and Lohmann of Bremen selling in Dahomey (nowadays South Benin); and I. P. Werner and Co of Manchester, representing the BMTC in the English colonies except the Gold Coast. Meeles I, 96. He also gives a summary of the sales per design, per merchant and quantities for various destinations.

61   Meeles I, 81

62   Meeles I, 98-102

63   Meeles I, 103

64   The numbers of copies of the designs of the Brown Fleming collection: 5325,5500 and 5550, based on instructions of the BMTC: 5300, 5350, 5375, 5475, 5525 and 5575 and the three by Ankersmit designers: 5400, 5425 and 5450. Meeles I, 62

65   Report of BMTC, Akuse, 25 May 1914 from UTC: Westafrika Generalagent 1912-1914 in Basel Mission Archives.

66   Examples of early Grafton designs that are probably imitations of popular Brown Fleming designs: D389 *Sunrise* designed by Davidson and engraved 25 Nov 1909, D570 *Old Peacock* designed by Woolhouse & Cleveland and engraved 16 Dec 1909 and D1310 of July 1910 (reg.275500) is *Skin*. Personal communication Philip Sykas 12 October 2023.

67   Personal communication, Philip Sykas 17 March 2015. He suggests that at least one pattern with a hand and coins seems to relate to Brown Fleming design, 250495, registered on 1 March 1895. Another design, registered by Brown Fleming on 3 March 1895 with a diamond motif, seems related to a Welch design. There are five books from the Calico Printers' Association library with Thomas Welch book plates in the Brunnschweiler Archive.

68   Report of BMTC, Akuse, 25 May 1914 from UTC: Westafrika Generalagent 1912-1914 in Basel Mission Archives.

69   'Die neuesten Muster scheinen Grossen Anklang zu finden.' (The new samples seem a great success), see Letter from M. Binhammer to A. Opferkuch, Ravensburg, 6 May 1913 in 4412 UTC: Westafrika Generalagent 1912-1914 in Basel Mission Archives

70   Numbers 5600-5875 were added.

71   Meeles I, 120. From then on, about 15-20% of all designs would be printed on 48/50" cloth.

72   Figures from 1911 until 1917 show that Brown Fleming related designs sold on average five times as much as their own designs. 'Overzicht van de in de jaren 1911 tot en met 1918 bestelde dessins' (Overview of the designs ordered in the years 1911 to 1918) Vlisco Archive, @ Vlisco BV.

73   A limited partnership (LP) in the Netherlands is a business entity that requires at least one general partner and one or more limited partners. The general partner has unlimited financial liability. LPs are pass-through entities that have little or no reporting requirements.

74   The commanditaire vennootschap (limited partnership) became necessary to manage the inheritance of Pieter II between Pieter III and Jan Matthijsen, the son of Frederik Jacob Matthijsen. His father was a partner in the company since 1852. Bijlsma and Rodenburg, 19, 34-35.

75   Verschueren, 28-29

76   His father was Jan Willem Sutorius (1772-1834).

77   Verschueren, 96

78   Sutorius moved to Weesp (The Netherlands) where he started a dyeing and printing company. In 1854 he tried to start a limited company to dye and print, among other things, batiks, but he did not manage to find sufficient funds. Verbong 1988, 208

79   Verschueren 95-96

80   In 1857 contracts were signed with Anderson Folson & Co. in Batavia, P. Kervel & Co. in Soerabaya and Oliphant & Co. in Semarang. Bijlsma, 27-28 and Brommer 1993, 126

81   Verbong 1988, 209. For Van Vlissingen, this period lasted less than one year.

82   LKM book 19, page 917, Vlisco Archive, @ Vlisco BV.

83   For a detailed description of the various engravers during this period, see Verschueren, 67-68.

84   After Deutsch and Hayder no colourists from abroad were hired. Verbong 1986, 227

85   Jacobs and Maas, 26; 2009, 62

86   The other samples were for various regions in Indonesia: Batavia, Samarang, Macassar, Soerabaya and Padang. Louis Pierre Bienfait, Aanteekeningen gemaakt bij de Heeren P. F. van Vlissingen & Co. 1876. A photocopy of this report is in the Vlisco Archive. The original remains with members of the Van Vlissingen family. Bienfait made this report during an internship at Van Vlissingen & Co. in Helmond. In 1881, he married Julia, daughter of Pieter II.

87   Verschueren, 50

88   See letter Cees Krantz to V. Arnoldus-Schröder of the Volkenkundig Museum at the University of Groningen dated 18 May 1979, 3. The letter is kept at the Vlisco Archive.

89   Bijlsma and Rodenburg, 38. These Java Prints were originally batik imitations printed without wax, so without the imperfections of a normal wax print.

90   Fentener van Vlissingen, 1

91   Verschueren, 68

92   Jan Veth was not related to Bas Veth, mentioned in chapter IV, who was part of a family of shippers.

93   Simon Thomas 2008, 33 . For more information about Duco Crop, see Joosten, 422; Simon Thomas 2008, 31, 33-34, 53; Simon Thomas 2008/2, 31, 32, 53; and E. G. M. Zeeman-Rutten, 'De Cretonnes van Michel Duco Crop' in *Spiegel Historiael*, 8:9 (Sep 1973), 491-495. See also https://www.kunstbus.nl/design/michel+duco+crop.html, last accessed 30 October 2022.

94   Bijlsma, 36

95   Because of the complexity of the printing process the company made little profit. The production was ceased in 1912. Bijlsma and Rodenburg, 36; Jacobs and Maas, 26; Simon Thomas 2008, 33

96   In 2011 an exhibition of his work was organised by the Gemeentemuseum in Helmond: *Johan. Made by Vlisco. Stofontwerpen en tekeningen 1896-1954*. A catalogue was published: Ger Jacobs, Majelle Janssen, Hans van de Laarschot and Lia van Zalinge, Johan Jacobs (1881-1955). O*ntwerper, beeldend kunstenaar en opleider uit Helmond*, Helmond 2011.

97   Jacobs 11-12. For a detailed history of the school in Helmond, see Jacobs, 19-29.

98   Jacobs, 19

99   He remained active as an independent artist until his death in 1955.

100   Verschueren, 67

101   Internal Vlisco document about machine printing of hand printed items, 73. Vlisco Archive, @ Vlisco BV.

102   See appendix with list of designers, based on list in the Vlisco Archive, @ Vlisco BV.

103   Jacobs, 13-14

104   Jacobs and Maas, 53

105   Krantz 1990, 99

106   For more information about the Koloniaal Instituut in Amsterdam, see chapter 4.

107   Frans van Rood reported that both Van Vlissingen and Jacobs practically forced the designers to visit the museum. Personal information Frans van Rood, Helmond (The Netherlands) 31 January 2023.

108   W. I. van Beusekom was also director, replaced in 1930 by T(obie). P. K. Hoogenboom. Verschueren, 47

109   Both Charles Henri Jacques and his brother Jean Jacques junior

were trained by Jean Jacques's father, Jean Joseph Jacques, colourist at the HKM from 1835 until his death in 1905. His book of recipes is in the Brunnschweiler Archive, Whitworth Art Gallery. The recipe books of both Jean Jacques and Charles Henri Jacques are in the Vlisco Archive. For further information about the position of a colourist and the Jean Jacques family see the appendix on colourists.

[110] Verschueren 18, 56 and personal information Frans van Rood, Helmond (The Netherlands) 31 January 2023.

[111] The book, entitled S. W. lijmdruk. Kantoor A. P. M. is in the Vlisco archive.

[112] Personal communication: Joop Martens, 18 March 2024.

[113] The invoices mention, amongst others, ten bales of V.9 design, consisting of 519 pieces of wax block garments 36 inches wide, 500 pieces of 12 yards, and 19 pieces of 6 yards length. Kopie Factuurboek 16 October 1906 – 28 December 1914. no. 27. Vlisco Archive, @ Vlisco BV.

[114] This system was only abandoned in the 1980s. Meij, 18

[115] Verschueren, 19

[116] See also the appendices of these three companies for more detailed information.

[117] Verbong 1988, 237

[118] Verbong 1988, 226

[119] Graham states that the largest quantity done in one year in 1834 or 1835 was 106.000 pieces of madder plates printed. John Graham, Chemistry of Calico Printing 1790-1835 and History of Printworks in the Manchester District 1760-1846, 393-394 (https://www.flickr.com/photos/manchesterarchiveplus/8318501091/in/album-72157632369315534/lightbox/), last accessed 23 October 2023. Philip Sykas suggests 28 yards per piece as a rule of thumb, estimating 106.000 pieces at 2,968,000 yards or 2714 kilometres. Personal communication, 24 October 2023.

[120] For more information about the Calico Printers' Association, see the appendix.

[121] Unfortunately, there is no illustration to get an idea what this design might have looked like. *Newton Bank Printworks Hyde 1812-2007 and European Involvement in Batik Printing*. Undated and unpublished document Brunnschweiler Archive, held at the Whitworth Art Gallery, University of Manchester (UK), 5.

[122] 'History of wax printing in the UK for the West African market', unpublished document 1 August 1977 Brunnschweiler Archive, held at the Whitworth Art Gallery, University of Manchester (UK). Four boxes with many samples of these experiments with wax printing are kept at the Brunnschweiler Archive, held at the Whitworth Art Gallery, University of Manchester (UK). The first box from 1908 contains cloth with tie and dye and hand block. This type of cloth would later not be commercialised. A second box from 1909 contains all hand blocked cloth. The remaining two boxes are from 1911. The first box contains cloth partly machine printed, partly hand blocked. The second box is machine printed with a paste resist and the colours are hand blocked.

[123] Personal communication Philip Sykas, 24 October 2023.

[124] Personal communication Philip Sykas, 12 October 2023.

[125] https://www.heritagegateway.org.uk/Gateway/Results_Single.aspx?uid=1585141&resourceID=19191, last accessed 16 March 2023, and John Graham, Chemistry of Calico Printing 1790-1835 and History of Printworks in the Manchester District 1760-1846, 356 (https://www.flickr.com/photos/manchesterarchiveplus/8318501091/in/album-72157632369315534/lightbox/), last accessed 12 October 2023.

[126] https://eprints.oxfordarchaeology.com/4621/1/Hargreavespercent27%20Warehouse%20Archaeological%20Appraisal.pdf, last accessed 15 March 2023. See also: T. E. Lightfoot, *The History of Broad Oak*, 1926. Typescript ABC Archives

[127] Hargreaves, 31. Lightfoot, transcript, 1. See also https://amazingaccrington.co.uk/flippingbook/26-27/#zoom=z, last accessed 15 March 2023, and chapter 3.

[128] http://genealogy.bathgatehall.co.uk/JEL.pdf, last accessed 11 March 2023. His brother Thomas (1811-1866), Thomas' son John (1832-1872) and his grandson John would also work as colourists for the company. Thomas' son John started in 1846, the grandson would start in 1876. Lightfoot transcript. Memoranda books, notes, diaries, trial and recipe books, swatch books, pattern books and samples from 1818 to the beginning of the twentieth century of the three generations are kept as part of the Calico Printers' Association Archives at Manchester Libraries.

[129] Verbong 1988, 250 and 360

[130] Lightfoot, 62

[131] Among the first were D389 *Sunrise*, designed by Davidson and engraved 25 November 1909, D570 *Old Peacock*, designed by Woolhouse & Cleveland and engraved 16 December 1909 and D1310 of July 1910 (reg.275500) *Skin*. However, patterns like *Football* and *Little Horse*, engraved 2 November 1909, imply greater originality. Personal communication 23 October 2023 Philip Sykas.

[132] 'History of wax printing in the UK for the West African market', unpublished document 1 August 1977 Brunnschweiler Archive, held at the Whitworth Art Gallery, University of Manchester (UK)

[133] Ankersmit 2009, 67

[134] Verbong 1988, 225. This company would become in 1924 Hohlenstein AG.

[135] Hand woven cloth from Madras in India made its appearance in West Africa already in the seventeenth century but became popular in the nineteenth century, especially in Nigeria and Sierra Leone. In 1872 two Swiss families Fröhlich and Brunnschweiler started industrial weaving of this type of cloth in Ennenda-Glarus. A family member of Brunnschweiler was sent to Liverpool to set up a separate branch in 1874, which moved to Manchester in 1882. In 1924 it was established as a separate company under the name of A. Brunnschweiler and Co. See Laurens van der Laan 1983 and *Kreuz und Quer der Farben. Karo- und Streifenstoffe der Schweiz für Afrika, Indonesien und die Türkei*, Exhibition Catalogue Museum Bellerive Zürich (1997), Modemuseum im Münchner Stadtmuseum München (1998) and Museum des Landes Glarus, Näfels (Switzerland) (1999)

[136] Wanner 1959, 176

[137] Wanner-Jean Richard, 49-77

[138] In 1928, after a decade of protest of the Swiss government against the violation of the rights of a neutral nation the British returned the assets including £250,000 for compensation. See Gannon, 513-515.

[139] Nielsen 1974, 38

The process of wax printing

5.
A second wash removes any wax dust. The cloth is then fed through a machine to seal the wax and straighten the cloth.

Production and trade of wax prints during the First World War and the interwar period

Eagerness to enter the wax print market pioneered by Brown Fleming had resulted in successful endeavours by companies in the Netherlands, the United Kingdom, and Switzerland to produce an equivalent product. The market was buoyant, and its potential inspired other companies. The years of the First World War posed a great hindrance to textile production and trade, but shortages were also a stimulus to innovation. More serious were the consequences that reshaped trade relations in Europe profoundly, and resulted in a dominant position for the British.

The surviving players and new entrants in wax print production

The production in the Netherlands was dominated by Ankersmit and Van Vlissingen. The three other companies, the LKM, the KKM and Roessingh did not survive the period. The production of the LKM stagnated after wartime due to a continuing lack of supplies. From 1926 to 1929 the company made a short recovery, including in exports to West Africa, but production stopped in 1934. It could not compete with foreign mechanised production while paying the higher salaries that handprinted cottons entailed. Sluggishness in their main export markets, Indonesia and Africa, made the company's position untenable, and in 1936, a hundred years after it opened its doors, the LKM went into liquidation.[1]

After the war, exports from the KKM to Africa restarted slowly. These included small quantities of wax prints,[2] but in 1920 production was still centred on batik styles for Dutch and English colonies in South East Asia. It never managed to become a serious competitor in the West African trade. The company could not survive the economic downturn of the Great Depression and the economic crises of the 1930s, and was forced to close in 1932.[3]

Roessingh did well into the 1920s but experienced a sharp downturn of sales when exports to West Africa slumped around 1930; its profits were curtailed and operations ceased in 1935.[4] The three companies shared the ability to prosper in a thriving market, but their wax prints could not match the value of those marketed by Brown Fleming, and in a time of recession closure was inevitable. On the other hand, Ankersmit and Van Vlissingen had developed a better-quality print that held its place in the West African market.

About a dozen wax printers were active in the United Kingdom, but Broad Oak (F. W. Grafton) and Newton Bank Printworks (F. W. Ashton), along with United Turkey Red (UTR) near Glasgow were the major innovators in the field, as well as the most long-lasting.[5] UTR was a relatively late bloomer when it started wax printing in the early 1920s with the help of the Dutch colourist Jean Jacques. Production was initially low, but took off in the mid-1930s, possibly linked to the company abandoning Turkey red dyeing altogether in 1936.

At the end of 1933, the Calico Printers' Association (CPA) took the decision to transfer wax printing from Broad Oak to Newton Bank. This gave Newton Bank a leading position among wax printers in the United Kingdom. This position was reinforced in 1941 by the closure of Rhodes Print Works, and the transfer of its batik styles to Newton Bank. The CPA was able to establish control and strongly influence policy in this specialist market with much closer monitoring of materials, production and expertise on one site.

In Switzerland most of the companies had closed by the beginning of the twentieth century.[6] Wax printing resumed after the First World War, this time no longer for the Indonesian market but for export to West Africa. In 1924, the BMTC acquired the *AG Baumwolldruckerei Hohlenstein* in Ennenda-Glarus. Four years later the company was able to produce marketable prints for West Africa.[7] In 1974 it was the last Swiss imitation batik printing factory to close its doors.[8]

The Netherlands

Deventer Katoen Maatschappij, formerly Ankersmit & Co.
The start of the First World War on 28 July 1914, began a challenging period for Ankersmit exacerbated by the company's export focus largely dependent on a single client, the BMTC.[9] Soon after the war commenced, the BMTC, although a Swiss organisation, was considered by the British government too *German* and its trade with British colonies in West Africa was forbidden. In 1915, when the Board of Trade realised that exports from neutral countries such as the Netherlands were increasing, they extended trade controls. With their own freedom of trade restricted, British firms wanted to ensure that the activity of their competitors in neutral countries was also limited.[10] With the trade of the BMTC halted, stock built up in the Netherlands and in Africa, but the BMTC wanted Ankersmit to retain it for post-war trade.[11] The production

of wax prints was reduced to a third, while prices were going down. Ankersmit approached Swanzy, knowing that they were one of the most important firms handling wax prints on the Gold Coast.[12] They already managed the recently established trade of Van Vlissingen in West Africa.[13] By representing Ankersmit as well, Swanzy obtained a dominant position in the sale of wax prints to West Africa.

Swanzy was willing to sell the stock initially prepared for the BMTC, and to place new orders. It acquired the exclusive right to market Ankersmit for the whole of West Africa, with the exception of Ivory Coast and Portuguese Guinea, for five years.[14] This meant that Ankersmit could resume usual production, especially because initial demand was substantial. Although wartime sales stagnated, and exports ceased in 1920, they resumed in the second half of 1921, which meant that Ankersmit production returned quickly to normal.

At the end of the war, the company had a portfolio of about sixty-four designs carrying its own signature style, even though many designs drew heavily on Brown Fleming models, which enjoyed continuous demand. The next year no new designs were added, but in the period 1919-1922, the collection grew by an average of twelve new designs per year. All but six were printed on 36-inch cloth, the others on 48-inch. Fourteen were based on instructions from Swanzy's Manchester office, the others from in-house designers.[15] Again, those *copied* from or *inspired* by Brown Fleming designs proved a reliable source of profit.[16] In 1923, nine designs were added, bringing the total to 120, with about twenty colourways available. A colour card of twenty shades facilitated ordering.[17] The new patterns were successful and in 1924 another sixteen designs were added, alongside five new shades.[18]

In 1930, Ankersmit invited Reyer Stolk, an artist and teacher at the *Instituut voor Kunstnijverheidsonderwijs* (Arts and Crafts Education Institute) in Amsterdam since 1926, to create designs for wax prints. It is not known how Stolk came to the attention of the company. He was born in Java in 1896, of a Javanese mother and Dutch father, and came to the Netherlands as a boy, where he received training from the batik artist Chris Lebeau, among others. In the 1920s he began to design batiks himself, which he signed as *Reyer Stolk Soegina*. He was also active as a decorative artist and graphic designer.[19] With one of the directors, Anton Ankersmit, Stolk undertook a two-month trip to Nigeria and the Gold Coast to obtain a better understanding of the market.[20] He recorded his impressions of this trip in masks, etchings, drawings, textile designs and a textile book.[21]

Stolk's first design, no. 21450, produced in 1930, was to make him familiar with the specific possibilities of wax printing. In the years 1931 to 1935, Ankersmit added sixty-four Stolk designs to make a total of just over two hundred designs.[22] The company took a risk in allowing an artist unfamiliar with wax print techniques to contribute so many designs. However, the designs testify to the significant effort Stolk made to become familiar with the visual language of wax prints, but most of them were too graphic and stylised to fit into the Ankersmit house style.[23] It is not known if they were commercially as successful as the established styles of wax prints.

In the early 1930s, against the backdrop of the worldwide economic crisis, sales in Africa slowed significantly, and the UAC tried to use its dominant position to force not only Ankersmit but also Van Vlissingen to lower their prices. Competition with much cheaper, but lesser quality prints from Manchester was fierce. A proposal from A. T. MacLaren, a manager of the UAC, to set up a separate business to profit from the high status of the products of both Dutch companies, showed that the UAC realised how much there was at stake. But it also made the companies aware of their unique position at the top of the market. The Dutch companies decided to collaborate instead of compete with each other and forced the UAC to continue to do business on existing terms.[24]

In 1932, the two Dutch firms gave the UAC monopoly over sales of all wax prints they produced.[25] In return the UAC would share orders for wax prints between the companies, and if placing orders with others, seek their approval.[26] But the economic situation deteriorated and sales languished. In 1934, in consultation with the UAC, Ankersmit decided to experiment with machine-printed imitation wax prints. They were recognisable through the image of a cockrell printed on the selvedge, but were not the success the company had hoped for.[27] Similar initiatives in later years continued to seek lower-cost alternatives.[28] The number of Ankersmit designs had been growing steadily and by 1937, 324 designs in 36-inch and 111 in 48-inch were available. The UAC had a strong influence on design choice.[29] The decade ended with a new competitor: cheaper prints began to come from Japan, which had added Africa to its export horizons.[30]

Van Vlissingen

After the First World War Van Vlissingen decided to throw itself *als een leeuw in de strijd* (as a lion into battle) despite the difficult post-war circumstances and uncertain prospects.[31] In July 1919, the English had re-opened their colonial markets in West Africa.[32] Sales of batik imitations in South East Asia, especially Indonesia, had gone downhill after a good start; the Indonesians had started using a new type of printing blocks that made production much cheaper.[33] The German dye manufacturer IG Farben had sent chemists to Indonesia to teach the use of synthetic dyes. However, protectionist measures of the Indonesian government were impacting the profitability of the market for Europeans.[34] In East and West Africa, so-called *Java Prints*, hand printed articles with traditional batik designs, were sought after but returned little profit because the hand work increased production costs. Most promising were the duplex machine wax prints. Swanzy had faith in growth of their sales and insisted on doubling production. Its managers in West Africa advised on designs and colours to improve their style features.[35] Articles made with the new printing technique – *lijmdruk* – were successful in West Africa. Haijkens would become a major seller of these products. He had been selling these *Java Prints* since 1905 and started selling wax prints in 1925; from 1928 onwards, he would be guaranteed his own collection of designs, exclusively printed for his business.[36] In 1929 Van Vlissingen employed fourteen designers.[37]

From 1920 until 1927 Van Vlissingen's position on the Gold Coast was getting stronger with Swanzy their biggest client, but competitors later advanced their positions.[38] Ankersmit was market leader for the rest of the West African market. The quality of Ankersmit was then superior to Van Vlissingen, and Ankersmit had a better knowledge of local markets, having experience on the ground in Africa since 1912.

It was only in 1932 that a Van Vlissingen employee, its commercial director Tobie Hoogenboom, paid a visit to the Gold Coast.[39] Van Vlissingen had seen its role more as a producer, serving their client merchants, but had so far not been investigating opportunities to market for themselves.[40] The stimulus for Hoogenboom's visit was the UAC's move to forcibly lower the prices of Ankersmit and Van Vlissingen in the competitive market.[41]

As stated earlier, the attempt of a UAC manager to set up a separate business for top-end producers made the companies realise their strength lay in collaboration, and forcing the UAC to more favourable terms. With some exceptions the UAC obtained exclusive rights to sell their wax prints, but had to promise to buy only from Ankersmit and Van Vlissingen.[42]

Hoogenboom's visit was important for the company because fierce Japanese competition had made export to Indonesia impossible. To increase their export to West Africa the company needed a better understanding of the market, the importance of which had so far not been appreciated. He discussed samples with West African customers of the two largest buyers UAC and G. B. Ollivant.[43]

The trade with Ollivant was organised via Haijkens.[44] Hoogenboom found out that in Kumasi, a major town in Ghana, Ankersmit fabrics sold well and Van Vlissingen's almost nil. The local market did not like the *dull and gloomy* colours of Van Vlissingen although the designs were acceptable.[45] Hoogenboom's trip resulted in a new commercial policy with increased activity and profits, in parallel with quality improvements to rival the Ankersmit cloth.[46] To improve profits on the *Java Prints*, designs on the rollers were no longer hand-engraved but applied by photography and etching, which were less costly. This made these prints a successful addition to the wax prints on the African market.[47]

Visits from Africa to Helmond slowly started as well. Before the Second World War it was only Antonio Nogueira, merchant for Congo for Haijkens, who travelled to Helmond on a regular basis.[48] After the war the UAC started sending company representatives in Africa to Helmond to place their orders. But when Van Vlissingen's sales representatives visited the African market, they were always accompanied by a representative of the UAC to avoid direct contact.[49]

Jan Fentener van Vlissingen, responsible for the export markets since 1927, embarked on his first visit to Africa in January 1934. His aim was to gain an insight into the creation of new designs instead of rearranging the designs of others.[50] During his trip he wrote reports in the form of letters to Hoogenboom, which provide a window into his thoughts and experiences.[51] He had prepared himself with knowledge of his competitors such as the Dutch companies Ankersmit and LKM, the British CPA and Hohlenstein in Switzerland, aiming for a distinctive positioning of his firm.[52]

It was also useful to observe their largest clients, the UAC and Ollivant (via Haijkens), operating on the market, and to present his company samples to market women, the *mammy* traders. He saw that relatively expensive good-quality cloth and print was selling well in spite of the economic turndown.[53] Jan understood that certain ethnic groups had a preference for Dutch products with particular designs and colours.[54] He was impressed by the beauty of the wax print colours under the African sun, and realised that prints with individual character, improved over the years, would become classics that would hold a lasting place in the market.[55]

His visit changed the way of operating in Helmond profoundly. From then on, the company became more market oriented. Strict planning was introduced based on production capacity. Exports represented 85 per cent of sales, focused on the West African trade, while the domestic market represented the remaining 15 per cent.[56] Hoogenboom and Jan Fentener van Vlissingen took personal responsibility for choice of new designs. In 1936 the studio was split between the home market and export. About 90 per cent of designs were commission-based, with only 10 per cent in-house creations.[57]

During his visit Jan also became aware of the drawbacks of being a market leader. Many of the most popular designs were copied by competitors:

Production and trade of wax prints during the First World War and the interwar period

Iedereen copieert nu maar naar hartelust en het is werkelijk kinderachting on aan te hooren hoe ze allen elkaar de schuld geven (Everyone is now copying to their heart's content and it's really childish to hear them all blaming each other).

He was particularly irritated by 'the Syrians, who live like hyenas on bargains', especially a certain Zacca.[58] Even the UAC and Ollivant were selling copies without being informed by their Manchester office which designs were officially registered.[59] To counter this, but also to cope with the economic downturn of the early 1930s, production was pushed to a maximum with the introduction of *fancy prints*, a relatively cheap product, and *imiwax*, a cheap imitation of the real wax prints. New ways of mechanisation were introduced to reduce production costs. For machine-printed wax prints, only extra colours were hand fitted. A laboratory was installed for the colourist Jan Lotichius to research colourants and printing processes. The transition from hand- to machine-printed cloth entailed changes in dye proportions and additives used, requiring technical formulation.

During Jan Fentener van Vlissingen's visit to the Gold Coast, Anton Ankersmit was also on a business trip and the two met. Both men returned home on the same steamship. Each had collected market samples to bring home and, to their mutual amusement, it turned out that Ankersmit had a suitcase full of samples from Van Vlissingen and Jan likewise had samples from Ankersmit.[60]

In Helmond the position of the employees of the studio was comparable to before the First World War. The designers were encouraged to create more *African* designs, but based strictly on instructions and comments from Jan. Personal interpretations were not allowed. To create designs to please African clients, they had to be familiar with the differing tastes in the market regions of Africa and the specific engraving and technical possibilities of the company. For Jan, a design had to be unique, well drawn and executed in fresh colours. Variations and a regular change of patterns were necessary to maintain market interest. He was critical of the quality of new engravings, and it was not unknown for rollers to be re-engraved if they were not to his liking.[61]

The number of designs increased and they were no longer based mainly on the instructions of clients, but increasingly originated in-house. Photobooks with these designs were sent to major clients in West Africa for feedback. Changes came at a price, but production increased despite the difficult economic climate. From 1936 onwards the company made a profit while other companies were struggling or had to cease operations. And although the Dutch home market was significant, the West African market had grown comparatively in importance.[62]

During the 1930s, Ankersmit still held the largest market share, with production of wax prints twice as great as Van Vlissingen. Van Vlissingen had the disadvantage that the UAC provided the printing cloth, which reduced their ability to control the final quality.[63] It also resulted in less focus due to their attention on a wider variety of products for export.

Efforts to improve the quality of wax prints were ongoing at Van Vlissingen. The firm recruited the head of the technical department of the HKM after its closure in 1918, also acquiring a printing machine to which changes were made to improve the fitting. Cracking of the cloth to get the desired *craquelure* effect was no longer done by hand – a very laborious task – but by a rotating washing machine. Lotichius, an engineer responsible for research and technical development from 1928, managed to obtain better control of production of several colours, while the colourist G. H. Rodenburg developed improved bleeding of indigo for a softer effect.[64] Tobie Hoogenboom, who had pushed Van Vlissingen in a more commercial direction, died in 1939. Brothers Pieter IV and Jan decided to continue together as directors, but the outbreak of the Second World War brought all exports to a halt.

United Kingdom
F. W. Ashton and Co. of Newton Bank Print Works in Hyde
In Britain, the war did not stop textile production but caused shortages of dyestuffs and loss of experienced personnel. Newton Bank retooled around 1920 with a new duplex wax printing machine that enabled up to 500 yards of fabric to be printed continuously, which sped up operations and

---

1. Jan Fentener van Vlissingen and Anton Ankersmit returning to the Netherlands after a business trip to Africa with samples from each other's company in their suitcases
Designer unknown, Collection Martin Frensel, Akkrum (The Netherlands)

lowered costs. Extra colours were still applied by hand-block printing. Sales were good until the slump of 1930-1931, which left the company with a significant amount of cloth in stock, which eventually was bought by the merchant H. J. Barrett. Both Newton Bank and Broad Oak had to reduce production. The CPA decided to transfer all wax printing from Broad Oak to Newton Bank by the end of 1933 to concentrate the *dirty* indigo dyeing in one place.[65] Concurrently, Grafton African was formed as the main African merchanting branch of the CPA.

In 1933, Frank Crompton, a member of the family business B. F. Crompton in Manchester, developed a machine that allowed extra colours to be applied continuously via an engraved roller. Although the method was somewhat imprecise, the machine improved productivity immensely, but it could only be used for simple designs with others still requiring hand-block additions. Crompton sold the patent to Rhodes Print Works, also part of the CPA. Wax printed cloth from Newton Bank would be transferred to Rhodes for the *Crompton* fitting and back for fixing, wax removal and finishing.[66] The technique made larger volumes and more economical production possible and pushed the company to a dominant position among British wax printers. The so-called *Drop Ons*, another new technique, were introduced in 1935. Wax bubbles were retained on the cloth, and a colour was machine padded between the selvedges or applied by fitter rollers. There was no necessity to fit to the design, so it was a quick and cheap way to enhance the cloth.[67]

By 1935 Newton Bank Works had attained a leading position among the wax printers in the United Kingdom. Managed through the powerful CPA, it benefited from the conglomerate's influence over policy in a specialist market. A regulating committee was formed, known as the *Wax Ring*, including H. J. Barrett, Brown Fleming, Elson & Neill and Grafton African as members. Members would only sell to selected merchants, who functioned as warehousemen and carried large stocks for recognised shippers. This policy was aimed at improving sales by limiting production, fixing prices for certain styles and maintaining a common response to issues in the wax print trade. For twenty years the Wax Ring held formal meetings and continued afterwards on a more informal basis.[68] Brown Flemings' membership ended in 1939. The Gold Coast cocoa crisis of 1937-1938 meant a boycott of all British goods, and Brown Flemings was caught with a large stock and printing commitment. This forced Herbertson, at that time its director, to sell the company to Ashton.[69]

F. W. Grafton and Company at Broad Oak Works
After 1920, a major modernisation and reconstruction took place and new print shops were built in the early 1930s. During the Great Depression in the late 1920s the African print trade was the only thriving textile business. But a slump of sales in 1930-1931 affected Broad Oak, which had to curtail production. The CPA decided to transfer all wax printing from Broad Oak to Newton Bank.[70]

United Turkey Red
In the 1920s United Turkey Red (UTR) would become a new player in the field. The speciality of the company since 1785 was the Turkey red dyeing process, introduced by two Scottish entrepreneurs who brought the Rouennais practitioner Pierre Jacques Papillon to Glasgow.[71] Turkey red would develop into a large industry, focused primarily on the export market, with India a principal destination. Several of the Turkey red companies that flourished in the nineteenth century had roots going back to the eighteenth century.[72] Turkey red production required a higher percentage of skilled workers than ordinary calico printing, and designing for export markets entailed specialist knowledge. The Scottish industry had a few competitors in the Manchester area, and by the end of the nineteenth century Asian manufacturers had entered the market. To strengthen their market position, three prominent firms based in the Vale of Leven, William Stirling & Sons, John Orr Ewing & Co. and Archibald Orr Ewing & Co., merged in 1898 to create UTR. William Stirling & Sons had been first to settle in the area and by the mid-nineteenth century had the widest distribution with exports not only to India, but also to South East Asia, China and Japan.[73] John Orr Ewing & Co. was to become the largest Turkey red manufacturer in the Vale of Leven, known for high-quality design and technically sophisticated production.[74] Archibald Orr Ewing set up his business in 1845 after having trained under his brother John. He was as successful as his brother but invested his wealth beyond the Vale of Leven for his business and personal interests.[75]

UTR had its production base in the town of Alexandria, northwest of Glasgow, but commercial managers and sales agents were eventually based in offices at 10 Charlotte Street, Manchester, which separation often brought conflicts. Production was focused on dyeing yarn and weaving plain cloth rather than printing. Frederick Steiner of Accrington provided strong competition, and later the rise of cheap foreign production brought further rivalry. In the 1930s and 1940s, several sections of works were closed and in 1936, the Turkey red process was abandoned in favour of more efficient modern dyestuffs.[76]

Efforts were made to move away from Turkey red into calico printing and indigo dyeing. In 1919, the Board of Directors invited Jean Jacques, who had been colourist at Ankersmit from 1910 until 1915, to work for UTR. Jacques was most problably introduced by Haijkens, a Dutch merchant who sold products from the UTR and who had worked with British and Dutch companies selling wax prints for the West African market since 1905. Jean Jacques sold the details of a cheaper way of batik printing to the company, and from 1920 to 1922, he helped in setting up the printing process there.[77] UTR experimented with fitting colours by the flat copperplate press, but the cost of plates and engraving made this method uneconomical.[78] With Jean Jacques's help, UTR was able to produce marketable wax prints in a relatively short time. In 1927, the UTR obtained sole rights to the process along with Jean Jacques's process notebook: *Livre de Fabrication appartenant a Jean Jacques 18 décembre 1889.*[79]

Haijkens probably used his long experience in selling imitation batik to West Africa to advise on the necessary quality of the cloth and the choice of designs. He had the cloths shipped to Holland where they were labelled Dutch Block Garments before being exported, demonstrating the appreciation for wax print from the Netherlands in this period.[80] His reputation as merchant gained the confidence of the firm to grant him exclusive rights to sell their wax prints.[81]

Although by 1924 Haijkens had 58 wax and fancy print designs produced at UTR, in 1925 he started to buy from Van Vlissingen, probably because the early production of wax prints at UTR was too slow to meet his demands.[82] According to Verschueren, the sales of wax prints of UTR were unimpressive around 1930, although considered to have significant potential.[83] Documents in the Brunnschweiler archives show that only a small number of designs were engraved in the 1920s, increasing from 1935 until 1939 once Turkey red printing had stopped, in accordance with the need for a new commercial impetus.[84] The company was to become a serious player in the business, with the merchants Elson and Neill as their main client, and also serving John Holt and the UAC.[85]

2. Egyptian-style design inspired by Brown Fleming in the collection of Haijkens, probably produced by UTR around 1922
Sample book Haijkens 500 tot 3035, p. 5
Vlisco Archive, @ Vlisco BV

3. Handshake, inspired by Brown Fleming design from 1897 in the collection of Haijkens, probably produced by UTR around 1922
Sample book Haijkens 500 tot 3035, p. 9
Vlisco Archive, @ Vlisco BV

4. Design of a garden fork in the style of Brown Fleming in the collection of Haijkens, probably produced by UTR around 1922
Sample book Haijkens 500 tot 3035, p. 1
Vlisco Archive, @ Vlisco BV

Switzerland

In 1915, the BMTC was forced by the United Kingdom to halt all trading. In 1918, the Colonial Office went even further and ordered the expulsion of the Basel missionaries and the seizure of all BMTC properties on the Gold Coast. The British had become increasingly reluctant to tolerate non-British activities on the Gold Coast, even trusteeships. The Commonwealth Trust Ltd had been formed to manage the resources of the Basel Mission and the BMTC with the promise to provide some of its profits to philanthropic activities for the native population, although this was not fulfilled because financial difficulties were encountered.[86] In 1919, the British government still refused the BMTC permission to resume trading on the West Coast of Africa.

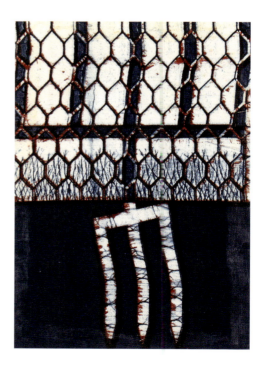

When Ankersmit started selling to Swanzy in 1919, the BMTC was left without a provider of wax prints.

Attempts to obtain wax prints for trade via the UAC were unsuccessful.[87] In 1921, the *Union Handels-Gesellschaft AG* (Union Trading Company Ltd, hereafter UTC) was founded with the intention of recommencing trade with West Africa, despite ongoing legal proceedings with the UK government to recover BMTC rights and property.[88] With a booming market for wax prints in West Africa marked by many new entrants from Europe, it was difficult to regain its market position.

In 1924, the UTC bought the AG *Baumwolldruckerei Hohlenstein, vormals R. Leuzinger* in Ennenda, Glarus (hereafter Hohlenstein) to work as their contract printer. Small dyeing companies had occupied the Ennenda site since the seventeenth century, with calico printing beginnning by the end of the eighteenth century. The year 1852 saw a merger with another Glarus firm, Blumer & Tschudi. In 1872 Rudolf Hösli and Heinrich Leuzinger became the new owners, continuing to improve the imitation batik printing in which their predecessors had specialised. The company stayed in Leuzinger hands until it was sold to the UTC.[89] The buildings needed modernisation and new machines were installed. Designs to be produced were ordered from the UAC.[90] In 1928, when the UTC, supplanting the former BMTC, was allowed to re-enter the Gold Coast, they were ready with marketable wax prints, *Swiss Real Wax*.[91] A report from the UTC General Agent's office in 1933 states that the company had produced about 30,000 pieces of wax print, mentioning six specific designs that were their best sellers and that represented a third of their total sales.[92] The BMTC had again become one of the leading trading houses on the Gold Coast, helping to extend the market for wax prints.

Trade of wax prints during the interwar period

The First World War had hindered the African trade, but it picked up quickly afterwards. With German interests and influences banned from import and export between Europe and West Africa, the trade was now dominated by the British. Some twenty companies were active, not only resulting in fierce competition, but also in relatively high overheads. In 1919, they associated as the African and Eastern Trade Corporation (AETC) with establishments in several African colonies. One of the most important members was Swanzy, established in 1789 and since 1850 trading as the brothers F. & A. Swanzy with a head office in London and agencies on the Gold Coast.[93] Swanzy's membership enhanced the competitiveness of the AETC. This model was followed by about twenty-five French trading companies operating in West Africa setting up the Compagnie du Niger Français (CNF).

On 3 March 1929, the AETC and the Royal Niger Company merged into the United Africa Company Limited (UAC) based in London.[94] The UAC got into financial difficulties in the early 1930s. It was saved by Unilever, a 1929 merger of Lever Brothers with the Dutch Magarine Union (*Margarine Unie*), and became a subsidiary of Unilever. Lever Brothers, the partnership of William Hesketh Lever and James Darcy Lever, had been effective owners of the Royal Niger Company from 1920 to 1929.[95] Swiss merchants, who thus far had their own export routes, began selling through the UAC in 1929.

The UAC would become in 1935 a large, complex and practically autonomous trading organisation in Africa with a quasi-governmental capacity having a strong influence on colonial rule.[96] It traded in the West African colonies of the British Empire, Gambia, Ghana, Nigeria and Sierra Leone. The UAC imported raw materials such as palm oil and timber, and exported finished goods such as textiles, building materials, refrigerators and cars. In their department stores across Ghana, Nigeria and Sierra Leone they sold British and other products. They organised the distribution of wax prints with their associate company G. B. Ollivant. Ollivant joined the UAC in 1933, but continued trading under its own name.[97]

Around 1935 only nine European printing companies remained active in wax print production. The Wall Street Crash of 1929, followed by the Great Depression, caused nearly a decade of economic hardship. Many textile printers ceased operation in the first five difficult years. The nine surviving printers were Ankersmit and Van Vlissingen in the Netherlands; Hohlenstein in Switzerland; Astbury & Pickford, B. F. Crompton, the Calico Printers' Association (at Broad Oak and Newton Bank), Horridge & Cornall, Marple Printing Company and United Turkey Red in the United Kingdom. The production of newly industrialised countries like Japan meant growing competition. The United Kingdom managed to make British West Africa the largest single market for British cotton goods outside India.[98] Formed in 1931, the British policy think tank Political and Economic Planning (PEP) counselled: 'Any expansion of British trade depends largely on the extent to which Lancashire can cater for the requirements of the native.'[99]

British firms in West Africa had the advantage that British merchant organizations dominated. Since the First World War, Dutch printers traded through British merchants, first Swanzy and later the UAC and Ollivant. The Swiss had their own trading company, the UTC, but British merchants benefited from a tightly organised trading structure for textiles in export markets evolved to optimise production capacity and minimise investment risks for wholesale distributors.[100]

The export trade in the United Kingdom was divided into different divisions: textile printers, merchant converters, commission agents and shippers, which spread the financial risk. Printing companies would sell mainly to merchants, who

Production and trade of wax prints during the First World War and the interwar period

would carry substantial amounts of printed stock ready for immediate delivery. The large printing companies had their own merchant branches, such as Grafton African for the CPA.

Merchant converters were central to the development of the West African textile trade. They ordered their cloth from specialist producers, commissioned the designs and provided cloth and design for printing on a commission basis. Their success was dependent on an intimate knowledge of the West African market, a network of trading contacts and the quality of their goods, often branded with their own trademarks. For example, all the wax print orders at Newton Bank were supplied by merchants until 1970.[101] Merchants might contract to sell only to recognised African shipping firms, or in some cases ship directly themselves. Shippers could have their own production department, trading directly with a printer, but this would then be separate from their dealings with merchants.

---

5. Detail of batik by Catharina Carolina van Oosterom 1380-1913 Beving Collection © The Trustees of the British Museum London, As1934,0307.51.

6. Imitation batik of Blakeley & Beving Manchester 1900-1913
Beving Collection © The Trustees of the British Museum London, inv.no. Af1934,0307.391

7. Vlisco imitation batik 13/0515
Vlisco Archives, @ Vlisco BV

Merchant converters in the United Kingdom

At the beginning of the twentieth century there was a rapid increase in merchant numbers resulting in extreme competition. After the First World War many of the smaller firms were taken over by larger ones.[102] The determinant for success or failure in the trade was an accurate reading of the market by the merchant to get appropriately designed goods, dependent on good contact with agents in West Africa.

One of the most important merchant organisations was the UAC. Another well-known company was Blakeley & Beving in Manchester, remembered now for Charles Beving's collection of Indonesian and African textiles begun around 1880. The collection consisted of about 200 textiles from West Africa, 100 pieces from Indonesia, mainly Java, and other cloth and objects, making up a total of about 400 pieces. Part of it was first displayed publicly from 12 December 1933 to 21 January 1934 in the Manchester Art Galleries with the title *Charles Beving Collection of West African Textiles*.[103] In 1934, when the company went out of business, the whole collection was donated to the British Museum.[104] About the company itself very little information has been kept, but its activities are known to have focused on export to West Africa, and a large number of designs had been registered.[105] Indonesian textiles were most likely collected as inspiration for imitation batik for export to West Africa, not to Indonesia which had become a less attractive market. The collection is important because it illustrates the common practice in the export trade to send samples of locally produced cloth to manufacturers and merchants for imitation. That Beving collected them at least partly himself is an exception.

Among other Indonesian pieces of textile, Beving bought an outstanding and unique batik attributed to Catharina Carolina van Oosterom, made sometime between 1880 and 1913.[106] Like the nutmeg tree batik of Franquemont, copied by the HKM, he made a wax print version of it, which must have been successful, because until 1956 it was available in the Vlisco collection.[107]

Paterson Zochonis was a merchant converter in Manchester, but also a trader in West Africa. George Henry Paterson (1845-1939) from Scotland and George Basil Zochonis (1852-1929) from Greece had been trading in Sierra Leone in the 1870s before setting up a business, first in Liverpool in 1884 and two years later in Manchester. They had an intimate knowledge of the West African market and a large network of trading contacts. They were known for the high quality of their goods, commissioned

Production and trade of wax prints during the First World War and the interwar period

8. Copy of *Peacock* design Brown Fleming registered in 1895 and design with Chinese figures, production Kralingsche Katoen Maatschappij. Rotterdam (The Netherlands)
Sample book Edwin Goodwin 1902-1903
Brunnschweiler Archive, held at the Whitworth Art Gallery, University of Manchester (UK)
Photo Philip Sykas

based on their own designs, and branded with their own trademarks.[108] Their major commodity was initially imitation batik and later also wax prints.[109]

Logan Muckelt had specialised in printed cottons for the African market since 1885. Initially they worked with the Pin Croft Dyeing & Printing Company but changed to Horridge and Cornall in 1928. This company operated the Bolholt Print Works near Bury, north of Manchester.

The company had been founded in 1857 to dye and produce indigo prints.[110] They are thought to have produced their first wax prints already in 1908, in advance of Newton Bank and Broad Oak.[111] From 1928 until 1961 when they stopped printing, Logan Muckelt was their main client for wax prints.

Another significant merchant was Edwin Goodwin, who sold prints sourced from the Kralingsche Katoen Maatschappij as *Dutch Wax* in the beginning of the twentieth century. He sold his business to A. H. Emery, who continued until the 1960s.

Other merchants working in the wax print market were J. A. Duke and Joseph Bridge active until the 1970s. Merchants Elson & Neill were for a long time the most important client of United Turkey Red as well as Newton Bank. During the 1950s and 1960s Newton Bank supplied half of its print volume to these merchants. The company was bought in 1970 by ABC (later ABC Wax). Hubert J. Barrett was a merchant converter, also a longstanding client of Ashton. Like Beving, Barrett made his own collection of West African cloth, which he donated to the Manchester City Art Galleries in 1938.[112] He used his collection to imitate traditionally produced African cloth. Barrett sold his business in 1958 to Richard Brotherton, who closed five years later.[113]

Shippers, distribution, retailing and marketing
Elder Dempster, founded in 1868 by Alexander Elder and John Dempster, was a well-known shipping company. Around 1890 they were the main shippers for West Africa alongside the Hamburg-based Carl Woermann, founded in 1837. Both tried to dominate the market, but other companies organised their own ships to protect their interests.[114] The UAC and G. B. Ollivant worked in close cooperation.[115] A rival of the UAC, with its own fleet, was Liverpool-based John Holt. These companies carried and wholesaled in Africa not only prints produced in the United Kingdom, but also Dutch and Swiss cloth as these were considered the better class of print and in good demand. The best developing markets from the 1900s were the Gold Coast and Nigeria, but also Gambia, Sierra Leone and Belgian Congo.[116] Shipping companies spread the imported merchandise between their own branches to be sold to wholesale customers or in their own retail stores. In these stores, sales could be to locals directly or to traders to sell on. This system was a necessity

in West Africa because of the lack of local finance for the wholesale distribution of goods. Africans were accustomed to buying in markets or from itinerant traders and street vendors. Competitive prices were not the first goal; the choice of appropriate goods was more important.[117]

Several companies were active in the French-speaking territories such as Senegal, Ivory Coast, Dahomey, Togo, Cameroon, Benin and Belgian Congo. Compagnie Niger Français (CNF), based in Paris, was the French branch of the UAC.[118] The Compagnie Française de l'Afrique Occidentale (CFAO) and the Société Commerciale de l'Ouest Africain (SCOA) were also major players. Protective tariffs in French-speaking countries made it difficult for British companies to compete there.

Distribution in West Africa is managed by the shippers, who each have their own organisation for importing and selling via large distribution centres, but also through depots in smaller towns and villages. Retailing is done either by shops owned by the shippers or by independent locals in the towns, stalls in local markets and itinerant pedlers in the countryside. In rural areas markets are held at regular intervals. In the shops a good variety of cloth is in general available, e.g. fancy prints and wax prints imitating tie dye, batik, embroidery and woven cloth. Retailers buy and sell on their own account or

9. Way to extend design from 36 inches to 48 inches by Vlisco Design *Good Husband** registered in 1902 by Brown Fleming. Actual Vlisco no. 14/0052, previously from Ankersmit collection
Vlisco Archive, @ Vlisco BV

Production and trade of wax prints during the First World War and the interwar period

work on commission. All cloth is prepared in such a way that it is acceptable for the region where it will be sold. Fabrics are mostly sold in lengths of 12 yards (11m), which are called *full piece*, or lengths of 6 yards (5.5m), half a piece, stamped and ticketed in a particular manner with the name of the local distributor.[119] The traditional way of shipping cloth was in bales covered in jute canvas, which in general contained five lumps. For ordinary printed textiles, a lump was ten pieces 22-30 yards long, so wax print lumps probably held twenty full pieces, and bales 100.[120]

An adjustment in relation to the original batik imitations was in width of the cloth. Initially the standard was 36 inches, but African women sewed 12-inch strips from other designs to get the desired width for their clothing.[121] Ankersmit already began to offer widths of 48 and 50 inches in the 1910s, in response to market demands. Other companies followed in the period between the wars.[122] After World War II, 48 inches became the norm, except for the people around Warri in Nigeria.[123] In order to get the necessary length, Warri people would cut up a piece of cloth and add a strip lengthwise to add the necessary twelve inches.[124] Vlisco imitated this method by keeping the designs at their original size and printing an extra third part of the design along the border. Krantz, head of design at Vlisco from 1952 until 1985, suggests that conservative consumers preferred this solution in order not to alter original proportions.[125] ABC opted to expand popular designs from 36-inch to 48-inch.

To identify the producer of the cloth and thereby its quality and prestige different methods were used. Stamps in pigment that washed out, which stated the pattern number, yardage and quality indicator could be added. Another method was to attach an impressive colourful label with the trademark of the company to each folded piece of cloth, already in practice when Brown Fleming started selling. The Basel Mission insisted on having its labels mention *Real Dutch Wax*.[126] A more recent method is marking the selvedge of the cloth with the name of the brand. Since the introduction of wax prints, the selvedge had been a crucial part of identifying the quality and maker of the cloth. African buyers would recognise original cloth of the HKM by its selvedge:

> *de zelfkanten mogen niet te breed en niet te small zijn, en, gelijk een echte Wasdruk, vooral een fijngeaderde indigo-blauwe breuk te zien geven* (the selvedges should not be too wide or too narrow, and, like a real wax print, show a finely veined indigo-blue break).[127]

For a long time, the selvedge was the principal way African clients identified the quality and the producer of the cloth.

Conclusion

With the closure of the HKM in 1917 and growing competition Brown Flemings Ltd was fast losing its monopoly. An important number of rivals had entered the market, but only the most committed and those with the strongest connections to the West African trade would manage to survive. Its competitors slowly developed new designs and their own style and signature, although the influence of Brown Fleming remained very strong. Clients would still compare new products of other companies with his original collections. The industry and trade came to be dominated by the British, supported by its government flexing its colonial muscle. The UAC used its dominant position to steer Dutch and Swiss manufacturers towards higher quality of wax prints at lower cost to stay competitive.

1 For more extensive information about the LKM, see the appendix.
2 Verbong describes a sample of wax print of the KKM of which the company in 1889 had sold only one single box, because the production had been too costly. Verbong 1988, 226
3 For more detailed information, see appendix on the Kralingsche Katoen Maatschappij.
4 For a detailed description of the history of Roessingh, see the appendix on the company.
5 See Agreement between Brown Flemings Limited, Ronald Richmond Herbertson and the Calico Printers' Association Limited, draft dated 16 May 1939. Brunnschweiler Archive, held at the Whitworth Art Gallery, University of Manchester (UK).
6 Nabholz-Karaschoff, 207
7 Ankersmit 2012, 67
8 Ankersmit 2009, 4
9 Meeles I, 123. With production only for export, the company realised it had to extend the range of products for more local markets. Gradually the assortment was extended and found its way to Dutch clients in fashion, home furnishings etc. Janszen and De Visser, 49
10 Dejung and Zangger, 187
11 See letter BMTC to Ankersmit dated 31 July 1914 in Meeles I, 154.
12 Letter Ankersmit to Swanzy, London dated 27 March 1919, Meeles I, 87
13 Verschueren, 56-57
14 Meeles I, 144-146
15 In this period, numbers 6660- 7775 were introduced. Meeles II, 15, 30. For information about further numbers, see the register with all design numbers and the year they came to the collection, from 1911/1912 (no. 5000) until 1964 (no 72950). This list is part of the Ankersmit holdings at the Vlisco Archive. The numbers jumped by increments of 25, e.g. 5000, 5025, 5050 etc. to allow for colourways. From 8350, increments of 50 were used. Personal information Gerhard Frensel Milsbeek (The Netherlands), 4 May 2022.
16 Krantz, head of design at Vlisco from 1952 until 1985, argues that Ankersmit relied heavily on the Brown Fleming collection until its closure. Krantz 1989, 118
17 For a detailed description of the twenty shades, see Meeles II, 31.
18 Meeles II, 40
19 De Bodt and Kapelle, 225. See also https://rkd.nl/nl/explore/artists/75434 and https://nl.wikipedia.org/wiki/Reijer_Stolk, both accessed 26 April 2022. See also the exhibition catalogue *Black is beautiful Rubens tot Dumas*, Amsterdam: Nieuwe Kerk, 2008, 304,311-312.
20 Meeles II, 112
21 Ester Schreuder mentions in her blog: 'The etchings, in total there are nine, are kept in a box decorated with batik', but does not mention where this box is kept. https://estherschreuder.wordpress.com/2011/11/06/javanese-dutch-batik-artist-visits-the-gold-coast-in-1930/, last accessed 26 April 2022. A sample book with 15 designs, made by hand, was exhibited in November 1936 at Het Handwerk dat zich Handhaaft at the Stedelijk Museum in Amsterdam.
22 For 1931, it was 28 out of 35; for 1932, 17 out of 24; for 1933, 14 out of 25; for 1934 ,none out of 4; and for 1935, 5 out of 13. Folder Dessinontwerpen 1911-1961 with photocopies of documents about Ankersmit, Vlisco Archive.
23 As far as I know, samples of cloth, designed by Reyer Stolk, have not been kept. What remains is a black faux-leather folder with black and white photos of designs 5000-30550 in the Vlisco Archives in Helmond (The Netherlands). Meeles asserts that not all his designs were appreciated in the Manchester office of the UAC and on the trading posts on the Gold Coast. Meeles II, 126
24 Janszen and De Visser, 57; Ingenbleek 1998, 268-269
25 https://www.archives-unilever.com/explore/search/gb1752-uac2122d151-gamma-holding-nv-agreement-between-p-f-van-vlissingen-van-ankersmit-and-uac-relating-to-the-purchase-of-dutch-wax-block-prints-for-re-sale-in-west-africa, last accessed 25 April 2024.
26 This was agreed with two exceptions: Van Vlissingen & Co was allowed to continue selling to Haykens & Co. and Ankersmit could sell on the Ivory Coast not only to the UAC, but to other merchants. Meeles II, 143
27 Meeles II, 164, 174
28 For example, machine-fitted wax blocks were introduced. They were obviously cheaper, but only possible for designs with a smaller repeat length. Meeles II, 180-181. For further information, see Meeles II, chapters 14-15.
29 Meeles II, 196
30 Meeles II, 195
31 Verschueren, 49
32 Verschueren, 20
33 Bijlsma and Rodenburg, 44
34 Verschueren, 52
35 It was only in 1932 that personnel of Van Vlissingen went to West Africa to see for themselves. Verschueren, 48
36 For more information about Haijkens, see the appendix.
37 Verschueren, 67
38 Bijlsma and Rodenburg, 47
39 Vollaard, 9
40 Meeles I, 88-89; Ingenbleek 1998, 266
41 See also the text about Ankersmit.
42 The two exceptions were Van Vlissingen's sale to Haijkens, and Ankersmit could sell on the Ivory Coast also to other traders. Jacobs and Maas, 44. See also Janszen and De Visser, 57 and Ingenbleek 1998, 268-269.
43 The company was founded in 1858 by Captain George Bent Ollivant, later to be known as G. B. Ollivant and Company Ltd in New Cannon Street Manchester, primarily to ship household and cotton goods to Africa and buy African produce for export to Europe. In 1894 his sons Alfred and Charles took over the business and made it a limited liability company in 1900. The company was purchased by the UAC in 1933. https://www.facebook.com/260326857424671/photos/a.282930865164270/2807134589410539/?type=3&eid=ARCo2gagZ0IIi-V3C48-7gUt4F0702imwrD1yXYIqpG5fBYZvcmA9e4VI_tMNIoAKrwtCdg-tL2cVkoh, last accessed 19 November 2022.
44 Ingenbleek 1998, 269
45 Verschueren, 62
46 Ingenbleek 1998, 269
47 Bijlsma and Rodenburg, 48 and Vollaard, 8. Vollaard mentions also that from 1932 photos were made of the various designs for future reference.
48 For more information about Antonio Nogueira, see https://www.kaowarsom.be/documents/bbom/Tome_VI/Nogueira.Antonio_Martins.pdf, last accessed 16 October 2022.
49 This only changed in 1994 when Vlisco took over the distribution of its products from the UAC. Personal information, Frans van Rood, Helmond, 31 January 2023.
50 Jacobs and Maas, 53
51 The original letters were typed by his wife H. E. Fentener van Vlissingen-Schroder in Helmond, dated 24 March 1982, kept at the Vlisco Archive. The whereabouts of the original letters and the samples sent with them are unknown.
52 Krantz 1990, 99
53 He gives as an example chintz produced by Grafton. Fentener van Vlissingen, 28
54 Ingenbleek 1998, 269; Fentener van Vlissingen, 17-18; Ingenbleek 1998/2, 99
55 Fentener van Vlissingen, 26, 38
56 Typed draft about Jan Fentener van Vlissingen by Jos M. Th. Verschueren, 72. Vlisco Archive, @ Vlisco BV.
57 This situation continued until the 1970s. New designers that were hired had to have trained at an art academy and from the 1980s were encouraged to travel to Africa for inspiration. Today all designs are in-house creations. Internal document Vlisco by Ruud Sanders, curator of the Vlisco Museum: Vlisco, 'De modekoning van Afrika', undated.
58 Fentener van Vlissingen, 16, 44. Zacca was probably not from Syria, but from Lebanon, which was until the collapse of the Ottoman Empire after the First World War, part of Syria. For more information about Lebanese traders in West Africa, see chapter 3.
59 Fentener van Vlissingen, 16
60 Fentener van Vlissingen, 59-60. Verschueren, 62-63
61 Verschueren 67, Krantz 1990, 99
62 Ingenbleek 1998, 271
63 Personal information Frans van Rood, Helmond (The Netherlands) 31 January 2023.
64 Jacobs and Maas, 52

Production and trade of wax prints during the First World War and the interwar period

65   'Wax Prints', typescript document dated 30 November 1939, Brunnschweiler Archive, Whitworth Art Gallery, The University of Manchester (UK).

66   Harrop, 6. See also 'Newton Bank Printworks Hyde 1812-2007 and European Involvement in Batik Printing'. Undated and unpublished document Brunnschweiler Archive, Whitworth Art Gallery, The University of Manchester (UK), 5. Initially only wax prints for Grafton and in 1934 also H. J. Barrett were executed in the newly developed fitter style. In June 1935 cloth of Brown Flemings Ltd and Elson & Neill would also be included. 'Wax Prints', typescript document dated 30 November 1939, Brunnschweiler Archive, Whitworth Art Gallery, The University of Manchester (UK).

67   'Newton Bank Printworks Hyde 1812-2007 and European Involvement in Batik Printing'. Undated and unpublished document, Brunnschweiler Archive, Whitworth Art Gallery, The University of Manchester (UK), 6.

68   'Newton Bank Printworks Hyde 1812-2007 and European Involvement in Batik Printing'. Undated and unpublished document, Brunnschweiler Archive, Whitworth Art Gallery, The University of Manchester (UK), 7.

69   Draft Agreement between Brown Flemings Ltd, Ronald Richmond Herbertson and the Calico Printers' Association Limited 16 May 1939, Brunnschweiler Archive, Whitworth Art Gallery, The University of Manchester (UK).

70   'Wax Prints', typescript document dated 30 November 1939, Brunnschweiler Archive, Whitworth Art Gallery, The University of Manchester (UK).

71   Arthur, Liz, *Seeing Red: Scotland's Exotic Textile Heritage*, Glasgow: Collins Gallery, University of Strathclyde, 2007, 6.

72   For example, Todd Shortridge & Co., bought by John Orr Ewing & Co. in 1860, had started calico printing in 1768. William Stirling & Sons, initially dealers in London-printed India cottons, started printing in Scotland in the 1760s. Nenadic and Tuckett, 2

73   For a more detailed description of the company, see Nenadic and Tuckett, 4-8.

74   For a more detailed description of John Orr Ewing & Co., see Nenadic and Tuckett, 9-11.

75   See Nenadic and Tuckett, 11-13 for more information about Archibald Orr and his company.

76   For more information, see https://colouringthenation.wordpress.com/, last accessed 17 March 2023.

77   Personal communication Philip Sykas, 9 September 2017, based on information in the United Turkey Red Minutes of Board Meetings, Manchester Central Library: Letter 24 September 1919.

78   'European Involvement in Batik Printing'. Unpublished document, Brunnschweiler Archive, Whitworth Art Gallery, University of Manchester (UK), 6.

79   Personal communication Philip Sykas, 2 October 2017, based on information of the United Turkey Red Minutes of Board Meetings, Manchester Central Library: Letter 29 January 1927. For more information about the notebook, see the Appendix on colourists.

80   Vershueren, 56-57

81   Ankersmit suggests that he had the exclusive rights except for F. Meyer in Manchester, possibly already a client of UTR. Ankersmit, 66. For more details about the input of Jean Jacques, see the appendix on colourists.

82   Baharini Baines, 56. It is not known how many of the 58 designs were specifically wax prints.

83   Verschueren, 56

84   There is unfortunately no information available about the possible designers.

85   'Wax Prints', typed document d.d. 30 November 1939 Brunnschweiler Archive, held at the Whitworth Art Gallery, University of Manchester (UK).

86   In 1928, after a decade of protest of the Swiss government against the violation of the rights of a neutral nation the British returned the assets including £250,000 for compensation. See Gannon, 513-515.

87   Nielsen 1974, 38

88   Letter: Ankersmit to Swanzy in London, dated 27 March 1919. Basel Mission Archives. Meeles I, 87

89   Wanner, 1968, 73,79; Arx, 141

90   Nielsen 1974, 56

91   Wanner 1959, 435-436

92   The best sellers were numbers 2040, 3741, 4261, 333, 3510 and 3715. See 4187 UTC: Map D83-06 Goldkuste Geschaftsjahr 1932-33 Statistik, Letter to the Union Handels Gesellschaft AG Basel dated 4 August 1933 from the General Agent's office UTC in Basel Mission Archives. Unfortunately, it was not possible to trace images of these specific designs.

93   For more information about the Swanzy family, see Henry Swanzy, 'A Trading Family in the Nineteenth Century Gold Coast' in *Transactions of the Gold Coast & Togoland Historical Society*, 2:2 (1956), 87-120.

94   The Royal Niger Company was a mercantile company, formed in 1879 by the British Government as the United African Company, renamed to National African Company in 1881, changed to Royal Niger Company in 1886. https://en.wikipedia.org/wiki/Royal_Niger_Company, last accessed 18 March 2023. See also Launert, 169-170. This company should not be confused with the trading company Compagnie du Niger Français, the CNF, based on the Boulevard Haussmann in Paris until 1995 (https://www.societe.com/etablissement/soc-niger-france-59204929000014.html last accessed 17 March 2023).

95   Janszen and De Visser, 47

96   For a detailed description of the various companies, see Verschueren, 57-60.

97   UAC activities changed from the 1930s and especially after the Second World War in response to African economic development. The emphasis shifted to the sale of sophisticated consumer goods and the equipment required for the industrial development that was expected to follow independence. Examples are docklands, warehouses, factories and even transport infrastructure, housing and town planning. There was also a shift from retail to wholesale and to the local manufacture of those goods which had previously been imported. How the UAC has contributed to the built environment in West Africa is researched by Iain Jackson of the Liverpool School of Architecture and Claire Tunstal, Global Head of Art, Archives and Records Management for the Unilever Archives and Records Management. They have started a research program in 2021 called *The Architecture of the United Africa Company* at the UAC archive held at Port Sunlight, Wirral (UK). See https://transnationalarchitecture.group/2021/06/15/3812/, last accessed 10 April 2024.

98   Based on figures of the Joint Committee of Cotton Trade Organisations in 1936. Launert, 157

99   Recommendation in report of Political and Economic Planning, Report on the British Cotton Industry 1936, 40. Launert 159

100   Launert, 172

101   The exception was Grafton African, part of the CPA, the merchanting arm set up when hand-blocked wax printing was transferred from Broad Oak Works.

102   Launert, 168

103   See also Launert, 181-182.

104   His son Charles Beving donated the collection. He had written labels with information for the cloths his father had collected, that are still attached to the cloth today. It gives information on how the designs could be adapted for the West African market, especially how particular motifs could be replaced, removed or added.

105   https://blog.nationalarchives.gov.uk/crossing-continents-textile-designs-west-african-market/, last accessed 3 September 2023

106   This batik can be found in the collection of the British Museum as As1934,0307.51.

107   The wax print of Beving and Blakeley, estimated production 1900-1913, in the collection of the British Museum is inventoried as Af1934,0307.391.

108   Archival material including fabric samples, registered design samples and certificates, shipping labels, photographs, hand printing blocks etc are kept at the Science Museum in Manchester: https://discovery.nationalarchives.gov.uk/details/c/F218284, last accessed 22 February 2023.

109   https://www.gracesguide.co.uk/Paterson_Zochonis, page visited 16 October 2022. The Museum of Science and Industry in Manchester has a collection of hand-printing blocks and samples of cloth of the company. Today the company is still active as PZ Cussons, specialising in health and beaty products. PZ is an abbreviation for Paterson Zochonis.

110 'Newton Bank Printworks Hyde 1812-2007 and European Involvement in Batik Printing'. Undated and unpublished document, Brunnschweiler Archive, Whitworth Art Gallery, University of Manchester (UK), 5-6.
111 'History of wax printing in the UK for the West African market', unpublished document, 1 August 1977, Brunnschweiler Archive, Whitworth Art Gallery, University of Manchester (UK), 5-6.
112 The collection is now held at The Gallery of Costume at Platt Hall in Manchester. Launert, 187
113 Some early archival material of Barrett is in the archives of ABC, possibly because it belonged to Ashton, Barrett being a customer of the company. The company archives of Barrett and Brotherton have been held in the Vlisco Archives in Helmond since 1994. Before they were kept by the Compagnie Niger Français in Paris, a trading house of African prints for the West African market, which was taken over by Vlisco.
114 Launert, 170
115 Before WW2, they sold products from the principal merchants F. W. Grafton, Brown Flemings Ltd, H. J. Barrett and Elson and Neill. 'Wax Prints', typescript dated 30 November 1939, Brunnschweiler Archive, Whitworth Art Gallery, University of Manchester (UK).
116 'Wax Prints', typescript dated 30 November 1939, Brunnschweiler Archive, Whitworth Art Gallery, University of Manchester (UK).
117 Launert, 172, 175
118 They were important distributors to, for example, John Walkden in Benin, UAC in Togo, Niger Afrique in Niger, Woodin in Ivory Coast etc. Personal information Frans van Rood 31 March 2023.
119 'West African Trade. Method of Production', 6 June 1940, Brunnschweiler Archive, Whitworth Art Gallery, University of Manchester (UK).
120 Personal communication, Philip Sykas, 19 October 2018. Vlisco still ships its cloth this way. Today, Vlisco packages contain about 120 half pieces per bale, although smaller bales can be sent if necessary. Personal communication Ruud Sanders 11 May 2023.
121 'Newton Bank Printworks Hyde 1812-2007 and European Involvement in Batik Printing', unpublished document p.9; and 'Wax Prints', typescript dated 30 November 1939, both at Brunnschweiler Archive, Whitworth Art Gallery, University of Manchester (UK).
122 Vlisco also changed the width of its Java Prints. Krantz 1985, 7
123 Krantz 1985, 6
124 Unilever Archive Oral History Programme Interview Ref. OH/80 with Ken Forrest, held on 3 March 2011 at Lever House, Port Sunlight. https://www.archives-unilever.com/media/_file/preservica/GB1752_OH/3b6f1de5-bf59-4aaf-8894-036b836d231c--OH80_Ken_Forrest.pdf, last accessed 10 April 2024.
125 Krantz 1985, 6-7. C. H. Krantz was head of the design department of Vlisco from 1952 until 1985.
126 Meeles I, 34-35
127 Meeles I, 93-94

The process of wax printing

6.
The first two colours (blue and brown) are applied to the fabric by using wooden print blocks or a printing machine. The wax will once again resist the dye.

Developments in the production and trade in wax prints after the Second World War

From the 1950s and 1960s, companies in the Netherlands, the United Kingdom and Switzerland began to leave the production of wax prints or transferred production to West Africa. After gaining independence, West African countries were keen to develop industrial textile production. A partnership of the CPA, Van Vlissingen and Ankersmit, called the Anglo Dutch African Textile Investigation Group (ADATIG), would create subsidiaries and collaboration with interested African countries. In 1965 the Ghana Textile Printing Company (GTP) was founded in Accra, followed by Uniwax in 1968 on the Ivory Coast. The CPA helped establish printing sites in Nigeria (Kaduna), Ghana (Akosombo) and Zaire. With the acquisition of the CPA by Tootal in 1970 and the Newton Bank site by Cha Textile Group in 1992, Ashton survived in a new incarnation as ABC Wax, working in cooperation with further African firms (Nichemtex, Supertex, Togotex). By continually adjusting its market position, it remained a viable producer until 2007, and then a design firm and brand until 2022. In the Netherlands, after the closure of Ankersmit in 1965, only Vlisco has survived and is the sole European company that continues to produce wax prints today.

Production and trade in the Netherlands, the United Kingdom and Switzerland after 1945

The Netherlands
Ankersmit

After the war, business for Ankersmit went smoothly for fifteen years. New designers were employed. Eduard Boll joined in 1946, and Cees Sistermans followed in 1949, while Wytse de Vries was responsible for engraving from 1948 onwards.[1] However, the role of the designer became increasingly *technical* rather than *creative*, following a lead set by the head of sales. Boll defended the artistic side, and when Teun Kloosterboer joined in 1957, the approach was changing and resulted in a more independent design studio focused on European as well as *export* markets. In 1959, the export side was split off, and designers could focus exclusively on the African market, creating *Real Dutch Wax Block Prints* or *Véritable Wax Hollandais*.[2] Sistermans developed as a natural leader of the team with a substantial share in new designs. Gerhard Frensel, trained as a designer at the art academy of Krefeld, joined in 1961. He initially worked for the European market, but from 1963 designed for the African market.[3] All designs were shown to a group of influential African women traders during their regular visits to the company in Deventer. Their opinion was decisive. If they appreciated a design and promised to order at least 10,000 yards, the design would be taken into production.[4] Sales of wide (50-inch) gradually overtook narrow (36-inch) cloth. In the postwar years, wide cloth accounted for two-thirds of sales.[5]

By the end of the 1950s, Ankersmit and Van Vlissingen were faced with internal and external challenges. In 1957, Ghana was the first West African colony to gain independence, to be followed by most other West African countries in 1960. In 1961 Nigeria also gained independence. The new governments wanted to develop their own industry and have a larger share in the import and export trade. This entailed licensing and higher tariffs. Over the next five years, Dutch companies saw their export halved. Pursuing survival, in 1964 Unilever, at the time the major shareholder of Van Vlissingen, prompted a merger with Ankersmit and Stoomweverij Nijverheid of Enschede. The new company was named Texoprint.[6]

To avoid over-production and increase efficiency, a reorganisation was considered necessary. This resulted in the closure of Ankersmit in 1965, a company that produced more than Van Vlissingen before the Second World War.[7]

After the conflict the relationship had reversed.[8] European production of wax prints was under pressure, and Unilever wanted to help the newly independent African nations to set up their own printing companies. Specialists from Deventer and Helmond travelled to West Africa to guardedly sharing their expertise. Competition from Japan, China and India was growing, and Unilever did not want to pass on knowledge of printing techniques to non-African competitors.

The closure of Ankersmit meant laying off 1,100 people. Exceptions were made for the designers and two sales personnel, who moved to Helmond to work for Texoprint. The idea was that Ankersmit's house style should not be lost, and to create an independent design unit within the Van Vlissingen studio, overseen by Sistermans.[9] The team in Helmond did not recognise the need for this, which resulted in difficult relations between the two. In the tense restructuring climate, Eduard Boll had already moved to Lagos in 1964 to work for Nigerian textile printers.[10] In the 1960s, kaftans and dashikis became fashionable in the West. In 1965, the Ankersmit designers were asked by Van Vlissingen to create a non-African collection with existing designs, registered under the name *Bouboudima* to cater for the new market.[11] Cees Sistermans and Hans van Gelder were responsible for the project.[12] Van Vlissingen was already producing this type of clothing for its West African customers, but the new range of designs was aimed at clients in tourist centres in the Caribbean, Florida, California, South Africa, Paris and London. Western clothing types, blouses, shirts, cocktail and evening dresses were introduced. Frank Govers, a Dutch couturier, created fashions to highlight these collections. The initiative faded with the fashion for kaftans and dashikis, and the last collection was released in 1972.[13]

Continuous pressure from the Van Vlissingen management to integrate the Ankersmit designers into the existing Vlisco studio exacerbated tensions that resulted in the loss of Frensel, Kloosterboer and Sistermans to the Chinese company Cha Chi Ming in 1969. Calling themselves Novi, they continued working in Helmond from a studio in the Heistraat to create designs for Kaduna Textiles Ltd in Nigeria (est. 1964) and Akosombo Textiles in Ghana (est. 1967).[14] The Novi studio closed in 1973.[15]

Van Vlissingen

Active planning during the war for postwar recovery resulted in a company in a better position than in 1940. The standstill was used for technical and organisational rearrangements. Ideas for improving export production prepared during the war were realised with the opening of a new laboratory and experimental production unit. Indigo dyeing was done using a more scientific approach, recycling of resin was improved and new colours were introduced.[16] Van Vlissingen had huge reserves of raw material hidden during the war. Two million meters of printed cloth for Africa was prepared for shipping as soon as the war was over.[17]

At the end of 1945 and in January 1946 Jan van Vlissingen, Anton Ankersmit and H. J. Haijkens visited business relations in London and Manchester. The orders of the UAC were so important that the directors decided to continue their pre-war collaboration. In August 1946 the first shipment was ready to leave the factory.[18] This early start gave Van Vlissingen a decisive advantage over its competitors. Within five years, Van Vlissingen managed to become the largest exporter of printed cloth in the Netherlands with 80 per cent of sales.[19]

The first shipment of Van Vlissingen did not resolve the problem of shortages of consumer goods after the wartime low. Textile shortages became a target of social unrest and anti-colonial sentiment. Wax prints had become more affordable, sought-after commodities for the middle-classes.[20] Proposals by Van Vlissingen to dramatically increase production were first met with scepticism by the UAC, but within a year they acknowledged the need. Ankersmit, producing about two-thirds of pre-1940 levels of wax print for the UAC, was not willing to increase production to meet the new demands, from concerns about quality control. Van Vlissingen, now able to make a comparable quality, was keen to invest in its production capacity. Van Vlissingen's initiatives meant that between 1946 and 1960 its production grew spectacularly, from 2 million yards per annum to 60 million yards. Although wax prints were its most expensive offering, they were no longer considered luxury goods, but everyday items within reach of an increasing sector of the population.[21]

Around 1955, the UAC were handling over a million yards per week in their warehouse in Manchester, mostly cloth from the Netherlands and the United Kingdom, but over time, also large quantities from Japan. All cloth that arrived was inspected, cut to the required lengths – 6, 8 or 12 yards – for the various markets in West Africa, packed and sent to Liverpool for shipment. The Compagnie du Niger-Français in Paris, part of the UAC, was responsible for the French territories.[22]

Van Vlissingen was printing for two very different markets: the specialised production of wax and fancy prints for export, and mass production for the domestic market with an aim of cost reduction. The two were run as separate businesses housed under one roof. Attempts to coordinate production were unsuccessful, and management remained indecisive, afraid of becoming too dependent on a single market.

Jan Fentener van Vlissingen was not only a director but continued as before to be responsible for new designs and colours. After his visit to Africa in 1934 he had developed a strong interest in African cultures. He was an active board member of the *Vereeniging Koloniaal Instituut* (Associated Colonial Institute) in Amsterdam. In 1948, Jan made a trip to Congo that reinforced his conviction of the importance of getting the right combination of design and colours for each specific market.[23] He was also convinced that it was important to regularly introduce new designs to sustain demand. Local agents, representatives of the various merchants, required a better grasp of the tastes of the local people.[24] In a speech to the annual meeting of the Royal Association 'East and West' in 1955, he criticised the colonial powers for their lack of sincere interest in the African people and their cultures, blaming the same deficiency for Europe's lost influence in Asia.[25] With better cultural understanding and more equal relations, the people of Asia would have perceived Europeans as partners instead of intruders. Only when attitudes towards the African people changed could the full potential for both

parties be realised. He perceived the growth of nationalism in some parts of Africa. The potential for economic benefit was huge, but only if Europeans were willing to cooperate with African partners.[26]

Gradually three types of cloth came to dominate exports. Most sought after and expensive were the wax prints, often with traditional designs used for special occasions. Java prints occupied the middle rank, and were more reflective of changes in fashion. The third type, imitation wax, copies after the more expensive originals, were considered as fancy prints, valued for cheapness. Van Vlissingen wax prints and Java prints held a prominent position, specially appreciated in the market, followed by the British, Swiss, Japanese and African factory production.

The high demand for Van Vlissingen's products during the 1950s and 1960s meant that the prices could be increased on a regular basis. A serious and quickly growing problem was the prolific copying of popular designs, especially of the expensive wax prints. One way to prevent copying was by continuously improving the quality and introducing novelties, but these tactics were never altogether successful.[27]

The company spent a substantial amount of money and time chasing imitators. Already in 1948 after having seen copies during a trip to Africa, Jan suggested the registration of designs. During the 1950s many designs were registered in England, which was successful for British export markets, but in Francophone Africa this was less effective.[28] Japanese copies were being perfected to imitate Dutch wax prints on the market.

---

1. Creation Frank Govers for Bouboudima Collection Vlisco, around 1970
Photo Vlisco Archive, @ Vlisco BV

2. Design *Leidsche Ruit** or *Lino**, shown by models for Vlisco in Eastern Nigeria, 1950s
Photo Vlisco Archive, @ Vlisco BV

Developments in the production and trade in wax prints after the Second World War

Printing company names on the selvedge

It was only in the 1950s that merchant firms such as Elson & Neill and Grafton African started printing company names on the selvedge, followed by *Guaranteed English Wax, for export to Africa*. For upcoming markets like the Ivory Coast and Togo the French translation, *Veritable Wax Anglais,* was added in the 1960s. ABC would print the CPA logo, a sun, with the text *Guaranteed Wax ABC Made in England*. Vlisco started around 1964 adding the text *Dutch Waxblock Print* and later *Real Dutch Wax* on the selvedge. From 1968 onwards the design number was also added. It also helped to discern the *right* side or the front of the cloth. Previously this was done by hiding the letter *R* (rechterkant, right side) somewhere in the design. The brand name was not mentioned, because the company assumed that the client would know anyway it was of the highest quality.[29] It was from 1980 that *Guaranteed Dutch Wax Vlisco* or *Vlisco Veritable Wax Hollandais* would be mentioned. However, even this did not stop the practice of copying, with copies becoming increasingly better over time and even duplicating the name of a prestigious company on lesser cloth.[30]

Constant innovation was necessary. This was done by introducing old designs in new colours as well as adding nearly 125 new designs by 1960. At that time, Van Vlissingen had a portfolio of about 1,400 current and obsolete wax print designs, and another 600 current and obsolete designs for Java prints.[31] Success of a design could be due to local factors entirely out of company control: getting an attractive name from female market traders, patronage by wealthy influential women, or gaining a reputation for being lucky. Paramount was that these coveted designs should be difficult to copy.

Van Vlissingen held an unquestionably dominant position for wax prints with 66.7 per cent of all production in the early 1950s. With Ankersmit's contribution of 18.9 per cent, the Dutch had a near monopoly of the market, with the United Kingdom and Switzerland contributing respectively only 10.8 and 3.6 per cent. At the end of this decade, however, Van Vlissingen saw its contribution reduced to 50.1 per cent and Ankersmit to 15.8 per cent because of growing competition from the United Kingdom (26.6 per cent). Switzerland (3.8 per cent) and Japan (3.7 per cent) remained minor competitors.[32] In this period six principal European and Japanese companies exported (imitation) wax prints to Africa. Even with this heavy reduction in market share, in 1960 Van Vlissingen remained market leader. It had seen a spectacular growth after the Second World War, especially under the direction of Jan. Investing more in sales to achieve greater market share had been his priority. To maintain market lead in the post-colonial era, Jan suggested starting a sales office in Ghana called *Dutch Waxblock Company* where African merchants could import directly, but his initiative was not a success.[33]

African governments wanted to develop their own industries, and Unilever was conscious that this would affect the position of the UAC. When Unilever had the opportunity to buy enough shares of Van Vlissingen to become the majority shareholder, it did not hesitate.[34] The UAC wanted to retain control of implementing Dutch wax print techniques in West African factories to prevent copying by the competition. The Van Vlissingen-Ankersmit Export Maatschappij (VAEM) was founded with the aim of selling fabric of both printers to trade organisations in West Africa. Unilever had 75 per cent of the shares, which gave it control over the sale of Dutch wax prints not only from Van Vlissingen, but importantly from Ankersmit as well.[35]

A further initiative was the start of a partnership, called the Anglo Dutch African Textile Investigation Group (ADATIG) with the UAC, Van Vlissingen, Ankersmit and the CPA in 1958.[36] Unilever was afraid that when production in West Africa started, Dutch companies would be set against each other and production compromised or stopped altogether. The idea was to create subsidiaries, collaborating with African countries as participants, not as opponents. This resulted in the UAC and Van Vlissingen acquiring interests in several companies.[37] In 1961 Van Vlissingen gained an interest in Congoprint SCRL in Leopoldville. Four years later the Ghana Textile Printing Company was founded with the help of the Ghanaian government, the UAC and Ankersmit and Van Vlissingen. In 1968 the company *Uniwax* was founded in Abidjan.[38] GTP and other West African wax printers co-founded by ADATIG used Van Vlissingen design and print technology. The overarching goal was to develop activities that allowed the company, now called Vlisco, to keep a firm place in the market, despite rising competition from Japan, Switzerland and the United Kingdom, countries also keen to increase production.

ADATIG was concerned that post-independence African socio-cultural developments would negatively impact a *colonial* product like wax print. In the winter of 1962/63, Ankersmit and Van Vlissingen commissioned an inquiry into whether social changes would affect demand for their cloth, especially in the crucial Ghanaian market where Van Vlissingen, the dominant partner, had good contacts with traders. While Ankersmit did more business in Nigeria, trading with the Igbo people there was already more complex than in Ghana.[39]

In September 1963, commissioned researcher F. L. van Holthoon presented a *Design Analysis Report* examining the turnover and geographic distribution of *old* (pre-1945), *middle-aged* (1945-1955) and *new* designs issued by Ankersmit and Van Vlissingen in the period 1956-1962.[40] In an article published with co-researcher W. J. Boelman, they concluded that textile consumption in Ghana was rather conservative. The customer had a strong preference for a limited range of well-established designs. They observed a shift from large, complicated designs with Indonesian origins to small recurring patterns with no specific origin. It seemed that new designs were more subject to *fashion* and reflected changes in taste. The analysis showed the vitality of patterns of established taste; although new designs sold well, designs based on the *Haarlem collection* were considered by consumers a serious investment.[41] For the Dutch printers, the report showed their anxieties were unfounded and confirmed that wax prints remained strongly embedded in West African cultures.[42]

This did not blind Vlisco to the need to manufacture as efficiently as possible for wax print production to remain profitable; the weaker product line for the European market was to be stopped completely in 1981.[43] A priority was replacing the expensive hand printed element of wax prints while retaining the desirable nuances of the hand printed look despite mechanisation. For some styles, hand printing remained necessary; only in 1993 was hand block work able to be dispensed with completely.[44] Despite all these measures, export was reduced by half between 1961 and 1966. It seemed that the West African market was no longer large enough for two Dutch wax printers. Their high wages could only be partly compensated by higher efficiency and productivity, especially in the face of competition from lower-wage countries.

As mentioned above in the section on Ankersmit, a merger arranged by Unilever of Van Vlissingen, Ankersmit and Stoomweverij Nijverheid was intended to sustain profitability. Van Vlissingen already worked with the weaving firm for their domestic production. The merger was listed as a holding company Texoprint.[45] Eventually, reorganisation to avoid overproduction and improve efficiency resulted in the closure of Ankersmit in 1965. Van Vlissingen was also required to reorganise production for the European market, refurbish its factory, mechanise indigo dyeing and keep only essential personnel.[46] On 1 July 1965, the company was officially renamed Vlisco Textieldrukkerijen NV (becoming widely known as Vlisco).[47]

Vlisco would focus on the top market segment, aiming to lead the wax print market with innovative design and a range of qualities of cloth. It would not neglect regular re-issues of the much appreciated classics; this *oldtimeren* – reprints of old designs in new colour ranges about every five years – was a conscious Vlisco policy. It kept the interest in these designs alive, limited the amount of new engraving for cost control, and led every time to substantial sales. Neil Whiteman, a representative of the UAC who worked in West Africa for several decades, observed:

> They [consumers] are very traditional and the wax block, just as they became wealthier they just wanted more wax blocks.

> I, okay the colour would change but a lot of the designs, the original designs sort of like *ABC* or *Butterfly*, just to quote a couple, would go on and on. Maybe you might order it in a different colour shade and colour way and that was it.[48]

Cees Krantz, head of the design department from 1952 until 1985, also suggested that in this way Vlisco helped to maintain local traditions in West and Central Africa and the Sahel region. To best understand what these clients wanted, the company wanted to study the local cultures in all their aspects. To Krantz it did not make sense to imitate their own symbols, motifs and other cultural elements. His idea was that people would only be interested in things they had not created themselves, but that were closely in tune with their own culture. To achieve this, one must travel extensively in the various regions and listen to consumers. What they said should be taken absolutely *au serieux*. Designers needed the cooperation of trade agents, African merchants and the various departments within the company.

Twice a year the company organised a presentation of about forty to fifty new designs for their agents. Six or seven representatives from every market region would be present. One event would take place in the Netherlands, the other on the African continent at places relevant to the trade. People from the UAC, the Compagnie Française de l'Afrique Occidentale (CFAO) and its most important competitor the Société Commerciale de l'Ouest Africain (SCOA), were invited and could choose their preferred designs.[49] They were also able to express their preferences for the various colour ranges.[50] When designs were initially rejected, re-introducing them in revised colours sometimes proved helpful. With

---

3. Women at market in Ghana, 1963
Picture taken during research trip for Design Analysis Report by Ankersmit and Van Vlissingen
Photo Vlisco Archive, @ Vlisco BV

Developments in the production and trade in wax prints after the Second World War

this policy, Krantz saw new collections achieve 99 per cent success. Analyses executed by the design department every five years tabulating the *visible features* of the design in conjunction with the quality of cloth, also proved valuable.[51]

GTP and other printing companies founded by ADATIG used specific Vlisco designs and print technology. To spread the risk, export was aimed at as many countries as possible. When some countries closed their borders to Dutch import, neighbouring countries became transit ports, such as Togo, and later Benin for Ghana and Nigeria. Although the greater part of wax and Java prints were now made locally, the clientele still had a strong preference for Dutch and English wax prints. While economic growth between 1981 and 1986 increased Vlisco's viability, import difficulties in Togo and political unrest in Nigeria led to an all-time low in 1994, necessitating further reorganisation and redundancies. The following year, the situation improved and Vlisco was able to remain in the highest market position even though the competition enhanced its products continuously. The brand name Vlisco, now printed on the cloth, was also easier to protect.[52]

Design has always been important for Vlisco. After its pioneer design directors Johan Jacobs (1900-1951) and Jan van Vlissingen (1923-1951), design-centred management continued under Cees Krantz from 1952 until 1985.[53] Frans van Rood was in charge from 1985 until 2010 and Roger Gerards during the next five years. From 2016, Zara Atelj was given the responsibility, replaced in 2020 by Gabriele Sanchez y Sanchez de la Barquera until 2023.

The profile of the designers slowly changed over the years. Until the 1970s they were recruited locally and learned their craft on the job by copying designs or completing the designs of senior designers and eventually training further outside the studio. Most designs were commissioned by clients, only 10 per cent were in-house creations. It was from 1985 under Frans van Rood that a single trip to West Africa was organised for every designer to allow them to discover the market and the critical desires of their clientele.[54] Apart from the enthusiasm to see their *own* designs used locally, it

---

4. Jan van Vlissingen and Cees Krantz visiting a market in Zaire, 1954
Photo Vlisco Archive, Vlisco Netherlands. B.V.

gave them an appreciation of and perspective on their role in renewing the collection.[55] But the market was as complex and incomprehensible as ever. The reason for success or failure of a specific design remained as unpredictable as before the trips started.

Slowly these trips became a regular event. The designers received more and more freedom and could gradually work almost as autonomous artists with their own individual handwriting. Designers hired since the 1990s came from all over the Netherlands and from other countries, having completed a formal academic training in graphic or textile design. Nowadays all designs are created in-house. The subjects for designs can be anything that catches the designer's attention. They are not asked to make something *African* if it is not their own choice. They create images with which they themselves are satisfied, not what they think African clients might appreciate. After all, they know clients will only buy what they like, and this is not predictable in any formulaic sense any more than in Europe.[56]

A careful respect for specific cultural motifs is important, of which Vlisco is abundantly conscious:

> A lot of the fabrics that are less embraced in our African markets have designs that can have a link to religion, either intentional or by interpretation. Designs with motives that can be interpreted as objects, gambling, masks, or parts of the human body can bring a negative association to a consumer, due to their religion or cultural heritage. For instance, Muslim communities would not wear objects or animals on their clothing. The most beloved designs are elegant designs with a botanical or decorative theme.[57]

Such caveats reflect recent practice but in the past, others applied, for example dice and playing card motifs enjoyed a run of popularity in the 1940s and 1950s. At ABC designers also learned which subjects were best avoided. A chameleon, which changes colour to blend in with its background, is interpreted as a sign of untrustworthiness.[58] Snakes likewise could have this association. Subjects directly linked to African proverbs or voodoo (Vodun-related religion) cosmology were avoided because these could evoke negative meanings or trangress metaphysical practices if handled ineptly.[59]

The choice of colours is crucial, and this varies from region to region for traditional designs, and can vary with the season.[60] Due to trading and emigration throughout the continent some beloved traditional colour combinations, like those originally linked to the Igbo in Nigeria, have crossed borders. Igbo communities like to dress collectively to show their group identity; preferred colour combinations are yellow and red or orange and blue. People in Congo like ochre and yellow, combined with strong colours like vibrant red, electric blue, intense green and bright orange.[61]

In Congo, indigo with small accents in yellow and red is a popular combination. In Ivory Coast, small all-over designs in indigo with yellow are prevalent. It is said that in Ghana, people prefer traditional batik designs without indigo, but red, yellow and turquoise and a strong effect of spots from resin resist.[62] Softer and less contrasting colour combinations have been developed for the less conservative consumer of wax, new preferences that are less defined by region or ethnicity.[63] Of course, these are generalisations that only serve as an indication of the importance of colour in the African marketplace.

Around 2000, Vlisco saw its sales decline. Cheap imitations had long been available in some West and Central African countries, but from the 1990s onwards better-quality wax print imitations from China started to compete not only with Vlisco, but also with African production. Since the early 1990s, the company enjoyed a virtual monopoly in the West African market for certain types of printed textiles, but it could not rest on its laurels. Vlisco realised that to maintain sales, it had to be more open to consumer demands, and continual refreshing its knowledge of the markets was essential.[64] Transformations of African society needed to be closely observed. When the mobile phone became available to the elite in the 1990s, it also became a popular motif for wax prints, but when the phones became more widely available, they became less popular for printing on cloth. Wearing wax prints had been for more than a century an important way to display wealth. Now more consumer prestige objects were available as subject matter, such as houses, cars and high-tech items. The introduction of Western clothing posed another challenge. Wax printers encouraged African fashion designers to use the cloth and create new interest in wearing wax, especially in big cities. This stimulated people to buy cloth more often and, because of the tight fit of fashion garments, to replace them more frequently.

The company decided not to compete with mass manufacture of textiles for Africa, but to position itself as a global luxury fashion and design brand with regularly changing collections, promoted by lavish print and online advertising campaigns. It tried to attract new customers among well-off urban Africans and those living in the diaspora. Commercially, this did not generate the expected results. The African market did not parallel Western countries with seasonally changing fashion styles. Since 2016, the company has focused again on the African market, avoiding superficial fashionability for a *design-driven* approach, more and more in collaboration with African fashion designers and artists, and cultivating the prestige of its brand. For consumers in West and Central Africa, Vlisco wax prints are deeply engrained in their cultures and widely embraced as symbol of *Africanness*.[65]

Developments in the production and trade in wax prints after the Second World War

United Kingdom

After the Second World War six companies were still printing in the United Kingdom, producing for the West African market. Astbury & Pickford in Oldham had gone into receivership in 1939, and an auction sale of its works was held in 1942. The company continued, but as a merchant converter, commissioning prints from others. Some who survived the Second World War did not continue for long, such as Marple Printing Company that had printed for the merchants Joseph Bridge and Edwin Goodwin, but stopped wax printing in 1952.

With wax print factories established in the newly independent African countries came import restrictions, sometimes bans, to protect the local production, provoking more British closures. United Turkey Red had to close in 1960 after four decades of wax printing. In the 1950s the works in Alexandria remained the largest and longest running of the UTR factories, but business was dwindling and even a more diverse product range could not guarantee survival. By the end of 1957, three years before the final closure of the company, UTR sold the rights to their wax print designs to the CPA.[66] Several designs came directly from the Brown Fleming collection, others were drawn in the spirit of his style. In 1960, the company formally closed under the British government's Cotton Finishing Reorganisation Scheme.[67] Horridge and Cornall, which printed wax styles mainly for Logan, Muckelt & Co., also decided to close in 1961 under the government redundancy scheme.[68] Logan Muckelt was able to transfer its printing to the CPA mills at Newton Bank and Rhodes Print Works.[69] The next works to tumble was B. F. Crompton, renowned for its invention of a roller-printed hand-block effect; its business was liquidated in 1966.[70]

Grafton's production at Broad Oak stagnated after the Second World War. Machine printing was stopped in 1959, and engraving in 1960, with Newton Bank taking over its roller printing.[71] Screen printing closed in 1966, and in 1970 the finishing operations were transferred to Loveclough.[72] The last remaining wax printer in the United Kingdom was then Ashton at Newton Bank, until 1968 part of the CPA.

F. W. Ashton and Co. of Newton Bank Print Works

Ashton managed to survive the hurdles in its business path by continually adjusting its market position. In 1940, Rhodes Print Works was converted to war work, and its *Crompton* fitter machines and hand-blocking machines were transferred to Newton Bank, but exploitation of this increased capacity had to await the end of the war. The Second World War led to severe shortages of raw materials and limited shipping facilities. At the end of the war there was a big demand for wax print, but supplies of cloth and dyestuffs were insufficient. New supplies were found in Japan and later in China. By 1950, wax print production was back to normal and reached 8 million yards, a quantity that would remain stable for the next five years. The main markets were Nigeria and Ghana, but Belgian Congo became increasingly important.[73] Production was supported by several technical improvements. In 1955, the first wax recovery plant was installed, reducing cost and easing effluent treatment problems. In the same year a step forward was taken by cracking the wax using rotary drum washing machines, which gave the company an advantage over its British competition. In the Netherlands this technology had already been perfected.

To have direct access to the markets of Nigeria, Ghana, Belgium Congo etc., the CPA acquired A. Brunnschweiler & Co. in 1959. This Swiss company, known as ABC, had subsidiaries in Nigeria and Sierra Leone.[74] The main attraction for the CPA was its distribution outlets. Further distribution capacity was created in 1960 by an agreement with the French company Société Générale du Golfe de Guinée (SGGG) in Togo, which gave Newton Bank production direct access to all the main markets. Soon the sales of wax prints, which had stagnated in the 1950s, exceeded 35 million yards per year. Newton Bank did not have sufficient space to accommodate all the necessary processing. The parent company, the CPA, allocated specialities to different sites, so processes such as bleaching, finishing, examination and packing could be outsourced to other CPA sites, along with engraving and printing for bulk orders when necessary. This involved complex record-keeping and logistics, but these had been developed during years of coordinating over forty separate component firms, now simplified on fewer sites.

Expansion was achieved while other British wax printers were closing down, as already described. With the closure of B. F. Crompton in 1966, Newton Bank became the last UK wax print works. Along with Vlisco, it was one of only two major manufacturers left in Europe, each with a capacity of around 25 million yards per annum. Hohlenstein in Switzerland had a capacity of around 5 million yards per annum.

By the 1960s, the CPA was facing rapid changes in the market. In 1968, it succumbed to a takeover, merging with English Sewing Cotton Co. to form English Calico Ltd. This textile group subsequently became Tootal Ltd in 1973.[75]

The opening of several print works in West Africa and Japan during the 1960s had an impact on the sales of Dutch and UK wax print. For the CPA, Congo had become the largest single market for export of English wax, a market shared since 1965 with the Ghana Textile Printing Company (GTP) opened under Dutch management. In 1967 Joseph Mobutu decided that certain major imports, including wax print, had to be substituted by local production. A year later, the CPA opened a wax print factory in Congo, CPA Zaire, with a capacity of 12 million yards per annum. By 1983, direct imports of English wax by Zaire had ceased.[76]

In October 1969, the CPA closed Birch Vale Printworks and transferred to Newton Bank the extra role of bleaching cloth ready for printing.[77] In the same year it was decided by the CPA that Newton Bank should drop the name F. W. Ashton, which it had been using for 114 years, and adopt the name of its subsidiary ABC, short for A. Brunnschweiler & Co., as the ABC brand was better known in the African markets. ABC became the tracing name for Newton Bank Printworks and its sales arm, as well as the principal brand name. The bulk of Newton Bank wax print production was now merchanted by ABC, either under the ABC or Grafton African brand.

The company employed forty designers and produced about 25 new designs every week. In their showroom they presented about 800 samples but had a range of 4,500 engraved designs available. In addition, they had records of 20,000 different patterns on rollers, with photographs and cloth samples. Patterns were removed from the collection if they received no sales for about five years, but could be re-introduced on demand. The huge archive was enhanced by the acquisition of several wax print collections, including Brown Fleming, United Turkey Red and Ashbury & Pickford.

Nevertheless, production fell to an all-time low at 4.7 million yards. However, closure was narrowly avoided by unexpected events: the end of the Nigerian civil war meant a boost in demand for wax prints, which was followed by the first 'oil shock' in 1973 that increased the profitability of Nigerian oil. This resulted in the doubling of sales in 1975, and an increase every year for the next seven years, despite Nigeria's complete ban on the importation of textiles since 1977 to protect its local producers. A well-organised smuggling trade was established through neighbouring countries of which Togo with its low rates of duty became most prominent. In 1977, ABC (under Tootal) decided to invest in new buildings, machinery and workflow in each department. The company was convinced that wax printing had a future despite decline in the trade and closure of all the other CPA printworks.[78]

Since 1945 Vlsco invested heavily in technical research and development and modernisation of wax print production, while the CPA had been reluctant to invest apart from in additional machinery. The product quality was lagging, which affected the sales price. While Vlisco could sell to more affluent people at a higher price, ABC became the brand for everyday wear. Wax prints were now sold throughout the whole of West Africa from Mauritania to Angola, Burundi and Rwanda. African clients were perfectly able to differentiate between a genuine wax print and a cheap screen-printed imitation. When demand outstripped supply in 1980, an attempt was made to import Malaysian and Javanese batiks, but despite the shortage this was not successful.[79]

In 1980 a major investment programme, based on years of growing demand for wax prints, started at Newton Bank. New buildings were erected, and old ones restored. Machinery was modernised with rotary screens rather than engraved rollers and workflow rationalised. When reorganisation was complete, the modernised factory reached full capacity with a production of 14 million yards in 1981. But due to the fall in oil prices the Nigerian economy collapsed, and with it the demand for wax prints. In 1984, sales fell to fewer than 6 million yards. However, ABC was able to take advantage of a stronger demand in French West Africa because of Britain's entry into the European Economic Community, and sales soon recovered to 12 million yards. The slump in trade and the lack of support from the remaining merchants convinced ABC that it was crucial to have total control of sales and marketing of all British wax prints. Consequently, the company stopped all commissioned printing on customers' cloth in 1987, only selling cloth and printing together. A consequence of this new policy was that two remaining merchants Logan Muckelt and Richard Brotherton ceased export trading in 1990.[80]

ABC had taken over control not only of the designs and production but also the marketing and sales of UK produced wax prints. It dedicated a designer specifically to each of the territories in which it sold its wax prints. Designers worked closely with regional marketing managers and made regular visits to consult customers in the field and monitor local trends within each area.[81] There was also development in design to suit the more sophisticated markets, helped by technical developments in the wax print process: greater ability to print on different weaves and fibres, varied base shades, marble effects, embossing and the use of metallic pigments and coloured foil.[82]

In 1991 the Tootal Group was taken over by Coats Viyella, a leading cotton manufacturer. This company was not interested in wax printing and a year later sold the wax printing division to the Cha Group, a Hong Kong based dyeing and printing company founded in 1949 by Cha Chi Ming (1914-2007) from Shanghai.

In 1964 the Cha company opened its first overseas business, the United Nigerian Textiles Limited (UNTL) in Kaduna and in 1967 Akosombo Textiles Limited in Ghana. Further companies were established or acquired across four African countries, but also elsewhere in the world which made it one of the world leaders in the textile industry.[83] Most of its factories were in Africa with mills spinning, weaving and printing including three wax print factories in Nigeria (UNTL, Supertex Ltd, Nichemtex Industries plc) and one in Ghana (Akosombo Textiles Ltd) with a total production of 100 million yards per annum in the 1990s. In 1995, the Cha Group claimed more than 60 per cent of the established market share of wax prints.[84] Over time the

Developments in the production and trade in wax prints after the Second World War

company's activities extended to technology, healthcare, financial services and property development.

Questions were raised as to why this group was interested in acquiring a struggling company. A mission statement was issued:

> To compete successfully in the premium segment of the Wax Print market by progressively improving quality and effectiveness at every level throughout the business and to contribute to overall Group success through the achievement of excellence and sharing of expertise in Marketing, Design, Technology and Management of People.[85]

In 1993, the first full year with the Cha Group, the company saw a return to profit. But a devaluation of the CFA franc (Coopération Financière en Afrique centrale) used in former French colonies affected 85 per cent of ABC sales, resulting in a drastic reduction of production and 100 redundancies. To improve communication and technical knowledge of the print process, in 1994 both the design studio and commercial department moved from Manchester to the manufacturing facility in Hyde. Different products and new colours and qualities were added, but the company did not recover quickly. It took until 1997 to reach profitability again in a climate of falling sales. Throughout this period the Cha group strengthened their West African factories through massive investment in machinery and facilities, design and marketing, and sharing of technical knowledge using the vast experience of the staff at ABC. Alongside the existing design studio of ABC, supervised by Rachel Wood, the Group Design Centre, supervised by Marilyn Hoyle, was created with studios in Togo (Lome), Ghana (Accra) and Nigeria (Kaduna and Onitsha).[86]

Even more pressure was added by the opening of several wax print factories in China that flooded the market with cheap products. Although the quality was inferior, the low price attracted sales, and factories in Africa began to suffer and some had to close. The European wax printers also felt the pressure. ABC transferred production of the standard wax prints to Akosombo Textiles Ltd (ATL) in Ghana, to concentrate on the higher value premium products like wax printing on brocade or poplin and in some cases with metallic foil added for further embellishment. Manufacturing these products proved to be demanding because the highest quality standards had to be met.

The company managed to survive on this reduced activity, but in 2005 the Cha Group started to transfer the remaining production and key staff to ATL in Ghana. Only a small team of designers continued to work in Hyde for the ABC brand and other group products in Ghana and Nigeria. On 20 December 2007, all UK manufacturing ceased, and printing at Newton Bank was finally closed. It was the last CPA works remaining, and the last wax printer in the United Kingdom. This left Vlisco as the last producer of wax prints in Europe.[87]

With most of the Newton Bank workforce made redundant, only the team of designers was kept on and a small team for management and site de-commissioning. Designing for wax print became less and less frequent. In 2009 the design studio produced the first range of designs of fancy prints for Da Viva, a new fashion brand for the West African market. The ABC designers, used to working within the strict technical requirements of wax print, were able to express their ideas more freely.[88] In 2014, the design studio relocated to another site in Hyde, where it was involved in a succession of initiatives to expand into new markets. Diminishing returns finally led to closure of the studio on 31 January 2021.[89]

Switzerland

After the war, sales of Swiss wax prints were slow-moving in the face of rising production costs at the Hohlenstein factory, and the restriction of UTC activities in its Ghanaian base in Accra due to caps on imports and high import duties. The UTC decided to start a joint venture with Cha Chi Ming of Hong Kong in establishing a new textile factory at Akosombo in Ghana, Akosombo Textiles Limited (ATL). In 1967, the Akosombo works began production of wax prints from the Hohlenstein repertoire, with UTL holding distribution rights. From Lagos in Nigeria, the prints were distributed to other markets.[90] The success of ATL meant that Hohlenstein started to struggle and had to close in 1974.[91]

Two post-war developments

The period after the Second World War saw two developments that had started before the war but afterwards expanded rapidly within the wax print industry and are associated with the postwar period: the rise of women traders and the increasing popularity of commemorative cloth.

Mama Benz

After the Second World War the UAC, G. B. Ollivant (GBO), the *Compagnie Française de l'Afrique Occidentale* (CFAO) and its most important competitor the *Société Commerciale de l'Ouest Africain* (SCOA) were the largest merchants of wax prints in Africa. Their representatives, mainly based in Londen and Liverpool, would visit the printing companies on a regular basis. Before the Second World War representatives of these companies, based in Africa, would pay such visits only occasionally.[92] After the

5. Visit of Mary Nzimoro and her daughter to the showroom of Ankersmit in Deventer (The Netherlands). Nzimoro was the main representative of the UAC in East Nigeria from 1948 onwards and visited on a regular basis Group photo Ankersmit. Standing (left to right): Gerrit Jan Meeles, Anton Ankersmit and Willem Wienbelt. Seated (left to right): Rudolf Ankersmit, Priscilla Nzimoro, Mary Nzimoro and Diderik Leonard Ankersmit (1949)
Photo by J. H. Rutgers, Deventer 1949
Collectie Overijssel NL-DvCO, ID 0895, inv.nr. 189

war these visits became more frequent. A novelty was visits of clients of the trade organisations. Most of these were women, who had used the growth of sales after the war to set up their own trading network.

The *Mama Benz* in English or *Nana Benz* in French, as women traders were called, saw a sharp increase in power and influence. Although in the 1950s African clothing was increasingly inspired by the West, the traditional female wax print costume remained popular and buying wax print became even more prevalent in post-independence African countries. Growing prosperity boosted the demand for Dutch wax prints which, by the 1950s, were no longer a luxury article for the elite but an aspirational commodity for many, at that time imported from Togo, but soon directly from Europe.[93] In 1952, Jan van Vlissingen considered that regular visits to West Africa were more important than ever:

de textielmanagers op de kust zijn onvoldoende vaklieden, zij weten te weinig van het wezenlijke van de inlandse smaak, van hun gewoonten, zeden en religie. Zij staan te ver van de zwarte af, begrijpen de quintessens waarom het gaat onvoldoende en weten last but not least veel te weinig van de fabricage mogelijkheden (the textile managers on the coast are insufficiently skilled, they know too little about the essence of the native taste, about their customs, manners and religion. They are too far removed from the black [population], insufficiently understand the quintessence of what is involved and, finally, know far too little about the manufacturing possibilities).[94]

These women traders were most knowledgeable, the local experts in understanding consumer preferences. They worked in close collaboration with the main merchants and had the rights to sell exclusive designs, sometimes based on their own sketches and colour ranges, which was a status symbol among themselves.[95] In the 1950s, this network of women traders was also used to circumvent import restrictions in specific countries. Togo was the centre for the main distributors of wax print with destinations in West and Central Africa, but fixed limits on the amount of imported cloth despite high demand. With the help of the women traders, about 70 per cent of the total export to Togo reached neighbouring countries. The traders who were not invited to travel to Europe to place orders had to rely on colleagues who made the trip and could order directly. The traders bought on credit, settling their accounts on the last day of every month. No interest was charged. Often the European merchant held deposit accounts for these traders. Most of them never learned to read, which did not hold them back in running successful businesses. Pedler describes their excitement when bales of wax cloth were opened for the inspection of the designs

Developments in the production and trade in wax prints after the Second World War

at the UAC's trading premises. The women vied with each other to get a first-hand into the bale. Attempts to impose discipline were resented as a restraint of their trade.[96]

Many of these women became prosperous, some became wealthy, which earned them their nickname of *Nana Benz*. *Nana* in Ewé, a Togolese language, means a respectable woman and *Benz* refers to the Mercedes Benz luxury brand. The phrase implied a respectable woman who could afford to drive an expensive car. Many of them did not limit their expenditure to luxury cars but invested in the stock market and real estate, even property in European capitals. Some sent their children to Europe and the United States for their education. But they also invested in political parties, health care and children's welfare.[97] Many Nana Benz businesses lasted several generations, their heads were called *Nanettes* or *Golden Ladies*. The 1970s and 1980s were the best years for these women. The 1990s were a turning point. Structural shifts in Togolese politics and economy were a major blow for the cloth traders. In 1994 the Banque de France decided to devalue the CFA franc, the currency used in 14 francophone African countries, which doubled the price of goods. The position of the Nana Benz has diminished further in recent times, because of competition and the influx of counterfeit.[98]

6. Classic design *Tie-up* and *Fishbone* from the Brown Fleming collection no. 253267 (17-4-1897) worn by East Nigerian women around 1960
Vlisco Archive, @ Vlisco BV

Commemorative cloth
Another rising phenomenon after the Second World War was commemorative cloth.[99] It was a phenomenon that had twentieth-century origins. After the First World War the end of export restrictions resulted in an economic boom for Nigeria from 1918 until 1920. This sudden prosperity ushered in a culture of dress, *aso ebi*.[100] *Aso* means cloth while *ebi* means family. Initially the term applied to a uniform dress, worn by family members of the Yoruba ethnic group during social events. This developed into a wider practice seen as an integral part of national culture in Nigeria during social events such as weddings, birthdays, burial ceremonies, political gatherings etc. Most Nigerian communities have a thriving associational culture based on informal and semi-formal organizations which help to construct participants' individual social identity, as well as a sense of solidarity:

Co-operation and mutual helpfulness are virtues among the Yoruba. There is a limitation to what a single individual can achieve all alone. The co-operation of others is highly

196 — 197

7. L'escalier de Gue, designed by Jos Reniers, Vlisco, worn by a group of people in Benin, 2006
Archives Missions Africaines, Rome

important in achieving most goals. It is believed that when two hands join in washing each other, one will have a truly clean hand ... It is also taught that while it is easy to break a broomstick, it is not easy to break a full bunch of them.[101]

The realisation of a goal with only an individual's opportunities is restricted, but in co-operation with others, achievements are unlimited.

The phenomenon of commemorative cloth spread to other parts of West Africa from Ghana to Liberia, Gambia to Zambia and the diaspora.[102] The idea of the uniform dress is that it transcends class barriers: everybody has access, both rich and poor. Some can wear the best quality, others will only be able to afford less expensive fabrics, but still with the same motif. *Aso ebi* seeks an alternative, a special cloth designed and printed to be within the reach of everyone concerned.[103] The likelihood of this special fabric becoming a classic is very slim, because of its short-lived use. According to Neil Whiteman, a representative of the UAC, in the 1950s and 1960s, the cloth was still mainly used as a wrapper.[104] But later, lengths of fabric were also cut to make clothing, like dresses, skirts, blouses, trousers or even three-piece suits. Such clothes were kept afterwards to save them for future generations like the whole lengths of fabric.

Aso oke, the woven cloth of the Yoruba worn for special occasions, lies within a tradition that goes back centuries. It is necessarily limited because production is not mechanised. Imported prints, on the other hand, could meet mass demand. They were faster and cheaper to produce and enabled the accelerating popularity of commemorative cloth.[105] In general, these were fancy prints and not the more costly wax prints. Already in 1908, some early examples were registered for copyright protection in the United Kingdom, but these were an exception. They were probably meant to commemorate an event, but not yet to be worn by a group of people.[106]

Faber claims that the earliest known examples of this type of cloth with portraits date from 1928.[107] In the sample books of the United Africa Company in the Brunnschweiler Archives, Picton found examples from 1929.[108] Portrait photography was introduced relatively early into Africa, especially in colonial urban centres, but became more widespread at the beginning of the twentieth century.

Developments in the production and trade in wax prints after the Second World War

Studios brought portraits within easy reach, but especially newspapers and magazines helped the spread of photo-realist depictions of people, especially royalty and politicians. Printed textile designs incorporating such images were produced to order, and sometimes employed standardised framing devices or simple printing techniques for a quick turnaround.[109] Today political subjects form the largest group of commemoratives fabrics. These include portraits of political leaders, national colours, political party emblems, state or national flags. They reflect an iconography created by the newly independent African states, with their search for a unique national identity with its own colours and symbols in order to evoke national pride and solidarity. Other patterns commemorate events such as the inauguration of a church or a visit by the Pope. Popular events such as an important football match or the visit of a celebrity can lead to a new pattern. Alongside prints, woven stripes and checks and *George* fabrics (damasks) of silk, cotton and polyester are used to commemorate an event as a group.[110]

European textile design for the West African markets was never an autonomous activity pursued for its own aesthetic ends, but an essential marketing tool.[111] Before the 1970s, rotating seasonal collections were not a fashion phenomenon as they were in Europe. The West African calendar is punctuated by a rainy period from May to August that slows sales, which pick up again at times of harvest when people are earning money.[112] What can be observed in going through the engraving books of ABC and Vlisco is that the influences of stylistic periods are clearly visible. Especially after the Second World War, a new type of imagery, related to consumer culture with its symbols of modernity, became popular. Some of those became classics, but did not replace the old classics, which were reprinted again and again often in variations of quality, colour and cloth. Classic motifs were enlarged, reduced, re-arranged, combined and given new backgrounds and settings with updated colourings to stimulate new interest.

All this required a good knowledge of the market, which remained as crucial to success as when Brown Fleming started trading. Agents, contracted by European merchant firms and resident in Africa, reported on potential trends and collected and sent samples of promising designs and qualities of cloth from competitors. Agents informed their employers about regional and tribal preferences, not only motifs but specific colours and pattern treatments. Local agents knew that the African consumers had a sophisticated taste for quality and good design and would not be interested in imitations or lesser qualities as long as better were affordable. There was an ongoing interest in novelties, but it took time for goods to be made. Printed goods often required five to six weeks for production. Individual requests from agents could not always be met, because of difficulties in producing small quantities. Another issue was piracy. Copying rivals' designs was universal and registration resulted only in limited protection. For companies in the United Kingdom, the Netherlands and Switzerland, the best marketing research could provide no certainty about which designs would sell well. Designers could work from original ideas or rework pre-existing motifs, but it was the merchant who was the driving force behind the design decision-making. As we have seen, the merchant controlled the selection of design, along with the quality and type of cloth until the late 1980s.[113] Since the introduction of African-styled wax prints around 1890, the way the market worked had remained the same for nearly a hundred years – a century in which patterns, now deemed classics, became entangled with African cultures and embodied in African identities.

1   Personal communication Gerhard Frensel Milsbeek (The Netherlands), 4 May 2022
2   Janszen and De Visser, 139
3   Personal communication Gerhard Frensel Milsbeek (The Netherlands), 4 May 2022
4   Janszen and De Visser, 139
5   Meeles II, 213-227
6   See under 'Van Vlissingen' for more details of post-independence developments in West African countries.
7   Janszen en De Visser, 169
8   In the Vlisco Archive is a *Report on the Design-analyses* by F. L. van Holthoon from September 1963, kept with an analysis of the turnover and distribution of various design factors among Old (pre-1945), Middle-aged (1945-1955) and New designs between designs of Ankersmit and Van Vlissingen in the period 1956-1962, probably made to prepare for the merger of the two companies. The results are generic without naming specific designs.
9   Cees Sistermans wrote down what for him as a designer of Ankersmit this handwriting had to look like. He stipulated that it was crucial to work as a team with equal members and no internal competion. Creation, not copying, of designs should be central. He probably wrote these thoughts before moving to Helmond. Document dated December 1965 and January 1966. Personal archive Gerhard Frensel, Milsbeek (The Netherlands), kept by Martin Frensel Akkrum (The Netherlands).
10 Boll moved to Nigeria as chief designer for Kaduna Textiles Ltd, the first overseas enterprise of the Cha group (https://www.chatextiles.com/english/aboutUs/history.html). It was Boll who put Cha Chi Ming in touch with the Ankersmit designers in Helmond. He stayed in Nigeria until 1966 and was replaced by Ebe van der Meer. Personal communication Gerhard Frensel, Milsbeek (The Netherlands), 4 May 2022.
11 https://trademarks.justia.com/722/79/bouboudima-72279340.html, last accessed 7 June 2022. In Swahili *boubou* means skin, *dima* leopard, hence leopardskin.
12 Notes: Gerhard Frensel, 30 June 2007, Personal archive.
13 'Wat doet Vlisco', unpublished document about European and Exo-markets, Vlisco Archive, @ Vlisco BV and Exhibition catalogue *Six Yards. Guaranteed Dutch Design*, MMKA Museum of Modern Art Arnhem 2012, 6
14 The studio was called 'Novi, Industrial and Design Services BV'. Personal communication Gerhard Frensel, Milsbeek (The Netherlands), 4 May 2022.
15 Attempts of Van Vlissingen to take over the studio before its closure were unsuccessful. Personal communication Gerhard Frensel, Milsbeek (The Netherlands), 4 May 2022.
16 Jacobs and Maas, 64
17 Bijlsma and Rodenburg, 55
18 Bijlsma and Rodenburg, 63; Verschueren, 82
19 Jacobs and Maas, 63
20 Ingenbleek, 271-272; Jacobs and Maas, 78–82
21 Jacobs and Maas, 83
22 Unilever Archive Oral History Programme Interview Ref. OH/80 with Ken Forrest, 3 March 2011, at Lever House, Port Sunlight. https://www.archives-unilever.com/media/_file/preservica/GB1752_OH/3b6f1de5-bf57-4aaf-8894-036b836d231c--OH80_Ken_Forrest.pdf, last accessed 10 April 2024
23 He would go on to further trips in November 1951 to West Africa, in 1952 to Egypt and Sudan, in 1953 and 1955 to East and West Africa. Verschueren, 89, 92-93
24 Jacobs and Maas, 75
25 *Koninklijke Vereeniging 'Oost en West'*. This association was founded in 1899 to strengthen the ties between the Netherlands and its colonies. The association stopped its activities in 1971. https://nl.wikipedia.org/wiki/Vereeniging_Oost_en_West, last accessed 24 November 2022.
26 'Over Equatoriaal Afrika' in De Rakel (ed.), M*aandblad voor het personeel van de 'Vlisco' en 'de Kempen'*, 7 (1955), 79, 2.
27 Jacobs and Maas, 150-151; Ingenbleek 1998, 273. A good, but later example is the introduction of Super Wax in 1972, developed to the highest standards by Marie Althuizen. For this quality, the finest yarns and weave were chosen, printed with three instead of two colours, based on requests from the market. Initially seen as gilding the lily, it soon became a commercial success. Personal communication Frans van Rood, Helmond, 31 January 2023
28 Jacobs and Maas, 150
29 Ingenbleek 1998, 273
30 The reason to mention Vlisco as well was that in a period that the company was very viable, Ankersmit wanted to come back and could also put Real Dutch Waxprint on the selvedges of its cloth. Eventually Ankersmit decided not to restart its business. Ingenbleek 280-281 and 'Document Inscriptie lijmdruk', Vlisco Archive, @ Vlisco BV.
31 Arts, 65
32 Jacobs and Maas 86, 111
33 Verschueren, 107
34 A lingering conflict between members of the Fentener van Vlissingen family meant that Unilever was enabled to buy enough shares. See Ingenbleek 1998, 277
35 As main shareholder Unilever had a say in Van Vlissingen's business, but was dependent on Ankersmit. Their technology should not be shared with the competition. Ingenbleek 1998, 277
36 ADATIG was incorporated in the UK as Adatig Ltd. 12 October 1961, company no. 705498.
37 Personal communication Frans van Rood, Helmond, 31 January 2023.
38 For more information about the background of these developments, see Robin van Koert, *Dutch Wax Design and Technology van Helmond naar West-Afrika, Uniwax en GTP in postkoloniaal Ivoorkust en Ghana*, Helmond 2008.
39 Personal communication Frans van Rood, Helmond, 31 January 2023.
40 Unfortunately, the report does not give specific design numbers, so it is difficult to judge their conclusion. The report is kept at the Vlisco Archive, @ Vlisco BV.
41 The researchers only published their results ten years later: W. J. Boelman and F. L. van Holthoon, 'African Dress in Ghana' in *Kroniek van Afrika*, 13:3 (1973), 236-258.
42 Ingenbleek 1998, 276
43 Verschueren, 110; Jacobs and Maas, 145. For a description of the period 1980-1996, see Jacobs and Maas, chapter 6, 147-152.
44 Jacobs and Maas, 123
45 Since 1960, Unilever had become a majority shareholder of Van Vlissingen after a protracted conflict with members of the Fentener van Vlissingen family.
46 Jacobs and Maas, 123-134
47 In 1970 it was transformed from a limited liability company into a private company. Jacobs and Maas, 106. In 1972 Vlisco became part of Gamma Holding, in 2010 part of Actis, and since 2021 part of Parcom. The merger was, in retrospect, not necessary, because the market kept expanding. Personal communication Frans van Rood, Helmond, 31 January 2023.
48 Unilever Archive Oral History Programme Interview Ref. OH/32 Part 1 with Mr Neil Whiteman, held 2 May 2007 at UAC Old Coasters Reunion. Interviewer: William Meredith. https://www.archives-unilever.com/media/_file/preservica/GB1752_OH/5c8027dd-9c5f-45db-8f4a-1cb68809f84c--OH32_Neil_Whiteman_Part_1.pdf, last accessed 5 April 2024
49 The CNF, being part of the UAC, had sole rights to sell Dutch wax prints, until the CFAO and SCOA also obtained an allocation of Dutch wax prints in 1964. 'Newton Bank Printworks Hyde 1812-2007 and European Involvement in Batik Printing', undated and unpublished document Brunnschweiler Archive, held at the Whitworth Art Gallery, University of Manchester (UK), 8.
50 Personal communication Frans van Rood, Helmond, 31 January 2023.
51 He hoped that in the future the computer might become a useful tool, also for the production and planning department. For a detailed description and the criteria of this analysis, see Krantz 1985, 5.
52 Ingenbleek 1998, 280-281
53 Jan Fentener van Vlissingen kept ties with the company until the early 1970s. Verschueren, 123
54 C. H. Krantz, head of design from 1952 until 1985, did not approve of his designers travelling to Africa, because it could influence their originality and focus. Personal communication Frans van Rood,

Helmond, 31 January 2023. For more information about designing at Vlisco, see M. Amah Edoh, 62-63.
55 Personal communication Frans van Rood, 29 June 2023.
56 Edoh 2016, 97
57 Personal communication Janne van Pelt-Verberne, Head of Colour Vlisco, Helmond, 24 October 2023.
58 Personal communication Marilyn Hoyle, Former Head of Design, ABC Wax, 24 October 2023.
59 Personal communication Jo Pinder, Former Designer, ABC Wax, 25 October 2023.
60 Tabiou, 36. For more examples, see Tabiou's book: *Nana Benz. Le mythe devenu discret*, Lomé Togo: Editions Haho, 2011.
61 Personal communication Janne van Pelt-Verberne, Head of Colour Vlisco, Helmond, 24 October 2023.
62 Personal communication Frans van Rood, 3 September 2023.
63 Personal communication Janne van Pelt-Verberne, Head of Colour Vlisco, Helmond, 24 October 2023.
64 Hoogenboom, 34
65 Arts, 65; Edoh 2017, 62-63 and Delhaye, 256
66 In the Brunnschweiler Archives, documents, photographs, pattern books and cloth testify to the UTR transfer. Lists were drawn up with detailed information of about one hundred wax print designs with name, width, UTR number, original engraving date and the newly assigned 'A' number used at the Newton Bank works. Design engagements were also specified, with about three-quarters for Elson & Neill. The width was in general 36-inch, some designs were extended to 48-inch.
67 Nenadic and Tuckett, 15. The most important collection of pattern books, textile samples and printing blocks of United Turkey Red are kept at the National Museums Scotland in Edinburgh and at Glasgow University. Some pattern books are kept in the Dumbarton Library. Business records relating to the running of the company are kept at the Manchester Archives. Miscellaneous records of the company from 1898 until 1960 are kept at the University of Glasgow. Material related to wax printing is held in the Brunnschweiler archives, Whitworth Art Gallery, University of Manchester (UK).
68 Both UTR and Horridge and Cornall took advantage of the government's redundancy scheme 1960-61. Personal communication Philip Sykas, 24 October 2023. See BT175/173B: Reorganisation General file 1961.
69 Sykas 16, 26-27. In 1986 the pattern books from 1890 until 1969 were discovered whilst clearing Logan Muckelt's warehouse. They are now kept at Manchester Archives. The Manchester-based records of the Patent Office Design Registry were acquired by the Victoria and Albert Museum, adding to an existing group donated by the manufacturer in the 1930s and 40s, making a collection of 77 pieces of wax print. https://www.vam.ac.uk/search?q=logan+muckelt&astyped=, last accessed 25 March 2023.
70 Harrop, 11
71 Nielsen 1974, 48
72 https://www.heritagegateway.org.uk/Gateway/Results_Single.aspx?uid=1585141&resourceID=19191, page visited 17 March 2023
73 'Newton Bank Printworks Hyde 1812-2007 and European Involvement in Batik Printing'. Unpublished document Brunnschweiler Archive, Whitworth Art Gallery, University of Manchester (UK), 9.
74 For more information about Brunnschweiler, see the appendix. See also Laurens van der Laan 1983 and *Kreuz und Quer der Farben. Karo- und Streifenstoffe der Schweiz für Afrika, Indonesian und die Türkei*, Zürich: Museum Bellerive, 1997. Modemuseum im Müncher Stadtmuseum München (1998) and Museum des Landes Glarus, Näfels (Switzerland) (1999).
75 This became Tootal Group plc in 1982, and in 1991 the Coats Viyella group. In 1998, the group was forced to split into Coats and Viyella.
76 https://www.flickr.com/photos/30593522@N05/12237082584, last accessed 20 March 2023. Elson & Neil, their biggest client, was forced to sell to Brunnschweiler in 1970 and close their business.
77 In 1993 years of political turbulence caused the closure of CPA Zaire, which meant the loss of the bleaching business in the United Kingdom. Attempts to find new business were unsuccessful and in 2002 it was decided to end all the bleaching.
78 Newton Bank stopped its own conventional print business in 1983. In 1980, Loveclough Printworks closed. Its specialist work in high-quality roller prints, mainly for Liberty and Marks and Spencer, was transferred to Strines Printworks and Newton Bank. Producing these high-quality roller prints, alongside West African prints, and indigo and brown discharge for the South African market, proved to be a logistical and financial challenge. Eventually all the fine roller work was transferred to Strines. 'Newton Bank Printworks Hyde 1812-2007 and European Involvement in Batik Printing', unpublished document, Brunnschweiler Archive, Whitworth Art Gallery, University of Manchester (UK).
79 B. W. Anderton. 'European Involvement in Batik Printing' (1991), unpublished document, Brunnschweiler Archives, Whitworth Art Gallery, University of Manchester (UK).
80 Ibidem. The patterns of Logan Muckelt were transferred to Newton Bank and Salis Schwabe, Middleton Print Works. Sykas 2005, 27
81 Copy script, Tootal Brand Book, 22 July 1992. Brunnschweiler Archive, Whitworth Art Gallery, University of Manchester (UK).
82 Personal communication David Bradley, Managing Director, ABC, Hyde, 23 November 2015.
83 https://www.chatextiles.com/english/aboutUs/history.html
84 For an extensive list of their factories in Africa, see: https://www.chatextiles.com/english/locations/globalLocations.html, last accessed 12 March 2023. See also: *The Cha Textile Group in Africa*, company brochure, 1995.
85 Harrop, 15
86 Personal communication Marilyn Hoyle, former Head of Design, ABC Wax, 23 February 2024,
87 For further information, see Gerald Harrop, 'Newton Bank Printworks Hyde 1812-2007 and European Involvement in Batik/Wax Block Prints', undated and unpublished document Brunnschweiler Archive, held at the Whitworth Art Gallery, University of Manchester (UK).
88 Personal communication David Bradley, manager at ABC Hyde UK 23 November 2015.
89 The cloth archive was sent to CHA in Hong Kong to be digitised in 2020. The historical archive was transferred to the Whitworth Art Gallery in Manchester in March 2023.
90 See also Stephan F. Miescher, 'Bringing Fabrics to Life. Akosombo Textiles Limited of Ghana' in Gott, Suzanne et al. (eds), *African-Print Fashion Now! A Story of Taste, Globalization and Style*, Los Angeles: Fowler Museum, 2017, 87-95.
91 Samples can be found in the Museum der Kulturen in Basel and Museum des Landes Glarus in the Freuler Palace in Näfels. This museum also holds UTC correspondence. Archival material concerning the UTC can also be found in the archives of the Basel Mission.
92 Meeles II, 85. See also Feld, Marit, *Adviesverslag ontsluiting Ankersmitarchief Collectie Overijssel*, Stichting Overijssel Zwolle/Deventer, 2024, 80, 83.
93 Meij, 12-13
94 Jacobs and Maas, 76
95 Ingenbleek 1998, 274
96 Pedler, 240
97 Tabiou, 21, 83
98 Tabiou, 40, 89. For more information, see also Rita Cordonnier, *Femmes Africaines et Commerce. Les revendeuses de tissu de la ville de Lomé* (Togo), Paris, 1987.
99 This type of cloth is different from a cloth that commemorates a specific event like Nigerian Railway and Postal Pattern, described in chapter 4. Those were worn by individuals; the 'commemorative' cloth that became popular in the 1950s was worn by specific groups.
100 Olukoju, 123. *Aso ebi* is distinct from *aso egbe* or *aso eke*, which history goes back to the fifteenth century.
101 Dopamu and Alana, 167
102 See also Ajani, 'Aso Ebi: The Dynamics of Fashion and Cultural Commodification in Nigeria' in *The Journal of Pan African Studies*, 5:6 (September 2012), 108-118.
103 The Asante already had new kente designs for special events. Stencils were used for the famous *adire aleko* fabrics from Nigeria to depict events.
104 Unilever Archive Oral History Programme Interview Ref. OH/32 Part 1 with Mr Neil Whiteman, held on 2 May 2007 at JAC Old

Coasters Reunion. Interviewer: William Meredith https://www.archives-unilever.com/media/_file/preservica/GB1752_OH/5c8027dd-9c5f-45db-8f4a-1cb68809f84c--OH32_Neil_Whiteman_Part_1.pdf, last accessed 5 April 2024
105 Faber 2010, 11-13
106 This design was registered as 1440 on 13 March 1908. The occasion has not yet been identified.
107 Faber 2011, 150
108 See Picton 1995, 29.

109 Faber 2011, 149-150. See also P*aul Faber, Long Live the President! Portrait-cloths from Africa,* Amsterdam: KIT Publishers, 2010.
110 George fabrics originated from India for the traditional use of saris. The cloth became first very popular with the African royal and noble families, later also with the general public. They are often hand-finished with gold thread, sequins and beading.
111 Elands, 66
112 Jacobs and Maas, 77
113 Launert, 205-207

The process of wax printing

7.
All wax is removed and the dye is fixed, creating a marble effect where the wax resisted the colours.

Epilogue
The *Contentious* Designs: the legacy of Brown Fleming

By the 1920s, wax prints, especially with designs from the 'Haarlem collection' introduced by Brown Fleming, were produced by many companies, not only in Europe but worldwide, and had become engrained in West African culture. The ownership of these classic designs was disputed for a long time, partly because companies were not aware of the rights held by Brown Flemings Ltd. until 1939 and by the CPA afterwards. But importantly, these companies all eventually had to accept that the designs from Haarlem had become so embedded as to constitute a common cultural language. Africans had transformed a colonial commodity, through naming, application of meanings and generational inheritance into authentic African material. It would take producers decades to acknowledge this.

Brown Flemings Limited

Almost a year before Brown Fleming's death in 1912 his son William Elphinstone Fleming and his son-in-law Ronald Richmond Herbertson, who had taken over the management of Brown Flemings Ltd, registered the design *Exhibition* with the British Patent Office, under number 36176, on 5 June 1911.[1]

Exhibition was an homage, a gathering together of Brown Fleming's most famous motifs that had been introduced since 1895. Each had acquired classic status relatively quickly. The company's printer was still the HKM. Both firms had been substantially successful with sales of wax prints in West Africa. The HKM was the first in the Netherlands to buy a *spring roller printing machine* in 1910.[2] In 1914, output reached 6 million yards.[3]

However, the First World War was fatal for the HKM, shrinking its West African exports. Sales fell sharply as export shipping became increasingly difficult. In 1916, employees numbered 243, but in 1917 they were reduced to 190.[4] When the Dutch government decided to seize resources and refused to contribute to redundancy payments, production was stopped in October 1917.[5] On 22 June 1918, the decision was taken to place the company in voluntary liquidation.[6]

Charles van de Poll had retired as director in 1914 and his son Andre (1884-1966) succeeded him. But as Driessen, director of the LKM, observed, Andre had no passion whatsoever for the profession ('*heeft hoegenaamd geen liefhebberij voor het vak*'). Verbong saw in Andre little of the usual strong drive to continue a business from father to son, little initiative to fight for the company's survival.[7] An auction was organised to sell off the closing inventory. Ankersmit tried to purchase part by private treaty, but this was refused by the HKM, still resentful of the copying of their printing process by their competitor.[8] Van Vlissingen purchased sample books, forty-two printing rollers and a wax print machine.[9] Most of the printing equipment was acquired by Roessingh of Veenendaal.[10] Employees, unhappy with the closure, attempted to re-start the business in 1919 as the NV Haarlemsche Katoendrukkerij with J. G. C. Sabel as director, but their initiative ended in liquidation on 11 December 1922.[11]

Brown Fleming also felt the consequences of the First World War. At the start of the conflict, William Elphinstone Fleming volunteered for the army and fought in Egypt and Italy. On his return to Glasgow in early 1919, he decided to leave the business he had been running with his brother-in-law. In February 1920 he sold his shares to Ronald Richmond Herbertson and his wife Frances Herbertson-Fleming.[12] Since the closure of the HKM in 1917, Herbertson had worked with Roessingh as printer. It may be that the London shipper Israel Werner suggested the collaboration. A letter in the archives of the Basel Mission dated 20 February 1919 shows that Werner claimed money for a delivery from Roessingh suggesting that the BMTC was already selling prints from Roessingh.[13] The choice was understandable as Van Vlissingen and Ankersmit were busy setting up their own wax print businesses and were probably not interested in *commission printing*.

In 1920, Herbertson registered a trademark for the company in the Netherlands: an open left hand with the letters *BF LTD* on the back. Registering a Dutch trademark is a sign that the collaboration had been formalised.[14] Herbertson had continued Brown Fleming's business at 164 Springfield Road in Dalmarnock, but soon relocated to 130 Robertson Street in Glasgow.[15] From 1925, Roessingh prospered as orders for wax prints for West Africa increased.[16] It is plausible that the commissions of Brown Flemings contributed to their success.

By 1927, F. W. Ashton and Co. also started printing for Brown Flemings.[17] When there was a rush of work all needed at the same time, it was not unusual for merchants to commission prints from more than one mill. But in 1929, the economic crisis brought a sharp downturn in sales and exports to West Africa stagnated. The first half of the 1930s was difficult for companies trading with Africa. Brown Flemings struggled with declining sales figures.[18]

The main clients during this period were the CFAO, the SCAO, the CGCA and G. B. Ollivant. Henry Werner, the son of Israel who had been a long-time shipper for Ebenezer Brown Fleming, was also a client. But Roessingh became a victim of the downturn of the early 1930s, and Wijnand Roessingh was forced to close the company in 1935. After its closure, Ankersmit and Van Vlissingen bought some of the machinery and agreed an annual stipend for Wijnand Roessingh on condition that he cease any commercial activities in the wax print business.

Brown Flemings was also in a difficult situation. In a letter to his brother-in-law William Elphinstone Fleming, Herbertson wrote on 17 August 1934 that he had decided to put the company into voluntary liquidation given the difficult economic situation in Africa: 'I can't tell you how sorry I am and how much my pride is hurt that the old firm has to put up the shutters while under my control'.[19] In 1935, perhaps in a final attempt to save the company, Herbertson decided to make Wijnand Roessingh co-director of Brown Flemings Ltd.[20] Despite his promise to Van Vlissingen and Ankersmit to stay out of the wax print business, Roessingh accepted this position.

It is not known for how long he worked with Herbertson or how much input he had in the business. In July 1935, F. W. Ashton and Co. started printing the most popular *classics* of the Brown Fleming collection for Brown Flemings.[21] The company, now entirely dependent on Ashton for the printing, also became a member of the so-called *Wax Ring* set up by the CPA to fix prices between merchants and shippers.[22] The sales figures for Brown Flemings Ltd went up significantly.[23] Unfortunately, the re-launch of Brown Flemings coincided with a boycott of all British goods during the Gold Coast cocoa crisis of 1937-1938. A coalition of farmers, brokers and chiefs refused to sell their produce to the major trading firms as a response to a collusive buying agreement that manipulated prices and fixed market shares.[24]

Brown Flemings Ltd was caught with a large stock as well as printing commitments. In 1939, Herbertson reluctantly decided to sell the company to the Calico Printers' Association. It was agreed that royalties would be paid on the use of any Brown Fleming designs for a period of five years.[25] Three hampers, containing all the swatches and designs in books and various company registers, were sent to Manchester.[26] On 12 May, the Chief Accountant of the Calico Printers' Association wrote to Daniel Forbes, partner of Moncrieff Warren Paterson & Co., solicitors in Glasgow:

---

1. *Exhibition*, BT reg.no. 36176, 5 June 1911 by Brown Flemings Ltd as an homage to its founder with the most famous motifs he had introduced since 1895
Brunnschweiler Archive, held at the Whitworth Art Gallery, University of Manchester (UK)

it seemed to us desirable that there should be an authoritative list of designs taken over. When these come here, they will all have a distinctive number, and it would not give us much trouble to prepare a list to be attached to the agreement.[27]

A total of 220 samples were photographed and numbered to establish the designs for which royalties should be paid.[28] The first 162 samples originated from the collection before Brown Fleming's death in 1912; the remaining designs were introduced later.[29]

Designs becoming *contentious*

Although Brown Flemings Limited until 1939, and the CPA thereafter, had legal ownership of the Brown Fleming designs, the legacy of years of printing by various companies created significant confusion about their ownership status. These firms began to argue over the recurring question of ownership of the classics of the *Haarlem* collection, each assuming they belonged uniquely to them.

Already in 1916 there was a request from the BMTC that Ankersmit pay royalties for designs it had suggested. Most of these designs came from Brown Fleming and were not part of the intellectual property of the BMTC. Lacking proof of ownership, payments were never made.[30]

When the HKM closed its doors in 1918, the inventory was sold at auction to several companies in the Netherlands and, as previously stated, Van Vlissingen purchased printing rollers.[31] The company assumed that by doing so it also acquired the copyright of the designs.[32] Jacobs and Maas suggested that the position of Ankersmit was more favourable because they were able to purchase the most popular Brown Fleming designs even earlier than Van Vlissingen.[33] These companies were clearly not aware of the fact that the rights were still with the heirs and directors of Brown Flemings Ltd.

In 1922, Jean Jacques was negotiating with the UTR about delivering designs for their new wax print division. He was convinced that no liability would arise from engraving patterns exactly to their originals, but the company hesitated and eventually urged him to make them sufficiently different to prevent any claims due to the copying of patterns.[34]

In 1937 Ankersmit learned that G. B. Ollivant had copied their design no. 9950, called *Grammophone**. Ankersmit urged Ollivant to withdraw it from the market, because they had registered it, but Ollivant refused to do so. Ollivant argued that they had already been printing it for some years as had other companies:

> You may take it that it is not part of our policy to copy other people's designs, but in this individual case we submit that it

is an open design and further that as we have been marketing it for some considerable period and it has apparently not affected sales of your own production, that there is nothing dangerous in it to your connections.[35]

In 1957, Ankersmit wanted to register some designs at the request of the UAC that were imitations of classics, but the Manchester Branch of the Designs Registry responded that it was impossible to check if very old designs had been registered before, because it would cause 'interminable delays. The fact that we are regularly submitting these out-of-time-applications to register old designs is, of course, something we are treating as quite confidential.'[36]

The problem came to a head that year when the two leading companies Van Vlissingen (now Vlisco) and F. W. Ashton (later ABC) both wanted to register the same classic designs for production in Japan. The CFAO produced a document with evidence of the widespread practice of copying the classics. It shows examples of many other companies that had printed the same design since its introduction, citing designs like *Target**, *Dice**, *Alphabet**, *New Fine Trail**, *Canoe Peak**, *Snakeskin**, *Grammophone** and many more. The explanation, repeated at every design, underlines lack of knowledge as the cause of confusion:

> This Ankersmit production was almost identical with a motif from a design which was originally the property of Haarlemse Katoenmaatschappij who sold the rollers of their design – and the accompanying rights therein – to Vlissingen in 1923. Ankersmit produced and continue to produce their production with the authority of Vlissingen.[37]

Had it not been Ankersmit that first started copying designs of Brown Fleming? And how was it possible that Van Vlissingen bought the rights when his successors were still trading? The HKM had only been a provider for them and was not the owner.

On behalf of the CPA as *the heir and rightful owner of Brown Flemings*, Ashton compiled a similar document with even more designs to prove their point. Writing about the design *Sibi Saba*, they found it 'preposterous on the part of P. F. van Vlissingen to claim to be the copyright owners of the design by the fact that they bought, as scrap, the rollers of the Haarlemse Katoenmaatschappij.'[38] A meeting was held in 1957 with the CPA, represented by J. C. Bridgman, Ankersmit, represented by its director Anton Ankersmit, and Van Vlissingen (Vlisco), represented by Jan Fentener Van Vlissingen and Gerard Vollaard.

Eventually all parties realised none could claim unique rights of ownership after so many years and so much confusion. Instead, the same list of 220 photographs that was established in 1939 formed the basis of a determination for which designs could be printed by which firm:

> *Uitdrukkelijk is afgesproken, dat de verdeling op deze lijst niet inhoudt dat het eigendomsrecht van de dessins is toegekend aan de firma die de dessins in Japan gaat registreren* (It has been expressly agreed that the distribution of this list does not mean that the ownership rights of the designs have been assigned to the company that will register the designs in Japan).[39]

The list was updated in 1969 and was still in use in the early 1970s.[40] In 1971 the issue flared up again between ABC and Vlisco, this time about registration of designs in Nigeria. Both parties felt the need to register a collection of the same designs for production locally. G. J. Jagger of ABC wrote to his colleagues in Lagos:

> In the African Print trade design is tremendously important. Good designs in the right colours marketed soundly can command high premiums over the ruling average market

2. *Icons on a pedestal*. Design for Vlisco campaign 2013 *Hommage à l'Art*. In a celebration of the most famous motifs, designers literally put the *Hand**, the *Snail**, the *Eye** and *Record** on a pedestal
Photo Vlisco Archive, @ Vlisco BV

prices. Many of these designs continue to print in considerable quantities for many years, and quite a number still in use today were first produced eighty or more years ago. Almost all the best designs were, and still are, originated either in Holland or England. (…) These designs have become a most valuable asset.[41]

All the designs mentioned on the list were part of the Haarlem collection. It is interesting to note that both parties decided to use the same agent of the UAC to defend their rights before the Registrar of Patents & Design in Lagos, which had a Patents and Design Act in place since 1970. This time it was Nigerian production that had become a shared concern for the European companies. It is not known how effective these registrations turned out to be.

How sensitive the subject was only five years later in 1976 is shown by correspondence between the UAC and Vlisco. Vlisco sent the UAC the draft for publication of W. T. Kroese's book *The Origin of the Wax Block Prints on the Coast of West Africa* in which he claims that Brown Fleming registered designs from the existing HKM collection. The UAC rejected the claim that any design was from Brown Fleming. They were convinced that they were created by the HKM, possibly not even aware that Brown Fleming registered them in the UK. Brown Fleming was to them no more than an agent for the HKM.[42]

The intensified circulation of counterfeit patterns in West African markets continued to threaten major companies such as Vlisco and ABC. According to Philip Poole, who worked for ABC during the last decades of the twentieth century:

> the Dutch were market leaders everywhere and by a country mile at the quality end. Every batch of new designs onto the market were immediately copied by the local fancy printers and the Cha factories in Nigeria.[43]

As an example of his frustration about design piracy, he mentions Hasson et Frères. In 1988, they had seventeen already extant designs for the Congolese market printed by *Sotexki* and *Utexafrica*. Initially these local fancy prints did not affect the major companies, because the difference in quality was easily detectable. But when the quality of copies improved and purchasing power declined, people were more inclined to buy the copies. The efforts of ABC had resulted in a decrease in piracy among the *old and contentious designs*. Ideally, Poole wished for a collaboration with Vlisco to further expand protection, but that did not materialise.[44]

As piracy continued to become more widespread, this increasingly affected Vlisco's position. In 2007, it introduced a marketing campaign to promote its authenticity and originality with the slogan *Vlisco, The True Original since 1846*. This drew on the company's heritage position in African print as well as its commitment to innovation, the creation of original designs and printing technology. But this could be said to be somewhat of a distortion: while Vlisco was established in 1846 and made batik imitations for Indonesia and South East of Asia from its inception, wax prints were only exported to West Africa almost seventy years later, some twenty years after Brown Fleming.[45] But its advertising campaign was not meant to deal with such historical nuance: a clear message was adopted to reinforce Vlisco's prime position, especially in the face of the expanding dominance of Chinese firms in the African market. Vlisco was, in effect, fighting the same threat they themselves had caused when imitating batik at the start of their own business.

Today companies from all over the world continue printing designs from the *Haarlem* collection, many of which were introduced more than 125 years ago. Over time new designs have been introduced by other companies that have also become classics and these gained popularity equivalent to that of the Brown Fleming patterns.[46] For a company such as Vlisco, market leader and the last remaining wax printing company in Europe, some 80 per cent of sales continue to be based on classics.

A notable illustration is *Hommage à l'Art*, a Vlisco campaign of 2013 which pays tribute to the most iconic designs, re-created as gold statues and literally put on a pedestal, several of which go back to the *Haarlem* collection. It is a representation of *their* heritage, but it also shows that Vlisco, more than hundred years after the death of Brown Fleming, is acutely aware that classics are the *backbone* of their story.

Conclusion

The success of Brown Fleming was based on a unique combination of a superior quality of wax-printed fabric and carefully selected designs, drawn by the skilled personnel of the HKM in the Netherlands. As a small merchant in a very specific market, Brown Fleming had the necessary flexibility to gather information essential for effective marketing. He was the first to base his selection of patterns and colourings for wax prints on information from his West African patrons via his network of traders. Research carried out for this book also revealed the essential role of missionary traders in this design and cultural guidance.

After Brown Fleming's death, companies continued to print his designs, and although they eventually became joint proprietors of those designs after decades of discussion, communities in West and Central Africa meanwhile embraced the imported textiles as expressions of their own culture and a sign of individual as well as collective identity. Their interaction in design choices enabled African aesthetics and cultural values to pervade these products, allowing them to carry connotations of tradition and authenticity, becoming a marker of *Africanness*.

1   They had joined already in 1906 Brown Fleming's business at 164 Springfield Road in Dalmarnock. BT2/6243 1906, National Records of Scotland, General Register House, Edinburgh (UK). See also Postoffice Glasgow Directory 1907-1908, p. 254.
2   This was a machine with a jumping rouleau. One roller would print the edges. Once these were printed, the roller would move back and a second roller would print the centre piece. Verbong 1988, 157
3   Van Vlissingen would buy a similar machine in 1914. Verbong 1988, 180
4   Baars, 153
5   The last order was on 12 June and was shipped two months later on 8 September 1917. See HKM sample book 212 (9345-9453), p. 77 in the Vlisco Archive. An attempt to re-start the company failed and in 1922, it had to close its doors indefinitely.
6   Verbong, 181, 238 and Haarlems Dagblad, 25 June 1918.
7   Verbong 1988 181; 1989, 78
8   Janszen and De Visser, 47. See chapter 5.
9   Ingenbleek 1998, 266
10 For more information about the company, see its appendix.
11 Verbong 1988: 238
12 He kept 5000 Ordinary Shares until Herbertson was able to purchase them. Private communication Malcolm Fleming, 29 October 2018
13 In the archives of the Basel Mission is a letter of the president of the BMTC, W. Preiswerk-Imoff to Israel Werner, 20 February 1919, in which Werner claims a sum of Dfl 18.748,80 for Roessingh printing. See 4256 UTC: WK (Welt Krieg) letter from W. Preiswerk-Imhoff to I. P. Werner 20 February 1919, p. 5 in: Archives of the Basel Mission.
14 The registration was done by the company Vriesendorp & Gaade in The Hague, 22 October 1920, for twenty years on request of Herbertson. Document at the Brunnschweiler Archive, Whitworth Art Gallery, University of Manchester (UK)..
15 Postoffice Annual Glasgow Directory of 1921/1922, p. 130
16 'Plan tot oprichting eener katoendrukkerij'. Typescript Mr Roessingh 1935? Document dated 8 March 1983, Library Nederlands Textielmuseum Tilburg: M46 MT5-4-19.
17 Between 1912 and 1927, no engraving books survive. On 13 October 1927 the first X number was issued starting a new number series of patterns at Newton Bank. Newton Bank Engraving Book X1 to X1200, Brunnschweiler Archive, Whitworth Art Gallery, University of Manchester (UK).
18 The figures for 1931-1935: 1931: £10740, 1932: £4131, 1933: £1325, 1934: £519 and in 1935 only £323 Ledger Brown Flemings Limited January 1931 – January 1939. Brunnschweiler Archive, Whitworth Art Gallery, University of Manchester (UK).
19 Letter: Ronald Herbertson to William Elphinstone Fleming, 17 August 1934. Personal archive, Malcolm Fleming.
20 Company Records File of Brown Flemings Limited 1935, BT2/18350, National Records of Scotland, Edinburgh.
His name is added on memo paper detailing travel expenses for Ronald Richmond Herbertson and Wijnand Roessingh 'paid by cheque to Mr. Herbertson 30 October 1935'. Undated letter Brunnschweiler Archive, Whitworth Art Gallery, University of Manchester (UK).
21 The first design was Little Lion* (X4468), 8 July 1935. See engraving book X3601-4800, F. W. Ashton and Co. Brunnschweiler Archive, Whitworth Art Gallery, University of Manchester (UK).
22 B. W. Anderton. 'European Involvement in Batik Printing', 1991. Unpublished typescript, Brunnschweiler Archive, Whitworth Art Gallery, University of Manchester (UK), 7.
23 The company made little profit: a profit of £204 in 1936, followed by a loss of £145 in 1937; in 1938 again a profit of £828, but in 1939 a loss of £501. Ledger Brown Flemings Limited January 1931 – January 1939 and Trading and Profit and Loss Account and Balance Sheet 1936-1939. Brunnschweiler Archive, the Whitworth Art Gallery, University of Manchester (UK). Today those £500 would be worth around £30.000 (http://inflation.iamkate.com/, last accessed 20 October 2018).
One Newton Bank pattern book records cumulative sales totals to Brown Fleming in June 1937, December 1937 and December 1939. Based on these quantities, it can be seen that *Canoe Peak* alone accounted for over 10% of sales, and the five top patterns (*Canoe Peak**, *Slendang**, *Three Bells**, *Staff of Kingship** and *Shrimp Check**) accounted for one-third of sales. The next ranking patterns (*Day and Night**, *Exhibition**, *Diagonal Stripe**, *Dice**, *Light and Dark*) generated another one-fifth of sales. There appears to have been a minimum order quantity of 50 lumps. Patterns in this minimum category were: *Batik Ancienne**, *Capella**, *Capella Square**, *Large Circle* and *Little Lion**, making just 3% of sales. A calico printer's lump was usually ten pieces of 24-28 yards length. The wax printer's lump may have been based on 12-yard pieces, so half that amount. Order Book, Brunnschweiler Archive, Whitworth Art Gallery, University of Manchester (UK). Information supplied by Philip Sykas.
24 See Rod Alence, 'The 1937-1938 Gold Coast Cocoa Crisis: The Political Economy of Commercial Stalemate' in: *African Economic History* 19 (1990-1991), 77-104.
25 Draft Agreement between Brown Flemings Limited, Ronald Richmond Herbertson and the Calico Printers' Association Limited, 16 May 1939, Brunnschweiler Archive, Whitworth Art Gallery, University of Manchester (UK).
26 See letter dated 12 May 1939 of the Chief Accountant, CPA Glasgow Office. Brunnschweiler Archive, Whitworth Art Gallery, University of Manchester (UK). On 5 June 1939, a wooden case with remaining items was sent to Manchester with several files and books: Battick Day Book no. 3 (September 1928-1934), Day Book No 11 (May 1923-December 1938), Order Book (January 1928-November 1938), Purchase Book No 3 (September 1923-November 1938), 1 File completed CPA Contracts, 4 Files Correspondence, 1 File Debit and Credit Notes, 1 File Orders to CPA 1 File Works, 1 File Invoice Copies, 1 File Works Specification 1924-25-26, 1 File Orders delivered, 1 Files Contracts and Orders, 1 File Inward Invoices and 1 File Buying and Selling Prices and a Trade Mark Stamp on Wood. See letter, 2 June 1939 of the Chief Accountant, CPA Glasgow Office, to Mr. F. F. Grainiger of CPA, Manchester: Brunnschweiler Archive, Whitworth Art Gallery, University of Manchester (UK). Apart from some correspondence, documents and bills these items have not been found in the Brunnschweiler Archive. They were probably held at the CPA Head Office and would have passed to Coats plc over time.
27 Letter of Chief Accountant CPA to Daniel Forbes of Moncrieff Warren Paterson & Co, solicitors in Glasgow, 12 May 1939. Brunnschweiler Archive, Whitworth Art Gallery, University of Manchester (UK).
28 Correspondence between Brown Flemings Ltd and the Callico Printers' Association in Brunnschweiler Archive, held at the Whitworth Art Gallery, University of Manchester (UK). See also letter d.d. 12 May 1939 of Chief Accountant CPA to their solicitor Mr. Forbes, Moncrieff Warren Paterson & Co, 45 West George Street in Glasgow: '...but since for a period of five years to come we have to satify Mr. Herbertson that we are paying royalties on all his designs, it seemed to us desirable that here should be an authorative list of designs taken over. When these come here they will all have a distincitive number and it would not give us much trouble to prepare a list to be attached to the agreement'. Brunnschweiler Archive, held at the Whitworth Art Gallery, University of Manchester (UK). The glass plates of these photos are kept at Brunnschweiler Archive, held at the Whitworth Art Gallery, University of Manchester (UK).
29 On November 18, 1952, the Calico Printers' Association decided to liquidate Brown Flemings Ltd. Letter of the secretary of the Callico Printers' Association to E. Moir in Renfrewshire d.d. twentieth November 1952. Brunnschweiler Archive, held at the Whitworth Art Gallery, University of Manchester (UK).
30 Meeles II, 139-141
31 Verbong 1988: 238. It could have been a total of 42. https://www.scripophily.nl/scripophily/Vlisco.php, page visited 4 September 2023.
32 Verschueren, 99; Jacobs and Maas, 41; Nielsen 1979, 474
33 Jacobs and Maas, 42
34 Letters of Jean Jacques to the UTR, 17 March and 15 April 1922. Minutes from 5 April and 26 April 1922 in: Board Minute Book no. 15, 23 November 1921-28 June 1922. Manchester Archives and Local Studies Library. Personal communication, Philip Sykas, 25 September 2017
35 Meeles II, 196
36 Letter of Designs Registry, Manchester Branch (textiles), Baskerville House, Broncross Street Salford UK d.d. 28 January 1957 in Frensel, Gerhard, 'Real Dutch Wax Block Print', M Isbeek (The Netherlands) 1980, unpublished document, 140.
37 Some notes also refer to registrations of Brown Fleming himself, like *Staff of Kingship**, that according to the document was registered

in 1902. This design was never registered. Another example was *Good Husband**, apparently registered in 1900. It was registered, but only two years later. Document CFAO, no date, kept at the Vlisco Archive, @ Vlisco BV.

38   The typescript with detailed information and samples of various companies is held at the Vlisco Archive, @ Vlisco BV.

39   Typescript letter by Gerard Vollaard held at the Vlisco Archive, @ Vlisco BV.

40   See the photo books of Brown Fleming in the Brunnschweiler Archive, Whitworth Art Gallery, University of Manchester (UK); and the photo book with correspondence *Contentious Designs*, Vlisco Archive, @ Vlisco BV. Later notes regarding specific designs were added in 1972 and 1974.

41   Letter G. J. Jagger, ABC, to C. West, A. Brunnschweiler & Co, Lagos, 12 October 1972.

42   A meeting between the author and Maurice Gavan of the UAC, who had done very detailed research into the ownership of the contentious range, is suggested in the letter. It is not clear if this meeting indeed took place. Letter of H.E Wagster of UAC International, Textiles and Industrial Services Division to D. van Lookeren Campagne at Vlisco d.d. 14 September 1976, Vlisco Archive, @ Vlisco BV, U280/566. The typed version of his book is kept at the Vlisco Archive, @ Vlisco BV.

43   Letter Philip Poole 19 October 2023. Philip Poole was sales and marketing director, when ABC had become part of Tootal. When the Cha group bought ABC in 1992 he set up a distribution network in various countries in West Africa (Cha Textile Distribution). He left the company in 2000. Personal communication David Bradley 25 September 2023

44   Letter dated 17 November 1988 from Philip Poole to R. H. Bedford, Brunnschweiler Archive, Whitworth Art Gallery, University of Manchester (UK).

45   Historical fact was further massaged in a recent advertising campaign for Satin Royal, where the company claimed nearly 180 years of experience in wax printing. https://www.vlisco.com/vlisco-products/satin-royal, last accessed 12 December 2023.

46   Well-known examples are *Flying Duck**, registered by Blakeley and Beving on the 9 January 1914 (BT 52/2987/99128.) and *Jumping Horse**, introduced by Ankersmit in 1930 under number 20850.

The *Contentious* Designs: the legacy of Brown Fleming

The process of wax printing

8.
All wax has been previously removed and the cloth has been straightened. A third colour is printed, known as a solid colour without any spots.

Addenda

Contents

217
Appendices

217
A. Brunnschweiler & Co.

217
Archives of Dutch, English and Swiss Wax Printing

219
Brown Fleming, as mentioned in John Hildesheim's diary

220
Registrations of designs of the HKM in 1889 and Brown Fleming from 1895 until 1914, submitted to the Patents, Designs and Trade Marks Office, part of the Board of Trade, in London, kept at The National Archives in Kew (UK)

223
Brown Fleming, a biography

225
Calico Printers' Association Ltd (CPA)

226
Collecting Indonesian artefacts for Dutch museum collections around 1900

227
Colourists Prévinaire and Son and the Jean Jacques family

228
Haijkens

229
Sample books of the Haarlemsche Katoen Maatschappij in the Vlisco Archives in Helmond

230
Kangas

230
Kralingsche Katoen Maatschappij (Kralingen Cotton Company) (KKM)

232
Leidsche Katoen Maatschappij (Leiden Cotton Company) (LKM)

233
Numbering of designs of Ankersmit, Vlisco and ABC – In collaboration with Philip Sykas

234
Paterson Zochonis

234
Prévinaire before 1834

236
Roessingh or the *Maatschappij voor Textiel Industrie, voorheen* (previous) *C. Roessingh & Zoon in Veenendaal*

237
The *Teekenschool* (drawing school) in the Netherlands

237
United Turkey Red

238
Voortman and the Société Anonyme Texas

239
Werner

241
Terminology

243
Abbreviations

244
Literature

Appendices

A. BRUNNSCHWEILER & CO.

This company specialised in imitation Madras for the West African market. Hand-woven cloth from Madras in India had already made its appearance in West Africa in the seventeenth century. It became popular in the nineteenth century, particularly in Nigeria and Sierra Leone. It was first shipped from India to London and auctioned off at the Cotton Exchange to British trading firms with branches in West Africa.

In the nineteenth century, European companies started designing their own patterns, referred to as *imitation Madras*, which were produced on power looms. Similarly to batik imitations, insiders were able to discern the difference between original Indian and imitation Madras.

In 1872, two Swiss families, Brunnschweiler and Fröhlich, started industrial weaving of this type of cloth. Two years later, a member of the Brunnschweiler family was sent to Liverpool to set up a separate branch that moved to Manchester in 1882. Part of the Swiss production was sent to the UK to be traded directly for export to West Africa.

In 1907 a separate office, set up in Madras, focused on the production of real Madras, based on instructions from the Manchester branch about patterns that sold well. It took only three years for the sales of real Madras to become more important than the production of their own imitation Madras.

In 1924, the Manchester branch was established as a separate company under the name of A. Brunnschweiler and Co., referred to as ABC. Although the business was flourishing, sales were threatened by Indian companies exporting Madras directly to West Africa. In the 1930s, the company started direct sales in West Africa, which turned out to be difficult for a new firm in the beginning but, eventually, it became profitable. Even though supplies were limited after the Second World War, there was huge demand. Business picked up very quickly, this being supported by ABC's excellent reputation.

In 1959, Ashton, a member of the Calico Printers' Association (CPA), acquired *A. Brunnschweiler & Co.,* mostly to get access to the distribution outlets to increase the sale of wax prints.

[1] See Laurens van der Laan 1983 and *Kreuz und Quer der Farben. Karo- und Streifenstoffe der Schweiz für Afrika, Indonesien und die Türkei*, Exhibition Catalogue Museum Bellerive Zürich (1997), Modemuseum im Münchner Stadtmuseum, Munich (1998) and Museum des Landes Glarus, Näfels (Switzerland) (1999)

ARCHIVES OF DUTCH, ENGLISH AND SWISS WAX PRINTING

Swiss archives of wax printing

The archives of several companies have providentially been preserved. Not only do they contain written documents, but also cloth and sample books. Most material dates back to the nineteenth century, with very few of the first eighteenth-century prints having been retained. The information, kept in accountancy books, balance sheets, letters, recipes as well as sample books, is relatively complete. Most archives are in private hands, which makes them at times complicated to access.

Since 2002, the archive of Blumer, from Schwanden, and other companies are kept by the Glarner Wirtschaftsarchiv, a private foundation, in Glarus.[1] Another important archive is that of Daniel Jenny & Cie (previously Bartholome Jenny & Cie) in the former company buildings in Ennenda, a neighbourhood of Glarus. The printing business was closed in 1907, but the office – *Comptoir* – is not much changed and is now a private museum.

The legacy of Adolf Jenny-Trümpy (1855-1941) in particular is worth mentioning. After he studied chemistry at the University of Zurich and further study of colour chemistry in Mulhouse (1875-1876), he worked as a colourist for Bartholome Jenny & Co. Not only was he the author of a book detailing the history of the trade and industry in the province of Glarus, but equally and perhaps even more importantly he was a collector of prints.[2] He collected these not for their designs, but for their various techniques, which he especially collected from his own company after its closure in 1907, and from other companies in Glarus, with the aim of preserving existing knowledge of cotton printing. He made 9 series of sample books with the cloth samples he collected. Each contained twenty-two books related to a specific technique.[3] For each sample he included a card that detailed the number, colour and printing recipe. When he needed samples of a specific technique that were not available within the collection of his own company, he would collect them from other companies, mainly French and English. Samples from his own company were stamped; those from other companies were annotated with the name and year of production. The Comptoir Archive has an incomplete collection of these books, but the Textile Museum in Sankt Gallen keeps a complete collection. They are an excellent tool for detailed study of the Swiss production.[4] They would use expensive printing techniques like copper plates more frequently than their English or Dutch counterparts, which made their Batik samples of very high quality.

[1] Rast Eicher 2009, 6. See also http://www.glarnerwirtschaftsarchiv.ch/
[2] See Adolf Jenny-Trümpy, 'Handel und Industrie des Kantons Glarus. Geschichtlich dargestellt' in *Jahrbuch des Historischen Vereins des Kanton Glarus*, vol 33-34, 1898.
[3] Interesting for the study of imitation batik are the following volumes: 1. Indigo Druckartikel 1904 – samples from 1820-1903; 14. Gedruckte Glarner Batik als Nachahmungen echt javanischer Batik 1931 – samples from 1840-1930; 15. Glarner Druckwaren fur Ost- und Westafrika 1931 – samples from 1890-1910; 23. Gedruckte Glarner Batik als Nachahmungen echt javanischer Batik; 24. Glarner Druckwaren fur Ost- und Westafrika
[4] The Textile Museum in Sankt Gallen (Switzerland) has one of these series in their library. The archives of Daniel Jenny & Cie publish on a regular basis on the printing industry in their *Comptoir Blatter*.
No 10/11 (2017) contains several articles about imitation batik printing in Glarus.
For a detailed description of these books, see Anne Wanner-Jean Richard, 'Die Musterbände aus Ennenda. Adolf Jenny-Trümpy und seine Sammlungen von Stoffmustern' in *Glarner Tuch Gespräche. Kunst und geschichte des Glarner und europäischen Zeugdrucks,* Ennenda (Glarus, Switzerland) 2017, pp. 184-197.

The Vlisco Archives

Vlisco has been creating an archive since 1856, but suffered from fire in 1876 and 1883, when an important part of the collection was destroyed. But it continued its archival activities and started collecting cloth from various regions of the world.

In 1960 Vlisco donated the archives to Jan van Vlissingen, director at the time. Two years after his death in 1978 the *Stichting Pieter Fentener van Vlissingen* was created in 1980 In order to protect the archives in case the company closed. The archives have always been located on the premises of the company, Vlisco BV. The ownership was never officially transferred to the foundation and, therefore, the collection still belongs officially to Vlisco BV. The archives are now treated as an integral part of the company. A few years ago Vlisco started digitising the archive. The foundation plays an advisory role.

The archives contain a library and company archive for designers, researchers and museum curators. The collection contains about 350,000 samples of (wax) prints not only from Vlisco, but also from many other companies and different periods: Vlisco, Ankersmit, Uniwax, GTP, the Haijkens collection etc. About 200 sample books are kept. Most are not classified and also not only from Vlisco but also from various other firms like Ankersmit, HKM, LKM, Haijkens, and others.

Garments, made with Vlisco cloth for promotion or as results of projects with (design)academies, are also held.

An estimated 18,000 original drawings for designs are kept. A small collection of old drawings by Johan Jacobs can be found, but most are from 1949 onwards. Drawings have been systematically kept since that year.

Objects, related to the production of (wax)prints as block prints, not only from Vlisco but also for example from the KKM, can be found in the archives.

Textile samples from various countries and companies, mainly Indonesian batik, and African cloth from various sources are kept in two special rooms. For example, batik samples, bought before the Second World War from Gallery Aalderink in Amsterdam, exhibited at the World Exhibition 1931 in Paris in the Dutch Pavillon, rare samples of the HKM and textile designs by Jaap Gidding and Michel Duco Crop. This part of the collection was photographed in 1982 and is available online: https://geheugen.delpher.nl/nl/geheugen/pages/collectie/Vlisco%2C+een+Hollandse+fabrikant+van+bedrukt+textiel+voor+West+en+Midden+Afrika/Familiebedrijf.

The archives also contain a library specialising in the (wax-) printing business with a focus on art, design and history, and offering chemical and technical information, including some 10,000 references. Written and printed material, photographs, videos and film referring to the history of the company or made for publicity are also kept.

The Brunnschweiler Archive: a summary description by Philip Sykas

The Brunnschweiler Archive is an archive that was consolidated at Newton Bank Print Works in Hyde, the site of the last export printing company in the Manchester region. Newton Bank stopped printing in 2007 and its allied design studio closed in 2022. Newton Bank was a major printworks of the Calico Printers' Association (CPA) and became the central site of its African export printing. The CPA was a conglomerate formed in 1899 that brought together forty-six printworks and thirteen merchant firms from the Glasgow and Manchester regions. In the tradition of calico printers, when a works stopped printing, their pattern rollers with the supporting pattern books were passed on to an active firm to complete existing orders. As the 'last man standing', Newton Bank added to its own records (the firm *F. W. Ashton and Co.*) significant runs of pattern records from CPA works at:

Broad Oak (F. W. Grafton and Co.),
Dinting Vale (Edmund Potter and Co.),
Loveclough (the Rossendale Printing Company) and
Rhodes (Salis Schwabe and Co.).

These design records representing the larger English printworks of the Calico Printers' Association, and covering in some depth the period from 1910 to 1980, form the core of the historical archive and its bound pattern books. Table 1 summarises these records.

As the CPA restructured its operations, the export patterns from Steiner's Church Bank came to Newton Bank in 1956 (covering 1930-1956). With the reorganisation of the industry, the CPA passed to Tootal's in the 1970s. In 1979, the mill engraved grounding patterns from Strines (covering 1925-1979) joined the archives at Newton Bank. From 1956, the CPA kept books covering registration of designs outside the United Kingdom, most notably Japan, and these duly entered the archive. Covering some twenty years of production, pattern books also document the African printing branch set up in 1971, CPA Zaire.

In addition, several important acquisitions of export market patterns were made; the first of these were the patterns of Brown Fleming in 1929. The CPA eventually transferred printing away from F. W. Grafton at Broad Oak, but created a merchant firm focused on the African export market around 1932, called Grafton African. This firm handled the most prestigious and best-selling wax-printed patterns. Until 1971, Grafton African patterns are thoroughly covered in the archive, both the company's function as originators of designs and their role as printing clients. In 1958, as part of the winding down of the Scottish conglomerate – the United Turkey Red company, rights to about 100 of their most important African export patterns were purchased by the CPA. Rollers came to Newton Bank and sample lengths entered the archive. Sadly, related pattern books are not present.

Finally, the Wigan-based Blue Printers Limited was purchased by the CPA in 1966. This firm was founded in 1934 by the Deutsch family from D'vur Králové in the first Czech Republic. It specialised in the indigo discharge patterns appreciated not only in Eastern Europe, but also in South Africa. Printing was transferred to Newton Bank, along with the record books, but the Blue Printers brand was retained. In 1983, Tootal signed a franchise agreement with Da Gama Textiles in South Africa, and in 1987 agreed to transfer production to Da Gama. And in 1992, Da Gama is said to have acquired sole rights to the patterns, but pattern books remained at Newton Bank, possibly because Da Gama had equivalent material.

Export patterns from several merchant firms were also acquired by Newton Bank. Anticipating the closure of Alfred Heathcote Emery, the firm's export patterns were first assigned to Astbury and Pickford around 1965, but when Astbury and Pickford was wound up in 1969, the pattern records of both firms joined the archives at Newton Bank. Newton Bank's long-standing commission printing for other merchants serving the African market led to significant design records being represented in the archive. Literally hundreds of merchant firms are recorded within engraving records, but the largest clients were given their own pattern books. Table 2 lists the most significant holdings of merchant pattern books.

The Manchester branch of the Swiss firm A. Brunnschweiler and Co. was set up in 1924, to expand its trade in woven

Broad Oak (F. W. Grafton)	Registration books Engraving books Block books Showroom books Client books	1878-1909 1930-1963 c. 1900-1930 1911-1960 1942-1960
Dinting Vale (E. Potter)	Engraving books	1913-1966
Loveclough (Rossendale)	Engraving books Impression books	1951-1980 1950-1969
Rhodes (S. Schwabe)	Engraving books Client books Strike-off books	1932-1966 1926-1955 c. 1910-1952
Newton Bank (F. W. Ashton)	Engraving books Client books Designs Competitors' samples	1927-1989 1932-1970 1966-1988 1912-1959

Table 1. Core Calico Printers' Association holdings

Elson and Neill	30 vols.
Hubert J. Barrett	11 vols.
United African Company	10 vols.
Obadiah Haber	6 vols.
Morreau Spiegelberg	6 vols.
J. A. Duke	5 vols.
Joseph Bridge	4 vols.
Logan Muckelt	2 vols.
Neuss Hesslein Kempton	2 vols.
Gibson and Costobadie	1 vol.

Table 2. Merchant firms with significant holdings in the archive

Madras checks from India, and also cotton damasks for Africa, known as 'brocades'. Some of these were marketed under the brand *Intorica* (standing for India to Africa). Brunnschweiler (UK) is comprehensively represented in the archive with business records as well as design records. In 1960, The CPA acquired Brunnschweiler, and in 1970, when the CPA itself was acquired by English Calico, it was decided to discard Newton Bank's old name of F. W. Ashton in favour of the name Brunnschweiler which had a widely recognised reputation in Africa as the brand ABC.

From 1970, Newton Bank became known as ABC, and when the firm was purchased by the Cha Textile Group in 1992, it was decided to rebrand the firm as *ABC Wax*. The records of ABC Wax take the archive into the contemporary arena, covering thirty years from 1992 to 2022. In this era, design and pattern records moved from paint and paper records to digital files, and from bound ledgers to spreadsheets and loose-leaf files. ABC Wax and its various brands, such as Elite, Superwax, Elegance, Top Wax, VIP Wax, Excellence and Da Viva as well as its collaborations with its various Nigerian and Ghanaian affiliate companies, take the archive up to the closure of the design studio, and the end of 200 years of calico printing at Newton Bank in Hyde.

The peculiar nature of the multi-site Calico Printer's Association and its transfer of printing and finishing between sites means that the same pattern can appear in up to four different works under different pattern numbers. A cataloguing system that combines archive and museum practice tries to capture printworks and merchant firms, and how they overlap. Three letter codes designate companies (or archival 'divisions'), but the 'series' number which follows indicates the type of material. This system reveals how records are distributed among the various functions of design, printing, warehousing and sales.

Although pattern books are the most quantifiable aspect of the archive, there is also a large quantity of textile samples, and a panoply of business papers, photographs, postcards, trade labels, office paraphernalia and memorabilia. There is, too, a significant design library that contains the remnants of the Calico Printers' Association Subscription Library. The CPA Subscription Library held design reference material for use by designers across the organisation. It contains early colour-printed design albums, lavish portfolios of *pochoir* prints, trade catalogues and rare books produced by leading Victorian designers.

Only a few of the many engraving books in the archive record the names of designers, but these precious few open a considerable field for study. An important story is that of the firm's female designers. Outstanding amongst these is Lorna Holcroft (1912-1999), who painted over 200 designs between 1934 and 1946. She left her design career in 1954 to go homesteading in Canada and later wrote a book about her adventurous life.

Although the African export side of the archive is undoubtedly its strength, the archive also contains work for the domestic market. CPA printworks produced work for Zika and Lida Ascher, Horrockses, Hoyles Prints, Liberty, Potter's Dress, Sekers and many other leading brands. Since the printer worked on commission for these firms, copyright was not acquired, and there may be some issues to resolve in making such material available beyond private study. The engraving books also record a significant number of designs for children's wear of the 1950s and 1960s.

In this archive, we can see how British designers educated themselves about African taste, and how to serve the African customer. We find not only cultural exchange, but cross-fertilisation, and it is doubtful that many British post-war modern styles would have arisen without the experience in producing for the African consumer – an experience that allowed the designer a freer range of expression and wider ability to experiment with colour.

BROWN FLEMING, AS MENTIONED IN JOHN HILDESHEIM'S DIARY

The diaries of John Hildesheim (1845-1928), a friend of Brown Fleming, present a more intimate picture of Brown Fleming and provide a good illustration of business relations around 1900, a time when business interest and personal contact were often interlinked. It is quite likely that Brown Fleming enjoyed a similar relationship with Van de Poll, the director of the HKM, with whom he regularly spent time at his second home in Scotland and at Van de Poll's properties in the Netherlands.[1]

John Hildesheim was born into a merchant family in 1845. From 1864 until 1868, he travelled extensively throughout South America. In 1868 he became engaged to Pauline Meyer. They settled in Glasgow to open an office for Lipman and Co. in Dundee, a manufacturer and exporter of jute products. Jute was, among other things, also used to pack textiles for transport. He married Pauline in 1869 and stayed in Glasgow until 1887, at which time they returned to Hamburg. He continued to meet with Brown Fleming, but also with other acquaintances who were of importance in the British and Scottish textile industry and whom he met in Germany, England and Scotland. His diaries are concise, business-related entries and provide only vague insights on many important subjects, but they do give an idea of his relationship with Brown Fleming. Considering the extent of their trips together in Scotland and Germany, they seemed to enjoy each other's company and must have been more than business partners.[2] John Hildesheim died on May 1st, 1928, at the age of 83.[3]

1884 October: first mention of 'E. Fleming', together they visisted Dollar, Castle Campbell, Glendevon and Rumbling Bridge
1885 went with Fleming on a tour of Lennoxtown, Fintry, Balfron, Drymen and back via Balloch
1888 May: '*we had a visit from E. B. Fleming*' (Note HE: in Hamburg)
December: '*we had another visit from E. B. Fleming*'
1889 22 October: '*I met Fleming at Hotel Hillmanns*' (Note HE: in Bremen, Germany). '*On 29 October Fleming and I went to Leith and Glasgow on the Breslau with Captain Thomas.*'
1891 visited E. B. Fleming in Lochanbrae, Fleming's second home in Garelochhead, Argyllshire.[4]
1895 visited by Fleming at his home in Hamburg.
1896 travels with Fleming from Glasgow to Lochanbrae
1899 stayed at Fleming's home in Lochanbrae from 10 to 12 August, traveled with him to Preston.
1900 travelled with Fleming to Lübeck, Eutin, Grevesmühlen, Holsteinische Schweiz and Kiel
1901 met Fleming at the Grand Hotel Manchester on 15 August and visited Fleming in Lochanbrae from 20 to 22 August.
1902 Fleming visited on 6 February – the precise location is unclear.
1903 visited Fleming in Lochanbrae and went on a tour with him
1906 stayed at Fleming's, 19 Kensington Gate Glasgow, 15-18 March.
1908 on 9 July stayed at Caledonian Hotel in Oban, went with Fleming in his new 'trap' to Kilchoan via the Pass of Melford. 'On 10-11 July we caught trout. On Sunday 12 July we went on a walk over the hill. On 13 July I went with Fleming on his motorboat over

Loch Melford. From there we travelled by coach through Kilmartin, where we saw the Druidical Stone, then through Lochgilphead to Ardrishaig. Then we sailed on the 'Jones' through the channel called the Kyles of Bute to Rothesay and Ganroch, then went on the train to Glasgow. In the evening we visited Fleming's factory and had supper in Clarence Restaurant. I stayed at North British Station Hotel.'

1909 visit from E. B. Fleming from 26 to 28 February and later that year 'visit from Fleming on 29 July by steamer via Lübeck, Travemünde, Kellenhusen and Dahme to Burg auf Fehmarn. We stayed at Wissers Hotel in Burg auf Fehmarn. On 31 July we went by railroad until Burgstaken, then by steamer via Heiligenhafen to Kiel, staying at the hotel Germania. On 1 August I went back to Hamburg.'

1910 'In January, I went on a visit to see Fleming. In the morning of 10 June, I went on the 'Columba' via Gourock to Ardishaig. I saw cattle show in Lochgilphead and had dinner with Fleming and the judges. On June 11 I went via Crinan Canal and Kilmartin to Kilchoan. We had a visit (…) from Fleming and his son 2-4 October.'

1911 visit from Fleming on 8 February and on 16-17 July. 'On 21 September, there was the marriage of Frances Fleming to Ronald Richmond Herbertson. On 7 October he meets Brown Fleming at Hotel zum Riesen in Koblenz. On Sunday 8 October we travelled by train to Cochem, and the Union Hotel. We went on an excursion in the mountains. On 9 October, we went to Bullay-Alf, took a splendid trip to Bad Bertrich, then took the 'Little Train through Eskirch, Trarbach, Cröv, Uerzig, Rachtig, Zeltingen, etc. arriving the same day at the Hotel 3 Könige in Berncastel-Kues.' On 10 October they went to Trier, the 11th to Luxemburg and Cologne. A day later Brown Fleming went to Bremen and John Hildesheim back to Hamburg.

1912 On 31 January he had a visit from Fleming. On 15-16 April Fleming died. In June William Elphinstone Fleming was in Hamburg. 'On 20 July I went to Kilcreggan-Cove to visit Fleming's grave at the Barbour cemetery' and meets his son a day later at Melford House, Bearsden. In October he meets with Fleming's son and son-in-law.

1914 'On 16-18 June we were visited by W.E.Fleming' (Note HE: Fleming's son William)

1924 On 6 October he went to 4 Cullum Street in London where he looked for W. E. Fleming without success. On 8 October he had lunch with 'Mr. Herbertson' (Note HE: Fleming's son-in-law).

1925 On 21 October he was visited by R. R. Herbertson and Mr Wynand Roessingh from Veenendaal (Note HE: Roessingh had taken over the printing after the closure of the HKM).

[1] Initially, Brown Fleming had a second home in Lochanbrae in Mambeg, Garelochhead, Argyllshire. In 1906, he also bought a country house in Kilchoan, Loch Melfort, also in Argyllshire. Kroese (1), 53 and Kroese (3), 22. M. P. T. Prévinaire had bought the estate *Heerlijkheid Callantsoog*, a beach resort north of Amsterdam, and had three villas built at the entrance of the village. In 1990 Van de Poll inherited this estate and enjoyed private time there with his family. For more information, see Kees Zwaan, 'Van Heerlijkheid tot badplaats. De ontwikkeling van Callantsoog tot badplaats van 1876-1940', MA study 2023 Open University: https://research.ou.nl/ws/portalfiles/portal/61451661/Masterscriptie_Van_Heerlijkheid_tot_badplaats.pdf

[2] Personal information Mark Hill, great-grandson of John Hildesheim, who has inherited his diaries: 9 December 2016.

[3] For the full text of the diaries: https://hildesheimfamily.wordpress.com/2015/07/15/the-hildesheim-family/

[4] In 1895 the Valuation Rolls show he is the proprietor of a house, named Lochanbrae, in Garelochhead, Argyllshire. Valuations Rolls VR009600041 Year 1895, National Records of Scotland.

REGISTRATIONS OF DESIGNS OF THE HKM IN 1889 AND BROWN FLEMING FROM 1895 UNTIL 1914, SUBMITTED TO THE PATENTS, DESIGNS AND TRADE MARKS OFFICE, PART OF THE BOARD OF TRADE, IN LONDON, KEPT AT THE NATIONAL ARCHIVES IN KEW (UK)[1]

Record series BT 50 and BT51
These are the designs submitted to the Patents, Designs and Trade Marks Office under the terms of the Patents, Designs and Trade Marks Act 1883.
These are representations for all designs except sculptures. Design range 1-526397.
The registers are listed by design number. There is a name index (submitting firm or person) in BT 51//175.

Record series BT 52 and BT 53
These are the designs submitted to the Patents, Designs and Trade Marks Office under the terms of the Patents and Designs Act 1907 and Registered Design Act 1949.
These are representations of all textiles and non-textile designs, divided into the following categories and number ranges.
Textile design classes 13, 14 and 15 (1-26041 and 1-11532).
Textile designs (11533-495183).

HKM registrations

De Haarlemsche Katoenmaatschappij, Haarlem, the Netherlands, Calico printers

BT 51/53 15jan 1889 – 2 March 1889
  p. 373 12 February 1889
  119506-16 (BT 50/114)
  119507-11 Certificates not issued: See Correspondence – see BT 50/115
  p. 373 12 February 1889
  119517-38 – (BT 50/114)

BT 51/54 2 March 1889-18 April 1889
  p. 202 19 March 1889
  121628-32 Class 13 (BT 50/115)
  p. 202 19 March 1889
  121633-9 Class 14 (BT 50/115)
  p. 545 16 April 1889
  123514-16 Class 14 (50/117)

BT 51/55 23 March 1889 – 25 June 1889
  p. 121 4 May 1889
  124666-7 Class 14 (BT 50/118)

BT 51/56 25 June 1889 – 20 September 1889
  p. 2 25 June 1889
  127679-82 Class 14 (BT 50/120)
  p. 234 29 July 1889
  129785-90 Class 14 (BT 50/122)
  p. 291 4 August 1889
  130329-33 Class 14 (BT50/124)

Brown Flemings registrations

Brown Fleming and Company, 205 Buchanan Street Glasgow Manufacturers and merchants

BT 51-79 26 October 1894 – 9 January 1895
  p. 537 1 January 1895
  247016 Class 13 (BT50/221)

BT 51-80 9 January 1895 – 16 March 1895
  p. 467 1 March 1895
  250492-5 Class 13 BT (50/222)

BT 51-81 16 March 1895 – 13 June 1895
  p. 79 24 March 1895
  251960-1 Class 13 (BT 50/223)
  p. 227 17 April 1895
  253267 and *253268* (BT 50/224)
  p. 470 21 May 1895
  255139-41 Class 13 (BT 50/225)

BT 51-82 13 June 1895 – 10 September 1895
  p. 80 26 June 1895
  256953-6 Class 13 (BT 50/226)
  26 June 1895: 256953 stopped. Certificate not issued. See Correspondence papers 23883 BT19.
  p. 281 24 August 1895
  258586 Class 13 (BT 50/227)
  p. 539 31 August 1895
  260844-6 Class 13 (BT 50/230)
  p. 540 31 August 1895
  260847 Class 14 (BT 50/230)

BT 51-83 10 September 1895 – 21 November 1895
  p. 282 15 October 1895
  263770-1 Class 14 (BT 50/233)
  p. 282 15 October
  263772-9 Class 13 BT 50/233)

BT 51-85 5 February 1896 – 23 April 1896
  p. 478 4 April 1896
  274007-10 Class 13 (BT 50/244)

p. 478 4 April 1896
274011-13 Class 14 (BT 50/244)
(*274013* sample missing)
p. 523 14 April 1896
274331 Class 13 (BT 50/244)
p. 581 21 April 1896
274699 Class 13 (BT50/244)

BT 51/87 11 July 1896 – 25 September 1896
p. 111 27 July 1895
280290 Class 13 (BT 50/251)
p. 378 1 September 1896
282670 Class 13 (BT 50/254)

BT 51/89 28 November 1896 – 8 February 1897
p. 418 20 January 1897
292261-62 Class 14 (BT 50/265)
p. 418 20 January 1897
292263-68 Class 13 (BT 50/265)
(*292267* sample missing - design *Tree of Life*)

BT 51/90 8 February 1897 – 17 April 1897
p. 190 27 February 1897
294842 Class 13 (BT 50/270)
p. 374 20 March 1897
295956 Class 14 (BT 50/273)

BT 51/91 17 April 1897- 17 July 1897
p. 101 4 May 1897
298262-4 Class 13 (BT 50/278)
p. 211 18 May 1897
298983 Class 14 (BT 50/280)
Ebenezer Brown Fleming, 50 Renfrew Street Glasgow Merchant
p. 458 24 June 1897
300706-7 Class 13 (BT 50/283)
p. 539 9 July 1897
301272 Class 14 (BT 50/285)

BT 51/92 17 July 1897 – 12 October 1897
p. 38 23 July 1897
301997-2000 Class 14 (BT50/286)
p. 138 10 August 1897
303041 Class 13 (BT50/288)
p. 458 23 September 1897
305741 Class 13 (BT 50/293)

BT 51/93 12 October 1897 – 22 December 1897
p. 122 23 October 1897
307891-2 Class 13 (BT 50/297)
p. 122 23 October 1897
307893 Class 14 (BT 50/297)
p. 347 20 November 1897
309473 Class 13 (BT 50/300)

BT 51/94 22 December 1897 – 11 March 1898
p. 58 31 December 1897
311578 Class 13 (BT 50/304)

BT 51/103 9 February 1900 – 14 May 1900
p. 469 21 April 1900
356288-9 Class 13 BT 50/387

BT 51/110 12 December 1901 – 5 March 1902
p. 508 22 February 1902
387612 Class 14 (See BT 50/455)
p. 508 22 February 1902
387613-14 Class 13 (See BT 50/455)
Samples missing.
p. 517 24 February 1902
387659 Class 13 (See BT 50/455)
Sample missing.
p. 592 4 March 1902
388035 Class 13 (See BT 50/456)

BT 51/111 5 March 1902 – 6 June 1902
p. 89 15 March 1902
388579-87 Class 14 except *388587* Class 13 (see 50/458)
p. 144 22 March 1902
388955 Class 13 (See BT 50/459)

BT 51/112 6 June 1902 – 13 September 1902
p. 337 30 July 1902
394628 Class 13 (See BT50/472)

BT 51/113 13 September 1902 – 3 December 1902
p. 39 18 September 1902
397407 Class 14 (See BT 50/479)
p. 40 18 September 1902
397408 Class 13 18 (See BT 50/479)
p. 50 19 September 1902
397536 Class 14 19 (See BT 50/479)
p. 132 1 October 1902
398166 Class 13 (See BT 50/481)
p. 133 1 October 1902
398167 Class 14 (See BT 50/481)
p. 159 4 October 1902
398366 Class 13 (See BT 50/481)
p. 430 11 November 1902
400539-42 Class 14 (See BT 50/487)
p. 430 11 November 1902
400543 Class 13 (See BT 50/487)
p. 440 12 November 1902
400592-99 Class 13 (See BT 50/487)
p. 449 13 November 1902
400695-703 Class 13 (See BT 50/487)
p. 474 17 November 1902
400830-5 Class 13 (See BT 50/488)
p. 474 17 November 1902
400836-7 Class 14 (See BT 50/488)

BT 51/114 3 December 1902 – 24 February 1903
Brown Flemings Limited of 164 Springfield Road, Glasgow, Manufacturers
p. 65 11 December 1902
402047 Class 13 (See BT 50/491)
p. 111 17 December 1902
402351 Class 14 (See BT50/491)
p. 498 11 February 1903
405016 Class 13 (See BT 50 498)
1 February 1908 Copyright extended under Sec. 53 (2) of P&D Act 1907
1 August: In pursuance of an application received on 25 July 1912 Brown Flemings Limited, 164 Springfield Road Glasgow, Manufacturers, registered as proprietors.
p. 588 23 February 1903
405584 Class 14 (See BT 50/499)

BT 51/115 24 February 1903- 12 May 1903
p. 62 4 March 1903
406201 Class 13 4 March 1903 (See BT 50/501)
p. 243 26 March 1903
407381 Class 13 (See BT50/504)
p. 251 27 March 1903
407447 Class 13 (See BT 50/504)
18 March 1908 – Copyright extended under Sec. 53 (2) of P&D Act 1907
p. 281 31 March 1903
407613 Class 13 (See BT 50/505)

BT 51/116 12 May 1903 – 31 July 1903
p. 38 16 May 1903
410149-72 Class 13 (See BT50/510)
Nos. *410151, 410156, 410162, 410169, 41071-72* Certificates not issued.
See Correspondence Papers 641/9199.

BT 51/117 31 July 1903 – 24 October 1903
p. 13 13 4 August 1903
414966 Class (See BT 50/516)
15 July 1908 Copyright extended under Sec. 53 (2) of P&D Act 1907
1 August 1912 In Pursuance of an application, received on 25 July 1912 Brown Flemings Limited of 164 Springfield Road, Glasgow, Manufacturers, registered as proprietors.
Copyright extended under Sec. 53 (2) of P&D Act 1907
p. 13 4 August 1903
414967 Class 14 (See BT 50/516)
15 July 1908 Copyright extended under Sec. 53 (2) of P&D Act 1907
p. 506 13 October 1903
419327-31 Class 13 (See 50/523)
21 September 1908 Copyright extended under Sec. 53 (2) of P&D Act 1907
1 August 1912 - In Pursuance of an application, received on 25 July 1912 Brown Flemings Limited of 164 Springfield Road, Glasgow, Manufacturers, registered as proprietors.
22 November 1912 Copyright extended under Sec. 53 (2) of P&D Act 1907
p. 583 22 October 1903
419879 Class 13 (See 50/524)
24 September 1908 Copyright extended under Sec. 53 (2) of P&D Act 1907
1 August 1912 in Pursuance of an application, received on 25 July 1912 Brown Flemings Limited of 164 Springfield Road, Glasgow, Manufacturers, registered as proprietors.
22 November 1912 Copyright extended under Sec. 53 (2) of P&D Act 1907

BT 51/118 24 October 1903 – 5 January 1904
p. 81 2 November 1903 *420628-9* Class 13 (See 50/525)
Design *420628* Copyright extended 1 August 1912 in Pursuance of an application, received on 25 July 1912 Brown Flemings Limited of 164 Springfield Road, Glasgow, Manufacturers, registered as proprietors.
30 November 1912 copyright extended
420629 sample missing
p. 165 11 November 1903
421221 Class 13 (See 50/526)

BT 51/119 5 January 1904 – 9 March 1904
p. 322 10 February 1904

ADDENDA — Contents

426382 Class 14 (See 50/535)
Sample missing
18 January 1909 Copyright extended under Sec. 53(2) of P&D Act 1907
p. 376 16 February 1904
426746 Class 14 (See BT 50/535)
p. 377 16 February 1904
426747 Class 13 (See BT50/535)
10 February 1909 Copyright extended under Sec. 53(2) of P&D Act 1907
1 August 1912 in Pursuance of an application, received on 25 July 1912 Brown Flemings Limited of 164 Springfield Road, Glasgow, Manufacturers, registered as proprietors.
27 February 1913 Copyright extended under Sec. 53(2) of P&D Act 1907
p. 495 February 1904
427676-7 Class13 27 (See BT 50/537)
Copyright extended for *427676* 10 February 1909
1 August 1912 Design No *427676* in Pursuance of an application, received on 25 July 1912 Brown Flemings Limited of 164 Springfield Road, Glasgow, Manufacturers, registered as proprietors.
p. 495 27 February 1904
427678-9 Class 14 (See BT 50/537)
Design *427678* 10 February 1909 Copyright extended
1 August 1912 Design *427678* in Pursuance of an application, received on 25 July 1912 Brown Flemings Limited of 164 Springfield Road, Glasgow, Manufacturers, registered as proprietors.

BT 51/120 9 March 1904 – 21 May 1904
p. 518 - no date
432288-91 Class 13 (See BT50/544)
Design No *432291* 30 May 1913 In pursuance of an application received on 28 May 1913, Brown Flemings Limited, of 164, Springfield Road Glasgow, Manufacturers, registered as proprietors.
28 May 1913 *432291* Copyright extended
p. 519 13 May 1904
432289-91 Class 13 (See BT50/544)
Samples missing
April 1909 *432289-91* Copyright extended
1 August 1912 Designs 432289-90 Copyright extended

BT 51/121 21 May 1904 – 11 August 1904
p. 6 13 May 1904
433294 Class (See BT 50/546)
30 April 1909 Copyright extended under Sec. 53(2) of P&D Act 1907
p. 314 2 July 1904
435990 Class 13 (See BT 50/551)
p. 569 5 August 1904
438268-9 Class 13 (See BT50/555)
Design *438269* 9 July 1909 Copyright extended under Sec. 53(2) of P&D Act 1907

BT 51/122 11 August 1904 – 21 October 1904
p. 587 20 October 1904
443630 Class 13 (See BT50/565)
22 September 1909 Copyright extended under Sec. 53(2) of P&D Act 1907

BT 51/128 19 Octobre 1905 – 3 January 1906
p. 84 28 October 1905
467998-9 Class 14 (See BT 50/615)

For *467998* Certificate not issued See Correspondence 641/10741
p. 113 1 November 1905
468210-11 Class 14 (See BT 50/615)
468210: 8 October 1910 Copyright extended under Sec. 53(2) of P&D Act 1907
468211: 18 October 1910 Copyright extended under Sec. 53(2) of P&D Act 1907
p. 114 1 November 1905
468212-13 Class 13 (See BT 50/615)
8 October 1910 *468212-13* Copyright extended under Sec. 53(2) of P&D Act 1907
Design *468212* 1 August 1912 Copyright extended under Sec. 53(2) of P&D Act 1907

BT 51/129 4 January 1906 – 16 March 1906
p. 511 6 March 1906
475188-90 Class 14 (See BT 50/630)
475188 and *475190* Certificates not issued. See Correspondence Papers no 641/11007

BT 51/130 16 March 1906 – 8 June 1906
p. 96 28 March 1906
476385 Class 14 (See BT 50/633)
p. 598 7 June 1906
480430-1 Class 14 (See BT 50/642

BT 51/131 8 June 1906 – 3 September 1906
p. 198 6 July 1906
482072 Class 13 (See BT50/645)
p. 198 6 July 1906
482073-4 Class 14 (See BT50/645)
p. 231 11 July 1906
482645 Class 14 (See BT 50/646)
p. 496 20 August 1906
485228 Class 13 20 August 1906 (See BT50/651)
p. 576 30 August 1906
486074 Class 14 (See BT50/653)

BT 51/132 3 September 1906 – 19 November 1906
p. 327 15 October 1906
489319 Class 14 (See BT 50/659)

BT 51/133 19 November 1906 – 12 February 1907
p. 446 24 January 1907
494677 Class 13 (See BT50/669)

BT 51/134 12 February 1907 – 26 April 1907
p. 338 23 March 1907
498743 Class 14 (See BT50/676)
p. 356 26 March 1907
498881 Class 13 (See BT50/676)

BT 51/136 9 July 1907 –30 September 1907
p. 322 23 August 1907
509884 Class 14 (See BT 50/695)
p. 368 29 August 1907
510490 Class 13 (See BT 50/696)
Copyright extended under Sec. 53(2) of P&D Act 1907 – 6 August 1912

BT 51/137 30 September 1907 – 7 December 1907
p. 51 October 1907

513190 Class 13 5 (See BT 50/700)
Copyright extended under Sec. 53(2) of P&D Act 1907 – 13 September 1912
p. 422 16 November 1907
515999 Class 13 (See BT 50/705)
Copyright extended under Sec. 53(2) of P&D Act 1907 – 26 October 1912
p. 580 5 December 1907
517088-9 Class 14 (517088) and Class 13 (517089) (See BT 50/707)
Copyright extended under Sec. 53(2) of P&D Act 1907 – 6 November 1912

BT 50 – BT 52, BT51 – BT 53

BT 52

The records are arranged in the following way:
– textiles classes 13, 14 and 15, ranges 1-26041 and 1-11532, years 1908-1910 are in BT 52/56-165
– textiles, range 11533-495183, years 1908-1964 are in BT 52/2455-7880
– BT 52/7881 contains some individual representations missed from the other series

BT 53

– textiles classes 13, 14 and 15, ranges 1-26041 and 1-11532, years 1908-1910 are in BT 53/9 + 10
– textiles, range 11533-495183, years 1908-1964 are in BT 53/108-195
– textiles, range 495000-515454, years 1964-1989 are in BT 53/288-308

BT 53/9 1 January 1908 – 15 June 1909
p. 90 13 March 1908
1440 Class 13 (See BT 52/60)
1 August 1912 In pursuance of application received on 25 July 1912. Brown Flemings Limited of 164 Springfield Road Glasgow, Manufacturers registered as proprietors.
p. 104 21 March 1908
1716-17 Class 13 (See BT 52/61)
1 August 1912 In pursuance of application received on 25 July 1912. Brown Flemings Limited of 164 Springfield Road Glasgow, Manufacturers registered as proprietors.
p. 186 5 June 1908
3222 Class 13 (See BT 52/65)
1 August 1912 In pursuance of application received on 25 July 1912. Brown Flemings Limited of 164 Springfield Road Glasgow, Manufacturers registered as proprietors.
p. 324 5 October 1908
6840 Class 13 (See BT 52/73)
1 August 1912 In pursuance of application received on 25 July 1912. Brown Flemings Limited of 164 Springfield Road Glasgow, Manufacturers registered as proprietors.
p. 434 18 January 1909
8650 and *8651* Class 13 (See BT 52/77)
samples missing
1 August 1912 In pursuance of application received on 25 July 1912. Brown Flemings Limited of 164 Springfield Road Glasgow, Manufacturers registered as proprietors.

p. 491 8 March 1909
9652 Class 13 (See BT 52/79)
> 1 August 1912 In pursuance of application received on 25 July 1912. Brown Flemings Limited of 164 Springfield Road Glasgow, Manufacturers registered as proprietors.

BT 53/10 16 June 1909 – 15 December 1910 (See for details BT 53/108 (21-6 – 19-12 1909)
p. 71 28 August 1909
12593 Class 13
> 1 August 1912 In pursuance of application received on 25 July 1912. Brown Flemings Limited of 164 Springfield Road Glasgow, Manufacturers registered as proprietors.

p. 115 8 October 1909
13491-92 Class 13
> 1 August 1912 In pursuance of application received on 25 July 1912. Brown Flemings Limited of 164 Springfield Road Glasgow, Manufacturers registered as proprietors.

p. 148 10 November 1909
14026 Class 13
> 1 August 1912 In pursuance of application received on 25 July 1912. Brown Flemings Limited of 164 Springfield Road Glasgow, Manufacturers registered as proprietors.

p. 242 15 February 1910
15624-5 Class 13
> 1 August 1912 In pursuance of application received on 25 July 1912. Brown Flemings Limited of 164 Springfield Road Glasgow, Manufacturers registered as proprietors.

p. 296 12 April 1910
16869 Class 13
> 1 August 1912 In pursuance of application received on 25 July 1912. Brown Flemings Limited of 164 Springfield Road Glasgow, Manufacturers registered as proprietors.

p. 369 21 June 1910
18545-7 Class 13
> 1 August 1912 In pursuance of application received on 25 July 1912. Brown Flemings Limited of 164 Springfield Road Glasgow, Manufacturers registered as proprietors.

BT 53/108 21 June 1909 – 19 December 1909 – identiek aan BT 53/10
p.66 28 August 1909
12593 Class 13 (See BT 52/90)
> 1 August 1912 In pursuance of application received on 25 July 1912. Brown Flemings Limited of 164 Springfield Road Glasgow, Manufacturers registered as proprietors.

p. 110 8 October 1909
13491-2 Class 13 (See BT 52/95)
> 1 August 1912 In pursuance of application received on 25 July 1912. Brown Flemings Limited of 164 Springfield Road Glasgow, Manufacturers registered as proprietors.

p. 143 10 November 1909
14026 Class 13 (See BT 52/97)
> 1 August 1912 In pursuance of application received on 25 July 1912. Brown Flemings Limited of 164 Springfield Road Glasgow, Manufacturers registered as proprietors.

p. 237 15 February 1910
15624-5 Class 13 (See BT 52/107)
> 1 August 1912 In pursuance of application received on 25 July 1912. Brown Flemings Limited of 164 Springfield Road Glasgow, Manufacturers registered as proprietors.

p. 290 12 April 1910
16869 Class 13 (See BT 52/114)
> 1 August 1912 In pursuance of application received on 25 July 1912. Brown Flemings Limited of 164 Springfield Road Glasgow, Manufacturers registered as proprietors.

p. 364 21 June 1910
18545-7 Class 13 (See BT 52/123)
> 1 August 1912 In pursuance of application received on 25 July 1912. Brown Flemings Limited of 164 Springfield Road Glasgow, Manufacturers registered as proprietors.

BT 53/109 20 December 1909 – 28 February 1912
p. 27 11 January 1911
27018-9 Class 13 (See BT 52/2570)
> 1 August 1912 In pursuance of application received on 25 July 1912. Brown Flemings Limited of 164 Springfield Road Glasgow, Manufacturers registered as p. 232 36176-8 Class 13 5 June 1911 (See BT 52/2636)
> 1 August 1912 In pursuance of application received on 25 July 1912. Brown Flemings Limited of 164 Springfield Road Glasgow, Manufacturers registered as proprietors.

p. 313 15 August 1911
40819-20 Class 13 (See BT 52/2662)
> 1 August 1912 In pursuance of application received on 25 July 1912. Brown Flemings Limited of 164 Springfield Road Glasgow, Manufacturers registered as proprietors.

BT 53/110 29 February 1912 – 10 May 1913
p. 8 13 7 March 1912
54672-3 Class (See BT 52/2752)
> 1 August 1912 In pursuance of application received on 25 July 1912Brown Flemings Limited of 164 Springfield Road Glasgow, Manufacturers registered as proprietors.

p. 10 8 March 1912
54764 Class 13 (See BT 52/2753)
> 27 June 1912 In pursuance of application received on 3 June 1912. Brown Flemings Limited of 164 Springfield Road Glasgow, Manufacturers registered as proprietors.

p. 125 8 June 1912
60396 Class 13 (See BT 52/2786)
p. 206 1 August 1912
65565 Class 13 (See BT 52/2810)
p. 215 9 August 1912
66053 Class 13 (See BT 52/2812)
p. 360 11 November 1912
73290 Class 13 (See BT 52/2850)
p. 467 1 February 1913
78026 Class 13 (See BT 52/2877)
p. 513 8 March 1913
80650 Class 13 (See BT 52/2892)

BT 53/111 10 May 1913 – 11 September 1914
P. 84 18 July 1913
88682 Class 13 (See BT 52/2934)
P. 108 9 August 1913
90669 Class 13 (See BT 52/2944)
P. 241 2 December 1913
96756 (See BT 52/2974)

[1] For more information: http://discovery.nationalarchives.gov.uk/SearchUI/Details?uri=C3125 and
http://www.nationalarchives.gov.uk/documents/records/ifa-registered-designs-1839-1991.pdf

BROWN FLEMING, A BIOGRAPHY

Ebenezer Brown Fleming was born on 25 November 1858 in Inverkeithing in the County of Fife, just north of Edinburgh in Scotland. His parents were Reverend John Dick Fleming (1810-1895) and Mary Lancaster Lowrie McArthur (1824-1909),[1] who lived in the *manse* of the United Presbyterian Church.

The Fleming family had several United Presbyterian Ministers: Ebenezer's grandfather, William (1777-1845),[2] was a minister in West Calder, Lanarkshire; his uncle James (1816-1900) was a minister in Whithorn, Wigtownshire,[3] and so were his cousins: Thomas McClelland Fleming (1852-1895) in Cupar, Boston and John Dick Fleming (1863-1938) in Tranent.[4]

He was first named Thomas Fleming but a month after his birth – on 26 December – it was altered to Ebenezer Brown Fleming. The reason behind his parents' decision might have been their wish to name him after a former and much venerated colleague of his father, Ebenezer Brown. John Dick was ordained as a minister on 5 December 1835, and Brown died a year later at the age of 78. A volume of his sermons was published in 1838.[5]

His family name, Fleming, is a surname that indicates the nationality of its original bearers i.e., natives of Flanders. Many immigrants settled in Scotland between the eleventh and seventeenth centuries as merchants or weavers.[6] The Fleming Clan is an officially recognized Scottish clan with their own crest and tartan.[7]

John Dick and Mary Fleming had six sons and three daughters of whom 4 sons went into the textile trade. Ebenezer's older brother William (1846-1883) is described in the census of 1881 as an East India Merchant. Ebenezer, living from 1880 with his brother until William's death at 9 Hillsborough Terrace in Hillhead, was working at that time as a Turkey red salesman.[8] Both had their office at 172 West George Street in Glasgow, so presumably they had been working together.[9] They knew the trade of the United Kingdom with overseas territories in Asia, Africa and the Far East. At the beginning of the 1880s, Ebenezer also became the Scottish representative of F. Steiner & Company in Church Bank, close to Accrington.[10] The company was known for their specialism in Turkey red dyeing. They were a high-quality printer employing excellent designers.[11] Steiner was one of the major Turkey red printers but they also produced dyed Turkey red cloth and yarn, which Brown Fleming may already have been marketing in Africa. In Scotland, there were more than enough Turkey red companies to satisfy local needs.[12]

His brothers, James MacArthur Fleming (1848-1907) and Arthur Charles Fleming (1855-1899), also set up a business working as textile merchants. James lived for at least ten years in Manila in the Philippines and returned in 1895, whereas Arthur died in Manila in 1899.[13] The brothers likely shared interests in each other's businesses. In William Fleming's will, he owed his brother Arthur Charles Fleming £70 for 'passage money from Singapore'.[14]

When Ebenezer married his wife Alice Spence on 4 October 1883, he was registered as an East India merchant.[15] When his brother William died a month later Ebenezer continued to work at 172 West George Street.[16] In 1886 Ebenezer is mentioned as a member of the incorporation of weavers as a *Commission Merchant* at the same address.[17] On 10 February 1887, he was admitted as a *Burgess and Guild Brother* in Glasgow, a charitable and social organisation.[18] In 1892 he moved his business to 205 Buchanan Street, an address housing multiple companies in Glasgow.[19] Brown Fleming is mentioned in the Post Office Directory of Glasgow 1896-1897 as Brown Fleming & Co., dyers, and printers of African specialties.[20] In the same year, he also became president of the *Fife, Kinross and Clackmannan Charitable Society*.[21] In 1897 he moved again, this time to 50 Renfrew Street in Glasgow. In 1906 Brown Fleming changed the name of the company to *Brown Flemings Ltd*, an indication that his son William Elphinstone Fleming and his son-in-law Ronald Richmond Herbertson had joined the business.[22] In the same year, he moved his business to 164 Springfield Road in Dalmarnock, an industrial part of Glasgow, where he set up his own printing division.[23] It is unlikely that he produced roller-printed versions of the Dutch block prints. According to Kroese, the firm ' *was known to be concerned with Chintz block prints*'.[24] The new address appears in the Post Office Glasgow Directory: *Brown Fleming & Co., dyers and printers of African and Colonial specialties at Springfield Dye Works in Dalmarnock*.'[25] According to Kroese he employed at least one designer.[26] He was probably just adjusting designs that were acquired for printing. John Hildesheim, a friend and colleague of Brown Fleming, remembers visiting *Fleming's factory* in 1908.[27]

In the meantime, he also moved home with his family. After his marriage in 1883, he lived with his wife at 3 Huntley Terrace in Glasgow. In the same year, he rented or bought a second house, *Lochanbrae* in Garelochhead, Argyllshire.[28] He had three children, William Elphinstone Fleming (1884-1960), Ethel Spence Fleming (1886-1976) and Frances Rowland Fleming (1891-1948).[29] The Scottish census of 1901 shows that he moved to 15 Granville Street, Sandyford in Glasgow. He also became the owner of two other properties. In 1905 he became the owner of 19 Kensington Gate in Glasgow. This *Gate* was a serpentine of red brick houses, designed by the architects Hugh and David Barclay in 1902,[30] where he would live until 1911.[31] A year later, in 1906, he also became the owner of *Kilchoan,* Loch Melfort (today Kilmelford) in Argyllshire, a very substantial country house with beautiful views over the loch.[32]

The census of 1911 reveals that he was a visitor to a hydrotherapy establishment in Dunblane with his daughter Frances and her husband-to-be Ronald Richmond Herbertson.[33]

Fleming died on 16 April 1912, at *Kilchoan*, Loch Melfort, in the county of Argyll. In the death register, he is mentioned as a manufacturer and the widower of Alice Spence. His wife had died on 18 February 1908, at the age of 45, after having suffered from ill health for more than fourteen years.[34] After her death, Brown Fleming seemed to suffer from poor health, however a newspaper cutting, written after his death, suggests that his physical vitality allowed him to take care of the management and improvement of his property Kilchoan at Loch Melfort and many local – agricultural – activities.[35] It suggests that he was less involved in his business than he had been in previous years.

He left a will referring to Ebenezer Brown Fleming from *Kilchoan,* Loch Melfort, Argyllshire and of Brown Flemings Limited in Glasgow, which was entered into the Legal Records of Wills and testaments on 7 May 1912.[36] His son William and two daughters Ethel and Frances outlived him.[37]

Brown Fleming wanted William and his son-in-law Ronald Richmond Herbertson to continue his business. Not only did he leave his property in Glasgow and the country houses in *Lochanbrae* and *Kilchoan* at Loch Melfort, but also stocks, shares and deposits at banks in the United Kingdom and several other countries in Africa and Asia totalling some £55,000.[38] The Scotsman added that his holding in Brown Fleming & Co. was valued for probate at £13,000.[39]

In his will, he leaves William '*all my travelling cases to be found anywhere* and *all my books of African travel and exploration*'.[40] Kroese describes him as an '*extrovert personality with flair and considerable acumen* and as a *much-travelled trader*'.[41] The diaries of John Hildesheim, also a textile merchant and his good friend, reveal several trips Brown Fleming took to Germany, where Hildesheim lived from 1887.[42] In 1903 he travelled to New York. A passenger list of the S. S. *Columbia* shows that he arrived there on 14 September 1903, *on a visit*.[43] He returned on 8 October 1903, on the S. S. *Teutonic* to Liverpool.[44] But there is no evidence that he went to Africa: his great-grandson doubts that he ever visited this continent.[45]

William also inherited a sick, given to Brown Fleming ' *by the Steiner employees*,[46] as he had worked as a representative for the company. Steiner was one of the major Turkey red printers but also produced dyed Turkey red cloth and yarn, which Brown Fleming could have been marketing in Africa.[47]

He left his son William Elphinstone Fleming a portrait of Van de Poll, director of the HKM. According to Kroese, Van de Poll and his family visited Brown Fleming in Scotland several times, first at his house called *Lochanbreae* and after 1906 at *Kilchoan*.[48] It is likely that Brown Fleming also visited Van de Poll in the Netherlands, especially after 1900 when Van de Poll inherited the estate *Heerlijkheid Callantsoog*.[49] The collaboration between the two had turned out to be the key to the success of wax print exports to West Africa.

[1] Statutory Registers Birth 132/92, National Records of Scotland.
[2] Small, 467, 617
[3] http://roegenealogy.com. FH%20Website/fam1747.html. Last accessed 11 November 2016.
[4] Small, 184, 541 and personal information of Malcolm Fleming d.d. 21 November 2016.
[5] See chapter 'Presbytery of Dunfermline and Kinross' in Small, 364-365.
[6] http://flemish.wp.st-andrews.ac.uk/2015/05/29/the-formation-of-the-fleming-surname/. Last accessed 9 November 2016. Two main groups can be discerned: a knight who came over with William the Conqueror and other Flemish immigrants, particularly from lower classes. Personal information George English d.d. 13 November 2016. See also http://www.selectsurnames.com/fleming.html and http://www.st-andrews.ac.uk/ishr/flemish/index.htm.
[7] https://en.wikipedia.org/wiki/Clan_Fleming and http://www.thetreemaker.com/family-crest-f/fleming/scotland.html. Visited 24 November 2016. See also Hunter, 469.
[8] 1881 Census 646/2 30/ 36 page 36, National Records of Scotland. https://glasgowwestaddress.co.uk/Hillsborough_Terrace/9_Hillsborough_Terrace.htm, last accessed 20 March 2023. On this site 1884 is mentioned. He might have moved out earlier, because not only William had died, but he wed on 4 October 1883 and started living with his wife at 3 Huntley Terrace in Glasgow.
[9] Post Office Glasgow Directory 1881-1882, 214.
[10] Kroese, 50
[11] Parry, 490
[12] Personal communication Philip Sykas 24 April 2017.

13   Personal information Malcolm Fleming d.d. 21 November 2016.
14   Will of William Fleming Legal Records Wills and testaments Reference Sc36/48/104, Glasgow Sheriff Court Inventories. National Records of Scotland pp. 385-389. Little is known about the two other brothers: his brother John Dick Fleming (1852-191?), who died in the Corowa Hospital in New South Wales in Australia, and Alexander Macarthur Fleming, born in 1854. He died only 27 days old. Information of Malcolm Fleming's family tree, information sent by email 24 March 2023.
15   He lived at 4 Bruce Street (today Bower Street) in Hillhead, a part of Glasgow. Statutory Registers Marriages 646/3 314, National Records of Scotland.
16   See Will of William Fleming Legal Records Wills and testaments Reference Sc36/48/104, Glasgow Sheriff Court Inventories. National Records of Scotland.
17   Robert Dugald, Old Glasgow Weavers: Being Records of the Incorporation of Weavers, 1916, p. 204.
18   http://www.tradeshouse.org.uk/about-us/associated-organisations/the-grand-antiquity-society.aspx. Last accessed 22 November 2016. His brother William had already joined this organisation on 21 August 1876. Scanned from original documents, collection Malcolm Fleming.
19   Post Office Glasgow Directory 1892-1893, p. 263.
20   Post Office Glasgow Directory 1896-1897, p. 89.
21   Alloa Advertiser 6 June 1896.
22   BT2/6243 1906, National Records of Scotland, General Register House, Edinburgh (UK). See also Post Office Glasgow Directory 1907-1908, p. 254.
23   For later developments of this site: http://www.glasgowhistory.co.uk/Books/Bridgeton/BridgetonChapters/Housing.htm.
24   Kroese, p. 53.
25   Post Office Glasgow Directory 1906-1907, p. 292.
26   Kroese (3), 22. Information based on an interview with Ethel Spence Wylie, daughter of Brown Fleming on 1 December 1975, Helensburgh, Dunbartonshire.
27   See part 3: https://hildesheimfamily.wordpress.com/2015/07/15/the-hildesheim-family/.
28   It is not clear if he was already the owner of the property at that time. In 1895 the Valuation Rolls show he is the proprietor of the house. Valuations Rolls VR009600041 Year 1895, National Records of Scotland.
29   Report The Descendants of Ebenezer Fleming. Report on the Family of Ebenezer Brown Fleming, George English, Research through People, https://researchthroughpeople.com/2016, 3,6.
30   http://www.scottisharchitects.org.uk/building_full.php?id=200437. Last accessed 1 november 2016.
31   http://www.glasgowwestaddress.co.uk/Kensington_Gate/19_Kensington_Gate.htm. Last accessed 1 november 2016.
32   In 2015 the house was put up for sale. The estate agent Robert McCulloch from Strutt and Parker called it the most picturesque estate he had been instructed to sell in Scotland. The Scotsman 17 April 2015. The house, dating back to 1798, was demolished and replaced by a modern building. https://www.pressreader.com/uk/the-scottish-mail-on-sunday/20180527/282003263095786.
33   Census 1911 348/4/14, National Records of Scotland. This establishment is still functioning: http://www.doubletreedunblane.com/.
34   Deaths in the district of Hillhead, Glasgow 1908, page 52, Statutory Registers Death 515/6, National Records of Scotland.
35   Newspaper cutting in possession of Malcolm Fleming, sent 12 October 2023.
36   Legal Records Wills and Testaments Reference Sc51/32/65 Dunoon Sheriff Court Wills, National Records of Scotland, pp. 149-154.
37   For William Elphinstone Fleming: Births. Patrick, Glasgow. 646/3. 24 August 1884. FLEMING, William. 646/3 1267 and Deaths. Surrey NW, Surrey. 14 December 1960. FLEMING, William. Vol 5g p. 695. For Ethel Spence Fleming: Patrick, Glasgow. 646/3. 30 Aug 1886. FLEMING, Ethel. 646/3 1079 and Death 31 December 1976 Glasgow. Frances Rowland Fleming born in 1890 in Glasgow And Deaths. Rhu, Dunbartonshire. 503. 19 July 1948 as HERBERTSON, Frances. 503/87.
38   This would be today worth about £ 5,500,000. http://www.thisismoney.co.uk/money/bills/article-1633409/Historic-inflation-calculator-value-money-changed-1900.html. Figures from before 1948 are based on estimates of the Office for National Statistics (ONS). Last accessed 3 November 2016.
39   The Scotsman d.d. 4 June 1912. Scotsman Digital Archive.
40   Legal Records Wills and Testaments Reference Sc51/32/65 Dunoon Sheriff Court Wills, National Records of Scotland, p. 151.
41   Kroese, 53
42   See the appendix Ebenezer Brown Fleming mentioned in John Hildesheim's Diary (https://hildesheimfamily.wordpress.com/2015/07/15/the-hildesheim-family/).
43   List of Manifest of Alien Passengers for the US Immigration Officer at Port of Arrival – S. S. Columbia sailing from Glasgow to New York, departing on 5 September 1903, arriving on 14 September 1903. Passenger Lists of Vessels Arriving at New York, New York, 1820-1897. Microfilm Publication M237, 675 rolls. NAI: 6256867. Records of the US Customs Service, Record Group 36. National Archives at Washington, D.C.
44   List of Passengers S. S. Teutonic. The National Archives of the UK; Kew, Surrey, England; Board of Trade: Commercial and Statistical Department and successors: Inwards Passenger Lists.; Class: BT26; Piece: 211; Item: 22.
45   He remembers that his aunt Hellen Seath Fleming told him that Brown Fleming teamed up with Thomas Bollen Seath, a shipbuilder and grandfather of Brown Fleming's daughter-in-law – Malcolm Fleming's grandmother – to use one of his ships for a trip to West Africa. Personal communication Malcolm Fleming 21 November 2016. I was unable to find any proof of this mention.
46   Legal Records Wills and Testaments Reference Sc51/32/65 Dunoon Sheriff Court Wills, National Records of Scotland, p. 151.
47   Linda Parry, 490
48   Kroese, 53
49   See also chapter 2.

CALICO PRINTERS' ASSOCIATION LTD (CPA)

In the second half of the nineteenth century the UK had enjoyed a monopoly of manufacturing cotton goods thanks to the development of steam machinery. This enormous expansion meant that production capacity greatly exceeded demand, driving prices below the cost of production and leading many printers to lower their standard of quality. Too many firms were catering to certain markets, too few to others, resulting in an immense waste in sampling, engraving and pattern development. It had become *a scramble for business which was sapping its vitality*.[1]

In 1899, 46 manufacturers and 13 textile merchants from England and Scotland, representing 85 per cent of the British textile printing industry merged into the Calico Printers' Association (CPA). Leading firms in the textile trade with the oldest dating back to 1750 decided to join. The goal was to preserve the tradition and standing of calico printing and to produce textiles of a high standard at reasonable prices. The headquarters were initially located at 2 Charlotte Street, later at 56 Mosley Street and from 1912 in the St James' Buildings on Oxford Street in Manchester. The company also had premises on Princess Street in Manchester. The association with F. F. Grafton as chairman had a small board of directors with sub-committees to deal with production, design, styles, prices, trading, buying, etc. A separate research department was set up in 1906.

After the First World War the association still had 29 print works in operation. The CPA faced competition from exports from America, Germany and Japan, with output increasing at a faster rate than that of Britain. The CPA had also lost markets because other countries began to produce their own textiles. These difficulties were worsened by the implementation of protectionist policies in the US and various European countries.[2] A solution was sought in establishing works outside the UK, either independently or as joint ventures. The main countries involved were China, Japan and India. In Africa, subsidiaries were established in Uganda and Nigeria in the 1950s and 1960s. But despite all the efforts there was a catastrophic decline in the textile trade in 1939 with only 11 print works left in the country.

The period after the Second World War brought even more foreign competition. The organisation was improved: by 1949 the Association was divided into four main groups: the *Mills Group*, which supplied some of the company's cloth and developed new fabrics, the *Commission Printing Group*, the *Merchanting Group* of trading departments and the *Overseas Group*, which supervised works established abroad. The four groups were supported by service departments including research, accounting, advertising and publicity. But production by countries that had previously been the best markets for the United Kingdom combined with relatively cheap labour and high tariff protection continued to be a serious concern. The association also engaged in research and development of textiles. It expanded its operations with the production and wholesale as well as retail distribution of textiles, textile engineering and the manufacture and distribution of chemicals.

In 1968 the CPA merged with English Sewing Cotton Co. to form English Calico Ltd. This textile group subsequently became Tootal Ltd in 1973, Tootal Group PLC in 1982 and eventually in 1992 the Coats Viyella group, today operating as Coats.[3]

[1] *Fifty Years of Calico Printing. A Jubilee History of the CPA*, Manchester 1949, 17.
[2] Launert, 14
[3] https://manchester.spydus.co.uk/cgi-bin/spydus.exe/ENQ/WPAC/ARCENQ?SETLVL=&RNI=7188712, last accessed 18 March 2023. And *Fifty Years of Calico Printing. A Jubilee History of the CPA*, Manchester 1949.

COLLECTING INDONESIAN ARTEFACTS FOR DUTCH MUSEUM COLLECTIONS AROUND 1900

Designers for specific markets, such as Indonesia, required very specific knowledge of local production to make the trade successful. With the exception of those working in the batik imitation industry, around 1900 there was little interest from Dutch designers in Indonesian arts and crafts, for the adaptation of ornaments or decorative principles.

The Netherlands had already had a long relationship with Indonesia. Since the early seventeenth century there had been trading posts in the East Indies (now Indonesia) and since 1817 the country had been a colony. In 1778, the Bataviaasch Genootschap van Kunsten en Wetenschappen (Batavian Society of Arts and Sciences) was founded in Indonesia by Jacob C. M. Rademacher. He was a pioneer anthropologist, describing the people and their way of life.[1] In 1813, Sir Thomas Stamford Raffles would become its chairman.

Private collectors had already been bringing objects to the Netherlands, but the first national museums in the Netherlands, which started around 1800, collected very few objects from Indonesia. There was more focus on Chinese and Japanese objects because these cultures were considered to be superior to that of Indonesia. The first and most important collection of original Indonesian objects, including batiks, was shown by the *Koloniaal Museum* (Colonial Museum) in Haarlem, founded in 1865 and officially opened in 1871 by Frederik Willem van Eeden. This museum, the first of its kind, was a private institution and was owned by the *Nederlandsche Maatschappij voor Nijverheid en Handel* (Dutch Society for Industry and Trade).[2] Van Eeden was not interested in creating a cabinet of curiosities to show the marvels of the world. He was more interested in the study of arts and crafts as they were practised in the Indonesian colony. The museum was equipped with a laboratory to experiment. Different dyes and batik techniques were explored.[3] Its core function was to gather, catalogue and study what was colonial wealth. This included examples of distinctive craftsmanship, which according to Van Eeden deserved respect and admiration and should be supported for preservation. The public should see it as an impetus to improve their own designs. Eduard von Saher, appointed in 1880 as the director and curator of the museum, went on several trips to London, Vienna, Berlin and Munich, but also to the US and Indonesia to collect objects.[4] Samuel van Musschenbroek, who worked until 1877 for the Dutch government in Indonesia, supported the initiative and donated a collection of 79 pieces of batik to the museum.[5]

A second museum, dedicated to ethnography, had been housed at a zoo in Amsterdam since 1858. This zoo was founded in 1838 by the Royal Zoological Society *Natura Artis Magistra* and focused on presenting wildlife from the Dutch colonial territories.[6] In 1910, the *Vereeniging Koloniaal Instituut* (Colonial Institute Association) was founded in Amsterdam. The Colonial Museum in Haarlem became part of this institute. The three institutions were united in one new building that opened in 1926.[7]

Since 1864, Leiden had its own ethnographic museum. It had already opened its doors in 1837 as the *Collectie Van Siebold*, an initiative taken in 1825 by the medical doctor Philipp Franz von Siebold (who collected Japanese artefacts), which was supported by King Willem I. In 1864, it became the *Rijks Ethnographisch Museum* (National Ethnographical Museum).[8] In 1891 and 1892, Dr J. Groneman, who worked as a private doctor for the sultan of Jogjakarta, donated an important collection of 118 pieces of batik all with different motifs, ordered by him and made in Jogjakarta.[9]

In Rotterdam, the *Museum voor Land- en Volkenkunde* (Museum of Geography and Ethnology) was housed in the building of the former Royal Yacht Association, opened in 1852 by King William III. The donation of batik cloth by the scientist Elie van Rijckevorsel (1845-1928), collected between 1872 and 1877 in Java, was especially important.[10]

Another interesting institution worth mentioning, which was not a museum, was the *Indische Instelling* (Indian – read: Indonesian – Institution) in Delft (1864-1900), which focused on education for future civil servants. The institute had a collection of objects which provided a picture of the history and culture of various Indonesian population groups and cultures.[11]

This relatively recent interest in products from the colonies was no surprise. It was sparked in the last quarter of the nineteenth century when colonies were opened to entrepreneurs and private capital. In 1870, for example, the Netherlands abolished their *cultuurstelsel* (cultivation system), a revenue system in Indonesia that forced farmers to pay part of their revenues to the treasury of the Netherlands in the form of export crops or compulsory labour. New investors were keen to gain more knowledge about local products and to explore investment possibilities for import, but also in the potential of exporting to Indonesia.[12]

This phenomenon was not limited to the Netherlands. In several European capitals, colonial exhibitions were organised to show the wealth of their possessions, with the aim of growing the public's interest and stimulating inspiring activities. Colonial exhibitions were organised in cities like Paris (1878) and Berlin (1880). Amsterdam organised the *Internationale Koloniale en Uitvoertentoonstelling* (International Colonial and Export Trade Exhibition) in 1883 with a focus on Indonesia, Suriname and the Antilles.[13]

[1] Hout 13-14.
[2] Bergvelt and Elands, 86. See also *Gids voor de bezoekers van het Koloniaal Museum te Haarlem*, Amsterdam 1902. The collection was eventually transferred to the Koloniaal Instituut, later Royal Tropical Institute and Tropenmuseum in Amsterdam, opened in 1926. Today, the Tropenmuseum is part of the National Museum of World Cultures. For more information, see Daan van Dartel, 'Het Tropenmuseum and Trade: product and source' in *Journal of Museum Ethnography*, 20(2008) 82-93. C. F. van de Poll, director of the HKM, was president of this association from 1902 until 1914. De Clercq 1936, 17.
[3] For details, see Herman A. J. Baanders,

226 — 227

'Over nieuwe proeven van batik-techniek in Nederland', *Bulletin Koloniaal Museum Haarlem*, Amsterdam 1901.

[4] Enschede, 27

[5] Legêne, 127; Rouffaer and Juynboll V

[6] The idea behind this was based on Linnaeus' efforts to comprehend Creation as a ladder from low to high development, where the human being is represented at the top. Therefore, collecting not only animals, but also minerals and objects created by humans made sense to him.

[7] In 2014, the *Tropenmuseum* (Tropical Museum) became part of *the Stichting Nationaal Museum van Wereldculturen* (Foundation National Museum of World Cultures): it has a collection of 3,000 pieces of batik, the oldest dating back to 1840.

[8] In 2014 it became, with the *Tropenmuseum* in Amsterdam and the *Afrika Museum* in Berg en Dal, part of the National Museum of World Cultures.

[9] This collection formed the basis of the important study of batik by Rouffaer and Juynboll, *Het batikwerk in Nederlands Oost-Indië en haar geschiedenis,* 1899.

[10] Simon Thomas 1998, 157

[11] Most objects were acquired after the colonial exhibitions in various capitals, the most important donation being after the exhibition in Amsterdam in 1883. After the closure of the institution in 1900, the collection of objects was housed in the Ethnographic Museum in Delft, which opened in 1911. In 1977 it was renamed Museum Nusantara and it closed in 2013. The archive of the institution is in the City Archive of Delft. See Leur, J. L. W. van, *De Indische Instelling te Delft. Méér dan een opleiding to bestuursambtenaar*, Volkenkundig Museum Nusantara, Delft 1989.

[12] Duuren, 15; Simon Thomas 1998, 152.

[13] Duuren, 10. Many objects were donated by their owners to museums in Amsterdam (Artis), Leiden, Delft and Haarlem.

COLOURISTS PRÉVINAIRE AND SON AND THE JEAN JACQUES FAMILY

Prévinaire and Son

The process of dyeing and printing cotton cloth needed several specialist operations. The role of a colourist was crucial. His main task was to provide the recipe, which indicated not only which dyes and other ingredients needed to be used, but also the quantities and in which order, as well as the duration and temperature. He decided on the most suitable printing process, judging new designs on their copying possibilities and economic profitability. A second important task was to analyse the necessary ingredients and other products that were to be used for printing. The strength and quality of products could vary, so he would determine in advance the necessary quantities to obtain a satisfactory result. Regularly checking the quality of the water was also useful. Another task was to solve problems during the production process by adjusting recipes or adapting machines. The colourist's essential knowledge resulted in him playing an important role in production but often also in the running of the company – from the selection of new machines to investments.

A textile printer could not afford to see his expensive products ruined by the poor quality of dyes and other products necessary for production, as well as failing recipes or defective machinery. To avoid becoming overly reliant on the expertise of an outside colourist, it was often a family member who would take up this important role and become part of the company's management. In the Netherlands, colourists received their training mostly outside the country. When a colourist from abroad had to be recruited he would rarely be offered a management position.[1]

The colourist's most important and unique tool was a recipe book, often with small samples of the results. These recipes were collected by the colourist himself, the foreman and the dyers, and were jealously guarded. To become a colourist, it was essential to obtain training within companies that often had their own specialities. From 1800, knowledge about chemicals slowly evolved. It was only from 1870 onwards that colourists attended technical schools that were better equipped to teach the use of newly invented synthetic dyes. From then on, colourists were even more capable of analysing samples from other companies, a practice as old as the branch itself. Colourists were working increasingly in laboratories and less in production. The direct importance of their role within the company diminished.

Between 1880 and 1910 natural dyes were slowly replaced. In the first decade of the twentieth century, natural indigo was completely replaced by its chemical counterpart. Producers of chemical dyes, such as the *Badische Anilin- und Soda Fabrik* (BASF) and the Swiss company *Ciba Geigy,* took over the work of colourists and provided a more controlled way of dyeing, thanks to their specific expertise.[2]

Prévinaire had himself received training as a colourist in Rouen in the early 1800s, where he learned the art of Turkey red dyeing. In Brussels, he worked together with his brother-in-law Auguste-Donat de Hemptinne, a pharmacist, to develop new products. His cloth, *Toile Adrinople,* was able to compete with market leaders in the Alsace.[3] On his arrival in Haarlem in 1835, he installed a small experimental laboratory within the company. Mansvelt suggested that this was the first industrial laboratory in the Netherlands.[4] His son Marie Prosper Theodore was introduced to the techniques by his father starting around 1842. Both were extremely innovative. According to Verbong, he also employed Célestin Le Roux, Laurent Joseph Genicot and Jean Joseph Jacques, the latter having received training in the Elzas.[5] He, his son and two of his grandsons would play a crucial role in the most important batik imitation printing businesses of the Netherlands.[6]

Jean Joseph Jacques family

Jean Joseph Jacques, born in 1815 at Opprebais, moved with Prévinaire to Haarlem and died there in 1874. His son, Joseph Jacques (1843-1905), also worked for Prévinaire as a *foreman,* but it is most likely that he was trained by his father as a colourist. Joseph Jacques' two sons, Jean Joseph Jacques (1872-1950) and Charles Henri Jacques (1874-1943), were also trained as colourists at the HKM.

Jean Joseph Jacques Jr. worked for the HKM until 1910 and then moved on to Ankersmit, a company that had just started attempting to imitate Prévinaire's wax printing process. In 1899, his father wrote a recipe book for him, probably as part of his training at the HKM, which he took with him to Ankersmit. This book, with the title *18 Décembre 1889 Livre de Fabrication appartenant à Jean Jacques,* is written in French and is now kept at the Brunnschweiler Archive, held at the Whitworth Art Gallery, University of Manchester (UK).[7] Judging from the handwriting, the book was most probably written by his father in French. It describes recipes for various imitation batik cloth items.

In 1910, Jean Jacques Jr wrote his own recipe book *Livre de Fabrication Deventer Katoen Maatschappij 29 Juin 1910* in Dutch, which is kept at the Vlisco Archives in Helmond (The Netherlands). Several of the small samples in the book could be from the HKM. During this period, Ankersmit had just started trying to copy designs by Brown Fleming, printed by the HKM. Jean Jacques turned out to be a difficult and secretive character. Hendrik Jan Ankersmit felt the need to protect Jean Jacques Jr because of his crucial knowledge of wax printing, but in March 1915, his behaviour had become untenable, and he was summarily dismissed.[8]

It is quite possible that Haijkens, who was selling United Turkey Red products in Scotland, suggested Jean Jacques Jr. sell his knowledge of wax printing to the Scottish company.[9] In 1919, Jean Jacques Jr sold the details of a cheaper and simpler method of the *Batik Printing Process* which he had developed himself to United Turkey Red in Scotland.[10] The factory would be based at Levenbank Works.[11] From 1920 to 1922, he moved to Scotland to help install the printing process. Upon his return to the Netherlands, he sent designs for engraving to UTR, which he purchased on behalf of the company.[12] Haijkens started selling wax prints for the UTR until 1925.[13]

ADDENDA — Contents

In 1927, the UTR obtained the sole rights of the process and Jean Joseph Jacques sent them the abovementioned book, *Livre de Fabrication appartenant à Jean Jacques 18 decembre 1889*.[14] At the bottom of each page is a hand-written English translation of the recipe. The handwriting is like that of the recipe book in the Vlisco archives dating from 1910. The recipes seemed to still prove useful and worth a summary translation. His brother Charles Henri Jacques worked from 1899 until 1910 for Van Vlissingen & Co. in Helmond (Netherlands), where he managed to produce a satisfactory quality of wax prints. Upon his departure, Van Vlissingen offered him for an advisory role until 1915. In 1913, he advised the company on a printing procedure for batik and donated batik cloth, recipe books and lab supplies.[15] He subsequently became a teacher at the School for Textiles in Deventer.[16] He died in 1943.

[1] Verbong 1988, 256

[2] The best study of colourists in the textile industry in the Netherlands in the nineteenth century is G. P. J. Verbong's PhD study: 'Technische Innovaties in de Katoendrukkerij en -ververij in Nederland 1835-1920', NEHA Amsterdam, 1988.

[3] Kroese 1979, 62. For more information about Prévinaire, see the appendix *Prévinaire before 1834*.

[4] Verbong 1986, 221(79)

[5] Verbong 1988, 356

[6] For a detailed family tree, see: https://genealogie.hintzbergen.nl/family.php?famid=F829, last accessed 15 February 2019. Although it is unclear when they began working for the company as colourists, Jean Disch and J.G.C Sabel worked there until its closure in 1917. Disch continued working for the DKM until 1930, after the closure of the HKM. In 1919, Sabel became the new director of the re-launch of the HKM, but the company was liquidated on 11 December 1922. Verbong 1988, 238.

[7] The book is also referred to as 'United Turkey Red... their wax batik process book written by Mr Rankin', because an inscription at the front of the notebook is signed by Mr Mankin of Levenshulme Works, who donated the volume to the CPA Library. Email correspondence with Philip Sykas d.d. 3 April 2023.

[8] Meeles I, 52-53

[9] Verschueren, 57. It could well have been Haijkens' revenge on Ankersmit. According to Verbong, it might have been Haijkens who had given samples from the HKM to Ankersmit in the period in which they contemplated starting with wax printing. Verbong 1988, 232. About three years later, in 1911, he wanted to sell Ankersmit's wax prints. At his request, Ankersmit gave him a sample to show a client, in confidence, but Haijkens also showed it to members of the BMTC, who consequently claimed the sole rights to selling Ankersmit's wax prints. Meeles I, 23.

[10] Email correspondence with Philip Sykas d.d. 9 September 2017, based on information in the United Turkey Red – Minutes of Board Meetings, held at Manchester Central Library: Letter 24 September 1919.

[11] Email correspondence with Philip Sykas d.d. 14 September 2017, based on information in the United Turkey Red – Minutes of Board Meetings, held at Manchester Central Library: Letter 28 January 1920. A letter of 24 February 1920 to the Standard Bank of Amsterdam gives details of the process, patterns and drawings.

[12] Email correspondence with Philip Sykas d.d. 25 September 2017, based on information in the United Turkey Red – Minutes of Board Meetings, held at Manchester Central Library: Board Minute Book No. 15 23 November 1921 – 28 June 1922, 5 April 1922.

[13] For more information, see the appendix on Haijkens.

[14] Email correspondence with Philip Sykas d.d. 27 September 2017, based on information of the United Red – Minutes of Board Meetings, held at Manchester Central Library: Letter 29 January 1927. Little is known about the two other brothers: his brother John Dick Fleming (1852-1911), who died in the Corowa Hospital in New South Wales in Australia, and Alexander Macarthur Fleming, born in 1854. He died only 27 days old. Information of Malcolm Fleming's family tree, information sent by email 24 March 2023.

[15] Verschueren, 56.

[16] Verbong 1988, 355. Interestingly, the school he worked for was founded by Charles de Maere, a Belgian textile producer who came to Enschede in 1830. Two years later, De Maere began a weaving school with the local municipality, which in 1922 became a higher school for textiles. It is still a leading academy today. https://www.1twente.nl/artikel/1851955/hoogere-textielschool-de-maere-bestaat-vandaag-100-jaar-een-terugblik-op-de-geschiedenis, last accessed 1 November 2022.

HAIJKENS

Henricus Jan Haijkens was the only merchant in the Netherlands who worked like the English merchants exporting to Africa by having cloth produced at several companies to ship and sell it directly to his African customers. Verschueren suggested that despite the intensive export trade he had with Africa, he never visited the Gold Coast personally.[1]

He was born in Beerta (The Netherlands) in 1880 and moved around 1900 to Chicago to work for the upscale department store *Marshall Fields'*, later sold to *Macy's*. In 1905 he moved to Paris where he started working as a textile merchant, already selling *Java Prints* from Van Vlissingen.[2] From Paris he moved to Hamburg in 1909, but before the First World War he moved to Hoek van Holland (The Netherlands), where he traded under the name *Haijkens and Co.'s Katoenmaatschappij*.[3]

A very important client was G. B. Ollivant Ltd, for which he organised the buying of wax prints and imitation batik. The company was founded by Captain George Bent Ollivant in 1858 in New Cannon Street in Manchester, primarily to ship cotton goods to Africa and buy African produce for export to Europe. A partnership was formed in 1894 by his sons Alfred and Charles under the name of G. B. Ollivant & Company that was converted to a limited liability company in 1900. By the 1950s the company had a network of 58 branches in Nigeria. They had their own warehouses in Manchester for the cloth that was to be exported. In 1933 the UAC bought and reorganised the company, but it continued to trade under its own name.[4] Haijkens also sold to the Commonwealth Trust in London.[5]

He initially traded cloth of United Turkey Red and Co. (UTR) in Scotland for which he had the exclusive rights to sell until 1925.[6] The UTR minute books do suggest he was their largest client.[7] In 1924 he had a total of 58 designs printed at UTR.[8] The cloth was transported to the Netherlands to be cut to the right size. A sticker was applied with the text *Dutch* Block Garments, as products from the Netherlands were especially appreciated.[9] He also ordered his fabric from companies like the LKM, Van Vlissingen and from Brown Flemings Ltd through Brown Fleming's son-in-law Ronald Herbertson.

From 1905 he sold *Block Prints* or *Javaprints*, so-called fancy prints, made by Van Vlissingen. Twenty years later he also started selling wax prints from Van Vlissingen, probably because he was not satisfied with the number of wax prints, he was able to sell from UTR. Van Vlissingen agreed on selling wax prints to him, but required him to halt trading with United Turkey Red. He soon became the second customer for wax prints from Van Vlissingen after the *African and Eastern Trade Association,* itself the result of a merger of the *African Association*, Miller and Swanzy in 1919.[10] From 1928 the company gave orders from Haijkens special numbers, always starting with an H.[11] He came on a regular basis with his own ideas that were transformed by the designers of Van Vlissingen into new motifs. Many, especially the early ones, are clearly inspired by the designs of the HKM. The only other person who could eventually introduce new designs in the *H* collection was Antonio Nogueira, a Portuguese merchant working for Haijkens in Congo and who knew this market particularly well. Nogueira introduced in 1940 the idea of *Six bougies* (H313).[12] Other popular designs with the H range were *Speed Bird* (H524), *Flying Duck* (H563) and *Taj Mahal* (H522). Haijkens had designs registered at the Patent Office in the United Kingdom.[13] He died in 1952

Haijkens' sample books can be found in the Vlisco Archives in Helmond (five books, of which one covering the Hamburg period) and the archive of Museum De Lakenhal in Leiden (Inventory no. 10719-21 and 10758). Boxes 03000-0177 and 03000-00061 in the Vlisco archives also contain information about Haijkens.[14] Useful for further study are all the order cards of the LKM with references to Haijkens from 1910 until the closure of the LKM, that are kept by Erfgoed Leiden. The notes on the cards reveal how closely connected he was with his English counterparts.

[1] Verschueren, 56
[2] Ankersmit 2009, 66
[3] Meeles I, 22, Vollaard, 85. Before moving to Hoek van Holland, he lived for a short period at Spoorsingel 1 in Rotterdam. He then moved first to Duinweg 39 and later to Grootzand 6 in Hoek van Holland. 'Rapporten over zijn zakenreis naar West-Afrika in 1934, in brieven geschreven aan zijn collega Tobie Hoogenboom, mede export-directeur van de NV P. F. van Vlissingen & Co's Katoenfabrieken Helmond.' Jan Fentener van Vlissingen, Helmond 24 March 1982, 2.
[4] https://transnationalarchitecture.group/2021/11/09/the-united-africa-company-uac-archive-october-updates/ and Kwara Nigeria Facebook page, https://www.facebook.com/260326857424671/photos/a.282930865164270/2807134589410539/?type=3&eid=ARCo2gagZ0IIi-V3C48-7gUt4F0702imwrD1yXYIqpG5fBYZvcmA9e4VI_tMNIoAKrwtCdg-tL2cVkoh, last accessed 19 November 2022.
[5] 'Rapporten over zijn zakenreis naar West-Afrika in 1934, in brieven geschreven aan zijn collega Tobie Hoogenboom, mede export-directeur van de NV P. F. van Vlissingen & Co's Katoenfabrieken Helmond.' Jan Fentener van Vlissingen, Helmond 24 March 1982, 3.
[6] Ankersmit 2009, 66
[7] In 1922 Haijkens ordered the company's total production of imitation batik. United Turkey Red minute books at Manchester Central Library: Board Minute Book No. 16. 5 July 1922-31 January 1923 (195pp). Partially indexed: 18 October 1922: Battik Prints. In 1924 they even agreed to sell exclusively to Haijkens with the exeption of F. Meyer in Manchester if he could guarantee large enough orders. United Turkey Red minute books at Manchester Central Library: 9 April 1924. Battiks Haykens & Co.
[8] Baharini Baines, 56
[9] Verschueren, 56
[10] Ankersmit 2009, 66
[11] Vollaard, 48. The numbers can be related to several dates: H1 was issued by the end of 1928, H500 on 2 May 1949, H1000 on June 1957, H1500 on 13 December 1961 and the final number, H1694, was released on 28 May 1965.
[12] Email correspondence with Philip Sykas d.d. 25 September 2017, based on information in the United Turkey Red – Minutes of Board Meetings, held at Manchester Central Library: Board Minute Book No 15 23 November 1921 – 28 June 1922, 5 April 1922.
[13] See correspondence of the Patent Office: Designs Branch at the Manchester Office 9 April 1940 with Elson and Neill Ltd Manchester d.d. 13 June 1930. Archives ABC Hyde (UK).
[14] Email Ruud Sanders Vlisco 1 October 2014.

SAMPLE BOOKS OF THE HAARLEMSCHE KATOEN MAATSCHAPPIJ IN THE VLISCO ARCHIVES IN HELMOND

A collection of a total of 60 sample books from around 1875 until July 1915 can be found in the Vlisco Archives in Helmond. Such books were used by manufacturers in the textile trade and were only intended for internal use. In general, they contain recipes, notes and technical details of the production process. Most of the books of the HKM were rebound in the 1960s by the Vlisco Company. The new numbering is random and the text on the cover not descriptive of the actual content. The books provide a general description. On some books LKM (Leidsche Katoen Maatschappij) is mentioned, although the content quite clearly shows HKM cloth. As an example, book 309 mentions *L. K. M. stalen v slendangs sarongs lijmdruk 1907-1911*, but contains HKM cloth. This is not only confusing, but also makes it difficult to determine the origin of the book.

The books were used for different purposes, varying from colourists' recipes, orders, samples with roller and design numbers, etc. There are no typical *sales-books* such as, for example, the Leidsche Katoen Maatschappij produced.[1] The HKM only printed based on orders from specific exporting merchants.

The numbers on similar designs are not identical in the various books, which is not unusual. Often separate sequences were kept for the various parts of the printing process, carried out in different workshops.[2]

My research has enabled me to identify a series of twenty-three books with roller and design numbers which could be identified by closely comparing the designs by Brown Fleming produced by the HKM and the numbers from the HKM with the information of the registration of several designs at The National Archives in Kew (London).[3] This made it possible for me to classify them so as to obtain an idea of the period of production. For the first time this allowed a unique insight into the production of the HKM over the period 1880-1917, which was initially only focused on export to Indonesia and South East Asia, but gradually moved to West and East Africa. An interesting addition to these books is book 212 with designs 9345-9453. This book resembles more an order book, with probably the very last design of the company before its closure, design 9345: 30-7-1915.

The books were most probably acquired after the closure of the HKM in 1917. Verbong suggests that Dutch printers were fighting over the heritage of the company.[4] It was common among calico printers to buy the designs, blocks and plates after a company's closure. They would frequently make use of these to create copies or adaptations, and in the case of the HKM it is not difficult to understand why. Many of Brown Fleming's designs, printed by the HKM, were extremely successful.

Twenty-three books with roller and design numbers

As already mentioned, the twenty-three books with roller and design numbers that are in the archives, starting from around 1880 or possibly even earlier, are the most interesting. As the first five books appear to be missing, it is difficult to know exactly when this series was started. It could go back to 1875 when the company changed its name, which corresponds to the sequence of the later books. The first books give a fascinating insight into some of the high quality and beauty of the imitation batiks of Prévinaire. These are the last samples of this kind that are left.

The series stops with book 309, if indeed book 312 can be considered an order book.

The original collection with roller and design numbers must have consisted of thirty-three books, based on the assumption that every book has an average number of approximately 290 designs.

Design numbers*:
– 1-1574: books missing
– 1575-1875: book 213
– 1876-2168: book 226 (some samples taken out and replaced with later samples for Brown Fleming)
– 2169-2363: book 223
– 2364-2669: book 211
– 2670-2966: book missing – partly covered by a smaller sample book with only roller numbers 2746-2909
– 2967-3261: book 266
– 3262-3559: book 233
– 3560-3850: book 214 First match with registered design: design 3844 matches with number 121636 (19 March 1889) BT50/115, p. 202 The National Archives, Kew (London)
– 3851-4142: book 248 (1890)
– 4143-4442: book 228 (1895)
– 4444-4736: book 210 (design 4443 missing) (1895)
– 4737-5040: book 224 (1895)
– 5041-5353: book 255 - 1897
– 5354-5589: book missing
– 5590-5889: book 246 (1897)
– 5890-6182: book 247
– 6183-6402: book 245
– 6403-6652: book 262
– 6653-6927: book 244
– 6928-7201: book 232

- 7202-7514: book 310 (designs 7515-7517 missing) (1902- 1903)
- 7518-7828: book 311 (design 7829 missing) (1903 -1904)
- 7830-8140: book 312 (1905)
- 8141- 8445: book 220 (1906)
- 8446-8792: book 309 (1907 – 1911)
- 8793-9345: three books missing
- 9345-9491: book 212 (1917)

A collection of eight smaller sample books, containing only roller numbers (corresponding to the numbers in the twenty-three books with the design and roller numbers)
- 2746-2909 (this book covers a part of the numbers, missing in the sample books 2670-2966 with roller and design numbers)
- 2910-3076
- One book missing
- 3243-3448 no. 237
- 3449-3620 no. 239
- 3621-3786 no. 240 (dessin 3635 = 20 October 1901)
- Two to three books missing
- 4330-4531
- 4531-4737
- Three books missing?
- 5344-5643 no. 253

A sticker on design 5627 mentions the fact that samples are delivered by the end of 1916, which means that this could well be the last book before the closure of the company.

The fact that the series only starts with number 2746 suggests that about 13 previous books are missing. The whole series may have consisted of about 27-28 books of which only 8 have survived.[5]

Sixteen very large books
- 1-308 no. 285
- (On the front cover is a note '19 September 1907')
- 309-620 no. 286
- Book missing
- 897-1190 no. 293
- 1191-1488 no. 296
- 1783-2078 no. 287
- 2079-2378 no. 292
- 2379-2678 no. 295
- 2679-2976 no. 304
- 2977-3274 no. 303
- 3275-3572 no. 297
- 3573-3870 no. 291
- 3871-4168 no. 288
- 4169-4460 no. 298
- 4467-4764 no. 289

Last design no 4764 is dated 18 June 1917.

Five books with roller and design numbers
with so-called 'interior designs' (badan - main field of the sarong) and suggestions for boarders (nos. 294, 299, 300, 302 and 305)

Remaining books
- Two books with small samples and recipes of the colourist 1892-1893 and an order book 1904-1906
- Book 308 'Rotatie 1-848' (Rotation) and book 209 'Rotatie 849' with samples from 24 September 1910 until 29 May 1913 and some from 1917, that gives the exact circumference of the used printing roll.
- Book 219 (paper copies of 'interior designs' for sarongs) and book 229, probably after 1910

* Year is approximate, based on link between specific design number and registration date of the design, but the time between printing and registration can vary. In the archives there is also an important collection of cloth from the HKM, probably taken at the closure of the company. It consists mainly of printing samples and experiments in various sizes. A closer study also revealed the presence of early Ankersmit wax prints.

[1] Examples of these typical sales books are kept at Museum De Lakenhal in Leiden.
[2] For an excellent introduction to textile pattern books within companies, see Philip Anthony Sykas, *Textile pattern books in the Northwest Region* in *The Secret Life of Textiles. Six Pattern Book Archives in Northwest England*, Bolton 2005, 11-15.
[3] On each sample are two round stickers with serrated edge: on the stickers on the left one can read the design number, on the sticker on the right the roller number.
[4] Verbong 1988, 181.
[5] The design numbers of these series do not correspond to the numbers in the books with the roller and design numbers.

KANGAS

Kangas, produced for the East African Market, mainly Kenya and Tanzania, would become increasingly popular after 1865 when the price of cotton dropped. They consisted mostly of pieces of cloth of about 100cm by 150cm with a border along all four sides and a central section with a different design. Initially kangas were block printed locally, but in response to growing demand merchants began sending orders to European textile companies, where larger quantities could be produced more economically. The first examples were sketched by merchants based on the wishes of their clients on the Swahili Coast and sent to the producers.[1] The cloth was mostly printed in only one or two colours, was relatively cheap to print and sold in pairs. They would be used for skirts, head-wraps and aprons, among other items, and worn by men, women and children. From the early 1900s, proverbs, sayings and slogans were added to the design. Texts in Arabic or Swahili would be hand copied by the European designers, who were, however, unfamiliar with these languages. As a result, words were often misspelled or even printed upside down. A kanga with its specific design and meaning represented a value for each person, community or ethnic group.

For more information about the history of kangas see three publications of Mackenzie Moon Ryan:
- 'The Global Reach of a Fashionable Commodity: A Manufacturing and Design History of Kanga Textiles', PhD University of Florida, Gainesville 2013
- 'A Decade of Design: The Global Invention of the Kanga 1376-1889' in *Textile History* 48 (1) 2017 101-132
- 'Kanga Cloths at Vlisco: An Object-Based Study of Dutch Printing for the Colonial East African Market 1876-1971' in *African Arts* (2023) 56 (3): 56-71.

[1] Ressler, 5, 15.

KRALINGSCHE KATOEN MAATSCHAPPIJ (KRALINGEN COTTON COMPANY) (KKM)

The precursor of this company, named *Non Plus Ultra,* was established in 1701 in Hillegersberg, a village bordering Rotterdam, on the shore of the river Rotte. It was owned by Pieter Barbet who moved to Kralingen, another village now part of Rotterdam, ten years later.[1] Initially he produced simple cotton prints for the Dutch market, but later specialised in copying chintz from India. In the eighteenth century, there were at least five other textile printing companies in the Rotterdam area, all attracted by the ample supply of water. However, all except *Non Plus Ultra* existed only for a short time.[2]

After Barbet's death in 1751, his family sold the company to Pieter van Eyck. Business had declined, although the sales advertisement mentioned more than 1800 printing blocks and thirty printing tables, indicating a respectably-sized establishment.[3] In the ensuing decades the company changed ownership several times, pointing towards an unpropitious economic climate. In 1772 Pieter van Eyck sold it to his brother Clement, who just three years later sold it to Nicolaas Riemersma. In 1809, it was bought by Isäac Benedictus, who sold it in 1813 to Petrus Landt and Martinus van Marle. After the death of Landt in 1829, Van Marle was joined by an associate in 1832, Andres Plemp van Duiveland, but Van Marle himself died two years later.[4] It is quite likely that the company already printed batik imitations, having received the help of the NHM to promote trade between the Netherlands and its colonies.[5] In spite of a loan of 40,000 guilders from the government in 1834, the company had to close its doors in 1836 because of a lack of orders.[6] Attempts to revive the textile industry in the Netherlands in the form of further subsidies from the Dutch government allowed G. Van Sillevoldt to buy the company in 1839.[7] It was renamed *De Hollandsche Katoendrukkerij van G. van Sillevoldt* and in 1857, when his son became co-director, it was named *G. van Sillevoldt & Zoon*. The company became a successful printer of batik imitations, although it is not clear when exactly imitation batik production started. Their product package was comparable to those of the LKM and Van Vlissingen, but the quality was lagging. Production of wax prints was minimal. It was aimed at export to Dutch and English colonies. Turkey red was one of their specialties, although according to Verbong the quality was not comparable to Steiner in Scotland.[8] Their production methods were outdated, and they did not have a colourist who was aware of the latest developments.[9]

In 1861, another printer of batik imitations, dyer and bleacher was founded in Kralingen, *Blom, De Lange and Braun*. After two years Blom left the company, which continued under the name De Lange, Braun & Co. Jacques Braun, born in 1815 in Mulhouse, worked as a colourist for Van Vlissingen from 1849 onwards, but moved in 1861 to work as a business associate for the newly started company.[10] In 1864 the company was renamed *Rotterdamsche Katoendrukkerij*. The company suffered from the contraction of sales of imitation batiks after 1867. This is illustrated by the fact that when De Lange wanted to leave the company in 1868, he approached Arnold Ledeboer, who was looking to start a cotton printing company, as a potential successor. Ledeboer was not interested and declined the offer, given the difficult market for imitation batiks.[11] When in 1870 a fire demolished part of the company, the shareholders decided it was time to sell. The buyer was the son of Van Sillevoldt, who had by then taken over his father's company.[12] With his business partner J. F. Kesting he began a new firm in 1871, *Van Sillevoldt en Kesting*.[13] One advantage of the acquisition of the Rotterdamsche Katoendrukkerij was that they finally had a real colourist.

In 1882 the company was renamed *NV Kralingsche Katoen Maatschappij*. Water supply problems, created by the draining of local lakes and lack of space to expand, drove the company to move from 's Gravenweg to the Oostzeedijk in Kralingen.[14] The production was focused on the domestic market. Around 1900 the export market for imitation batik was still difficult. The company made wax prints, but only in small volumes. The production was too costly to enable the company to become profitable.[15] Gradually, export to Indonesia, and an entry into the African market, turned out to be more promising.[16] Around 1920 the production was mainly imitation batik for export to Dutch and English colonies in South East Asia, as well as several countries in Europe, Africa, China and to the US.[17] Later, the heavy competition from the Far East, especially Japan, made export more and more difficult and in 1932 the company had to close.[18]

Wiersum and Van Sillevoldt concluded in their article published in 1921 that little remained of the old records about the company. Two fires, in 1870 and 1872, had destroyed most of the archives. Wiersum and Van Sillevoldt described some surviving samples and printing blocks, price lists, correspondence and two sample books. One sample book covering over 3,400 designs of *indiennes* from 1813 until 1832 is kept by the Museumfabriek in Enschede (The Netherlands).[19] This book was donated by J. van Sillevoldt, the author of the article and director of the KKM. In 1935 he became director of the Twentse Textielfabriek in Goor, close to Enschede. The second sample book is described as a book with samples of imitation batik on cotton. If this book originated from Non Plus Ultra, which changed its name in 1839, it would mean that the company must have been one of the first to print imitation batik in the Netherlands.[20] Unfortunately, the origin of this sample book can no longer be traced.

The Museum Rotterdam holds twelve sample books in its collection, along with printing blocks and samples of sarongs.[21] The books range from around 1880 until 1931, a year before closure of the company. A closer study of these books reveals how various companies *copied* the same designs. The first books show traditional imitation batik with some of the motifs that were also printed by other imitation batik printers. An interesting example is the print of a boat, dated 22 May 1885. An exact copy was registered by the *Haarlemsche Katoen Maatschappij* (HKM) in the United Kingdom on 16 April 1889.[22] In 1909, the KKM printed this design in a version clearly adapted for the African market with the characteristic veining and irregularities.[23]

Another intriguing design is *Peacock*. Early examples can be found in the sample books of the HKM from the end of the 1870s.[24] Brown Fleming registered this design in 1895 in three variations.[25] In the sample book of the KKM that covers the period 1891-1901, no. 1570 is a clear example of this peacock design, dated 11 June 1898.[26] The same peacock appears also in a sample book of 1902, kept in the archives of *ABC Wax* in Hyde, and linked to the Manchester merchant Edwin Goodwin.[27] Goodwin was a regular client of the KKM.[28] In this sample book the design appears next to samples of Chinese figures, also dated 1902, that correspond with identical samples of the KKM at the Museum of Rotterdam.[29] Later samples from Goodwin show stickers with not only his own marks but indicating *Guaranteed Dutch Wax Block Prints*. British merchants certainly bought *Dutch* wax prints for trade in Africa and coming from the Netherlands was clearly a sign of quality.

The sample book of the KKM covering 1912-1931 shows various designs inspired by motifs introduced by Brown Fleming like *Sunray* and *Hand and Fingers*, but these are not wax prints and of mediocre quality.[30]

[1] The company was initially founded by Barbet and Jan Dustoe, but only one month after the start Dustoe pulled back. See H. C. Hazewinkel, *De aanvang der katoendrukkerij te Rotterdam*, Rotterdamsch Jaarboekje 1933, 31-32.
[2] Smit, 56
[3] Wiersum and Van Sillevoldt, 69-70; Hartkamp-Jonxis 1989, 20.
[4] Verbong (1989), 53 and Smit, 72
[5] Wiersum and Van Sillevoldt, 77 and Verbong 1988, 30
[6] Griffiths, 153
[7] For more information about the early years of this company, see Verbong 1988, 143-144.
[8] Verbong 1988, 116
[9] Verbong, 144
[10] Verbong 1988, 209
[11] Letters H. A. Ledeboer to Abraham Ledeboer d.d. 26 February 1868 (Archief Twentse Textielfamilies, familiearchief Ledeboer, inv.no. 203, LA01377), 21 February 1879 (Archief Twentse Textielfamilies, familiearchief Ledeboer, inv.no. 254, LA02444) and 27 February 1870 (Archief Twentse Textielfamilies, familiearchief Ledeboer, inv.no. 254, LA02445), seen as scans in email Derk Jordaan 17 December 2022. The brothers H. A. 'Arnold' and J. B. (Bernard) Ledeboer would eventually start in 1871 a cotton printing business in Mottram, east of Manchester with the help of their uncle H. J. van Heek, a wealthy Dutch textile entrepreneur. Bernard was head of printing in Mottram, Arnold was responsible for their office in Manchester. https://www.derkjordaan.com/het-treinongeluk-van-arnold-ledeboer-1876/ and personal communication Derk Jordaan 12 January 2023.
[12] Two letters dated 24 February 1868 and 4 June 1870 from De Lange to Hendrik Jan van Heek (1814-1872), one of the shareholders, in the Archief Twentse Textielfamilies in Enschede (The Netherlands) indicate the financial struggle the company had. Given the difficulties of the batik trade, they seemed to prefer to focus on prints for the domestic market. Personal communication Derk Jordaan 11 December 2022.
[13] Verbong 1988, 30 and personal communication Derk Jordaan 9 December 2022: *Nederlandsche Staatscourant*, 11 September 1871.
[14] Unpublished document 11 February 1983, Vlisco archives, Helmond (The Netherlands) and Wiersum. and Sillevoldt, 84
[15] Verbong describes a sample of wax print of the KKM of which the company in 1889 had sold only one single box, because the production had been too costly. Verbong 1988, 226
[16] Wiersum and Van Sillevoldt, 71, 78-79. https://www.modemuze.nl/blog/rotterdams-katoen-aanwinst-museum-rotterdam, last accessed 21 November 2014.
[17] Wiersum and Van Sillevoldt, 85.
[18] https://www.modemuze.nl/blog/rotterdams-katoen-aanwinst-museum-rotterdam, last accessed 21 November 2014. See also unpublished

document about the Kralingsche Katoen Maatschappij, dated 11 February 1983, in the Vlisco Archives in Helmond (The Netherlands).

[19] The Museumfabriek also holds two sample books of the KKM from around 1890 with printed satins under numbers 5541 and 5542.

[20] Wiersum and Van Sillevoldt, 78.

[21] https://www.modemuze.nl/blog/van-depot-tot-digitalisering-de-stalenboeken-van-de-kralingsche-katoenmaatschappij, last accessed 15 December 2017. For a detailed description of the various sample books see Ernestine van Herwerden, 'De stalenboeken van de Kralingsche Katoendrukmaatschappij', MA, University of Amsterdam 2010.

[22] The design is registered under number 123514, see: TNA. BT50/117 and BT51/54.

[23] See sample 2472 in book 20984 Kralingsche Katoen Maatschappij, Museum Rotterdam (The Netherlands).

[24] See chapter IV.

[25] The first version with peacocks on a green background on the border and flowers in the middle on a white background was registered on 17 April 1895 under no. 253268. A striped version was registered under no. 260846 and the square version as 260847 on 31 August 1895.

[26] Stalenboek van de Kralingse Katoen Maatschappij, 944-1839, 1891-1901, inventory no. 20983, Rotterdam Museum, Rotterdam. The book can be seen on https://www.youtube.com/watch?v=6P3_MNAPACQ.

[27] Edwin Goodwin was a merchant in Manchester and traded with Albert Heathcote Emery, who took over the business in 1927. See *The London Gazette,* 3 May 1927, 2909.

[28] Meeles II, 105

[29] See inventory number 23604-98, Museum Rotterdam.

[30] This book, no. 22162, covers the numbers 2770-3416.

LEIDSCHE KATOEN MAATSCHAPPIJ (LEIDEN COTTON COMPANY) (LKM)

Initially named De Heyder & Co., the Leidsche Katoen Maatschappij was an important cotton printer. In 1757 Peter Jacob de Heyder started as a manufacturer of woven and printed cloth in Lier, close to Antwerp in Belgium. By the turn of the century, it had become one of the most important textile companies in the south of the Netherlands.[1]

After the separation of Belgium from the Netherlands in 1830, the company struggled because of a lack of orders. The loss of Indonesia as an export country proved to be a disaster. In 1831 the owner, the well-known *orangist* baron F. Van den Berghe, had to close his company and lay off 1,200 employees in Lier. In 1835 he decided to move the company to Leiden.[2] Managers were Ten Sande and P. J. F. Van Ael. From Van Ael a collection of recipes has been kept, especially for the dyeing of Turkey red.[3]

They also specialised in the production of imitation batiks. According to Rouffaer and Juynboll the company started systematically collecting original batiks, recording the exact place of origin and year of production as inspiration for their own collection.[4] An inventory of the company from 1835 shows the presence of a *rouleau* printing machine. During the first years after their arrival in the Netherlands the company made a very good profit with the deliveries to the NHM, which bought their entire production of Turkey red, but this went into a quick decline after 1840.[5] The company took a passive attitude towards the difficult economic situation and stopped investing.[6] Ten Sande started his own company in 1840 and when Van Ael died in 1846, the company was in a poor state with only 32 workers. With the arrival of the new owners Heinrich Driessen, a textile producer and merchant, and his brother-in-law Ignatz van Wensen in 1846, the situation changed for the better. Driessen's son Louis became director. He had trained in several English textile companies.[7] In 1848 Pierre, Louis' brother, started his training as a colourist within the company. In 1851 he moved to Rouen for several years to pursue his education.[8] Quickly the production of *rouleau*- and hand printing resumed to a profitable level. In 1849 a substantial investment was made in new equipment such as a three- and four-colour *perrotine*. In 1851 a machine to print six colours was bought. This investment allowed the company to produce series on a smaller scale, ideal for sale to various, smaller markets that needed their own specific products such as imitation batiks. Rouleau printing was mainly used for the domestic market; batik imitations were entirely done by hand. It was too difficult, if not impossible to compete with English mass-production.[9]

Overall business was flourishing, which allowed the company in 1854 to move to new premises with a separate laboratory and a small library.[10] Two years later Driessen made a study trip to England and Scotland to see how he could modernise the printing facilities of the company. After a fire in 1861, which destroyed a major part of the factory, the factory was rebuilt, even better and larger than the one dating from 1856. A steam driven mill was installed, replacing handweavers who were working from home.[11]

The NHM was no longer the exclusive client and other ways of selling were explored. When the export of imitation batiks stagnated at the end of the 1860s, the company was faced with an important amount of unsold cloth and ended up having serious problems. Driessen decided to focus only on saleable products and on other international markets.[12] At the same time efforts to produce real wax prints were accelerated, especially because Van Vlissingen and some Swiss companies were already able to do so. In one way or another Pierre Driessen obtained at least some notion of the recipes of Prévinaire and in 1865 a machine that would imitate the *Javanaise* was buildt. Although the results were promising, the machine was no longer in use by 1870 for production; however, experimentation continued. The company had started taking the production of wax print seriously, too late so it had not been able to profit from the boom of the 1860s. In addition, the results of their hand printed cloth were mediocre.[13]

In 1874 Driessen became sole owner of the company. Three years later he decided to change its name from *De Heyder and Co.* into *Leidsche Katoen maatschappij voorheen De Heyder and Co.* It employed almost 1,200 people. To gain more knowledge of the technique of textile production and become less dependent on the experience of employees, Driessen's son Felix had spent a year in the company as an intern and then specialised at the *École de Chimie* in Mulhouse from 1873 until 1875 to become a colourist.[14] To obtain practical experience he did an internship in Hollingworth and at the Fowhill Bank Printing Company in Accrington (United KIngdom).[15] From 1877 onwards he worked as the company's colourist.[15] From the beginning of 1878 until the end of 1879, he travelled to South East Asia and in 1884 and 1897 he made study trips to Java.[17] Felix did extensive research on batik imitations made by other European companies on the local markets to expand his knowledge.[18]

In 1878 the company stopped its production of Turkey red, but Felix Driessen continued to experiment with the technique. He presented a resume *Etude sur le Rouge Turc (Ancien Procédé)* at the *Société Industrielle de Mulhouse* in 1901 for which he received a medal of honour.[19] In 1889 Charles Casanovas was hired to help Felix Driessen. He attended the same *Ecole de Chimie*, founded in 1825 by the *Société Industrielle de Mulhouse,* as Felix.[20]

In 1897 a second fire again destroyed a major part of the company which was rebuilt very quickly.[21] However, the associated costs took a toll on the financial situation of the company and as a result it was more reluctant to invest in new machinery. It kept using perrotine machines for the various markets they printed for at a time when other companies were already investing in more modern and efficient rouleau printing machines, often combined with hand printing.[22] Around 1900 the company still made wax prints, but in very small volumes. Only 1 per cent of the production was double-sided printed and the wax prints formed just a small part of this. Like Van Vlissingen, in this period the company started to print and export kangas to East Africa. Interest in the West African market only took off around 1910 with the production of prints of imitation batik.[23]

In 1889 both sons of Louis became directors. While Felix (1855-1936) became general director, Carl was responsible for the weaving mill.[24] A fire at the company unfortunately destroyed the collection of original batiks, with which they had started already in 1835.[25] When Louis Driessen died in 1904 the company had a workforce of 950, which is impressive compared to the 32 who were working at the LKM on its arrival in Leiden.[26]

There was an interest in producing wax prints, but the company had difficulty in finding the right colourist. It did not have the advantage of Van Vlissingen and Ankersmit in being able to employ the sons of Jean Jacques. Eventually they hired Alfred Kunig from 1911 until 1913. He had finished his studies in Mulhouse in 1901 and previously worked for Roessingh in Enschede. He wanted to develop a new way of printing double-sided wax prints, but the LKM could only produce single-sided prints. His experiments failed and he left. His ideas about developing a double-sided printing machine were explored and proved to work, but the company did not have a specific interest or the necessary money to develop this way of printing any further.

In the meantime, the son of Felix, Louis (1890-1954), trained like his father as a colourist at the Ecole de Chimie in Mulhouse. His apprenticeship was at the Schlüsselburg Print Works near Saint Petersburg and at the Lowerhouse Printworks in Burnley (United Kingdom).[27]

During the public sale of the machinery of the HKM, the LKM was able to buy a wax printing machine. Especially English merchants were interested in the possibility of buying wax prints from the LKM, but the company did not manage to print a satisfying quality with this machine let alone to compete with Ankersmit and Van Vlissingen. After 1922 production stagnated because of a lack of supplies, while exports had already slowed down after the First World War. From 1926 to 1929 orders from West Africa led to a short recovery, but the Great Depression starting in 1929 again affected product on. In 1934 the company halted its activities altogether. The crisis in their main export markets of Indonesia and Africa meant that the company was no longer viable. It could not cope with Japanese competition and the higher salaries made the hand printed cottons, which was its specialty, just too expensive. After being operational for a hundred years it was liquidated in 1936. The buildings were demolished.[28]

Felix van Driessen and his sons systematically kept detailed notes of their business, which provide unique insights. He also wrote various articles.[29] They also created a unique collection of books and documents about cotton printing. A major part of this legacy as well as the company archives has been kept in several collections in the Netherlands. The organisation *Erfgoed Leiden en omstreken* has a part that includes sample books and correspondence. *Museum De Lakenhal*, also in Leiden, has a major collection of sample books, from as early as 1848, among which are some samples from the NHM and Haijkens. The *Textielmuseum* in Tilburg has books, compiled during training of collaborators of the LKM at several companies in Europe as well as laboratory books in which tests for the dyeing and printing process were recorded. Books about textile printing and dyeing have also been kept as well as for batiks and printed cloth.[30] Vlisco in Helmond has about twenty books among which are from as early as 1846 as well as several books with samples and letters from Indonesia with ideas for production.

[1] For more information about the company's years in Belgium, see Catharina Lis and Hugo Soly, *Een groot bedrijf in een kleine stad. De firma De Heyder & Co te Lier 1757-1834*, Lier 1987.
[2] Visser, 197
[3] Verbong 1994, 274
[4] Unfortunately, this collection was destroyed in a fire at the factory in 1897. Rouffaer and Juynboll 1899, IX
[5] The NHM got into trouble, because of stagnating sales in Indonesia due to economic problems after a succession of crop failures. Verbong 1988, 28, 149 and Verbong 1994, 274
[6] Verbong 1988, 153
[7] Verbong 1988, 31
[8] Verbong 1994, 278
[9] Verbong 1988, 202
[10] Verbong 1994, 278
[11] Visser, 198
[12] Verbong 1988, 150
[13] For a detailed description of the experiments and production of the copy of the *Javanaise*, see Verbong 1988, 204-207.
[14] Visser, 200. For more information about Felix Driessen training as a colourist, see G. Verbong, 'Coloristen en Laboratoria. De ontwikkeling van het coloristische werk in de Nederlandse textielveredelingsindustrie' in *Tijdschrift voor de geschiedenis der geneeskunde, natuurwetenschappen, wiskunde en techniek* 9(1986)4, 221-226. For more information about the Ecole de Chimie in Mulhouse: https://fr.wikipedia.org/wiki/%C3%89cole_nationale_sup%C3%A9rieure_de_chimie_de_Mulhouse, last accessed 22 February 2023.
[15] The report he wrote about his apprenticeship with drawings of machines and samples is kept at the Textielmuseum in Tilburg (The Netherlands).
[16] Dicke *et al*, 200
[17] Rouffaer and Juynboll, XIV
[18] An extensive correspondence with his father with not only letters, but also samples and cloth is kept at the Textielmuseum in Tilburg.
[19] Verbong 1994, 285
[20] Verbong 1988, 250
[21] Verbong 1988, 170
[22] Verbong 1988, 183
[23] Verbong 1988, 227
[24] Felix Driessen, 'Peter Ludwig Carl Driessen' in *Leidsch Jaarboekje* 1906, Sijthoff Leiden 1906, 19-23.
[25] Rouffaer and Juynboll IX.
[26] Unpublished document 'De Leidsche Katoenmaatschappij 1835-1936', 4. This document is in the Vlisco Archives in Helmond (The Netherlands).
[27] Elk, 35-36
[28] Verbong 1988, 236-237, 358; LePoole, 35 and Dicke *et al*, 202
[29] See a complete list in LePoole 1943, 38 and https://adoc.pub/jaarboek-van-de-maatschappij-der-nederlandse-letterkunde-194.html, last accessed 22 February 2023
[30] The collection was bought in 1956 by the town of Tilburg prior to the opening of a textile museum. Elk, 30

NUMBERING OF DESIGNS OF ANKERSMIT, VLISCO AND ABC
In collaboration with Philip Sykas

Ankersmit 1912-1964
The numbers start with 5000. The company initially chose four digits because the Brown Fleming clients were already familiar with numbers of this style.[1] Designs numbers jumped in steps of twenty-five, so 5000, 5025, 5050 and so on, so 24 numbers were available to designate additional colourways for each design. In 1924, the numbers from 8350 onwards stepped fifty to allow even more colourways.

In 1929 the administration of the United Africa Company was mechanised and a new numbering system was needed. For 36-inch widths the prefix 13 was introduced, and for 48-inch widths, the prefix 14. The existing 180 narrow-width patterns received 'record numbers' starting with 0001, as did the existing 40 wide-width patterns. For the new 36-inch designs the company started with 20000, for the new 48-inch designs with 40000. The various colourways were now recorded with a suffix number.

Fortunately, the company has kept extensive records of these changes. The Ankersmit holdings in the Vlisco Archives in Helmond and the files of Gerhard Frensel in Milsbeek give a *complete* insight into the various designs and their specific numbers, which is quite unique for a company that closed its doors in 1965.[2]

Vlisco
The first merchant who received his own code within the Vlisco collection was Haijkens. From late 1928, all designs printed for him started with an H. In the 1930s, the

numbers of designs for Vlisco were given the prefix 14/. The very first number was 14/0510. Afterwards all numbers would start with 14/4 for Vlisco designs and 14/5 for Ankersmit. Other merchant companies had their own codes. The last number was 14/5146, replaced in 2000 with numbers starting with the letter A, for example the first one was A0001. Since 2018 separate codes are used for super wax, beginning with an S, and for wax block, beginning with a W.[3]

ABC 1816-2022

F. W. Ashton and Co. at Newton Bank joined the Calico Printers' Association (CPA) in 1899 when the conglomerate was formed. It was soon using pattern numbers beginning with the letter D for duplex engraved rollers, and later for all rollers. In the 1920s, the CPA had begun a major restructuring that would lead to the closure of around twenty works. It is likely that this prompted a rationalisation of pattern numbering across the organisation. In 1927, D numbers at Newton Bank had reached as high as D18575 when a new sequence was begun using numbers beginning with X. This possibly stood for 'export', although all patterns at Newton Bank received X numbers, or it might have been simply a letter not previously used at any CPA works. Between 1927 and 1939 these X numbers ran in a consecutive series from X1 to X6025. When the Brown Fleming designs joined Newton Bank works, they were assigned numbers in the current X sequence. As patterns were re-engraved, their X numbers were updated: for example, *Two Fishes* which had been X2759 became X4443 on re-engraving in June 1935. Because the engraving book covering numbers X2401 to X3600 is missing, it is not possible to trace the precise pattern number sequence for many Brown Fleming designs. In 1939, a changeover in pattern numbering was probably prompted by government assignment of several CPA works to war production. The first A (Ashton) number was given out on 9 November 1939 beginning a new sequence. In addition to X or A numbers, the letter G was used for products printed for Grafton African.

[1] Meeles I, 59-60
[2] Gerhard Frensel, 'Real Dutch Wax Block Print', Milsbeek 1980, unpublished document.
[3] Email correspondence Ruud Sanders, Vlisco 25 September 2023.

PATERSON ZOCHONIS

George Henry Paterson (1845-1930) from Scotland and George Basil Zochonis (1852-1929), a Greek national, had been working for the trading company Fisher & Randall in Freetown, Sierra Leone. In 1879 they set up a trading post of their own. In 1884 they started a business in Liverpool, two years later in Manchester, specialising in the export of textiles and food to and import of produce such as groundnuts, coffee, hides, skins and timber from Sierra Leone.

They had an intimate knowledge of the West African market and a vast network of trading contacts. The role they played was of a *merchant converter*. Their major commodity was imitation batik and later wax prints. They acquired their own *greycloth* – unbleached cotton fabric – and commissioned cotton printing from companies such as the Manchester based R. Brotherton and A. Brunnschweiler & Co to produce finished fabrics. They would use patterns that were produced by their own designers and branded with their own trademarks. The fabrics were stored and packed for export in their own warehouse.

The business expanded rapidly and in 1896 it opened offices in Liberia and Guinea and in 1899 in Nigeria. In 1920 it also started trading in Cameroon. George Zochonis died in 1929, George Paterson three years later. Family members took over.

The company experienced an exceptional growth in trade after the Second World War. With West African countries preparing for independence, the company tried to increase its industrial base rather than acting solely as merchants. In 1948 the company bought a soap factory in Nigeria that would also produce toiletries and pharmaceuticals from the 1960s. During the 1970s it discontinued its trade in cotton fabrics. In 1973 it started operating in the refrigerator market. It also established companies in Ghana.

Back in the United Kingdom they acquired Roberts Laboratories Ltd in Bolton in 1972 and the Cussons Group Ltd in 1975. In the 1990s the company established a more global sales network and adopted PZ Cussons as the group name.[1]

Archive material, including fabric samples, registered design samples and certificates, shipping labels, photographs, hand printing blocks etc. are kept at the Science Museum in Manchester.[2]

[1] PZ is an abbreviation of Paterson Zochonis. https://www.gracesguide.co.uk/Paterson_Zochonis, page visited 27 February 2023 and unpublished document about Paterson Zochonis, Collections Department Museum of Science and Industry Manchester, not dated. See also: https://www.pzcussons.com/about-us/our-history/?fbclid=IwAR2N3R-I1w-iGf2Bv29MwXy4bZbNFGP45fHMUIg98bFIk7eUfRicVvxROCw#:~:text=An%20extraordinary%20journey%20PZ%20Cussons%20began,commodities%20with%20the%20UK%20in%201884&text=An%20extraordinary%20journey%20PZ,the%20UK%20in%201884&text=journey%20PZ%20Cussons%20began,commodities%20with%20the%20UK, last accessed 27 February 2023.

[2] https://discovery.nationalarchives.gov.uk/details/c/F218284, last accessed 22 February 2023. Anne Grosfilley researched the material, Paterson Zochonis Collection of Textile Samples, and produced a research report in 1996, kept at the Museum of Science and Industry Manchester. The goal of the report was mainly to make the collection more accessible for further research by explaining the different codes of letters and numbers, used by the company for different types of cloth and different markets. A collection of stickers for the cloth with the brand of the company is also kept.

PRÉVINAIRE BEFORE 1834

The founder of what in 1875 would be named the HKM was Jean Baptiste Theodore Prévinaire, born in 1783 in Jodoigne in Belgium.[1] De Herckenrode suggests he first studied humanities and philosophy at Leuven (Belgium) before pursuing a career in commerce and industry.[2] He trained in Rouen, where he learned the technique of Turkey red dyeing and most likely resist printing.[3] His French language skills also gave him access to cutting-edge French professional literature.

Rouen was in that period in France the second centre of *indiennes* printing after Mulhouse for quality and volume. A speciality of Rouen and its surroundings, particularly at Bolbec, close to Lehavre, was the printing of the *toiles bleu reserve*, whereby white motifs on an indigo background were created by using wax. It was introduced around 1780.[4] It is quite possible that Prévinaire was introduced to this technique during his training and would use it later to improve his batik imitations.

In 1812 he married Marie Aldegonde De Hemptinne (1779-1862) with whom he had four children. He had three daughters: Séraphine Aldegone (1815-1884), Victoire Françoise (1817-1894) and Thérèse Octavie (1819-1894) and one son Marie Prosper Theodore Prévinaire (1821-1900), who would take over his business in 1854. In 1880, his son's daughter Eugénie (1858-1928) married Charles Frederik van de Poll (1855-1936) who would be the third generation to oversee the company, from 1886 until its closure in 1917.[5]

Not much is known of his early years, but in 1814 and 1815 he worked with M. Walkiers and benefited from the help and advice of Auguste-Donat De Hemptinne (1781-1854), his brother-in-law, who was a pharmacist and professor at the Free University of Brussels. They developed the production of *huile de pied de boeuf*, a yellow coloured oil, until then imported from France.[6] Together with Walkiers he worked in 1816 on the production of *noir animal* (bone black dye) for which they opened a factory close to the *Pont du Diable* in Molenbeek (Brussels).[7]

234 — 235

He started his first company in 1817 in the Rue Ransfort in Molenbeek with his partner Dieudonne Sény (1783-1870).[8] He was the first in Belgium to start printing on mousseline.[9] He was, too, the only one in Belgium to use the specific method of dyeing he had learned in Rouen. After a period of experimenting, their Turkey red products were considered the best in Belgium and could be compared as equal with those from the Alzace.[10] At a first exhibition of industrial products in Gent in 1820 both were awarded a bronze medal for their products.[11] Five years later their products, exhibited in 1825 in Haarlem at the second exhibition of *Voortbrengselen van Nederlandsche Volks- en Kunstvlijt (Creations of Dutch Popular and Art Industry)*, earned them a gold medal.[12] In 1830 they exhibited a selection of woven and printed cottons, among which were sarongs and slendangs.[13] These exhibitions were initiated by the Dutch government and were aimed at acquainting the public with products of its industry, mainly dominated by textiles. The aesthetic element was initially not important. Only at the exhibition of 1825 some credit was given to the design of some products.[14]

Prévinaire specialised in the dyeing of Turkey red yarn and cottons. De Hemptinne revealed to Prévinaire and Sény a secret Swiss process that allowed to print a variety of colours on the dyed cloth in such a way that the results equalled the Alsatian prints in quality. It made it possible for them to print on the dyed cottons by etching patterns using a bleaching agent to remove the colour from certain areas and subsequently printing the etched parts partly or completely with different colours.[15]

Prévinaire's business of exporting Turkey red and imitation batik cloth was flourishing, which allowed him in 1828 to start with Sény another company, in Cureghem, close to Brussels, which had a *stoomwerktuig* (steam engine) installed as well as several perrotines.[16] The company quickly expanded, exploying 2,500 workers by 1830.[17] For a short period until 22 September 1830, this *fabricant d'indiennes* was mayor of Molenbeek, today part of Brussels.[18] He continuously searched for innovation. One of the first to do so in Belgium, in 1834 he introduced the *perrotine* together with his colleagues Sény, De Hemptinne and M. Poelman-Hamelinck. This machine, invented by Perrot in Rouen, could print three colours one after another, replacing the block prints done by hand. This allowed him to reduce the number of workmen needed. *L'avantage de la pérotine est d'abord de produire une perfection ou les rapports des planches ne sont point aperçus, et en second lieu, de faire le travail de dix à quinze ouvriers imprimeurs* (The advantage of the perrotine is firstly to produce a perfection where the seams between the blocks can hardly be seen, and secondly, to do the work of ten to fifteen printing workers).[19]

De Herckenrode describes him as *un homme fort distingué sous tous les rapports* (a very distinguished man in all respects) and a person with *de vastes connaissances* (vast knowledge).[20] After the separation of Belgium from the Netherlands in 1830 the economic future for the textile industry in the south was bleak. Prévinaire was an *orangist*, a strong supporter of King William I and against the separation of Belgium from the Netherlands. Supporters of *orangisme* belonged to the upper classes of society and most of them were very influential. Directors of quickly expanding textile companies were afraid that the separation would be detrimental for their business. This movement was strongly opposed by the working classes. His workshop in Molenbeek was pillaged and ransacked in 1830 and 1834 by opponents of the king. The police did little to interfere or protect him.[21] In 1834 he decided with the help of the king to transfer his business to Haarlem. Together with a certain Leclerc, Sény continued to run the company in Cureghem until its closure in 1870.[22] The only *souvenir* left is the Rue Prévinaire in Cureghem, now part of Anderlecht in Brussels.

On his way to the Netherlands, he carried a portrait of King William I, painted by François Joseph Navez in 1823. At the time of the unrest in Brussels, Navez had the painting in his atelier. Anxious about the problems this might cause, he handed it to Prévinaire, who placed it in a prime position in his office in Haarlem until the closure of the company.[23]

[1] His parents were Alexandre Prévinaire (1749-1787) and Marie Françoise Laurent (1746-1833). https://gw.geneanet.org/ froment?n=previnaire&oc=1&p=theodore+jean+baptiste, last accessed 8 November 2018. His father was born in Incourt. First, he became mayor of Incourt, later of Jodoigne. Report Baron Leon de Herckenrode, Brussels 25 January 1859 in Brussels, Noord-Hollands Archief in Haarlem (The Netherlands), files 1-3, access number 663.

[2] Report Baron Leon de Herckenrode, Brussels 25 January 1859 in Brussels, Noord-Hollands Archief in Haarlem (The Netherlands), file 3, page 27, access number 663. The university was officially closed between 1797 and 1816, but teaching may have continued.

[3] Briavoinne 1837, 154 and Briavoinne, 1839, 390. Besides Rouen Mulhouse in the Alsace, Elberfeld in Wuppertal and Scotland became centres of these new methods of dyeing. G.P.J Verbong, *Technische innovaties in de katoendrukkerij en -ververij in Nederland 1835-1920*, Amsterdam 1988, 71.

[4] Doré, 37 and Avenel, 27-30

[5] https://www.genealogieonline.nl/en/stamboom-driessen/I73231012.php, last accessed 9 November 2018.

[6] In 1842, De Hemptinne opened the first school of pharmacy at the Free University of Brussels. *Annuaire de l'Académie Royale des sciences, des lettres et des beaux-arts de Belgique*, Brussels 1854, p. 113. https://www.bestor.be/wiki/index.php/Hemptinne,_Auguste-Donat_de_(1781-1854), last accessed 22 November 2018.

[7] Briavoinne 1837, 148 and Briavoinne 1839, 390.

[8] Personal information Jean Boterdael, founder, and president of the local history research group 'Molenbecca' d.d. 29 November 2018.

[9] Briavoinne 188, 85 and Lévy-Leboyer, 71.

[10] Briavoinne 1837, 154 and Briavoinne 1839, 339.

[11] They sent in cottons, a *tafel- of toiletkleed van geitenhaar* (table- or toilet cloth of goat hair) and an experiment with woollen yarns. The jury found it difficult to estimate the full potential of the company but wanted to encourage their initiatives. Rapport der Hoofdcommissie ter beoordeeling der voorwerpen van de Nationale Nijverheid ten toon gesteld te Gent in de maand augustus 1820, The Hague 1820, 92.

[12] There are four entries for Prévinaire and Sény in the catalogue that mention yarns and cottons, dyed and printed in various colours and white cloth for the Indonesian market: *Catalogus der Voortbrengselen van Nederlandsche Volks- en Kunstvlijt toegelaten der tweede algemeene tentoonstelling binnen Haarlem*, Haarlem 1825. The report of the jury can be found in *Rapport der Hoofdcommissie ter beoordeeling der voorwerpen van nationale nijverheid ten toon gesteld te Haarlem in de maanden julij en augustus 1825*, The Hague 1825.

[13] *Catalogus der Voortbrengselen van de Nationale Nijverheid, toegelaten ter derde Algemeene Tentoonstelling te Brussel in de maand Julij 1830*, no 949, p. 268. It is not mentioned if or which medal they received.

[14] Eliëns 1990, 216

[15] Briavoinne 1837, 85, Briavoinne 1839, 339 and *Annuaire de l'Académie Royal de Belgique des Sciences, des Lettres et des Beaux Arts de Belgique*, Brussels 1854, 113.

[16] Beke, 767

[17] See a letter of Pierre van Gobbelschroy, the Belgian Minister of Interior, to Prins Frederik, the son of King William I d.d. 18 September 1830, cited in C. Gerretson, *Muiterij en Scheuring*, 1830. vol II, Leiden 1936, 16.

[18] Antoon-Willem Maurissen, *Bijdrage tot de geschiedenis van Sint-Jans Molenbeek*, Puurs 1980, 245. https://fr.wikipedia.org/wiki/Liste_des_bourgmestres_de_Molenbeek-Saint-Jean, last accessed 8 November 2018.

[19] Briavoinne 1837, 85.

[20] Report Baron Leon de Herckenrode, Brussels 25 January 1859 in Brussels, Noord-Hollands Archief in Haarlem (The Netherlands), file 3, page 27, access number 663.

[21] Personal information Jean Boterdael, founder, and president of the local history research group 'Molenbecca' d.d. 29 November 2018.

[22] Herten, 65

[23] https://rkd.nl/nl/explore/images/125783, last accessed 29 August 2023. After the closure of the HKM the painting went to Marie Henriëtte

Previnaire, a sister of Eugénie, who was married to the director of the HKM, Charles van de Poll. Marie Henriëtte's husband was Albrecht Arent Del Court van Krimpen. She decided to give the painting to their daughter Theodora Marie Albertine Del Court van Krimpen, married to Reinhard Jan Christiaan, baron van Pallandt. They lived in castle Keppel in Laag-Keppel (The Netherlands), where the painting is still kept.

ROESSINGH OR THE *MAATSCHAPPIJ VOOR TEXTIEL INDUSTRIE, VOORHEEN (PREVIOUS) C. ROESSINGH & ZOON* IN VEENENDAAL

The company was founded in 1804 by Carel Roessingh (1779-1844) in Enschede (The Netherlands). Roessingh, son of a baker, started with the weaving and (indigo) dyeing of cotton and linen cloth. Most of the production was *bombazijn*, linen with a cotton weft, which was much sought after.[1] In the same year he married Bertina Hegerink (1781-1863) and had a substantial home built in Langestraat 41 in Enschede.[2] In 1817 he bought another substantial property, the *Van Loenshof* where he built a factory behind the house. In 1834 he also acquired *Van Lochemsbleek*. A *bleek* is a lawn on which textiles are left to *bleach*, soon called *Roessinghsbleek*.[3]

His son Wijnandus (1818-1890) introduced hand printing. At least a part of the production was for export, probably including imitation batiks.[4] In 1869 he bought a perrotine machine, which accelerated production.[5] In 1873 Wijnandus' sons Carel and Theodorus became partners, followed by son Bartinus in 1878. The company was expanding rapidly.[6] In 1898 the three sons set up a limited company, named Maatschappij voor Textiel Industrie voorheen C. Roessingh & Zoon. Of the three brothers only Carel had a son. A year later a separate weaving mill was created in Veenendaal.[7] Roessingh was, like its competitors, also working on improvements to the wax prints. Around 1910 a colourist, A. Kunig, carried out experiments, but no further details are known.[8]

In 1910 the family decided to sell off all their property in Enschede and Carel Roessingh, director of the company, started building a completely new factory in Veenendaal.[9] The reason was that the company continued to expand, but could not find enough land with access to the necessary amount of water for production.[10] In 1912 the transfer from Enschede to Veenendaal was completed with the modern factory fully functional.[11] The company specialised in weaving and perrotine and rouleau printing of linen and cotton cloth. Their wax print imitations competed with other comparable businesses such as the LKM and KKM, but di not really consistute for the HKM and Van Vlissingen.[12]

When a restart of the earlier liquidated HKM proved to be unsuccessful, Roessingh had the opportunity to buy most of its inventory in 1918.[13] Brown Flemings Ltd, which had its cloth printed by the HKM until its closure, became a new client. But in 1921 the company only had a three-day working week.[14] The many changes in the history of the company from 1921 onwards might indicate that business was not always going as they wished for.[15] From 1925 until 1928 the company did good business. Half of the production was for export with *batikdoeken met de vreemdste patronen naar de smaak van de inlanders van Britsche, Portugeesche en Nederlandsche en andere koloniën* (batik cloths with the strangest patterns to the taste of the natives of British, Portuguese, Dutch and other colonies).[6]

Demand exceeded production capacity, so the company expanded its buildings, bought new machinery and invested in more cloth to print on.[17] At its 125th anniversary in 1929, 376 people worked in Veenendaal.[18] But in the same year a sharp downturn of sales occurred because the export to West Africa stagnated, a problem which other textile companies also faced at the time. To survive, a new method of engraving was developed. The new method sought to create effects and colour combinations that were impossible before, but also enabled a sharp reduction in the number of dyes. Financial problems blocked the implementation of this new method.

After a fire on 25 December 1933 that demolished a major part of the buildings, the company could no longer make a profit.[19] However, Roessingh bought the inventory and took over the workforce of the KKM after its closure in 1932 and when the LKM stopped its activities in 1934.[20] The company ceased to exist in 1935.[21] His son, Wijnand, tried to re-start the company, continuing to print batik imitations, but without success.[22]

Ankersmit and Van Vlissingen decided to buy the duplex roller resin printing machines together with the engraved cylinders. The engravings were scraped off and the rollers sold for scrap.[23] The main reason to buy together was to reduce the risk of any new competition. Wijnand Roessingh, director since 1913, would receive a yearly allowance paid by both companies, but had to promise not to pursue any commercial activities in the wax print business.[24] A promise he did not keep, because he continued working with Ronald Herbertson, the son-in-law of Brown Fleming who had taken over his business and for which Roessingh had been printing since the closure of the HKM.[25] He died in 1953.[26]

The cause for the failure of the company was that, in a thriving market, Roessingh did relatively well, but when the market became more difficult, it was obvious that Roessingh's products never met the high expectations of Brown Fleming's clients, who were used to HKM quality.[27] Other companies such as Ankersmit and Van Vlissingen & Co. had developed a better quality product in the meantime and were able to gain a stronger position in the market.

---

[1] https://www.canonvannederland.nl/nl/overijssel/twente/enschede/een-octrooi-, last accessed 26 April 2023. In a document of 1830, he is mentioned as a manufacturer of linen, cotton and *bombazijn* Bedrijfsarchieven C. Roessingh en Zoon Enschede in Archief Gemeente Enschede inventarisno. 1-23.

[2] https://cultureelerfgoedenschede.nl/wordpressnew/het-jannink-huis/, last accessed 5 December 2022 and email correspondence Derk Jordaan 7 December 2022. The Hegerink family, farmers, was already wealthy at that time.

[3] https://www.derkjordaan.com/het-loenshof-van-de-familie-roessingh-1856-1912/, last accessed 5 December 2022.

[4] The Stadsarchief (City Archives) of Enschede keeps a small archive of Roessingh 1804-1870 with a file of insurance for the transfer of goods (*twee kisten met manufacturen* – two boxes with piece goods) d.d. 21 November 1852 between Amsterdam and Batavia (Djakarta, Indonesia). Bedrijfsarchieven C. Roessingh en Zoon Enschede in Archief Gemeente Enschede inventarisno. 1-23.

[5] Handwritten document C. Roessingh from archive Roessingh 1804-1879 in *Stadsarchief Enschede*, sent by Derk Jordaan 7 December 2022.

[6] Handwritten document C. Roessingh from archive Roessingh 1804-1879 in *Stadsarchief Enschede*, sent by Derk Jordaan 7 December 2022.

[7] Just de la Paisières, 277-273.

[8] Correspondence of A. Kunig with the LKM January 1913, Verbong 1988, 233-235.

[9] 'Agenda van den burgemeester en de wethouders van Veenendaal 1911' – permission to construct textile factory, designed by Heijgers in Enschede, and office buildings, designed by J. J. Hellendoorn in Lochem. See also https://www.derkjordaan.com/het-loenshof-van-de-familie-roessingh-1856-1912/, last accessed 5 December 2022. Archives Municipality of Veenendaal, 1811-1941, inv. no. 306.

[10] Handwritten document C. Roessingh from archive Roessingh 1804-1879 in *Stadsarchief Enschede*, sent by Derk Jordaan 7 December 2022.

[11] Thoomes, 105-106 and Verbong 34

[12] Verbong, 235

[13] Meelis II, 175-177

[14] Dossier De Maatschappij voor Textiel-Industrie voorheen C. Roessingh & Zoon, Veenendaal 8 March 1983 in Vlisco Archives Helmond (The Netherlands), 3.

[15] These changes are described in dossier Vnr 4216G14347 of de *Kamer van Koophandel*

(Chamber of Commerce) in Amersfoort (The Netherlands), 1. Dossier De Maatschappij voor Textiel-Industrie voorheen C. Roessingh & Zoon, Veenendaal 8 March 1983 in Vlisco Archives Helmond (The Netherlands).

[16] *De Nederlander,* 25 april 1928.

[17] 'Plan tot oprichting eener katoendrukkerij', C. Roessingh, 1935. Document dated 8 March 1983, Library Nederlands Textielmuseum Tilburg (The Netherlands) M46 MT5-4-19.

[18] Gedenkboek (Commemorative Book) 1804-4 May 1929 of the Maatschappij voor Textielindustrie voorheen C. Roessingh en zoon for its 125th anniversary, kept in Museum Veenendaal, Veenendaal (The Netherlands).

[19] Grootheest, 243.

[20] Janszen and Visser, 57.

[21] Unpublished document in portfolio 03000-00061, Vlisco Museum, Foundation Pieter Fentener van Vlissingen, Helmond, The Netherlands.

[22] Copy of unpublished document, written by W. (?) Roessingh 8 March 1983 about the creation of a new company 'Roessingh's Textiel-Maatschappij' after the closure of the NV Maatschappij voor Textiel Industrie voorheen C. Roessingh en Zoon at Veenendaal. Portfolio 03000-00061, Vlisco Museum, Foundation Pieter Fentener van Vlissingen, Helmond, The Netherlands. Original in Dutch Textile Museum Tilburg: M46 MT 5-4-19 d.d. 29 March 1983. The company continued in a smaller version as the 'NV Textielfabriek "Veenendaal"', founded by B. H. Walkotten and D. Sandbrink, specialising in cotton for work clothing. Production ceased in 1968. Thoomes, 106 and Grootheest, 243.

[23] Copy of unpublished document, author unknown, 8 March 1983 about the creation of a new company 'Roessingh's Textiel-Maatschappij' after the closure of the NV Maatschappij voor Textiel Industrie voorheen C. Roessingh en Zoon at Veenendaal. Portfolio 03000-00061, Vlisco Museum, Foundation Pieter Fentener van Vlissingen, Helmond, The Netherlands. Original in Dutch Textile Museum Tilburg: M46 MT 5-4-19.

[24] Meeles I, 178

[25] His name is added on brief paper, detailing travel expenses for Ronald Richmond Herbertson and Wijnand Roessingh 'paid by cheque to Mr. Herbertson 30 October 1935'. Herbertson was Brown Fleming's son in law and director of Brown Flemings Ltd at the time. Undated letter Brunnschweiler Archive, held at the Whitworth Art Gallery, University of Manchester (UK).

[26] North Holland Archives, Haarlem (Netherlands), Civil registration deaths. Naarden / Naarden, 12 December 1953, record number 147.

[27] Meeles II, 175-178

THE *TEEKENSCHOOL* (DRAWING SCHOOL) IN THE NETHERLANDS

Already in the seventeenth, but especially during the eighteenth century, art schools and academies were founded in the Netherlands, mostly with the idea of raising the artistic level of artists and dilettantes by using drawing models. Lessons were in the evenings, mostly twice a week. The first one was founded in 1682 in The Hague; other cities soon followed. In 1765 the schools became more formalised.[1]

Where these schools were aiming at teaching art for artists, the *Maatschappij tot Nut van 't Algemeen* (Society for the benefit of the public), founded in 1784, was intended for all classes of society. It was a national organization with local branches all over the country. The goal was both individual and social development with a high cultural level, focused on issues of general interest. Around 1800, the Society started to open special drawing schools, aimed at low-income artisans and anybody else interested in improving their drawing skills.

It thereby also replaced the teaching which the traditional guilds had provided, but having lost much of their influence during the eighteenth century the guilds were completely suspended in 1798.[2]

The idea came from France, where artistic education was organised by the *École des Beaux Arts* or the *grande école*, based on classical principles. Drawing was the basis for all artists whether painters, sculptors or architects. Because the school was predominantly accessible for the upper part of society, the *École Spéciale de Dessin et de Mathématique, appliqué aux arts industrielles* was founded in 1766. The school, free of charge, focused on improving drawing skills for artisans. The students not only copied classical examples, but also drew from nature.

The fact that French ideas permeated Dutch society was no surprise. In 1795 the Batavian Republic was founded with the armed support of the French revolutionary forces and part of the Empire of Napoléon. Its politics were deeply influenced by the French. Louis Napoleon Bonaparte, the younger brother of Napoleon I, ruling over the Netherlands from 1806 until 1810, was a strong supporter of encouraging the arts.[3]

On 13 April 1817 King William I issued a royal decree on art education at three different levels. As many places as possible were to get a drawing school of the first degree. All major towns were to get a school of the second degree, while Antwerp and Amsterdam would get a Royal Academy for the Visual Arts. For the first- and second-degree schools, local governments were supposed to provide the necessary funding. They mostly offered classroom space, but even with donations, they were not always able to pay the salaries. In many cases the *Maatschappij tot Nut van het Algemeen* was able to give the required extra help. The schools within the first degree would attract future craftsmen and architects, who could enrol at very low or no cost. Classes were given in the evening. The directors of local companies often comprised part of the supervisory committee of the schools. Students could choose from hand, architectural or technical drawing, often depending on the need of local industries. The aim was not to turn the students into artists, but to improve their skills.[4] To this end, courses in geometry and perspectival theory were added. The academies in Antwerp and Amsterdam had a more artistic approach.[5]

Textile designers followed courses in hand drawing, over a period of three years. The first year was aimed at improving observation and drawing skills by copying examples the teacher had put on the drawing board, printed plates, objects and plaster casts. Anatomy was taught with plates, plaster casts from classical examples and by life drawing. The last two years were focused on drawing from nature with an in-depth study of real plants and flowers. Gradually, students were encouraged in styling their objects and to transfer them into a pattern with a repeat, suitable for industrial production.[6]

[1] Knolle, Paul, De Amsterdamse stadstekenacademie, een 18de eeuwse 'oefenschool' voor modeltekenaars in *Nederlands Kunsthistorisch Jaarboek (NKJ) - Netherlands Yearbook for History of Art* 30(1979) Leiden, 1-2.

[2] Kuijl, van der 17, Simon Thomas 2008, 17.

[3] Reynaerts, 31.

[4] Herweijer and De Visser, 146.

[5] Lintsen V, 61.

[6] Jacobs 20-21. For more information on this subject, see Simon Thomas, Mienke, *De Leer van het Ornament. Versieren volgens voorschrift 1850-1930*, Amsterdam 1996.

UNITED TURKEY RED

It was in 1785 that the dyeing process of Turkey red was introduced into Scotland by a French entrepreneur. It quickly developed into a large industry, focused on export mainly to India. Several of the Turkey red companies that flourished in the nineteenth century had begun as calico printers in the second half of the eighteenth century.[1] Production required a higher percentage of skilled workers and excellent knowledge of the international market. Although it was profitable, this industry faced stiff competition from factories in the Manchester area and by the end of the nineteenth century also from Asian manufacturers. India had also started to introduce protectionist measures in the form of import duties. Three prominent companies, situated in the Vale of Leven, William Stirling & Sons, John Orr Ewing & Co. and Archibald Orr Ewing & Co. merged to create the United Turkey Red Company Ltd

(UTR) in 1898. William Stirling & Sons had been the first to settle in the area and were by the mid nineteenth century the largest with exports not only to India, but also the South East of Asia, China and Japan.[2] John Orr Ewing & Co. was known for its high-quality design department and technically sophisticated way of producing.[3] Archibald Orr Ewing set up his business in 1845 after having had his training at his brother John's firm. He was as successful as his brother but invested his wealth beyond the Vale of Leven for his business and personal interests.[4]

The UTR had its production in the town of Alexandria in Dunbartonshire, north-west of Glasgow, but decisions were often made in the offices at 10 Charlotte Street in Manchester, where the commercial managers and sales agents were based, which often caused conflicts. The production was focused on the dyeing of yarn rather than the printed cloth. It turned out that it was more and more difficult to compete with Manchester based companies. The rise of cheap foreign production made the situation even more difficult. In the 1930s and 1940s several works fell into disuse. The original Turkey red process was abandoned in 1936.[5]

Efforts were made to move away from Turkey red with calico printing and indigo dyeing. One attempt to create more business was the invitation of Jean Jacques by the Board of Directors in 1919. He may have been introduced by Haijkens, a Dutch merchant who already sold products of the UTR. Haijkens worked with other UK and Dutch companies selling wax prints that were in high demand for the West African market. Jean Jacques sold to the company the details of a method, which he had developed, of a *Batik Printing Process* that was cheaper to execute.[6] From 1920 to 1922 he helped install the printing process. Little is known about the details, but United Turkey Red did experiment with fitting colours by mechanical flat press copper plates; however, the cost of the copper plates and the constant re-engraving made this method of applying colour uneconomical.[7] With Jean Jacques' help UTR was able to produce marketable wax prints in a relatively short time. Haijkens may have used his extensive experience in selling imitation batik to West Africa to advise on the necessary quality of the cloth and the choice of designs.[8] He managed to get the exclusive rights to sell their wax prints, but soon, in 1925, he started buying from Van Vlissingen in Helmond (The Netherlands) as well, probably because the start of the production at UTR was too slow to meet his demands.[9] Van Vlissingen insisted he stop buying from UTR.[10] Verschueren mentions that he had the cloth shipped to the Netherlands and added stickers with *Dutch Block Garments* on them before export, which shows the appreciation for wax prints from the Netherlands in this period. But he also states that the sales of wax prints of UTR were not encouraging around 1930, albeit he considered them to have the right potential.[11]

Documents in the archives of ABC show that only a small number were engraved in the 1920s, with most from 1935 until 1939.[12] This is perhaps related to the fact that UTR stopped its Turkey red dyeing in 1936 and the company needed a new commercial goal. The company indeed managed to become a serious player in the business for some time, with Elson & Neill as their main client, but in the 1950s business slowed down.[13]

The works in Alexandria remained the largest and longest lived of the UTR factories, but even a more diverse product range could not guarantee their survival. By the end of 1957, three years before the final closure of the company, UTR transferred the rights of their wax prints to the CPA. In the Brunnschweiler Archive, held at the Whitworth Art Gallery, University of Manchester (UK) documents, photos, sample books and cloth related to the transfer can be found. Lists were drawn up with detailed information about 88 designs with the name, size or width, the number within the UTR collection, the new number with an A (Ashton) and the original engraving date.[14] Also mentioned is for whom the design was made. About 75 per cent were printed for Elson & Neill. Several designs came directly from the Brown Fleming collection, others are drawn in the spirit of his style. In 1960 the company was closed and taken over by the CPA.[15]

The most important collection of pattern books, textile samples and printing blocks of United Turkey Red is kept at the National Museum Scotland in Edinburgh and Glasgow. Some pattern books are kept in the Dumbarton Library. Records relating to the creation of the company are kept at the Greater Manchester County Record Office. Records of the company from 1898 until 1960 are kept at the Scottish Business Archives of the University of Glasgow. Material related to wax printing is kept at the Brunnschweiler Archive, held at the Whitworth Art Gallery, University of Manchester (UK).

[1] For example, the previous owners of John Orr Ewing & Co., bought in 1860, Todd Shortridge & Co., started calico printing in 1768. William Stirling & Sons, initially dealers in London-printed India cottons, started printing in Scotland in the 1760s. Nenadic and Tuckett, 2.
[2] For a more detailed description of the company, see Nenadic and Tuckett, 4-8.
[3] For a more detailed description of John Orr Ewing & Co, see Nenadic and Tuckett, 9-11.
[4] See Nenadic and Tuckett, 11-13 for more information about Archibald Orr and his company.
[5] See for more information https://colouringthenation.wordpress.com/, last accessed 17 March 2023.
[6] Email correspondence with Philip Sykas d.d. 9 September 2017, based on information in the United Turkey Red-Minutes of Board Meetings, held at Manchester Central Library: Letter 24 September 1919.
[7] Harrop, 6
[8] Vlisco was in that period more reliant on the expertise of Swanzy to start their wax print business. See chapter 5.
[9] Ankersmit suggests that he had the exclusive rights except for F. Meyer in Manchester, possibly already a client of UTR. Ankersmit, 66. For more details about the input of Jean Jacques, see the appendix about *The importance of the colourist in the nineteenth century*.
[10] Jacobs and Maas, 41.
[11] Verschueren, 56.
[12] Unfortunately, there is no information available about the possible designers.
[13] That the designs were engraved from 1935 onwards is perhaps related to the fact that UTR stopped its Turkey dyeing in 1936.
[14] The width was in general 36 inches: some designs were extended to 48 inches.
[15] Nenadic and Tuckett, 15.

VOORTMAN AND THE *SOCIÉTÉ ANONYME TEXAS*

The company was founded in 1790 by Abraham Voortman from Weesp (The Netherlands) and Frans de Vos, brother-in-law of Lievens Bauwens, from Ghent (Belgium).[1] When De Vos retired in 1805 Voortman was director of a cotton printing company with 200 employees, the largest in Ghent at the time. After his death in 1810 his widow Maria Francisca took over the business and from 1824 onwards worked with the help of her son Jean Baptiste and her son-in-law Guillaume van Zantvoorde.[2] Initially cloth was imported from India and printed by hand with wooden blocks.

At the beginning of the nineteenth century, it was the leading firm of *indiennerie* thanks to very innovative production methods such as the use of steam engines in 1817, followed by the further mechanisation of printing and weaving in 1824 and spinning in 1826. Sales were stimulated with the help of the Nederlandsche Handels Maatschappij (NHM).[3] Alongside printed cloth for the European market the company also made imitation batiks, probably already around 1820.[4]

The company directors were supporters of the Dutch king William I, so called *orangists* and were not in favour of Belgium separating from the Netherlands. They feared that losing the possibility to sell to Indonesia and other places in South East Asia would damage their businesses.

Opponents wrecked the buildings of the company and attacked Jean Baptiste Voortman in the night of 3-4 of April 1830.[5] The separation was the start of a very difficult period for those companies that did not move to the Netherlands upon invitation of King William I. The market for imitation batiks stagnated so badly that the company decided to stop the production from 1830 until 1832.[6] It had become difficult to compete with foreign competition. The position of Ghent as the centre of textile printing was lost.

In 1842 the widow of Abraham Voortman decided to retire, so her son and son-in-law changed the name of the company to *A. Voortman NV*. Jean Baptiste Voortman died in 1862 and his son Jules took over. From 1865 it struggled because of the American Civil War that resulted in a reduced importation of cottons.[7]

The first orders of imitation batiks and *copies* of traditional West African woven cottons for West Africa were received in 1869.[8] The imitation batiks they had made for the Indonesian market were traditional motifs, carefully copied and well printed on a refined cloth. The printing, although done by hand, was very precise. The chosen colours were close to those of original batiks.[9]

The batik imitations for the African market were printed in a less refined way than those for the Indonesian market. Sometimes motifs were juxtaposed without any relation with one another. The resist print were in general of a poor quality. Sorber suggests that the main goal was to produce quickly and cheaply to gain the maximum profit.[10] It may also have been done on purpose because the Africans liked the irregularities of wax print.

The *copies* of traditional cloth for the West African market were made of quite heavy cottons of a cheap quality with thicker yarns or bundles of yarns creating ribs every 5cm, giving the impression that woven bands were sewn together and decorated with motifs by resist dyeing imitating locally made cloth.[11]

In 1876 Jules renamed the company *Société Anonyme Texas* (Texas Limited) and tried to create more work for his printing business by increasing the sales to export companies in Africa and Indonesia despite the extra costs for new designs. A year later, stagnating sales to Indonesia resulted in a loss and were stopped immediately. In 1878 export to Africa slowed down because of the fraudulent bankruptcy of the *Afrikaanse Handelsvereeniging* with which the company had close ties. Belgian textile printers found it increasingly difficult to stay competitive, which caused a sharp decline in exports, which also affected Voortman's business. In 1889 the company had to close its printing business. The last orders left in 1890. Final orders were printed by Van Vlissingen & Co. in Helmond.[12]

The company decided to concentrate on the more profitable activities of weaving and spinning. In 1926 Jacques Voortman, grandson of Jules, took over as director of the company. In 1957 he organised a merger with *La Louisiane* under the name *Loutex*. *Loutex* eventually merged in 1967 with the *Union Cottonière* into *UCO*, that would continue until 1988.[13]

In particular from the last years of activity of the company significant archival material has been kept. Sample books are kept in the Archive of the City of Ghent, the *Museum of Industry* in Ghent, the *Mudel* (Museum van Deinze en de Leiestreek) in Deinze and the *MoMu* in Antwerp. The latter museum also keeps about hundred printing plates for the perrotine and about five hundred plates for hand printing. As part of the closure of the company, printing plates were also sold to Van Vlissingen & Co. (Vlisco) in Helmond. Order books and extensive correspondence between Jean Voortman and Louis Driessen, director of the Leidsche Katoen Maatschappij (Leiden Cotton Company), are kept at the Dutch Textile Museum in Tilburg. The Archive of the City of Ghent has the fabrication books with the recipes of the colourists, the Museum of Industry in Ghent two sales books from 1877-1878 and 1879-1881 with samples from their collection.[14]

[1] Bauwens (1769-1822) was an entrepreneur and industrial spy who copied innovations in the English textile industry to improve Belgian production. https://en.wikipedia.org/wiki/Lieven_Bauwens, last accessed 3 March 2019. See also Chapter I.
[2] Scholliers, 119.
[3] Scholliers, 120
[4] Frieda Sorber, Drukblokken uit de Gentse Katoendrukkerij Voortman', MA Thesis University of Ghent 1976, 195. See also: Frieda Sorber, *De evolutie van de katoendruk in de Gentse onderneming Voortman 1790-1890* in Vijfde Nationaal Kongres voor Industriële Archeologie Textiel 1977, Werkgroep Industriële Archeologie Rijksuniversiteit Gent 1978, 154
[5] Scholliers, 120-121
[6] Scholliers, 120
[7] See Schollier, 'Het Katoenbedrijf A. Voortman en de Secessieoorlog' in *Belgische Tijdschrift voor Nieuwste Geschiedenis* VI 1975, 117-144.
[8] https://www.industriemuseum.be/nl/collectie-item/afrikadrukken-van-de-firma-voortman-texas, last accessed 25 August 2023.
[9] Sorber (1976) 195
[10] Sorber (1976), 191
[11] Sorber (1976), 191
[12] Frieda Sorber (1989), 46
[13] http://community.dewereldmorgen.be/blog/frankdepreitere/2017/06/30/de-grote-gentse-textielfamilies-en-de-petites-histoires, last accessed 3 March 2019.
[14] See also https://www.industriemuseum.be/nl/collectie-item/afrikadrukken-van-de-firma-voortman-texas, last accessed 13 June 2022.

WERNER

Israel Paulus Werner was born in Württemberg (Germany) in 1841 into a protestant family.[1] He moved to London in 1870 to work as a shipper or consignor, being responsible for organising and transporting goods from one point to another for various clients. According to a document in the archives of the Basel Mission in Basel (Switzerland), he took over the business with the missionaries in India and West Africa in 1874 from John Hall and Son, who had their offices at 23 Lombard Street in London.[2]

In 1872 Werner became a member of the German *Jünglingsverein* (youth club), in 1885 vice-president and three years later president of the German YMCA in London from 1888 until his death in 1931.[3] This association was known for its strong missionary programme.[4] An important part of his family, about thirty members, served in the Basel Mission and worked in India and Africa.

Manuscripts in the archives of the Basel Mission in Basel reveal that in 1904 he had his office in 27 Finsbury Square and branches on 36 Cooper Street in Manchester and Irwell Chambers in Liverpool.[5] From 1907 he was a member of the Manchester Chamber of Commerce.[6] He used, possibly among others, the British and African Steam Navigation Company Ltd with as agents Elder, Dempster and Co. and the African Steam Company in Liverpool.[7]

He exported all kinds of necessities, such as cloth of various companies. Edwards, Cunliff and Wilson was one of those.[8]

A major client for Werner was the BMTC, which he represented in England and for which he dealt with all kinds of issues concerning their trade.[9] Some companies were willing to offer specific prints in exclusivity for the BMTC if they were interested.[10]

Probably at the beginning of the 1890s the BMTC started buying HKM wax prints via Brown Fleming through Werner. The BMTC would send instructions about designs and colours to Werner, who transferred this information to Brown Fleming. From 1912 onwards the BMTC also started trading with Ankersmit via Werner. Meeles writes that Werner had the complete collection of Ankersmit in stock and was sent new samples on a regular basis. He was also involved in advising on new designs, but always supervised by the BMTC. Ankersmit had no direct contact with Werner but communicated with him via the BMTC. A dispute about the monopoly of English versus German agents on the West Coast meant that the collaboration with

Werner was stopped in December 1913.[11] His son Charles Henry Werner, born in 1875, became a partner in 1910 and manager of the company from 1919 until 1922. In 1923 the firm became 'Henry Werner Ltd'.[12] Israel Werner died in 1931.

[1] https://www.familysearch.org/ark:/61903/1:1:N8S9-TG9, last accessed 8 October 2018.

[2] See letter from I. P. Werner 15 January 1874 in 4267 UTC: Ausgewahlte Korrespondenz Zusammenfassung – I. P. Werner London 1874-1914 in Archives of the Basel Mission, Basel (Switzerland). This move might be explained by the fact that Hall was also a gunpowder manufacturer, an activity that was not acceptable for members of the Basel Mission. https://www.gracesguide.co.uk/John_Hall_and_Son, last accessed 3 March 2022.

[3] Email Martina Hildebrandt, German YMCA London 13 November 2015. See also Hildebrandt, 17 and 367 with pictures of Werner on pages 38 and 73.

[4] For more information, see Porter, 301-306.

[5] 4004 UTC: M. Binhammer Korrespondenz 1901-06 – letter fom I. P. Werner and S. F. Bryan Manchester d.d. 29 November 1904.

[6] Email correspondence Philip Sykas 2 November 2015.

[7] The BMTC also used the Afrikanische Dampfschiffs-Actiengesellschaft Woermann-Linie. See shipping letters in the archives of the Basel Mission, Basel (Switzerland).

[8] Letter of I. P. Werner 27 January 1888 in 4267 UTC: Ausgewahlte Korrespondenz Zusammenfassung I. P. Werner London 1874-1914 in Archives of the Basel Mission, Basel (Switzerland). Edward, Cunliff and Wilson, a company in Glasgow, produced designs specifically for the African market. See the article by Lisa Aronson, *A Documentation of African Trade Cloths in the Philadelphia Port of History Museum*, paper for Textile Society of America Symposium 1990, University of Nebraska, Lincoln. This collection of cloth is today kept at the African American Museum in Philadelphia.

[9] See the Annual Review 2010: 150 Years German YMCA in London 1860-2010: http://www.german-ymca.org.uk/german-ymca-annual-review-2010-low-res.pdf, last accessed 12 november 2015.

[10] Letter of I. P. Werner 22 July 1895 in 4267 UTC: Ausgewahlte Korrespondenz Zusammenfassung – I. P. Werner London 1874-1914 in Archives of the Basel Mission, Basel (Switzerland).

[11] Meeles I, 109-110

[12] Venn, vol 2, 8406. See also *The London Gazette* 14 August 1923, p. 5582.

Terminology

Written with advice of Joop Martens, retired Product and Knowledge Manager, Vlisco BV

Batik
Batik (tulis) is created by applying decorative patterns with a spouted tool, called *canting* or *tjanting* in wax on cloth, preferably on both sides, after which the fabric is dyed. The areas covered with wax resist the dye and thus remain uncoulored. The wax needs to be removed by washing or scratching. This process must be repeated for each individual colour. It is a complicated process and very labour intensive.

The most important pieces of cloth that can be decorated with the batik technique are the *sarong* – a long piece of cloth with the ends stitched together wrapped around the waist like a skirt. the *kain* – also worn like a sarong but not stitched together, the *slendang* – worn over the shoulders, and the headcloth. A sarong was 1 metre wide and 2 metres long, the kain was about 2.5 metres long, while slendangs had the same length but only half of the width (50cm). A headcloth was about 1 square metre. Integral were not only the material, the colour and the design but also the way of presenting the products. The pieces of cloth could be woven to the right size and sold in packets of twenty or cut to size from pieces of 12 to 24 yards with a width of 24 to 35 inches.[1] Wearing batik cloth was one of the most important status symbols. There was great variability in colours and patterns and these were specific to groups. This allowed one to identify the wearer as belonging to a specific class, age, gender and region or district.[2]

Bleeding
The running of colour from a dyed spot into a section next to it. This can be done on purpose for the desired effect or accidentally when washing cloth with colours that have not been properly fixed or washed before use.

The effect can also be created by mechanised printing. The – preferably wet printing – technique was first developed by the English printer Horridge & Cornall when working on the imitation of tie-dyed cloth. The company developed a controlled bleeding of colour by block printing the wet cloth with a citric acid resist agent before dyeing. Eventually machine-made versions were developed.[3]

Bubbling
Part of the wax print process, developed to add imperfections into a signature feature of the cloth. On purpose, not all remaining resin is cleaned off after (indigo-) dyeing, leaving spots that resisted successive dye or printed colours, which gave the cloth *sparkle*.

Crackles
Wax is applied where dye should not penetrate the cloth. The wax hardens on cooling and provides a protective layer. When the wax is accidently or deliberately cracked prior to immersion in dye, the dye will seep through creating an unpredictable pattern of little veins.

Prévinaire even developed a way of directly printing artificial veining to imitate the effect that was normally caused during the process. The designer can incorporate crackles into the design by drawing lines that look like veining but are in fact printed on both sides of the cloth, but these will of course be repeated at intervals. Initially printed veining was a solution to avoid excess wax usage, although the non-repeating veining patterns engineered by the deliberate vertical and horizontal breaking of the wax gave the most sought-after effect. Soon it became a signature and is still in use today as part of the typical wax print iconography.[4]

Cretonnes
Was originally a strong white fabric with a hempen warp and linen weft. The word is now used more for a strong, printed cotton cloth and may be printed on both sides.

Discharge printing
The cloth is dyed and then a bleaching agent is used to remove or *discharge* the colour from certain areas, creating the desired pattern. Additional colours can be printed on top.

Emily Jiagge procedure[5]
A technique that was developed in West Africa whereby parts of a piece of European printed cloth were prepared with wax or by tying up so the dye, in general indigo, cannot penetrate. On the prepared parts the initial design of the printed cloth would still be visible after the wax was taken off and/or the tying up taken off. Especially the colour yellow was a successful combination with indigo. Brown Fleming but also later wax printers did use this technique to enhance their cloth. He would rather not use existing cloth but print a simple motif before applying a second design with wax, which allowed him to have more control over the final effect. The same motif was used as a base for various designs. The technique may have acquired the name of Emily Jiagge because she introduced this technique to Vlisco in the 1950s or 1960s.[6]

Fancy
See non-wax prints.

Gingham
Originally a woven striped fabric, but in the mid-eighteenth century it changed to a pattern of woven coloured squares on a white background.

Ikat
A resist-dyeing technique in which yarns are tie-dyed before they are woven into cloth. In double-ikat both warp and weft yarns are resist-dyed to create patterns prior to weaving, which process demands exceptional weaving skills.

Imi-wax (imitation-wax) print
See non-wax prints.

Indiennes
Initially these were pieces of printed cotton, made in India – mainly from regions like Gujarat, Bengal and the Coromandel Coast – imported by various commercial companies in the seventeenth century. They were predominantly used as exchange for products in countries without currency. The more refined prints started to become sought-after by the more affluent classes in Europe. By the middle of the eighteenth century printers in various places in Europe managed to copy the technique of using mordants and resist printing in the way that hitherto only the Indians had been able to do. Facsimiles of Indian cloth, defined by its own, specific style were produced and became popular all over Europe; they were mainly used for interior decoration and clothing. A large portion was also destined for export to Africa, but with the end of slavery, this trade came to an end.

Java print
See non-wax prints.

Mastic
Is a resin obtained from the mastic tree, dries into *tears* or droplets and can be used in textile printing as a resist.

Non-wax prints
Fancy, imi-wax and Java are all non-wax prints. Fancy prints use designs that are visually unrelated to wax prints and are printed on one side of the cloth only. Initially this was done with roller printing, using engraved metal rollers. A faster and more cost-effective method is rotary-screen printing. The pattern shows only on one side. In general, cheaper quality of cloth and dyes are used, which makes them less expensive but also less colourfast than the more expensive wax print. These products show a static repeating look because each yard is identical.

Imi-wax are not real wax look-a-like products. They use designs of the same repertoire as the wax (resin-resist) prints, but without any resin-resist and dye-bath processes. The difference between a real and an imitation wax print can be established by looking at the *bubbles* and *crackles*, associated with the wax-printing process. An imitation will show a regular, predictable repetition at 1- to 2-yard intervals.

For Java Print no resin resist or dye-bath process is used as in wax prints, but often a chemical resist. Both sides of the cloth are identical. By applying high pressure on engraved screens and rollers the dyes are rigorously pressed onto the cloth, enabling small details to be printed with precision. Java prints can carry up to nine different colours, which are in general vivid in style and enhanced by the sheen and soft surface of the fabric.

Perrotine
A printing machine, developed by Perrot in 1834, that could print three different colours at the same time. It had some considerable advantages over the hand-block. The production is increased and the joining up of the various impressions is much more precise. In well-executed work no sign of a break in continuity of line is noticeable. The disadvantages were that only three colours could be applied and the design could not exceed 5 inches in a vertical repeat. Hand block printing can cope with patterns of almost any size and up to a dozen different block colours. Both processes have their own advantages and disadvantages and can therefore not be compared on the same basis.

Rakel (Dutch) or Doctor blade (from ductor blade)
In printing, the *rakel* or *doctor blade* removes the excess dye or resin from the smooth non-engraved portions. The design of a wax print must therefore be adapted to the fact that, during the resin printing process, the contact of the resin printing machine under fairly strong pressure can remove the excess resin from the printing rollers. Therefore, the *rakel* or *doctor blade* requires support at regular, not too great intervals. This is achieved by ingeniously arranging the motifs. If this is not possible or desired, the background must be processed, often by means of so-called hand crack or support veins (*doctor blade* support), which are repeated at regular intervals.

Resist-printing
Can be achieved by two different methods: mechanical and chemical.

Mechanical resist can be achieved by using materials such as resin, clay or wax that form a physical barrier between the fabric and the dye. Stitches or clamps can also be used to shield areas of the fabric from the dye.

Chemical resist printing is a modern printing method in which the fabric is printed with the resist paste followed by printing the colour. The resist paste prevents fixation or development of the overprinted colour by chemically reacting with either the dye or the reagents necessary for the fixation of the dye.

Touché effect
This special effect is created along indigo dyed lines with wax pastels in a lighter shade of indigo, which should give a smooth, veiled shadow effect.[7] Today companies such as Vlisco still apply this technique, which is now called *halftone effect* or the *Haarlem gravure*. It is created by using unequally engraved rollers on the front and back of the cloth.[8]

Turkey red
Turkey red is a complex way of dyeing cloth in an intense red, highly resistant to, for example, washing, sunlight and corrosive substances. Cloth and yarn were dyed in this colour. The fabric, sold in plain red, but also printed with patterns, was in high demand on several markets. It was the highlight of the dyeing technique in the nineteenth century. The dyeing process used natural alizarin, which was extracted from madder root and a metal component such as iron. A serious disadvantage was the complexity and highly time-consuming process of which the outcome was never guaranteed. The whole process could take from six weeks to several months. Slight differences in the process or unforeseen circumstances could ruin the work of weeks of labour. A thorough training and years of experience were necessary to be successful.

Turkish red dyed cloth and yarns were first introduced into Europe in the seventeenth and eighteenth centuries by the Turks. From 1750 French textile producers, especially in the Rouen area, hired Turkish dyers to teach them the technique. It quickly became popular in other areas like Elberfeld in Germany, Scotland, the Alsace and the province of Glarus in Switzerland. In Belgium the first attemps were made in 1808 by Guillaume-Jacques Vanesse et Comp.[9] In 1817 Previnaire started a company that specialised in dyeing Turkey red, in the neighbourhood of Brussels. In the Netherlands the production of Turkey red only really started, when Previnaire moved his business to the Netherlands in 1834.[10]

The introduction of synthetic dyes around 1870 seemed to provide an easier way of production, but the results were not comparable. Only an adaptation of the technical process – applying oil by steam on the cloth instead of soaking – proved to facilitate the technique. Now printing directly on the cloth instead of etching became possible.

By the end of the nineteenth century the complex way of dyeing was simplified using synthetic dyes.[11]

Turkey red Discharge Style
The fabric is initially dyed plain, all one colour. A so-called discharge paste is applied, which through a chemical reaction will destroy the colour. The areas where the colour disappears are called discharged. These can consequently be over printed with other colours. Alternatively, a colour can be added to the discharge paste, which will simultaneously bleach the existing colour and add another.

Wax-prints (see also lijmdruk)
The so-called *African* wax prints are a mechanised version of batik, which is based on a method of resist printing. Wax prints are produced by printing a design with resin onto both face and back of the cloth, fitting as much as possible (unless special effects are desired) with a duplex-roller system or engraved copper rollers. As the fabric is handled by hand or machinery the resist will create minute irregular cracks. Dye will be able to seep through these cracks, resulting in the unique crackle effect simulating the imperfections of handcrafted batiks. The cloth is dyed, originally in indigo, today in any colour. The areas of the fabric that are not printed with resist turn into the indigo blue shade.

Following the dye bath, the resin is partly removed, leaving small spots of resin that will result in unpredictable bubbling effects in the added colour(s) or cracks. Other colours can be added. Until the last decade of the twentieth century this was done by hand using wooden printing blocks covered with felt; today the cloth is overprinted by machine using screen techniques in the case of absence of bubbling and with felt covered rollers in the case of bubbling.

Because it was and is almost impossible to get a perfect alignment of pattern with each overprint of colour, coupled with the accidental crackle effect and spots of resin each single yard of wax print fabric is totally unique.

[1] Veth 1889, 119
[2] Raffles 1817 (second edition 1833), 95-101
[3] Sykas, 28
[4] Interview Gerhard Frensel, Milsbeek (The Netherlands) 4 May 2022.
[5] Emily Jiagge (1913-2003) was the first wife of Nii Amaa Ollennu, a lawyer and in 1970 for a short period president of Ghana. It is not known why or how the technique acquired her name.
[6] Personal communication Joop Martens 8 May 2024.
[7] Frensel, Gerhard, 'Real Dutch Wax Block Print', Milsbeek 1980, unpublished document, 141.
[8] Personal communication Ruud Sanders, Vlisco 15 November and 24 December 2023.
[9] Briavoinne 1839, vol I, 338
[10] Verbong 1994, vol V, 273-274
[11] Verbong gives an overview of Turkey red in H. W. Lintsen (ed.), *Geschiedenis van de techniek in Nederland. De wording van een moderne samenleving 1800-1890*, Zutphen 1994, vol V, 271-287. For more detailed information, see his PhD study: *Technische innovaties in de katoendrukkerij en -ververij in Nederland 1835-1920*, Amsterdam 1988.

Abbreviations

ABC – A. Brunnschweiler & Co. (abbreviation of)
ADATIG – Anglo Dutch African Textile Investigation Group
AETC – African and Eastern Trade Company
ATL – Akosombo Textiles Limited
BF – Brown Fleming
BMTC – Basel Mission Trading Company
CFAO – Compagnie Française de l'Afrique Occidentale
CGCA – Compagnie Générale des Comptoirs Africains
CNF – Compagnie du Niger Français
CPA – Calico Printers' Association
GBO – G. B. Ollivant
GTP – Ghana Textile Printing Company
HC – Haarlem Collection
HKM – Haarlemsche Katoen Maatschappij (Haarlem Cotton Company)
KKM – Kralingsche Katoen Maatschappij (Kralingen Cotton Company)
NHM – Nederlandsche Handel-Maatschappij (Dutch Trading Company)
SCOA – Société Commerciale de l'Ouest Africain
UAC – United Africa Company Limited
UTC – Union Trade Company, since 1921 as follow-up of BMTC
UTR – United Turkey Red
VAEM – Van Vlissingen-Ankersmit Export Maatschappij
VOC – Vereenigde Oost-Indische Compagne (East India Trading Company)

Literature

Ajani, O. A., *Aso Ebi,* 'The Dynamics of Fashion and Cultural Commodification in Nigeria' in *The Journal of Pan African Studies*, 5 (6) September 2012: 108-118

Alana, E. O. and Dopamu P. A., 'Ethical Systems' in Lawal, N. S., Sadiku, M. N. O. and Dopamu, A. (eds), *Understanding Yoruba Life and Culture*, Africa World Press, Trenton NJ 2004

Alence, Rod, 'The 1937-1938 Gold Coast Cocoa Crisis: The Political Economy of Commercial Stalemate' in *African Economic History* 19(1990-1991) 77-104

Allman, J., *Fashioning Africa. Power and the Politics of Dress*, Indiana University Press, Bloomington 2004

Ankersmit, Willem, 'The Wax Print. Its origin and its introduction on the Gold Coast', MA Thesis Leiden, 2009

Ankersmit, Willem, 'De opkomst van de waxprint, van imitatiebatik voor Nederlands-Indië tot statussymbool in West-Afrika' in *Textiel Historische Bijdragen* 52(2012) 7-33

Arlt, Veit, 'Christianity, Imperialism and Culture. The Expansion of the two Krobo States in Ghana c.1830 to 1930', PhD diss. Basel University 2005

Aronson, Lisa, 'A Documentation of African Trade Cloths in the Philiadelphia Port of History Museum', paper for Textile Society of America Symposium 1990, University of Nebraska, Lincoln

Arts, Jos, *Vlisco*, Artezpress Arnhem/Wbooks Zwolle 2012

Arx, Rolf von, Davatz, Jürg and Rohr, August, *Industriekultur im Kanton Glarus. Streifzüge durch 250 Jahre Geschichte und Architektur*, Glarus 2005

Auzias, Dominique and Labourdette, Jean-Paul, *Ghana 2015 Petit Futé*, Nouvelles Editions de l'Universite Paris 2014

Avenel, Alain, Lhommet Philippe and Levaray, Jacques, *Indiennes et indienneurs de Bolbec*, Association Au fil de la mémoire Bolbec, 2017

Baanders, Herman A. J., 'Over nieuwe proeven van batik-techniek in Nederland', *Bulletin Koloniaal Museum Haarlem*, Amsterdam 1901

Baars, Freek, 'De Haarlemse textielindustrie in de 19e en 20e eeuw' in H. Rombouts (ed.), *Haarlem ging op wollen zolen. Opkomst, bloei en ondergang van de textielnijverheid aan het Spaarne*, Schoorl (The Netherlands) 1995, 111-159

Baines, Emily Anne, 'Design and the Formation of Taste in the British Printed Calico Industry, 1919 to 1940', PhD diss. De Montfort University, Leicester 2002

Barley, Nigel, *The Golden Sword. Stamford Raffles and the East*, London 1999

Barnes, Ruth, *Indian Block-Printed Textiles in Egypt. The Newberry Collection in the Ashmolean Museum*. Clarendon Press Oxford 1997

Bayly, Christopher Alan, *The Birth of the Modern World 1780-1914*, London 2004

Beke, Philippe, 'Aspecten van de industriële ontplooiing in het Brusselse: een overzicht van de katoenverwerkende nijverheid in de Anderlechtse deelgemeente Kuregem (1787-1830)' in *Belgische Tijdschrift voor Nieuwste Geschiedenis,* 1981 4, 740-775

Bender, Wolfgang, 'Omo Laso (kinderen zijn onze kledingstukken). Over het omgaan met stoffen in Afrika' in Brommer, B. (ed.), *Katoendruk in Nederland*, Helmond/Tilburg 1989, 157-174

Benjamin, Jody A., 'The Texture of Change: Cloth, Commerce and History in West Africa 1700-1850', PhD diss. African and American Studies, Harvard University Cambridge, Massachusetts 2016

Bergvelt, Ellinoor and Elands, Helen, 'Colonial Inspiration in New Art and Industry in the Netherlands' in *Design Derby 1815-2015*, Museum Boijmans-van Beuningen Rotterdam 2015, 84-87

Breitenbach, Esther, 'Scots Churches and Missions' in MacKenzie, John M. and Devine T. M. (eds), *Scotland and the British Empire*, Oxford University Press 2011, 196-226

Bijlsma, G. W. and Rodenburg, G. H., *Van Vlissingen & Co's Gedenkboek 1846-1946. Honderd jaren Van Vlissingen & Co. Over de kunst van het drukken,* Helmond 1948

Bickford Berzock, Kathleen, 'African Prints/African Ownership. On Naming, Value and Classics' in Gott, Suzanne, Loughran, Kristyne S., Quick, Betsy D., Rabine, Leslie W. (eds) *African-Print Fashion Now! A Story of Taste, Globalization and Style*, Fowler Museum Los Angeles 2017, 71-79

Bloembergen, Marieke, *Colonial Spectacles. The Netherlands and the Dutch East Indies at the World Exhibitions 1880-1931*, Singapore University Press 2006

Boatema Boateng, Nsaasaawa, 'Ghanaian Patchwork from the Kitchen to the Catwalk' in Gott, Suzanne, Loughran, Kristyne S., Quick, Betsy D., Rabine, Leslie W. (eds), *African-Print Fashion Now! A Story of Taste, Globalization and Style*, Fowler Museum Los Angeles 2017, 156-159

Bodt, Saskia de and Kapelle, Jeroen, *Prentenboeken. Ideologie en Illustratie 1890-1950*, Amsterdam/Ghent 2003

Boeck, Juliette de and Janssen, Alsje, 'De Tissage de Bornhem' in Brommer, Bea (ed.), *Bontjes voor de Tropen. De export van imitatieweefsels naar de tropen*, Zwolle 1991, 90-93

Boelman W. J. and Holthoon, F. L. van, 'African Dress in Ghana' in *Kroniek van Afrika* 13(3) 1973, 236-258

Boot, J. A. P. G. and Blonk, A., *Van smiet- tot snelspoel. De opkomst van de Twents-Gelderse textielindustrie in het begin van de 19e eeuw*, Hengelo 1957

Bosman, Willem, *Nauwkeurige beschrijving van de Guinese Goud- Tand- en Slavekust*, Anthony Schouten Utrecht 1704

Boyd-Buggs, Debra, *Wax Prints of the Sahel: Cloth Portraits of Contemporary African History,* Africa World Press 2021

Braeckel, Hilde van, 'Een vergelijkende studie van Afrikadruk uit Gent en gereserveerde doeken uit Afrika' in *Echt, namaak en vals*, VVOHT Bulletin Ranst-Oelegem, 1996

Braeckel, Hilde van, Verfaille, Nike and Van der Vloet, Gonda, 'Voorbeeld en imitatie. West-Afrika en de Tissage de Bornhem' in Brommer, Bea (ed.), *Bontjes voor de Tropen. De export van imitatieweefsels naar de tropen*, Zwolle 1991, 101-127

Briavoinne, M. N., *Sur les inventions et perfectionnements dans l'industrie, depuis la fin du XVIIIe siècle jusqu'à nos jours*, Brussels 1837

Briavoinne, M. N., *De l'Industrie en Belgique. Causes de Decadence et de prospérité*, Brussels 1839

Brommer, Bea (ed.), *Katoendruk in Nederland*, Helmond/Tilburg, 1989

Brommer, Bea (ed.), *Bontjes voor de Tropen. De export van imitatieweefsels naar de tropen*, Zwolle 1991

Brommer, Bea (2), 'Bontjes voor de tropen. Imitatie en export 1800-1960' in *Bontjes voor de Tropen. De export van imitatieweefsels naar de tropen*, Zwolle 1991, 27-64

Brommer, Bea, 'Handel is handel. Imitatie en innovatie bij de produktie van exporttextiel' in *Textielhistorische Bijdragen* 33(1993) 120-134

Brouwer, Jaap W., Siesling, Jan Laurens and Vis, Jacques, *Anthon van Rappard. Companion and correspondent of Vincent van Gogh. His life and all his works*, Amsterdam 1974

Brugmans I. J., *De arbeidende klasse in Nederland in de 19e eeuw (1813-1870)*, Amsterdam 1928 (2nd edn)

Budge, Ernest Wallis, *A guide to the first and second Egyptian rooms. Predynastic antiquities, mummies, mummy-cases, and other objects connected with the funeral rites of the ancient Egyptians*, London 1904

Burg, Pieter van den, *Curieuse beschrijving van de gelegentheid, zeden, godsdienst, en ommegang van verscheyden Oost-Indische gewesten en machtige landschappen, en inzonderheid van Golkonda en Pegu*. Isaak Naeranus Rotterdam, 1677

Clerq, G. S. de, 'Charles Frederik van de Poll 1855-1936' in *Haerlem Jaarboek* 1936, 14-19

Colenbrander, H T., *De afscheiding van België*, Amsterdam 1936

Comaroff John L. and Comaroff, Jean, 'Fashioning the Colonial Subject. The Empire's Old Clothes' in *Cf Revelation and Revolution. The Dialectics of Modernity on a South African Frontier*, vol. 2, Chicago 1997, 218-273

Cordonnier, Rita *Femmes Africaines et Commerce. Les revendeuses de tissu de la ville de Lomé (Togo)*, Paris 1987

Cordwell, J. M. and Schwarz, R. A., *The Fabrics of Culture. The Anthropology of Clothing and Adornment*, The Hague 1979

Cosyns Rina, 'Afrikadrukken van de firma Voortman: een imitatie van traditionele West-Afrikaanse weefsels', PhD diss. Ghent University, Belgium 1989

Cousin, Françoise, 'Caché, Montré, Détourné. Quelques exemples pris dans des tissus imprimés et teints' in Charpigny, Florence and Cousin, Francoise, 'Transgression, Progression: l'Erreur dans le textile'. *Actes des journées d'études de l'Association Française pour l'Étude du Textile* 2003, 13-20

Craandijk, Jacobus, *Wandelingen door Nederland met pen en potlood*, vol. 3, 1878

John Crawfurd, *History of the Indian Archipelago. Containing an account of the manners, arts, languages, religions, institutions, and commerce of its inhabitants*, vol. 3, Edinburgh 1820

Crowley, Roger, *Conquerors. How Portugal forged the first global empire*, London 2015

Curtin, Philip D., *Cross-Cultural Trade in World History*, Cambridge 1984

Dantzig, Albert van, *Forts and Castles of Ghana*, Accra 1980

Dapper, Olfert, *Accurate Description of the African Regions* (*Naukeurige beschrijvinge der Afrikaensche Gewesten*), Jacob van Meurs Amsterdam 1676

Dartel, Daan van, 'Het Tropenmuseum and Trade: product and source' in *Journal of Museum Ethnography* 20(2008) 82-93

Davidson, Basil, *West Africa before the Colonial Era. A History to 1850*, London/New York 1998

Davidson, Julian, 'Getting to know Raffles: On reading Raffles and forming an opinion' in Murphy, Stephen A., Wang, Naomi and Green, Alexandra, *Raffles in Southeast Asia. Revisiting the Scholar and Statesman*, Asian Civilisations Museum Singapore/The British Museum London, Singapore 2019, 230-255

Davidson, Lola Sharon, 'Woven Webs, Trading textiles around the Indian Ocean' in *Portal, Journal of Multidisciplinary International Studies*, vol. 9 no. 1, 2012

Debo, Kaat, *Beyond Desire*, ModeMuseum Antwerpen 2005

Dejung, Christof and Zangger, Andreas, 'British wartime protectionism and Swiss trading companies' in *Asia during the First World War in Past & Present*, Oxford University Press 207 (2010), 181-213

Delhaye, Christine, 'The Production of African Wax Cloth in a Neoliberal Global Market. Vlisco and the Processes of Imitation and Appropriation' in Gaugele, Elke and Titton, Monica, *Fashion and Postcolonial Critique*, Berlin 2019, 246-259

Depierre, Joseph, 'Notes sur la fabrication des battiks' in *Bulletin de la Société Industrielle de Rouen*, July 1879, 260-265

Depierre Joseph, *Sur les industries de l'impression et de la teinture à l'Exposition universelle de 1878*, 1880

Doedens, A. and Huygers, P., 'Enige aspecten van de Haarlemse social-economische geschiedenis in de eerste helft van de negentiende eeuw' in A. Doedens (ed.), *De strijd om het bestaan. Bijdragen tot de lokale geschiedenis van Nederland in de eerste helft van de negentiende eeuw*, Amsterdam 1983, 15-39

Doedens, A. (ed.), *De strijd om het bestaan. Bijdragen tot de lokale geschiedenis van Nederland in de eerste helft van de negentiende eeuw*, Amsterdam 1983

Doorman, G., *Het Nederlandsch Octrooiwezen en de techniek der 19e eeuw*, The Hague 1947

Doré, Mylène, *Quand les toiles racontent des histoires. Les toiles d'ameublement Normandes au XIXieme siècle*, Rouen 2007

Dorward, David, 'Arthur London, Chief Agent of Swanzy and Co: A Biography of Imperial Commerce on the Gold Coast' in *African Economic History* 29(2001) 61-77

Driessen, Felix, 'Peter Ludwig Carl Driessen' in *Leidsch Jaarboekje* 1906, Sijthoff Leiden 1906, 3-23

Duplessis, Robert S., *The Material Atlantic. Clothing, Commerce and Colonization in the Atlantic World 1650-1800*, Cambridge 2016

Duuren, David van, *125 jaar verzamelen. Tropenmuseum, Koninklijk Instituut voor de Tropen*, Amsterdam 1990

Edoh, Amah, 'Doing Dutch Wax Cloth: Practice, Politics and "The New Africa"', PhD diss. Massachusettes Institute of Technology 2016

Edoh, Amah, 'Design at Vlisco' in S. Gott (ed.), *African-Print Fashion Now! A Story of Taste, Globalization and Style*, Fowler Museum at UCLA, Los Angeles 2017, 62-63

Eisenloeffel, Jan, 'Een stalenboek van Reyer Stolk' in *Elseviers Geïllustreerd Maandschrift* 47(1937) XCIII, 143-144

Elands, Helen, 'Designing for Wax Prints at ABC' in S. Gott (ed), *African-Print Fashion Now! A Story of Taste, Globalization and Style*, Fowler Museum at UCLA, Los Angeles 2017, 66-69

Elands, Helen, 'Dutch Wax Classics. The Designs introduced by Ebenezer Brown Fleming circa 1890-1912 and Their Legacy' in S. Gott (ed), *African-Print Fashion Now! A Story of Taste, Globalization and Style*, Fowler Museum at UCLA, Los Angeles 2017, 52-61

Elbers, W.. *Die Bedienung der Arbeitsmaschinen zur Herstellung bedruckter Baumwollstoffe,* Vieweg 1909

Eliëns, Titus, *Kunst. Nijverheid. Kunstnijverheid. De nationale nijverheidstentoonstellingen als spiegel van de Nederlandse kunstnijverheid in de negentiende eeuw*, Zutphen 1990

Elk, Jantiene van, 'De familie Driessen en de Leidsche Katoen Maatschappij. Reizen in de negentiende eeuw' in *Leidsche weefsels. Studies in Textiel* 14(2022) 30-37

Eliëns, Titus M., Leidelmeijer, Frans and Groot, Marjan, *Kunstnijverheid in Nederland 1880-1940*, Bussum 1996

Elliott, Inger McCabe, *Batik. Fabled Cloth of Java*, New York 1984, 2nd edn 2004

Eng, Pierre van der, 'Economic Benefits from Colonial Assets: The Case of the Netherlands and Indonesia 1870-1958', *Groningen Growth and Development Centre Research Memorandum* no 199839, University of Groningen, The Netherlands 1998

Eng, Pierre van der, 'De-industrialisation' and colonial rule: The cotton textile industry in Indonesia, 1820-1942', paper XIV for *Cotton Textiles as a Global Industry 1100-1848*, International Economic History Congress Helsinki, Finland, 21-25 August 2006

Enschede, A. J., *De geschiedenis van het museum van kunstnijverheid en de school voor bouwkunde, versierende kunsten en kunstambachten te Haarlem der Nederlandsche Maatschappij voor Nijverheid en Handel 1877-1927*, Haarlem 1928

Faber, Paul, *Long Live the President! Portrait-cloths from Africa*, Amsterdam 2010

Faber, Paul, *Africa at the Tropenmuseum*, Amsterdam 2011

Familusi O. O., 'The Yoruba Culture of Aso Ebi (Group Uniform) in Socio-Ethical Context' in *Lumina* (Holy Name University Tagbilaran Philippines), vol. 21(2), 2010, 1-11

Familusi O. O., 'African Culture and the Status of Women: The Yoruba Example' in *The Journal of Pan African Studies* vol. 5(1), 2012, 299-313

Feld, Marit, *Adviesverslag ontsluiting Ankersmitarchief Collectie Overijssel*, Stichting Overijssel Zwolle/Deventer, 2024

Fine, Julia, "Art Treasures' and the Aristocracy: Public Art Museums, Exhibitions, and Cultural Control in Victorian Britain' in *Penn History Review* 24(2017)1, 9-43

Forge, Anthony, 'Batik Patterns of the Early Nineteenth Century' in Gittinger, M. (ed.), *To Speak with Cloth. Studies in Indonesian Textiles*, Museum of Cultural History Los Angeles 1989, 91-10

Fothergill, J. B. and Knecht, E., *The Principles and Practice of Textile Printing,* London 1912

Frensel, Gerhard, 'Real Dutch Wax Block Print', Milsbeek 1980, unpublished document

Gannon, Margaret, 'The Basle Mission Trading Company and British Colonial Policy in the Gold Coast 1918-1928' in *The Journal of African History*, Cambridge University Press 24(1983)4, 503-515

Gerards, Roger and Suze May Sho (collective of Jessica Helbach, Rosell Heijmen and Connie Nijman), *Vlisco Fabrics*, Arnhem 2012

Gerlich, Gabriele, 'Waxprints im Soziokulturellen Kontext Ghanas', MA Thesis Johannes Gutenberg University Mainz, 2004

Gerretson, C., *Muiterij en Scheuring 1830*, vol. II, Leiden 1936

Giersberg, Bettina, *Die Kunst der Imitation. Glarner Textildruck*, Zürich 2022

Gillow, John, *African Textiles, Colour and Creativity across a Continent*, London 2003

Gillow, John and Barnard, Nicholas, *Indian Textiles,* London 2014

Gittinger, Mattiebelle, *Splendid Symbols. Textiles and Tradition in Indonesia*, Oxford University Press 1979

Gooswit, Sylvia M., 'Gebruik van Javaans goed onder creolen 1900-2023' in *De Ware Tijd*, 2 August 2023, A10

Gott, Edith Suzanne, 'In celebration of the female: dress, aesthetics, performance and identity in contemporary Asante', PhD diss. Indiana University 1984

Gott, Suzanne, 'The Ghana an Kaba: Fashion That Sustains Culture' in Gott, Suzanne and Loughran, Kristyne, *Contemporary African Fashion*, Indiana University Press, Bloomington and Indianapolis 2010, 11-28

Gott, Suzanne and Loughran, Kristyne S., 'Introducing African-Print Fashion' in Gott, Suzanne, Loughran, Kristyne S., Quick, Betsy D., Rabine, Leslie W (eds), *African-Print Fashion Now! A Story of Taste, Globalization and Style*, Fowler Museum Los Angeles 2017, 23-49

Gott, Suzanne, Loughran, Kristyne S., Quick, Betsy D., Rabine, Leslie W (eds), *African-Print Fashion Now! A Story of Taste, Globalization and Style*, Fowler Museum Los Angeles 2017

Graham, John, Chemistry of Calico Printing 1790-1835 and History of Printworks in the Manchester District 1760-1846, last accessed 16 March 2023. https://www.flickr.com/photos/manchesterarchiveplus/8318501091/in/album-72157632369315534/lightbox/

Green, Alexandra, 'Raffles' Collections from Java. European Evidence of Civilisation' in Murphy, Stephen A., Wang, Naomi and Green, Alexandra, *Raffles in Southeast Asia. Revisiting the Scholar and Statesman*, Asian Civilisations Museum Singapore/The British Museum London, Singapore 2019, 24-39

Griffiths, R. T., 'Iets meer over de Haarlemse katoenfabrieken' in *Textielhistorische Bijdragen* 15(1974) 38-59

Griffiths R T., *Industrial retardation in the Netherlands 1830-1850*, Den Haag 1979

Gril-Mariotte, Aziza, *Les Toiles de Jouy. Histoire d'un Art Décoratif 1760-1821*, Rennes 2015

Gril-Mariotte, Aziza, *Motifs d'Artistes. Une histoire du design dans l'industrie textile depuis le 18ieme siècle*, Musée de la Toile de Jouy, Jouy-en-Josas 2023

Grootheest, A. C. van, Bisschop, R., Groenleer, G. C., *Geschiedenis van Veenendaal*, Historische Vereniging Oud Veenendaal, Veenendaal (The Netherlands), vol. 2, 2005

Grosfilley, Anne, *Wax & Co. Anthologie des Tissus imprimés d'Afrique*, Paris 2017

Guy, John, *Woven Cargoes. Indian Textiles in the East*, London 1998

Haake, Annegret and Winotosastro, Hani, 'Batik or Plagiate? How to Distinguish Between Batik Tulis, Batik Cap and Direct Prints' in Marie-Nabholz-Kartaschoff, Marie-Louise, Barnes, Ruth and Stuard Fox, David eds - *Weaving Patterns of Life: Indonesian Textile Symposium 1991*, Museum der Kulturen Basel, 449-455

Halliday, Fred, 'The Millet of Manchester: Arab Merchants and Cotton Trade' in *British Journal of Middle Eastern Studies* 19(1992)2, 159-176

Halls, Julie and Martino, Allison, 'Cloth, Copyright and Cultural Exchange: Textile Designs for Export to Africa at The National Archives of the UK' in *Journal of Design History* 31(2018)3, 236-254

Hansen Trahnberg, K. and Madison Soyini, D., *African Dress. Fashion, Agency, Performance*, Bloomsbury 2013

Hargreaves, Benjamin, *Messrs. Hargreaves' Calico Print Works at Accrington and Recollections of Broad Oak*, Accrington 1882

Hartkamp-Jonxis, Ebeltje, 'Sits en katoendruk, handel en fabricage in Nederland' in Hartkamp-Jonxis, Ebeltje (ed.), *Sits. Oost-West Relaties in Textiel*, Zwolle 1987, 31-41

Hartkamp-Jonxis, Ebeltje, 'Katoendrukkerijen in de Noordelijke Nederlanden 1678-1820' in Brommer, Bea (ed.), *Katoendruk in Nederland*, Helmond/Tilburg 1989, 15-30

Hazewinkel, H. C., 'De aanvang der katoendrukkerij te Rotterdam', *Rotterdamsch Jaarboekje* 1933, 27-33

Hendrickson, H., *Clothing and Difference. Embodied Identities in Colonial and Post-colonial Africa*, Durham/London 1996

Heijer, Henk den, *Goud, ivoor en slaven. Scheepvaart en handel van de Tweede Westindische Compagnie op Afrika 1674-1740*, Walburg Pers, Zutphen 1997

Heijer, Henk den, *Geschiedenis van de WIC. Opkomst, bloei en ondergang*, Walburg Pers, Zutphen 2013

Heringa, Rens, 'Javaanse katoentjes' in Brommer, Bea (ed.), *Katoendruk in Nederland*, Helmond/Tilburg, 1989, 131-156

Heringa, Rens, 'Upland Tribe, Coastal Village, and Inland Court: Revised Parameters for Batik Research' in Barnes, Ruth and Kahlenberg, Mary Hunt (eds), *Five Centuries of Indonesian Textiles*, Prestel 2010, 120-131

Herten, Bart van der, Michel Oris and Jan Roegiers, *La Belgique Industrielle en 1850, deux cents images d'un monde nouveau*, Brussels 1995

Herwerden, Ernestine van, 'De stalenboeken van de Kralingsche Katoendrukmaatschappij', MA Thesis University of Amsterdam 2010

Herweijer, Nina and Sam de Visser, *Geknoopt en geweven. De kleurrijke geschiedenis van de Deventer tapijtindustrie (1797 tot heden)*, Deventer 2012

Hildebrandt, Bernd W., *It Can Be! 150 Years German YMCA in London 1860-2010*, German YMCA London 2010

Holenstein, Andre, 'The Indiennes and Switzerland – Far More Than the Story of a Colourful Fabric' in *Indiennes. Material for Thousand Stories*. Swiss National Museum, Christoph Merian Verlag Basel 2019, 40-51

Hoogenboom, Marcel, Bannink, Duco and Trommel, Willem, *'Fighting the Dragon'. The reorganization of a textile printing company in The Netherlands and West-Africa*, Amsterdam 2007 https://www.researchgate.net/publication/47341193_'Fighting_the_Dragon'_-_The_Reorganization_of_a_Textile_Printing_Company_in_The_Netherlands_and_West_Africa

Hout, Itie van, 'Of Love and Passion: Biographical Notes on the Batik Collection in the Tropenmuseum' in Hout, Itie van (ed.), *Batik. Drawn in Wax. 200 years of batik art from Indonesia in the Tropenmuseum collection*, Amsterdam 2001

Hout, Itie van (ed.), *Batik. Drawn in Wax. 200 years of batik art from Indonesia in the Tropenmuseum collection*, Amsterdam 2001

Hout, Itie van and Wijs, Sonja, *Indonesian Textiles at the Tropenmuseum*, Amsterdam 2017

Hunter, William, *Biggar and the House of Fleming*, Edinburgh 1862

Hurst, Christopher, *The View from King Street: An Essay in Autobiography*, London 1997

Huygers, H., 'De NHM en Haarlem. Gastarbeid en sociaal protest als gevolg van ondernemersbeleid en conjunctuur: een staking in 1841' in Doedens, A. (ed.), *De strijd om het bestaan. Bijdragen tot de locale geschiedenis van Nederland in de eerste helft van de negentiende eeuw*, Amsterdam 1983, 50-63

Ingenbleek, Paul, 'The part Elmina played in the popularisation of waxprints' in *Save Elmina*, vol. 3 (1996), publication of Save Elmina Association

Ingenbleek, Paul, 'Een overzeese afzetmarkt. De marketing van Vlisco in Ghana 1900-1996', PhD diss. Erasmus Universiteit Rotterdam 1997

Ingenbleek, Paul, 'Marketing als bedrijfshistorische invalshoek: de case van Vlisco in West-Afrika, 1900-1996' in Bielman, J. (ed.), *NEHA-jaarboek voor economische, bedrijfs- en techniekgeschiedenis*, Nederlandsch Economisch-Historisch Archief, Amsterdam vol. 60, 1998, 258-284

Ingenbleek, Paul, 'De introductie van de waxprint op de West-Afrikaanse textielmarkt' in *Textielhistorische bijdragen* 38(1998/2) 74-99

Inikori, Joseph E., 'English versus Indian Cotton Textiles: The Impact of Imports on Cotton Textile Production in West Africa' in Riello, Giorgio and Roy, Tirthankar, *How India Clothed the World. The World of South Asian Textiles 1500-1850*, Leiden/Boston 2013, 85-114

Isert, Paul Erdmann, *Reise nach Guinea und den Caribäischen Inseln in Columbien, in Briefen an seine Freunde beschrieben*, Kopenhagen, 1788

Iwanaga, Etsuko and Shoji, Sachiko, *Ages of Sarasa*, Fukuoka Art Museum, Fukuoka (Japan) 2014

Jacobs, Ger, Janssen, Majelle, Van de Laarschot, Hans and Van Zalinge, Lia, *Johan Jacobs (1881-1955). Ontwerper, beeldend kunstenaar en opleider uit Helmond*, Helmond 2011

Jacobs, M. G. P. A. and Maas, W. H. G., *Een leven in kleur. Textieldrukkerij Vlisco 1846-1996*, Helmond 1996

Janszen, Heleen and De Visser, Sam, *Ankersmit. Honderd jaar katoen in Deventer. Een fabrieksgeschiedenis vol. herinneringen van oud-werknemers*, Deventer 2006

Jenkins, Jennifer, 'Education for a Useful Life. Schools and industrial training in the Basel Mission' in *Mission Possible? The Basel Mission Collection Reflecting Cultural Encounters*, Catalogue Museum der Kulturen, Basel 2015, 90-108

Jenny-Trümpy, Adolf, 'Handel und Industrie des Kantons Glarus. Geschichtlich dargestellt' in *Jahrbuch des Historischen Vereins des Kanton Glarus*, vols 33 and 34, 1898

Jonge, J. A. de, *De industrialisatie in Nederland tussen 1850 en 1914*, Nijmegen 1976

Jewison, Deborah, 'Policy and practice: Design education in England from 1837-1992 with particular reference to furniture courses at Birmingham, Leicester and the Royal College of Art', PhD diss. De Montfort University Leicester 2015

Jonghe, Daniël de, 'De Tissage de Bornhem. Het weven van imitatiedoeken' in Brommer, Bea (ed.), *Bontjes voor de Tropen. De export van imitatieweefsels naar de tropen*, Zwolle 1991, 95-100

Joosse, Niek, 'Afrikaanse droom. De handel van Henry P. Kerdijk en Lodewijks Pincoffs in Afrika 1857-1879', MA Thesis Erasmus Universiteit Rotterdam 2016

Joosten, J. M., 'De batik en de vernieuwing van de nijverheidskunst in Nederland 1892-1905' in *Nederlands Kunsthistorisch Jaarboek* 23(1972) 407-429

Josson, Maurits, *De Belgische omwenteling van 1830*, Tielt 1930

Just de la Paisières, G. A. A., 'Maatschappij voor Textielindustrie voorheen C. Roessingh & Zoon te Veenendaal' in *Industrieel Nederland* Haarlem 2(1921), 276-280.

Kerlogue, Fiona, 'Batik: The Cloth of Kings' in Barley, Nigel (ed.), *The Golden Sword. Stamford Raffles and the East*, London 1999, 30-34

Kerlogue, Fiona, 'Islamic talismans: the calligraphy batiks' in Hout, Itie van (ed.), *Batik. Drawn in Wax. 200 years of batik art from Indonesia in the Tropenmuseum collection*, Amsterdam 2001, 124-135

Kerlogue, Fiona, *Batik. Design, Style and History*, London 2004

Kessel, Ineke van, 'The Black Dutchmen: African soldiers in the Netherlands East Indies' in Kessel, Ineke van (ed.), *Merchants, Missionaries & Migrants. 300 years of Dutch-Ghanaian Relations*, KIT Amsterdam 2002, 133-43

Kessel, Ineke van, *Zwarte Hollanders: Afrikaanse soldaten in Nederlands-Indie*, KIT Amsterdam 2005

Kessel, Ineke van, 'Wax Prints in West Africa: Unravelling the Myth of Dutch Colonial Soldiers as Cultural Brokers' in Osei-Tutu, John Kwadwo (eds), *Forts, castles and society in West Africa; Gold Coast and Dahomey, 1450-1960*, Brill Leiden 2019, 92-118

Knolle, Paul, 'De Amsterdamse stadstekenacademie, een 18de eeuwse 'oefenschool' voor modeltekenaars' in *Nederlands Kunsthistorisch Jaarboek* 30(1979) Leiden, 1-41

Kobayashi, Kazuo, *Indian Cotton Textiles in West Africa. African Agency, Consumer Demand and the Making of the Global Economy 1750-1850*, Palgrave Macmillan, Cham (Switzerland) 2019

Koert, Robin van, *Dutch Wax Design and Technology van Helmond naar West-Afrika, Uniwax en GTP in postkoloniaal Ivoorkust en Ghana*, Helmond 2008

Korteling, H. D., 'De vroegere avondtekenschool te Deventer' in Lugard, G. J. Jr. (ed.), *Overijssel: Jaarboek voor cultuur en historie*, Zwolle, 1955, 96-105

Kouoh, Koyo, *Hollandaise. A journey into an iconic fabric*, Stedelijk Museum Bureau Amsterdam, Newsletter 130, Amsterdam 2012

Kraamer, Malika, 'Sword of Kingship Design' in Fogg, Marnie and Steele, Valerie, *Fashion. The Whole Story*, London 2013, 162-163

Kraan, Alfons van der, 'Anglo-Dutch Rivalry in the Java Cotton Trade 1811-1830' in *Indonesia Circle*, 68(1996) 35-64

Krantz, C. H., 'De export van de Nederlandse bedrukte katoen naar het Verre Oosten en Afrika' in Brommer, Bea ed., *Katoendruk in Nederland*, Helmond/Tilburg, 1989, 111-130

Krantz, C. H., 'De culturele band tussen de volkeren van West-Afrika en het Vlisco-dessin met zijn specifiek daarop gerichte kenmerken', April 1985. Typed document, kept at the Vlisco Archives, @Vlisco BV Helmond (The Netherlands)

Krantz, C. H., 'Jan Fentener van Vlissingen en zijn collectie' in Verschueren, Jos, M. Th., *Jan Fentener van Vlissingen 1893-1978*, Helmond 1990

Kriegel, Lara, *Grand Designs. Labor, Empire and the Museum in Victorian Culture*, Durham/London 2007

Kriger, C. E., *Cloth in West African History*, Oxford 2006

Kroese (1), W. T., *The Origin of the Wax Block Prints on the Coast of West Africa*, Smit Hengelo 1976

Kroese (2), W. T., 'De oorsprong van wasdruktextiel op de kust van West-Afrika' in *Textielhistorische Bijdragen* 17(1976), 22-89

Kroese (3), W. T., 'De oorsprong van wasdruktextiel op de kust van West-Afrika', unpublished typed document Vlisco Archives, @Vlisco BV Helmond (The Netherlands)

Kroese, W. T., 'Haarlem, textielstad in de 19e eeuw' in *Textielhistorische Bijdragen* 20(1979) 53-91

Kuijl, Aart van der, *Kunst zij ons doel, 175 jaar wel & wee van een Haarlemse kunstenaarsvereniging. Van teekencollegie, teekengenootschap tot beroepsvereniging*, Haarlem 1996

Kwadwo Osei-Tutu, John ed., *Forts, Castles and Society in West Africa. Gold Coast and Dahomey 1450-1960*, Leiden 2018

Laarhoven, Ruurdje, 'The Power of Cloth: The Textile Trade of the Dutch East Indian Company (VOC) 1600-1780', PhD diss. Australian National University, Canberra https://digitalcollections.anu.edu.au/handle/1885/10888

Launert, Frederika, 'The Role of Design in the Lancashire Cotton Industry', PhD diss. University of Central Lancashire, Preston 2002

Laurens van der Laan, H., 'Modern Inland Transport and the European Trading Firms in Colonial West Africa (Transports modernes et firmes commerciales européennes dans les colonies d'Afrique occidentale)' in *Cahiers d'Études Africaines* no 84, 21(1981) 547-575

Laurens van der Laan, H., *The Lebanese Traders in Sierra Leone*, 's-Gravenhage 1975

Laurens van der Laan, H., 'A Swiss Family Firm in West Africa: A. Brunschweiler & Co., 1929-1959' in Clarence Smith, W. G., 'Business Empires in Equatorial Africa' in *African Economic History* 12(1983) 287-297

Legêne, Susan and Waaldijk, Berteke, 'Reverse Images – Patterns of Absence. Batik and the representation of colonialism in the Netherlands' in Hout Itie ed., *Batik. Drawn in Wax. 200 years of batik art from Indonesia in the Tropenmuseum collection*, Amsterdam 2001, 34-65

Legêne, Susan, *Spiegelreflex. Culturele sporen van de koloniale ervaring*, Amsterdam 2010

LePoole, F. A., 'Felix Hendrik August Driessen. Leiden 22 september 1855 – 18 october 1936' in *Jaarboek van de Maatschappij der Nederlandse Letterkunde* 1943, 34-38

Lee, Chonja, 'Chintzes as Printed Matter and Their Entanglement within the Transatlantic Slave Trade around 1800' in Biro, Yaelle and Etienne, Noemie, *Rhapsodic Objects, Art, Agency, and Materiality (1700–2000)*, 57-78

Leur, J. L. W. van, *De Indische Instelling te Delft. Méér dan een opleiding tot bestuursambtenaar*, Volkenkundig Museum Nusantara Delft 1989

Lévy-Leboyer, Maurice, *Les Banques Européennes et l'Industrialisation Internationale dans la première moitié du XIXieme siècle*, Paris 1964

Lightfoot, John Emanuel, *The chemical History and Progress of Aniline Black*, Burnley (UK) 1871

Lindblad, J. Thomas, 'De handel in katoentjes op Nederlands-Indië 1824-1939' in *Textielhistorische Bijdragen* 34(1994) 89-104

Lintsen, H. W. ed. *Geschiedenis van de techniek in Nederland. De wording van een moderne samenleving 1800-1890*, Zutphen 1994

Lis, Catharina and Hugo Soly, *Een groot bedrijf in een kleine stad. De firma De Heyder & Co te Lier 1757-1834*, Lier 1987

Lunsen, Dan van, 'De Previnaires', Julianadorp (The Netherlands) 2014, unpublished article

Lydon, Ghislaine, *On Trans-Saharan trails. Islamic Law, Trade Networks, and Cross-Cultural Exchange in Nineteenth-Century Western Africa*, Cambridge University Press 2009

MacKenzie, John M. and Devine, T. M., 'Scots in the Imperial Economy' in *Scotland and the British Empire*, Oxford University Press 2011, 227-254

MacCabe Elliott, Inger, *Batik. Fabled Cloth of Java*, New York 1984

Mansvelt, W. M. F., *Geschiedenis van de Nederlandsche Handel-Maatschappij*, Haarlem 1924 (2 volumes)

Mansvelt, W.M.F, 'Iets over de Haarlemsche Katoenfabrieken' in *Eigen Haard*, 50 (1924), 238-243

Marees, Pieter de, *Beschrijvynge ende historische verhael van het Gout Koninckrijck van Gunea anders de Gout-Custe de Mina genaemt liggende in het deel van Africa*, Cornelis Claesz Amsterdam 1602, reprint The Hague 1912

Martin P. M., 'Contesting Clothes in Colonial Brazzaville' in *Journal of African History* 35(1994) 401-426

Mault, Nathalie A., 'Java as a Western Construct: An Examination of Sir Thomas Stamford Raffles' The History of Java', MA Thesis Louisiana State University, 2005

Maurissen, Antoon Willem, *Bijdrage tot de geschiedenis van Sint-Jans Molenbeek*, Puurs 1980

Maynard, M., *Dress and Globalisation*, Manchester University Press 2004

Meeles, Gerrit-Jan, 'Geschiedenis van het wasdrukartikel van Ankersmit's Textielfabrieken NV', Helmond 1972 (unpublished)

Mehos, Donna C., *Science & Culture for members only: The Amsterdam Zoo Artis in the Nineteenth Century*, Amsterdam University Press 2006

Meij, Ietse, *Fashion and Ghana*, Gemeentemuseum Den Haag 2002

Messing, Franciscus Antonius Maria, 'Werken en leven in Haarlem (1850-1914). Een sociaal-economische geschiedenis van de stad', PhD diss. Rijksuniversiteit Utrecht 1972

Meylink, B., *Het Nut der Nijverheidstentoonstellingen*, Deventer 1853

Miller, Jon, *Missionary Zeal and Institutional Control: Organizational Contradictions in the Basel Mission on the Gold Coast 1828-1917*, Eerdmans Michigan/Cambridge UK and Routledge Curzon, London 2003

Mingoen, Hariëtte and Shoehirman, Patmo, 'Javanen hebben betaald voor afschaffin slavernij in Suriname en Caraïbisch-Nederland' in *De Ware Tijd* 19 January 2023

Moes, Jaap, *Onder aristocraten. Over hegemonie, welstand en aanzien van adel, patriciaat en andere notabelen in Nederland, 1848-1914*, Hilversum 2012

Morfini, Irene, 'An Egyptian collection held in the National Museum in Accra', *Göttinger Miszellen* 249(2016), 125–29

Murphy, Stephen A., Wang, Naomi and Green, Alexandra, *Raffles in Southeast Asia. Revisiting the Scholar and Statesman*, Asian Civilisations Museum Singapore/The British Museum London, Singapore 2019

Nabholz-Kartaschoff, Marie-Louise, 'Original und Nachahmung – Batik in Java und Glarus im 19. Jahrhundert' in *Glarner Tuch Gesprache. Kunst und geschichte des Glarner und europäischen Zeugdrucks*, Ennenda (Switzerland) 2017, 59-70

Nabholz-Kartaschoff, Marie-Louise, 'Original or Imitation? Batik in Java and Glarus (Switzerland) in the Nineteenth Century' in *The Textile Museum Journal* 46(2019), 190-209

Nenadic, Stana and Tuckett, Sally, *Colouring the Nation. The Turkey Red Printed Cotton Industry in Scotland 1840-1940*, Edinburgh 2013

Nielsen, Ruth, The History and Development of Wax-Printed Textiles Intended for West Africa and Zaire, MA Thesis Michigan University 1974

Nielsen, Ruth, 'The History and Development of Wax-Printed Textiles Intended for West Africa and Zaire' in Cordwell, J. M. and Schwarz, R. A. (eds), *The Fabrics of Culture. The Anthropology of Cloth and Adornment*, The Hague 1979, 467-494

Niemeijer, Frits, 'Verdwenen buitenhuizen. Een schets aan de hand van Elsenburg bij Maarssen' in *Vitruvius*, 53(2020) 4-16

Olukoju, Ayedele, 'Maritime Trade in Lagos in the Aftermath of the First World War' in *African Economic History* 20(1992), 119-135

Oppong-Boateng, Juliet, 'Economic Enterprises of the Basel Mission Society in the Gold Coast: A Study of the Basel Mission Trading Company from 1859 to 1917', PhD diss. University of Ghana, Accra 2014

Parry, Linda, *British Textiles 1700 to the present*, London 2010

Paeye, Koen, 'De Gentse katoennijverheid op de internationale katoenmarkt in de19e eeuw', MA Thesis Ghent University (Belgium) 2009

Peck, Amelia ed., *Interwoven Globe. The worldwide textile trade 1500-1800*, London 2013

Pedler, Frederick, *The Lion and the Unicorn in Africa. The United Africa Company 1787-1931*, London 1974

Perani, Judith and Wolff, Norma, *Cloth, Dress and Art Patronage in Africa*, Berg Publishers 1999

Phillips, Tom ed., *Africa: The Art of a Continent*, Royal Academy of Arts, London 1995

Picton, John, *The Art of African Textiles. Technology, Tradition and Lurex,* Barbican Art Gallery, London 1995

Picton, John, 'Notes on Fashioning Art across Africa' in Gott, Suzanne, Loughran, Kristyne S., Quick, Betsy D., Rabine, Leslie W. (ed), *African-Print Fashion Now! A Story of Taste, Globalization and Style*, Fowler Museum Los Angeles 2017, 18-22

Porter, Andrew, *Religion versus Empire? British Protestant missionaries and overseas expansion 1700-1914,* Manchester University Press 2004

Quaile, Sheilagh, 'Imitation and Piracy in Paisley Shawl Design 1805-1870' in *Journal of Design History* (Oxford University Press) 36(2022) 1-16

Rabine, L. W., *The Global circulation of African Fashion*, Berg Publishers 2002

Raffles, Sophia, *Memoir of the life and public services of Sir Thomas Stamford Raffles: particularly in the government of Java, 1811-1816, and of Bencoolen and its dependencies, 1817-1824: with details of the commerce and resources of the Eastern archipelago, and selections from his correspondence*, Murray, London 1830

Raffles, Thomas Stamford, *The History of Java*, vol. I, London 1817

Rast-Eicher, Antoinette, *Zeugdrucke der Firma Bartholome Jenny & Cie in Ennenda. Farben und Drucke und die Tricolori Mouchoirs,* Comptoir Blätter 4, Ennenda 2009

Rast-Eicher, Antoinette, 'Zeugdrucke im Kanton Glarus' in Hassler, Uta, *Maltechniek und Farbmittel der Semperzeit*, München 2014, 170-185

Reikat, Andrea, *Handelsstoffe. Grundzüge des Europäisch-Westafrikanischen Handels vor der Industriellen Revolution am Beispiel der Textilien*, Köln 1997

Renne, Elisha, 'Textile Manufacturing, Printing and Trade during Colonial Rule' in Renne, Elisha P. and Maiwada, Salihu (eds), *Textile Ascendancies. Aesthetics, Production and Trade in Northern Nigeria*, Michigan 2020, 45-68

Ressler, Phyllis and Ressler-Horst, Lara, *The Kanga. An African Cloth*, independently published 2019

Reynaerts, J. A. H., *Het karakter onzer Hollandsche school. De Koninklijke Akademie van Beeldende Kunsten te Amsterdam, 1817-1870.* Amsterdam 2000 https://pure.uva.nl/ws/files/3079302/11910_UBA002000111_06.pdf

Reynolds, Edward, *Trade and Economic Change on the Gold Coast 1807-1874*, Longman UK/New York 1974

Rodenburg, G. H., 'Dutch Wax-Block Garments' in *Textielhistorische Bijdragen* 8(1967), 18-51

Rombouts, H. ed., *Haarlem ging op wollen zolen. Opkomst, bloei en ondergang van de textielnijverheid aan het Spaarne*, Schoorl (The Netherlands) 1995

Rooyen, Pepin van, *Batikpatterns*, Amsterdam 2002

Ross, Robert, *Clothing. A Global History*, Cambridge (UK) and Malden (USA) 2008

Rouffaer, G. P. and Juynboll, H. H., *De Batikkunst in Nederlandsch-Indië en haar Geschiedenis.* Haarlem 1899

Ryan, Mackenzie Moon,' The Global reach of a Fashionable Commodity: A Manufacturing and Design History of Kanga Textiles', PhD diss. University of Florida, Gainesville 2013

Ryan, Mackenzie Moon, 'A Decade of Design: The Global Invention of the Kanga 1876-1889' in *Textile History* 48 (1) 2017 101-132

Ryan, Mackenzie Moon, 'Kanga Cloths at Vlisco: An Object-Based Study of Dutch Printing for the Colonial East African Market 1876-197' in *African Arts* 56(2023) vol. 3, 56–71

Sandberg, Lars, *Lancashire in Decline. A Study in Entrepreneurship, Technology and International Trade,* Ohio State University Press 1974

Schmid, Anna, 'Project Basel Mission' in *Mission Possible? The Basel Mission Collection Reflecting Cultural Encounters*, Catalogue Museum der Kulturen, Basel 2015, 8-13

Scholliers, Mark, 'Het Katoenbedrijf A. Voortman en de Secessieoorlog' in *Belgische Tijdschrift voor Nieuwste Geschiedenis* 6(1975), 117-144

Scholliers Marc, *Bedrijfsgeschiedenis van de firma A. Voortman - NV Texas*, Centrum voor hedendaagse sociale geschiedenis VUB Brussel 1977

Scholten, Frits, 'Het interieur 'op d'Indische Manier'' in Hartkamp-Jonxis, Ebeltje ed., *Sits. Oost-West Relaties in Textiel*, Zwolle 1987, 42-53

Schultz, M. A. 'Fabrication des Sarrongs Indiens Genre Batick' in *Le Moniteur Scientifique* March 1877, 327-329

Sill, Ulrike, *Encounters in Quest of Christian Womanhood. The Basel Mission in Pre- and Early Colonial Ghana*, Brill Leiden/Boston 2010

Sillevoldt, J. van and Wiersum, E, 'De Katoendrukkerij Non Plus Ultra' in *Rotterdamsch Jaarboekje* 1921, 67-90

Simon Thomas, Mienke, 'KVT' in *Industrie en Vormgeving 1850-1950*, Amsterdam 1985, 94-97

Simon Thomas, Mienke, 'Het ornament, het verleden en de natuur' in *Nederlands Kunsthistorisch Jaarboek* 39(1988), 27-60

Simon Thomas, Mienke, *De Leer van het Ornament. Versieren volgens voorschrift 1850-1930*, Amsterdam 1996

Simon Thomas, Mienke, *Goed in vorm. Honderd jaar ontwerpen in Nederland,* Rotterdam 2008

Simon Thomas, Mienke, *Dutch Design: A History*, London 2008/2

Sluyterman, K., 'Herinneringen aan de Haarlemsche School voor Kunstnijverheid' in *Elsevier's Geïllustreerd Maanschrift* 15(1905), 74-92

Small, R., *History of the Congregations of the United Presbyterian Church 1733-1900*, Edinburgh 1904

Smit, Willem Johannes, *De katoendrukkerij in Nederland tot 1813*, Amsterdam 1928

Smit-Muller, R., *De familie Bokhorst. Verrassend veelzijdig*, Waanders Zwolle 2014

Sorber, Frieda, 'Drukblokken uit de Gentse Katoendrukkerij Voortman', MA Thesis Ghent University (Belgium) 1976

Sorber, Frieda, 'De evolutie van de katoendruk in de Gentse onderneming Voortman 1790-1890' in *Vijfde Nationaal Kongres voor Industriële Archeologie Textiel* 1977, Werkgroep Industriële Archeologie Rijksuniversiteit Gent 1978 153-158

Sorber, Frieda, 'Vlaanderen-Nederland: een wisselwerking in katoendruk' in Brommer, Bea ed., *Katoendruk in Nederland*, Helmond 1989, 31-46

Spring, Chris, *African Textiles Today*, Smithsonian Books Washington 2012

Steiner, Christopher B., 'Another Image of Africa: Toward an Ethnohistory of European Cloth marketed in West-Africa 1873-1960' in *Ethnohistory* 32(2) 1985, 91-110

Stylianou, Nicola Stella, 'Producing and Collecting for Empire: African Textiles in the V&A 1852-2000'. PhD diss. University of the Arts, London 2012

Swanzy, A, 'On Trade in Western Africa with and without British Protection' in *Journal of the Society of Arts* no 1117, 22(1874) 478-488

Swanzy, Henry, 'A Trading Family in the Nineteenth Century Gold Coast' in *Transactions of the Gold Coast & Togoland Historical Society* 2(1956) 87-120

Sykas, Philip Anthony, *The Secret Life of Textiles. Six Pattern Book Archives in Northwest England*, Bolton 2005

Sykas, Philip Anthony, 'The public require spots: modernism and the nineteenth century calico designer' in *Journal of the Textile Institute* 89 (1998) 3-15, corrected version June 2023

Sylvanus, Nina, *Patterns in Circulation. Cloth, Gender and Materiality in West Africa,* University of Chicago Press 2016

Tabiou, Dolibe Dorothée, *Nana Benz. Le mythe devenu discret*, Editions Haho, Lomé Togo 2011

Taylor, William H., *Mission to Educate. A History of the Educational Work of the Scottish Presbyterian Mission in East Nigeria 1846-1960*, Brill Leiden 1996

Thompson, William, 'Glasgow and Africa: Connections and Attitudes 1870-1900', PhD diss. University of Strathclyde, Glasgow 1970

Thoomes, J. G.,*Veenendaal, toen en nu*, Ederveen 1982

Travis, A. S. (1995). Artificial Dyes in John Lightfoot's Broad Oak Laboratory' in *Ambix, Journal of the Society for the History of Alchemy and Chemistry 42*(1)1995, 10–27 https://doi.org/10.1179/amb.1995.42.1.10

Unwin, George, *Samuel Oldknow and the Arkwrights: The Industrial Revolution at Stockport and Marple*, Manchester/London 1924

Valsecchi, Perluigi, 'Free People, Slaves and Pawns in the Western Gold Coast: The Demography of Dependency in a Mid-Nineteenth-Century British Archival Source' in *Ghana Studies* 17(2014), 223-246

Veldhuisen, Harmen C., *Batik Belanda 1840-1940. Dutch Influence in Batik from Java, History and Stories*, Jakarta (Indonesia) 1993

Veldhuisen, Harmen C., 'From Home Craft to Batik Industry' in Heringa, Rens and Veldhuisen, Harmen C, *Fabric of Enchantement. Batik from the North Coast of Java from the Inger McCabe Elliott Collection at the Los Angeles County Museum of Art*, 1996

Venn, J and Venn, J. A. (eds), *Alumni cantabrigienses: a biographical list of all know students, graduates and holders of office at the University of Cambridge from the earliest times to 1900*, vol. 2

Verbong, G., 'Coloristen en Laboratoria. De ontwikkeling van het coloristische werk in de Nederlandse textielveredelingsindustrie: in *Tijdschrift voor de geschiedenis der geneeskunde, natuurwetenschappen, wiskunde en techniek* 9(1986)4 216-231

Verbong, G. P. J., *Technische innovaties in de katoendrukkerij en -ververij in Nederland 1835-1920*, Amsterdam 1988

Verbong, G. P. J., 'Katoendrukken in Nederland vanaf 1800' in Brommer, Bea ed., *Katoendruk in Nederland,* Helmond/Tilburg, 1989, 47-84

Verbong, G. P. J., 'Turks Rood' in Lintsen, H. W. ed., *Geschiedenis van de techniek in Nederland. De wording van een moderne samenleving 1800-1890*, Zutphen 1994, vol. V, 271-287

Verschueren, Jos, M.Th., *Jan Fentener van Vlissingen 1893-1978*, Helmond 1990

Veth, P. J., *Java: geografisch, ethnologisch, historisch*, Haarlem 1875

Veth, P. J., *Uit Oost en West*, Arnhem 1889

Veyrassat, Beatrice, 'Schweizer Erbe des Kolonialismus. Konsum, Kattunproduktion und Sklavenhandel im 18. Jahrhundert. Wo steht die Geschichte der schweizerischen Tuch-Industrie heute?' in *Glarner Tuch Gespräche. Kunst und geschichte des Glarner und europäischen Zeugdrucks,* Ennenda (Switzerland) 2017, 40-48

Visser, Joop, Dicke Matthijs and Zouwen, Annelies van der (eds) – 'Familie Driessen' in *Nederlandse Ondernemers 1850-1950 - Zuid Holland*, Zutphen 2011, 197-203

Visser, Joop, Dicke Matthijs and Zouwen, Annelies van der (eds), 'Jan Fentener van Vlissingen 1893-1978' in *Nederlandse Ondernemers 1850-1950 – Noord-Brabant, Limburg en Zeeland*, Zutphen 2011, 91-95

Vollaard, G., *Geschiedenis van de exporthandel tot 1960,* Helmond 1974, unpublished typescript Vlisco Archive, @ Vlisco BV Helmond (The Netherlands)

Voorst tot Voorst, J. M. W., 'Nederland op de Wereldtentoonstelling van 1851 te London' *Nederlands Kunsthistorisch Jaarboek* 31(1908) 475-492

Voortman, J., *Les Débuts de l'Industrie Cotonnière et les Crises Economiques. L'Industrie Cotonnière Gantoise sous le Régime Français et le Régime Hollandais*, Ghent 1940

Vries, Boudien de, *Een stad vol. lezers: leescultuur in Haarlem 1850-1920*, Nijmegen 2011

Wang, Naomi, 'Amass and disperse: Collecting the Malay Archipelago' in Murphy, Stephen A., Wang, Naomi and Green, Alexandra, *Raffles in Southeast Asia. Revisiting the Scholar and Statesman*, Asian Civilisations Museum Singapore/The British Museum London, Singapore 2019, 216-229

Wanner, Anne, 'Kattundrucke der Schweiz im 18. Jahrhundert. Ihre Vorläufer, orientalische und europäische Techniken, Zeugdruck-Manufakturen, die Weiterentwicklung', PhD diss. Basel, 1968

Wanner-Jean Richard, Anne, 'Die Musterbände aus Ennenda. Adolf Jenny-Trümpy und seine Sammlungen von Stoffmustern' in *Glarner Tuch Gespräche. Kunst und geschichte des Glarner und europäischen Zeugdrucks,* Ennenda (Switzerland) 2017, 184-197

Wanner, Gustaf Adolf, *Die Basel Handels-Gesellschaft AG 1859-1959*, Basel 1959

Weel, H. B. van der, *In die kunst en wetenschap gebruyckt. Gerrit Claeszoon Clinck (16461693), meester kunstschilder van Delft en koopman in dienst van de Verenigde Oostindische Compagnie*, Hilversum, 2002

Wertz, Julie, *Turkey Red*, Bloomsbury 2024

Wiersum and Van Sillevoldt, 'De katoendrukkerij Non Plus Ultra' *Rotterdamsch Jaarboekje* 1921, 67-90

Wilbrenninck, D. E. W., 'John Waterloo Wilson (1815-1883*)* in *Cahiers Bruxellois – Brusselse Cahiers* 2016/1 XLVIII, Editions Musées et Archives de la Ville de Bruxelles, 5-24

Wisseman Christie, Jan, 'Texts and Textiles in 'Medieval' Java' in *Bulletin de l'École française d'Extrême-Orient* 80(1983) 181-211

Witte, Els, *Het Verloren Koninkrijk. Het harde verzet van de Belgische orangisten tegen de revolutie 1828-1850*, Amsterdam/Antwerpen 2015

Wronska-Friend, Maria, 'Javanese batik for European Artists: Experiments at the Koloniaal Laboratorium in Haarlem' in Itie van Hout (ed), *Batik. Drawn in Wax. 200 years of batik art from Indonesia in the Tropenmuseum collection*, Amsterdam 2001, 106-123

Wronksa-Friend, Maria, 'Fernöstliche Faszination: Henry van de Velde und die javanische Batik' in Föhl, Thomas and Neumann, Antje (eds), *Raumkunst und Kunsthandwerk/Interior Design and Decorative Arts,* Band II Textilien, Klassik Stiftung Weimar 2014, 369-398

Wronska-Friend, Maria, *Batik Jawa Bati Dunia/Javanese Batik to the World*, Jakarta 2016

Wronska-Friend, Maria, 'The early production of Javanese batik imitations in Europe (1813-1840)' in *Glarner Tuch Gespräche. Kunst und geschichte des Glarner und europäischen Zeugdrucks,* Ennenda (Switzerland) 2017, 49-58

Zangger, Andreas P., 'Chops and Trademarks: Asian Trading Ports and Textile Branding 1840-1920' in *Enterprise & Society*, Cambridge University Press, vol. 15, 4(2014) p. 759-790

Zeeman-Rutten, E. G. M., 'De Cretonnes van Michel Duco Crop', *Spiegel Historiael* 8(1973)9, 491-495

Zinsou, Marie-Cecile ed., *Wax Stories*, Fondation Zinsou 2023 Ouidah, Benin

Zwaan, Kees, 'Van lichtgeraakte fabrieksdirecteur tot grootgrondbezitter' in *Historiek, online geschiedenis magazine* 8 november 2021, https://historiek.net/van-lichtgeraakte-fabrieksdirecteur-tot-grootgrondbezitter/130697/
Zwaan, Kees, 'Van Heerlijkheid tot badplaats. De ontwikkeling van Callantsoog tot badplaats 1876-1940', MA thesis 2023 Open University: https://research.ou.nl/ws/portalfiles/portal/61451661/Masterscriptie_Van_Heerlijkheid_tot_badplaats.pdf

Catalogues

Black is beautiful. Rubens to Dumas, Exhibition catalogue De Nieuwe Kerk Amsterdam 2008

Catalogus der Voortbrengselen van Nederlandsche Volks- en Kunstvlijt toegelaten der tweede Algemeene Tentoonstelling binnen Haarlem, Haarlem 1825

Catalogus der Voortbrengselen van de Nationale Nijverheid, toegelaten ter derde Algemeene Tentoonstelling te Brussel in de maand Juli 1830, Brussel 1830

Catalogus der Voortbrengselen van Inlandsche Nijverheid en Kunst ingezonden voor de Tentoonstelling te Utrecht, Utrecht 1847

Catalogus der Voorbrengselen van Inlandsche Nijverheid en Kunst voor de Provincien Zuid- en Noord-Holland te Delft, Delft 1849

Catalogus der afdeeling Nederlandsche Koloniën van de international koloniale en uitvoerhandel tentoonstelling, Amsterdam 1883

Gids voor de bezoekers van het Koloniaal Museum te Haarlem, Amsterdam 1902

Indiennes. Material for Thousand Stories. Swiss National Museum, Christoph Merian Verlag 2019
Kreuz und Quer der Farben. Karo- und Streifenstoffe der Schweiz für Afrika, Indonesien und die Türkei, Exhibition Catalogue Museum Bellerive Zürich (1997), Modemuseum im Müncher Stadtmuseum München (1998) and Museum des Landes Glarus, Näfels (Switzerland) (1999)

Seeing Red: Scotland's Exotic Textile Heritage, Collins Gallery, Glasgow 2007

Six Yards. Guaranteed Dutch Design, MMKA Museum of Modern Art Arnhem 2012

Various

Annuaire de l'Academie Royal de Belgique des Sciences, des Lettres et des Beaux-Arts de Belgique, Brussels 1854

Bolk, Sabine: https://www.journeytobatik.org/2018/05/arabic-calligraphy-in-dutch-traditional.html (23-10-2021)

Carter-Silk, Alexander and Lewiston, Michelle, *The Development of Design Law. Past and Future. From History to Policy*, independent report commissioned by the Intellectual Property Office (IPO) 2022

Cortenbach, Frank, 'Cultuurinvloed op de kleding in West Africa', unpublished document Vlisco Archives, @ Vlisco BV Helmond (The Netherlands) 1997

Fentener van Vlissingen, Jan, 'Rapporten over zijn zakenreis naar West-Afrika in 1934, in brieven geschreven aan zijn collega Tobie Hoogenboom, mede expcrt-directeur van de NV P. F. van Vlissingen & Co's Katoenfabrieken', Helmond 24 maart 1982, Vlisco Archives, @ Vlisco BV Helmond (The Netherlands)

Fifty Years of Calico Printing. A Jubilee History of the CPA, Manchester 1949
Forrest: Unilever Archive Oral History Programme Interview Ref. OH/80 with Ken Forrest, held on 3 March 2011at Lever House, Port Sunlight. Transcript: https://www.archives-unilever.com/media/_file/preservica/GB1752_OH/3b6f1de5-bf59-4aaf-8894-036b836d231c--OH80_Ken_Forrest.pdf

Gedenkboek 1804-1929 van de Maatschappij voor Textielindustrie voorheen C. Roessingh en zoon, Viseum Veenendaal (The Netherlands)

Gids voor de bezoekers van het Koloniaal Museum te Haarlem, Amsterdam 1902

Harrop, Gerald, 'Newton Bank Printworks Hyde 1812-2007 and European Involvement in Batik/Wax Block Prints', undated and unpublished document, Brunnschweiler Archive, Whitworth Art Gallery, Manchester University (UK)

Proclamations, Regulations, Advertisements and Orders, printed and published on the island of Java by the British Government, September 1811 to September 1813

Rapport der Hoofdcommissie ter beoordeeling der voorwerpen van de Nationale Nijverheid ten toon gesteld te Gent in de maand augustus 1820, The Hague 1820

Rapport der Hoofdcommissie ter beoordeeling der voorwerpen van nationale nijverheid ten toon gesteld te Haarlem in de maanden juli en augustus 1825, The Hague 1825

Jenny-Trümpy, Adolf, Series of 24 sample books, Textilmuseum Sankt Gallen, Switzerland

Whiteman: Unilever Archive Oral History Programme Interview Ref. OH/32 Part 1 with Mr Neil Whiteman, held on 2nd May 2007 at UAC Old Coasters Reunion. https://www.archives-unilever.com/media/_file/preservica/GB1752_OH/5c8027dd-9c5f-45db-8f4a-1cb68809f84c--OH32_Neil_Whiteman_Part_1.pdf

Photo credits

Ankersmit, Willem. The Hague/Museum Helmond (The Netherlands) 2-7

Archives Missions Africaines, Rome (Italy) 4-2, 7-7

Basel Mission Archives/Mission 21, Basel (Switzerland) 3-6, 3-7, 4-11, 4-35, 4-37, 4-50, 4-72, 4-75

Brunnschweiler Archive, held at the Whitworth Art Gallery, University of Manchester (UK)
- Photos by Whitworth Art Gallery, University of Manchester
  The following designs depicted here were kindly donated to the Whitworth, The University of Manchester by the Cha Chi Ming family following their long involvement with the textile industry and ownership of A. Brunschweiler and Company in Hyde, Manchester (UK) 4-1, 4-19, 4-21, 4-25, 4-31, 4-34, 4-38, 4-49, 4-51, 4-53, 4-55, 4-59, 4-60, 4-62, 4-63, 4-66, 4-67, 4-70, 4-71, 4-74, 4-77, 4-78, 4-81, 4-87, 4-93, 4-94, 4-97, 4-98, 4-101
- Helen Elands, photos taken at Brunnschweiler Archive, Hyde (UK) 4-3, 4-4, 4-6, 4-9, 4-12, 4-13, 4-14, 4-15, 4-16, 4-20, 4-22, 4-32, 4-39, 4-40, 4-41, 4-42, 4-44, 4-45, 4-46, 4-47, 4-48, 4-61, 4-65, 4-73, 4-89, 4-91, 4-92, 4-95, 4-96, 4-99, 4-100, 4-102, 4-103, 4-104, 5-6, 5-7, 5-8, 6-8, E-1

Clarke, Duncan, Adire African Textiles, London (UK) 3-8, 4-54, 4-79, 4-83, 4-84, 4-90

Collectie Overijssel, Zwolle/Deventer (The Netherlands) 5-1

Collectie Vereniging Haerlem (The Netherlands) 1-7

Fleming, Malcolm, Porton (UK) 3-1

Frensel, Martin, Akkrum (The Netherlands) 6-1

Jenny, R. D., Sent (Switzerland) 5-9

Musee de la Marine, Honfleur (France) 2-1

Museum De Lakenhal, Leiden (The Netherlands) 1-4

Nationaal Archief, The Hague (The Netherlands) 1-3, 2-5

Noord-Hollands Archief (The Netherlands) 1-2, 1-6, 2-6, 3-5

RKD The Hague (The Netherlands) 1-1, 3-2

Science and Industry Museum Manchester (UK) 4-32

The National Archives Kew (UK) 3-4, 4-30, 4-33, 4-69, 4-76

The Trustees of the British Museum, London (UK) 6-5, 6-6

Vlisco Archive, © Vlisco BV (The Netherlands) 1-5, 1-8, 2-2, 2-3, 2-4, 3-3, 4-5, 4-7, 4-8, 4-10, 4-17, 4-18, 4-23, 4-24, 4-27, 4-28, 4-29, 4-36, 4-43, 4-52, 4-56, 4-57, 4-58, 4-64, 4-68, 4-80, 4-82, 4-85, 4-86, 4-88, 5-2, 5-3, 5-4, 5-5, 6-2, 6-3, 6-4, 6-7, 6-9, 7-1, 7-2, 7-3, 7-4, 7-6, E-2

Wereldmuseum Amsterdam (The Netherlands) 4-26

The process of wax printing (30-31, 46-47, 64-65, 144-145, 164-165, 182-183, 202-203 and 212-213): samples produced by ABC Wax, Hyde (UK), private collection, photos Laura Elands

The author has endeavoured to find out who owns the copyright, but has not succeeded in all cases.

This publication has been made possible
by Alixar BV Hasselt (Belgium)

Cover image
Hand and fingers*
BT reg.no. 260844, 1 August 1895
Brunnschweiler Archive,
held at the Whitworth Art Gallery,
University of Manchester (UK)

Silvana Editoriale

Chief Executive
Michele Pizzi

Editorial Director
Sergio Di Stefano

Art Director
Giacomo Merli

Editorial Coordinator
Laurianne Barban

Graphic Design
Annamaria Ardizzi

Copy Editing
Mariangela Palazzi-Williams

Layout
Diego Mantica

Production Coordinator
Antonio Micelli

Editorial Assistant
Giulia Mercanti

Photo Editor
Silvia Sala

Press Office
Alessandra Olivari,
press@silvanaeditoriale.it

All reproduction and translation rights
reserved for all countries
© 2024 Silvana Editoriale S.p.A.,
Cinisello Balsamo, Milano

ISBN 9788836658749

Under copyright and civil law this book
cannot be reproduced, wholly or in part,
in any form, original or derived, or by
any means: print, electronic, digital,
mechanical, including photocopy,
microfilm, film or any other medium,
without permission in writing from
the publisher.

Silvana Editoriale S.p.A.
via dei Lavoratori, 78
20092 Cinisello Balsamo, Milano
tel. 02 453 951 01
www.silvanaeditoriale.it

Reproduction, printing and binding
in Italy
Printed by I.G.P. Grafiche Pacini,
Ospedaletto (Pisa)
Printed in December 2024